MY GREEN AGE

To Bob & Kay   October 2010

With memories from a long time ago. Another time, another place, another me — and another you. And best wishes.

Jerry

TERRENCE KEOUGH, whose early life is recounted in this memoir, continued in later years to lead a life in which travel and education played a major role. After spending two dreary years in Port Alberni on the west coast of Vancouver Island, to which he was headed when the present account ends, he and his wife, Rosemary, went to Kenya for three years, where he trained teachers at Siriba College, near Lake Victoria. In 1968, he returned to university, completing an M.A. at the University of Alberta, and a Ph.D. at the University of Ottawa, both degrees in Old and Middle English Literature.

After seven years of marriage, he and Rosemary parted in 1969. While a student in the Ph.D. program at the University of Ottawa, he met a fellow doctoral candidate, Barbara Chase, whom he later married. He and Barbara taught for the next quarter of a century at Heritage College in Hull, Quebec. Upon retiring in the mid 1990s, the couple moved to Victoria, B.C., where they continue to reside.

MY GREEN AGE

The force that through the green fuse drives the flower
Drives my green age; that blasts the roots of trees
Is my destroyer.
And I am dumb to tell the crooked rose
My youth is bent by the same wintry fever.
                    Dylan Thomas (1933)

Terrence Keough

Order this book online at www.trafford.com
or email orders@trafford.com

Most Trafford titles are also available at major online book retailers.

© Copyright 2009 Terrence Keough.

All rights reserved. No part of this publication may be reproduced, stored in a retrieval system, or transmitted, in any form or by any means, electronic, mechanical, photocopying, recording, or otherwise, without the written prior permission of the author.

Printed in Victoria, BC, Canada.

ISBN: 978-1-4269-2322-7 (sc)

Library of Congress Control Number: 2009913327

Our mission is to efficiently provide the world's finest, most comprehensive book publishing service, enabling every author to experience success. To find out how to publish your book, your way, and have it available worldwide, visit us online at www.trafford.com

Trafford rev. 12/14/2009

 www.trafford.com

North America & international
toll-free: 1 888 232 4444 (USA & Canada)
phone: 250 383 6864 • fax: 812 355 4082

FOR BARBARA

My memory is proglottidean, like the tapeworm, but unlike the tapeworm it has no head, it wanders in a maze, and any point may be the beginning or the end of its journey.
        Umberto Echo, "The Gorge," ***The New Yorker*** (March 7, 2005)

Memoirists are not writing proper history but rather what they remember of it, or, more accurately, what they can't forget.
        Joseph Kertes, "The Truth about Lying," ***Walrus*** (June 2006)

There are moments which are not calculable, and cannot be assessed in words; they live on in the solution of memory, like wonderful creatures, unique of their kind, dredged up from the floors of some unexplored ocean.
        Lawrence Durrell, ***Justine*** (1957)

Errata

Dedication Page For "Echo" read "Eco"

p. 5 For "Wendy" read "Diane"

p. 320 For "James" Burston read "W. H." [Wyndham Hedley] Burston

p. 343 For "Francine" read "Françoise"

p. 347 For "Francine" in photo caption read "Françoise"

Back Cover For "Rhodes" read "Roads"

CONTENTS

The Arches of the Years

    Preface: A Proligerous Beginning

1.	From Out the Boundless Deep: Revelstoke 1935-53	1-36
2.	Wake Up the Echoes: Notre Dame 1953-55	37-60
3.	Hail and Health to Alma Mater: St. F. X. 1955-57	61-90
4.	It's Hard Not to Think of the Bay: Vancouver 1957-58	91-108
5.	Hitching Canada to Sail on the *S.S. Homeric* 1958	109-137
6.	Europe on a Moto Guzzi Cardellino 1958	138-166
7.	Dark Night of the Soul: London 1958	167-177
8.	A Young Man's Fancy: Peace Haven 1958-59	178-212
9.	That Summer in Jaca 1959	213-239
10.	Living in Franco's Spain 1959-60	240-277
11.	The Long Route Home 1960	278-289
12.	Interlude in Castlegar 1960-61	290-307
13.	Return to London 1961	308-325
14.	Autumn at the Institute 1961	326-347
15.	Bloomsbury, Brighton, and Blackheath 1962	348-386
16.	A London Last Hurrah 1962-63	387-407

A PROLIGEROUS BEGINNING

Just think! If a different one of the two million sperm your father deposited into your mother had penetrated the egg she provided, you would not exist. A quite different being would have been created, lived whatever life it had to live, and experienced the quotidian ups and downs and ins and outs of human existence. Finally, it would have (as the old Bible used to put it), like all mortal things, "given up the ghost" and gone on to whatever next life may or may not be out there. And before going, it might even have written its autobiography.

These pages are a recollection of five seminal years of my life, beginning at age twenty-three and ending at age twenty-eight. Since I was not plunked into life at twenty-three, I have written introductory chapters chronicling my early years in Revelstoke, at Notre Dame College, at St. F. X. University, and in Vancouver. As accounts of early years tend to be tedious, in the interest of not boring my reader—even family, friends, and acquaintances, who will, I assume, be less bored than others—I have written not so much a chronicle account of those years as a pastiche that offers some explanation as to why the young man who is the subject of this book was the way he was.

Chapter 1: From Out the Boundless Deep

REVELSTOKE MADE ME (1935-53 PLUS)

> I learned that to remember is, at least in part, to imagine, and that the act of transposing memory into written words is a creative act that transforms the memory itself.
> Joel Agee, "A Life that Tells the Truth: Memoir and the Art Of Memory," ***Harper's*** (Nov. 2007), 55

THE CITY OF REVELSTOKE, INTO WHICH I WAS BORN, THE SIXTH AND LAST CHILD OF JOHN PATRICK KEOUGH AND ESTHER ELIZABETH KEOUGH (NEÉ McCARTHY), IN THE QUEEN VICTORIA HOSPITAL, ON June 14, 1935, lies in a narrow valley of the Columbia River, which provides a brief level area between the Selkirk and Monashee mountains in south-central British Columbia. It is hardly a city in any sense other than a legal one. It was incorporated that way in the 1890s, when people thought it would grow much bigger than it eventually did, not an uncommon thing in the optimism that pervaded the province after the arrival of the Canadian Pacific Railway in 1885. Many of the cities incorporated at that time flourished for awhile and then died; others failed to fulfil their promised growth. So it was with Revelstoke. At the time of my birth it had fewer than 3,000 inhabitants, and the population remained at or near that level throughout the years I was growing up there.

Revelstoke is a railway town, a divisional point along the main line from Calgary to Vancouver, so the CPR was by far the main employer. The inhabitants of the town came from a number of ethnic backgrounds, and the CPR doled out jobs according to their ethnicity. If you were from the British Isles or Northern Europe, you were worthy of a job in the administration of the division: Superintendent, Assistant Superintendent, Clerk in the Division Offices, Train Dispatcher; or you could be a member of the Running Crew: Engineer, Fireman, Conductor, Brakeman; or a foreman in the Maintenance Shops; or a Telegraph Operator or Agent at one of the stations along the line. If you were from Southern or Eastern Europe—principally Italy and the Ukraine—

where the people were still known by the masters of the Empire as "dagos," "wogs," or "bohunks," you were allowed to labour in the Maintenance Shops, on an Extra Gang, or to maintain the track as a Section Man. If you were Chinese, you were condemned to the lowest of labouring jobs: building track, or cooking (not crew) on Extra Gangs, Paint Gangs, and any of the other gangs that were sent out into isolated mountain areas. It wasn't until after the Second World War that this ethnic racism began to break down.

But even though the CPR was the dominant factor in the working world of Revelstoke, there were many other smaller industries and places of work. A few people ran trap lines in the wilderness around the town; there was a smattering of logging; there were a few sawmills (e.g., Riverside Sawmill, run appropriately by R. H. Sawyer); a plant for creosoting polls; and a small sash and door factory. There was a blacksmith shop (Domke's), and a place to get fender-benders repaired (Ned's Body Shop). There was the Revelstoke Brewery (run by the Holdener family). There were dairies (Campbell's, McKinnon's, Olson's), which delivered their milk around the town in quart glass bottles.

> *We got our milk from Olson's Dairy, a small farm with a herd of Jersey cows. The milk was not homogenized. A winter memory: often, when I went to the back steps to bring in our quart, the large area of frozen cream had pushed the paper lid off the bottle, and the cream was standing a couple of inches in the air. A summer memory: My birthday, June 14, 1940. I heard from my upstairs bedroom my mother talking to Mr. Olson on the doorstep below. "Paris has fallen to the Germans," he said. My dad would now have to move the coloured pins on the map of Europe on the living room wall. And I wanted to watch.*

South of town there was subsistence farming, mostly done by immigrants from Eastern Europe. As these farms would not in themselves support a family, the husband often worked for the CPR as a section man, or something at that level, in order to bring in some ready money. While these men worked at their menial jobs, the farm was attended to by the wife, who ran a little business on the side selling chickens, eggs, and butter to people in the town. For example, when my mother wanted to cook a chicken—a treat in those days—she would telephone Mrs. Shura, and the chicken would be delivered to the back door, ready for the oven. During the war, when there were ration coupons for most food items, we (and much of the rest of the town) would often obtain (illegally, of course, but nobody cared about that) bits and pieces of food from these farmers.

Coming from Eastern Europe, these families were largely good Catholics, and when I was an altar boy in the mid- to late-Forties, I sometimes on a Sunday morning accompanied Father Flynn by car to one of two small, wooden churches in the area—wooden cabins, really—just big enough to hold a dozen people or so, where I assisted at Mass. It was all informal, except for the Latin and the ritual movements. We would kneel together in front of the small altar and begin: *P. Introibo ad altare dei. S. Ad deum qui laetificat juventutem meum.*[1]

---

[1] The beginning of the prayers at the Latin Mass: **P.** I will go unto the altar of God. **S.** To God, Who gives joy to my youth.

Revelstoke was laid out by CPR surveyors, divided into blocks on a grid, the lots of a standard size—streets in one direction, which were given numbers, and avenues in the other, which were given names. Alleys, where garbage could be picked up and bread and milk, ice, and groceries delivered, ran through the centres of the blocks at the backs of the houses. It was a standard CPR plan and is found in cities throughout the West.

Mackenzie Avenue

The Revelstoke Review, Ron Finn's Hitler, and Altar Boys

THE MAIN BUSINESS AREA, THE THREE BLOCKS OF MACKENZIE AVENUE FROM THE RAILWAY TO THIRD STREET, DEVELOPED AS THE CITY GREW. THERE WERE BANKS, THE IMPERIAL BANK AND the Bank of Commerce. The building that had housed the Bank of Montreal remained on the north-east corner of Mackenzie and First Street, the bank's name still carved in the lintel above the entrance, a symbol of permanence. But the bank itself was no longer there, having closed the branch during the Great Depression. The building was now occupied by the town paper, *The Revelstoke Review*, run by Arvid Lundell. Lundell was a prominent citizen throughout his lifetime, sometime MLA for the Revelstoke area, and Mayor from 1962 to 1969. He was a short man who wore a toothbrush moustache. One of my childhood friends, Ron Finn, told me many years later that during the war, when he was seven or eight years old, he had decided that Lundell was in fact that other bearer of a toothbrush moustache, much in the news at the time, Adolf Hitler. Ron told his mother that he was going to tell the police about it. She managed to convince him that it was not a good idea.

Ron and I were both altar boys and often served together at Sunday Mass. Ron had significant style and presence on the altar, carrying himself as if he were at least a bishop. Some people in the congregation thought he was a dead ringer to become a priest. But I, a bumbler on the altar, knew different. Neither one of us was devout. In spite of the solemnity he projected, Ron was having fun, and I was having fun with him. On one occasion, he surreptitiously shoved a handful of raisins into my hand while I was heading up the altar steps to move the big Mass book from the epistle side of the altar to the gospel side—a task that was precarious enough when you were wearing an ankle-length cassock—making it even more difficult than usual for me to move the book without dropping it or the raisins. After communion was distributed, when we went together to the communion rail to flip the cloth back to its normal hanging position, he would wait at the other end until I was just about to grab my end and snap it away from my hands. All of these shenanigans were done with solemnity, even beauty. He was a fine actor.

Inevitably, Ron was known to some of his friends, especially "Busher" MacDonald, as "Huck" Finn, one of those obvious nicknames, like the "Buck" that is so often attached to males with the surname "Rogers." But he was only one of many Revelstokians who were given nicknames, some of them startlingly original.

> *Why was Revelstoke a hive of nicknames? Nicknames that were applied and stuck and were used ever after? It may have had something to do with the influence of the sons and daughters of the large local Italian immigrant population. I come to this conclusion because major league baseball, which had many Italian stars in the thirties and forties, was a world of nicknames: "Scooter" Rizzuto, "Bocci" Lombardi, "Yogi" Berra, "Joltin' Joe" Dimaggio, and so on. Some of the Revelstoke nicknames were related to baseball: Vince "Choppy" Pratico, Bob "Busher" MacDonald. But most nicknames grew from personal attitudes or attributes. Dale Marino was called "Boogie-Woogie," later shortened to "Juggy," for the way he looked when running the 100 yard dash; Ron Belton was called "Froggie" (for his favourite fish bait); Harry Ludwig was "Cheesehound"; Chester Graham was "Gump"; there was Ukrainian "Yuke" Wasylik; there was "Bugs" Nelson, and his son, differentiated when necessary as "Young Bugs" and "Old Bugs"; the Ozeros: "Twenty-Below" and his sister, "Scratch Below," shortened later to "Scratchy"; "Ole the Bear" Westerberg, his son, "Ole the Cub," and his grandson, "Ole the Cub's Cub"; and so on. Was there another town at that time that had so many nicknames? I don't think so.*

Putting Together the High School Annual

When I was involved with it, the High School Annual was finished at the *Review* building, partly, I suspect, because another Lundell, Dorothea, a teacher at the high school, was the staff member in charge of the project. Apart from its picture pages, cover, and, usually, advertising pages (all ordered from a printer in Vancouver), the Annual was produced on a mimeograph and collated by lines of students at the high school before being taken to the *Review* to be stapled together on a large stapler and taped at the spine. I was always involved in these projects. I remember once while we were doing the stapling being fascinated by one of the *Review* staff who was operating a nifty small press. It stood on a pedestal at waist level and was round, like a clam shell, about two feet in diameter, with the type locked into the bottom half. The man operating it would insert a piece of paper in the brief interlude in which the shell was open, and the two sides would then automatically slam together, printing the piece of paper. The top shell would lift, and the operator would remove the newly-printed sheet as he inserted the next piece of paper. It took great rhythm and perfect timing and seemed to me to be incredibly dangerous and exciting.

I Get Fitted for My First Suit

Also on Mackenzie Avenue there were a couple of drug stores (Revelstoke Drugs, Donaldson's Drugs); Ramsden's Ladies' Wear; L. C. Masson's Grocery; Sturdy's Hardware (which disappeared when I was very young); Well's Men's Wear ("Well's Wear Wears Well"); F. G. Bews, Jeweller; Meehan's Meat Market; Taverna's Meat Market; Manning's Café and Restaurant (beautifully panelled with mahogany and plate-glass mirrors, where the fabulous *Manning's Broadway Chocolates* were made in the basement by Jack Pugsley); and the Avolie Theatre (the name derived from "Olive," the first name of the wife of the owner, Warren Cooper), the town's only cinema.

Art's Esquire Shop, owned and run by Art Switzer, was in the middle of the block on the West Side of Mackenzie Avenue that runs between Second and Third Street. I went there to have my first suit made, in preparation for the high school graduation ceremonies and dance. Art's suits were made in Vancouver, so he took measurements and put them on to a standard form and sent the form to the people who would be making the suit. I chose a hideous light blue woollen material. I also chose to have the pants made as "drapes." Still popular at the time in Revelstoke, but coming near the end of their run outside of the boondocks, these were the pants that went along with the "zoot suit"—the trousers had bulging 26" knees and narrow 13" cuffs—modified to be worn by ordinary decent people like me and my friends: no huge shoulder pads, exaggerated lapels, or chains hanging in a loop from waist to knee. I was, after all, the President of the Student Council and had to make a good impression.

Eddie Arnold, Hi-Lo and the Broken Skeleton Key

Stedmans chain of ten-cent stores arrived just at the war's end, opening up with a window display of the largest selection of candy I had ever seen (bad news for the teeth). There was MacDonald's Grocery, owned by the father of my friend, Bob "Busher" MacDonald. I remember walking by the store along a deserted Mackenzie Avenue early on a warm winter evening—the avenue was usually deserted on winter evenings—all of the stores closed except Louis Catlin's, the snow piled six feet high between the sidewalk and the road; you could pass someone on either side without knowing it. Inside the store, with only the night lights on, Bob's father was toting up the day's receipts, using an adding machine with a crank on the side and a roll of paper on top, standard technology at the time. As he never looked up and didn't know I was there, I felt vaguely uncomfortable, as if I were watching something private.

> *A cousin of Busher's, Diane Keyes, arrived in Revelstoke with her family when I was about thirteen and just beginning to get profoundly interested in the wonderful world of sex. She was not beautiful, but, as it turned out, she was willing to allow Terry Stringer and me glimpses of her body in return for certain favours. Terry had a horse called Kitty, which he kept on the edge of a field to the west of town. He would allow Wendy to ride Kitty only after she'd loosened the string on the top of her sexy, off-the-shoulder peasant blouse and let us look one at a time at her developing, braless bosom. It was not something that any other girls I knew would have agreed to do. I was too curious not to go along. But underneath, I knew it was unkind and unfair, and I was a little ashamed of myself for being a part of it.*

There was Stock's Photo Studio; the CPR Telegraph Office, which operated the CBC Radio booster station, the only radio in the midst of these mountains that could be heard during the day. At night, other stations mysteriously came in—as teenagers we liked to listen to "Lucky Lager Dance Time" from KIRO, Seattle; there was the City Hall, a fine art deco building put up in 1939; and the Chop House, where as a teenager, I watched one of the town drunks, Jock Inkster, arise from his booth late at night, hat in hand, sing swayingly, "That's How Much I Love You," which he introduced "with apologies to Eddie Arnold."

On the south-west corner of Mackenzie Avenue and Second Street stood Brandon's Furniture Store and Funeral Parlour, with its little cabin of used furniture behind it. This cabin became an important place in my life when I was in Grade 12. My friend, Bill Wood, had discovered that you could get into it from the back simply by climbing over a small fence—easy to do with the snow piled to the top of it—and opening the lock with a skeleton key. He started going there with his girl friend, Beverley Rudd; and since my girlfriend, Karen Abbott, and I were good friends of Bill and Bev, they told us about it and we started going there together. The place was heated, and, being a warehouse of used furniture, stuffed chairs, settees, and beds, it was an ideal spot for lovers to gather in the dark winter evenings. Beverley named it "Hi-Lo" for reasons I don't remember. We were always worried about getting caught there *in flagrante*. But Bill reasoned that since Karen's father was the Principal of the High School and I was the President of the Student Council, if we were caught, the situation would be covered up and dismissed. I'm not sure that would have been the case. Luckily, we were never caught, *in flagrante* or otherwise. One night when Bill and Bev went there on their own, Bill broke the key in the lock as they left, leaving half the key inside the mechanism. The next time we checked, the lock had been replaced with a sturdy, unopenable Yale lock. Our little Shangri-la was no longer available to us.

SUMMER JOBS

Catlin's was a kind of corner store in the middle of the block between First and Second Street, right next to the new City Hall, the only store that was open on Sundays and Holidays. It was presided over by old Louis Catlin, who sat on a stool behind the counter; and though he appeared to be only half awake, his eyelids drooping, his large grey moustache appearing to sag, he was very much aware of what you were doing in—and maybe stealing from—his store.

Feather Touch in CPR Red

I HAD AN ODD AND ENTIRELY PERIPHERAL GLANCE INTO THE WORLD OF THE CATLINS ONE SUMMER DURING MY HIGH SCHOOL YEARS. I WAS working on the CPR Paint Gang. We lived in outfit cars, box cars that had been modified into kind of dormitories, with double bunk beds on each side of the car made from two-by-fours, and two-inch-thick straw mattresses that lay on plain boards. Two rough, grey blankets were supplied. No sheets. To clean yourself up you poured water from a cistern into an enamelled pan, and with a bar of soap (not supplied) you did the best you could. There were no bathrooms. You just headed into the fields or the bush to do your thing—

quickly in mosquito country. These cars, along with a cook car, which contained a kitchen, a dining area for the crew, and separate living quarters for the cook and the foreman, were hauled on a freight train with the painting crew aboard to wherever along the line the CPR had buildings it wanted painted.

We painted everything: stations, section houses, water towers, stinking outhouses (one-holers and two-holers); inside and out; all ceilings and walls. Wooden floors were painted and, weirdly, given a faux wood pattern with a kind of trowel; roofs were creosoted. We did it all under the watchful eyes of our foreman, "Podger" Shaw, who constantly urged us to put on the CPR red, brown, and cream paint with "a feather touch." One of my fellow painters, a handsome man in the mode of Clark Gable, complete with pencil-line moustache, was Dean Staten. He was apparently working on the paint gang to escape a disastrous marriage to one of Louis Catlin's daughters, who, one assumes, was escaping from him by staying in Revelstoke. I liked Dean. He was a personable, gentle sort. Day after day, as he painted (in a world in which the ghetto blaster was still, mercifully, uninvented), he sang love ballads from the ladder tops and scaffolding in a soft and sentimental way—"You always hurt the one you love," "Ramona," and "Paper Doll" were favourites—all songs of romantic loss.

> *We usually tried to get home to Revelstoke for the weekend. One Friday after work we were hanging around the outfit car, which was parked at Monte Creek, a few miles east of Kamloops. A freight train, whose engineer was the father of our friend, Jack Hooley, lumbered by. He pointed east and shouted "Revelstoke!" We waved our yeses: Jim Craig, George Benson, and me. We needed no luggage; we were going home. Hooley slowed the train right down and we hopped on to the caboose. The conductor, who knew us, said: "I walked the street for thirty days once for doing this." But he didn't kick us off, merely told us to keep out of sight as we went under overpasses on the highway, from which the Assistant Superintendents tended to check the trains.*

Mosquitoes and Foreman Vic

THE PAINT GANG WAS NOT MY FIRST EXPERIENCE WITH A CPR GANG. THAT HAPPENED WHEN I WAS FIFTEEN AND LIED ABOUT MY age (you were not allowed to work on a CPR gang before you were sixteen), and got a job on an Extra Gang. We were employed ripping up track on the sidings—the places where trains on this single-track line waited for trains from the opposite direction to pass—and replacing them with a heavier type rail, allowing trains to haul heavier loads. We were also extending the sidings, as the diesel engines that were then on order would be pulling longer trains than the sidings, designed with steam engines in mind, could accommodate. Our foreman, a slave-driver if ever there was one, was an Italian immigrant by the name of Vic Fichicelli. Inevitably, behind his back we called him "Fuck-em-silly."

When I joined the gang, it was working near Beavermouth, a station about 25 miles west of Golden (50 miles east of Revelstoke), an area largely empty of people that is basically a huge swamp. So, even harder to get along with than Fichicelli were the swarms of mosquitoes. You would not believe how bad they were. We wore wide-brimmed hats with mosquito netting tucked into doubled shirts, and still the buggers got inside. If you took your netted hat off for a moment, a hundred would land on each side of your face. If you wiped off one side, and then the other, they were instantly back on both sides. We wore two pairs of pants, because they would instantly—and constantly—bite through one pair. It was impossible to work with any efficiency. Fichicelli, who it seemed even the mosquitoes didn't like, wore a wide straw hat with no netting. "Whats-a matter you?" he would say. "The mosquites a-bother you?" The ten of us in the gang would grip one of the thirty-nine foot rails, weighing an incredible 130 lbs. per foot, five on one side, five on the other—each pair sharing huge tongs that gripped the rail—and pull it along the ties, as Vic shouted "Montreal!" for one direction, "Vancouver!" for the other.

But even he could see that we could not work properly in our bug-infested world. So he convinced the powers-that-be in Revelstoke to move us to Palliser, just east of Golden, where huge cliffs towered above the Kicking Horse River. The Trans-Canada Highway had still not been driven through these canyons, so there was a sense of quiet isolation. High up on the cliffs we often caught sight of mountain goats clinging precariously. We loved the beauty that surrounded us, so different from Beavermouth. But most of all, we thanked God, or whoever was in charge of this area, that there were far fewer mosquitoes than at Beavermouth. After a few days there, we were moved to Field, where, because of its altitude (1243 metres), there were none.

But even without the mosquitoes, my friend Harvey Dean and I found the job impossible. We were working very hard ten-hour days—7 to 12, 1-6—for sixty-five cents an hour, minus an amount I don't remember for room and board. Living conditions were horrible. One of our fellow workers, a Swede who had learned his English in a logging camp full of Irishmen—"Begora! Wic! Yumpin' Yesus!"—got drunk on cheap wine one Saturday night and puked all over the outfit-car. It was the last straw. We told Vic that we were quitting, so would he get us a pass on the train to go back to Revelstoke. He said, "But you can't-a quit. I'm-a havin' nobody to do your work." Nonetheless, he was obliged by the rules to order our passes, and when he had done so, we returned to Revelstoke, gratefully unemployed.

> *On the way home to Revelstoke after Harvey Dean and I had quit the Extra Gang, we were pulled off the train during the stop in Golden and frisked by an RCMP officer. He found nothing. We didn't know what he was looking for or what this was all about. Later, we heard that there was a robbery in Field the night we left, and we were suspects. In the fall, the Mounties called my mother and said they would send someone around to the house to take a statement. "You didn't lie to the police, did you," my mother said.*

The Superintendent's 1927 Buick

IN THE SUMMER OF 1953, THE YEAR I GRADUATED FROM HIGH SCHOOL, I WORKED AS ONE OF THE HOSTLER'S HELPERS (USUALLY CALLED "Wipers") in the CPR maintenance shops. It was here that the big steam engines were stored and maintained. I worked the swing shift, covering the shifts of those who had days off: Sunday and Monday, midnight to eight; Tuesday and Wednesday, four to midnight; and Thursday, eight to four. I loved the hours, as I was free from Thursday at four until Sunday at midnight, a superb long weekend in which I could swim at Williamson's Lake, hang around with friends most evenings, and pay maximum attention to my girl friend. And the job was fun. Two of us helpers worked under the supervision of the Hostler. The engine crews, having pulled a train into Revelstoke, would leave the engine on what was known as the shop track. We would move the engine from there to the roundhouse, filling it along the way with oil, water, and sand.[2] To get it into one of the stalls in the shops, we would put it on a turntable and rotate the table until the engine was pointed at the right stall. We would then drive it into the stall, park it, and put a chain under its wheels to keep it from spontaneously backing out into the turntable pit.

Once, one of the helpers forgot to put the chain under the wheel. A short time later, the engine, puffing as if someone were running it, rolled back and dropped its tender into the turntable pit. Some oil and water gushed into the pit, but not much. Later, a crane was brought the scene and the engine was lifted back on to the track. It had suffered less damage than one might have expected.

When an engine was requested to go into service, we were told to fire it up. You opened the fire door, turned on the oil and atomiser, lit a handful of waste, and threw it into the fire chamber. Boom! The longer it took you to get the lighted waste in there, the bigger the boom. You would sit and watch the steam building up on the steam gauge, until it reached its maximum level and the safety release popped. The Hostler would then drive it to the shop track, leaving it there for the engine crew. By the summer of 1953, the first generation of diesel engines had also gone into service. We refuelled them as well and drove them to the diesel shop track for the engine crews to take away. The handwriting was on the wall for the iron horses.

These magnificent engines, 2700s, huge 5900s, and others, were always supposed to be driven by the Hostler. But in practice, we helpers often did the job. One of the hostlers, Sig Leonard, more often than not arrived to work the midnight shift three sheets to the wind. He would punch in on the time clock outside of the shop office and then head to the Superintendent's 1927 Buick, which was parked in one of the stalls in the roundhouse. It was a neat vehicle, which had been given a set of wheels so that it could travel on rails. But the days when superintendents flaunted their importance by travelling about the division in a luxury car were over. I never saw the car used by anyone except Sig Leonard, and he used it as a kind of bedroom in which to sleep off the evening's booze. Once or twice, when things were slow, I had a nap in there myself.

---

[2] Sand was stored in the upside-down cups you see on the tops of steam engines. It could be sifted on to the rails by the engineer to improve traction on slippery tracks.

> *We ate our lunches, mine made by my mother—usually tuna fish sandwiches, homemade pie in a plastic, triangular pie holder, fruit—on a bench outside the roundhouse about fifty feet from the sand house, where the sand for the engines was stored. Hobos often spent the night sleeping on the soft sand. One evening on a shift being worked by a couple of other guys, there was a hobo who was not quite right in the head. He kept sticking his face out the side of the shed and grinning at the guys as they ate their lunches. One of them picked up a stone, and, when the hobo's head was not visible, threw it where his head usually appeared. He was more accurate than he expected to be. Out came the head, just as the stone arrived, knocking out two teeth. The CPR paid for the repairs. The hostler's helper who did the deed was given demerit points, known to the workers as "brownies." He should have been fired.*

Lab Technician at the Test Pits

IN THE SUMMER BETWEEN GRADE 11 AND GRADE 12, I GOT A JOB, COURTESY OF MY CHEMISTRY TEACHER, SAM SMITH, WORKING IN A laboratory. The laboratory had been set up to determine how much gravel there was in the soil around Mica Creek, which emptied into the Columbia River about 80 miles north of Revelstoke, beside the winding and unpaved Big Bend Highway. Plans were already far advanced to build a large holding dam in this area, as part of a major hydro-electric power development. Fellow student, Ron Chisholm, and I, under the supervision of a young man whose name I don't remember, had the job of assessing how much gravel per cubic foot was in the soil samples that were brought into the lab.

The plan was that after three weeks in the lab, I was to go to Mica Creek, where I would gather and bag the samples to be sent to Revelstoke to be tested by Ron, and after another three weeks, Ron and I would switch jobs. My official title was "Lab Technician at the Test Pits," but I soon found out that I was expected to share in the grunt work involved in collecting the samples, an aspect of the job that I had not counted on and that I resented. We were camped in tents in a beautiful spot beside the Columbia River. There were four of us labourers, a cook, and the foreman, a man in his early sixties, who was in tremendous physical shape and could outwork the rest of us combined. The cook was a young Danish man, who looked a bit like Harpo Marx and who spoke English in a highly original way. For instance, he called the squirrels "monkey mouses," and refused to learn the word "squirrel," in spite of my efforts to teach it to him. If truth be told, I preferred his colourful descriptive phrase to our boring word.

The test pits, it seemed to me, were to be found on a whim, anywhere in the forest that the foreman decided we would test for gravel. What we would do is blow off the surface of the soil with dynamite, which I refused to have anything to do with, much to the foreman's disgust. Then we would take shovels and dig down about six feet, taking a sample every two feet. I was expected to help with the digging, and then at each two-foot level, run some of the soil through a portable sieve into a small gunny sack, which was sent to the lab to be analysed.

After I had been in the camp for only a few days, we began in the evenings to get spectacular thunder and lightning storms. The lightning would zigzag down and hit trees on the mountains on the other side of the river, and the trees would burst into flame. Most of the fires burned out in the trees where the lightning hit and that was the end of them. One evening, a couple of days after this all started, while we were enjoying the fireworks, a truck pulled into our campsite and a forestry officer emerged. He told us that in the morning we were going to be trucked to a location north of us to fight a large fire. There was nothing we could do about this. When you were conscripted by the forestry service, you had to go. It was dangerous, for example, to be drinking in the hotel beer parlours in Revelstoke during fire season. The forestry press gang used to go there first in search of "volunteers."

In the morning, we climbed on to the high-sided deck of a 3-ton truck, joining a group of others who had been picked up along the way—there might have been twenty of us—and headed to the fire. We were dropped off at a bulldozed trail a few miles north of our camp. We hiked the trail for an hour or so, much of it gently uphill, to an area about a half mile from the fire. We could not see the actual fire. But there was the smell of smoke; though, luckily, because of the wind direction, the bulk of the smoke was blowing away from where we were. The heavy equipment that had built the trail was busy building a fire line. The idea was that, if the wind held, the foresters would light a back-fire and burn the fire into itself.

Men were cutting down trees with chain saws, and the bulldozer was pushing the debris aside. We were each given a grub hoe—a tool with the head of a pick on one side and an axe-like hoe on the other—and told to cut roots behind where the bulldozer was working. It struck the three of us young people in the group that it was absurd to be cutting roots by hand in the wake of all that power equipment, so we sauntered as far up the line as we could go, out of sight of the head forester, and sat down on a fallen tree. We had been there for about an hour, when the smoke began to thicken. Suddenly, a forestry man came running our way. "Take your tools to the bulldozer. We have to get out," he said. "The wind has shifted." The bulldozer operator had made a large open circle around the machine, so it would be relatively safe if and when the fire reached it. He was just heading down the trail to the highway. We dropped our tools by his machine and followed him.

A camp had been set up in a meadow area beside the highway. Thirty or forty men were gathered there, some of them putting up tents. We lined up for food. Each of us was given a metal plate, on which were placed a keyed can of Argentinean bully beef, a couple of boiled potatoes, and a dollop of overcooked canned peas. There were piles of white, sliced bread. There were tin cups, tea, and canned milk. We sat on whatever piece of ground we could find. Elegant it was not.

But the fire-fighting was soon over for those of us working on the Mica Dam project. Apparently, the powers-that-be, whoever they were, told the forestry people that our work was too important for us to be conscripted to fighting forest fires. After our strange lunch, we were loaded into the back of a truck and taken back to our camp. In a few days the fire had been brought under control without our help.

When my three weeks at the Test Pits were up, I returned to the lab in Revelstoke, where I spent the rest of the summer. It was at this time that I started going out with Karen Abbott.

> *When I was elected President of the Student Council, I suddenly found that I was popular with the girls in a way that I had not been before. It was my first lesson in the fact that women tend to favour successful men. At a school dance, I was approached one at a time by three different girls who were letting me know, on behalf of three different friends, that these friends would be happy if I chose them for the "home waltz." You got to walk home the girl you danced the home waltz with. Karen Abbott was one of these interested girls. She had recently returned from her tour of England with the Vancouver-based Elgar Choir, and though we had not actually dated—I was too shy to ask for a date— we had spent time together in the company of others. For me it was a no-brainer. On the way to her house, she said, "I've got an itchy nose." I said, "My mother says that means you are about to kiss a fool." And so it proved to be. From that night on, we were, as we said in those days, "going steady," and the noses itched and the fools were kissed on a regular basis.*

The Boring World of Icing Trains

MY LAST SUMMER JOB, IN 1956, BETWEEN MY THIRD AND FOURTH YEARS AT UNIVERSITY, WAS WORKING ON THE ICE GANG. OUR JOB was to put air-conditioning ice, in 400 pound blocks, in the under-areas of coaches on passenger trains. Every day there were at least six trains going through Revelstoke, three in each direction. Often, in the summer, to carry the extra passengers, there were supplementary trains: e.g., Second No. 3, Third No. 4.

We iced the trains in the mornings and in the evenings. In the afternoons, we cleaned out refrigerator cars ("reefer cars") that were on their way back to the Okanagan Valley to be filled with fruit; or we moved coal for the next winter's heating from a gondola car into the basement of the station building; or we moved rock salt from a car beside the ice house, a large, two-storey, gabled building, into buckets, which we hoisted to the second floor with a primitive pulley system. It was a good job, lots of hours, lots of pay. The gang was run by a Vancouver contractor. Every two weeks our pay would come from Vancouver by train. We were paid in cash. The money was stuffed into small brown envelopes, on the front of which the contractor had stamped a form on which he wrote the details of our payment.

We had a small tractor and a string of flat wagons, open at the sides, but with metal bars at the ends, on which we carried the ice from the ice house to the trains.

Starting at one end of the train, a couple of us opened up the compartments under all of the cars. These were unhooked, pulled up from the bottom, and re-hooked at the top. Usually, it was necessary to reorganize the ice that still remained in the compartment before the new ice could be put in. A couple of our guys would be busy doing that. Another part of the crew would follow them with the new ice. They put a wooden-ladder-like device from the ice wagon to the compartment, and with tongs, two of them would flop the 400 pound blocks on to their sides on the ladder and shove them into the compartment. I don't remember how many blocks went into a car, maybe half a dozen in an empty compartment. On top of the ice we would throw salt, causing it to melt quickly, which created the cold air for the air-conditioning. And in this fashion we rapidly worked our way along the train, doing our best to finish the job within the 20 minutes or so that the trains normally stopped in Revelstoke. It was hard work, often made awkward by the droves of passengers who poured on to the platform to stretch their legs. But on most days the hard work was intermittent. When it was not, when the next section of the train was waiting right behind the one in the station, we would race back to the ice house, reload the wagons with new blocks, and hurry to the platform to install them.

When the trains were late, we sat around while the ice dripped from the wagons—getting paid, of course, which was nice. But I found the waiting acutely boring. And it wasn't just the waiting. My fellow gang members were not very inspiring company. From time to time, my boredom was somewhat alleviated by the ragging that went on among the boys while we waited. For example, one of the gang was a fellow named "Dennis," known by all as "Den." His best friend in the group, Larry (aka "Louse") Mercurio, who was not the brightest guy in the valley, began to call him "Den Bien Phu," after the place in French Indochina, much in the news that summer, where the French army was under siege. His friend, Ron "Lum" Lombardo, would pick this phrase up and repeat it over and over. If I had not before been convinced of the value of a university education, making it unnecessary for me to take this kind of job in the future, this summer confirmed the idea.

Louse Mercurio and Lum Lombardo were able to buy fancy cars with their full-time ice-gang earnings. Louse bought a salmon pink and grey Desoto, Lum a wine-red Buick convertible. Both cars had all the bells and whistles available at that time, even such things as power windows. Lombardo had some serious mental problems. When he worked on the rebuilding of the snow sheds at Three Valley Lake, about fifteen miles west of Revelstoke, he was working for the high school principal, Mel Abbott, who had taken on this summer CPR contract. Suddenly, in the midst of conversations on totally unrelated topics and away from the job site, he would say, "M-Eh-Boat: Monk!" over and over. He was shipped to Essondale, the provincial mental institution east of Vancouver, a couple of times for shock treatments. A few years after I left Revelstoke, he committed suicide by jumping into the raging, spring-swollen, Illecillewaet River. The last time I saw Mercurio was in Vancouver in 1957. He was working in a Kelly-Douglas jam factory. His ambition was to become "a peanut butter man," as peanut butter men could sit down on the job. He was killed in a car accident some time in the Sixties.

The Co-op and Grades 3 and 4 with "Horsey" Burn

On the corner of First and Mackenzie was the Revelstoke Co-op Store, where our family bought groceries and where my mother took me when I was in elementary school to buy school supplies. Everything was behind the counter, and a clerk, pad in hand, would write down the items you asked for and retrieve them from the shelves. He would then wrap them in brown paper and tie the parcel up with string that was fed from a giant ball. Groceries were put in large paper bags, much as they are in some stores today. If you weren't taking your groceries with you, they would be delivered free later that day. Those who weren't running a credit account (where you paid your bill at the end of each month) would either pay in the store or pay the delivery man, when he brought the groceries to your house.

> *Just before my brother joined the army in July 1943, he brought home a mongrel puppy called Pedro, a mixture of spaniel, collie, and most likely a number of other breeds. We called him "Paydee." The dog was a great family pet but was totally untrained. When I was walking with him near the police station, he went after a policeman's pant cuffs in a playful way. "Not a very obedient dog you have there," said the policeman. One day when the Co-op man was delivering groceries to our house, Pedro began jumping up on him in his overly-friendly way. "Paydee!" my mother shouted at him. "No," said the delivery man. "Pay day's next Tuesday."*

When I was going into Grade 3, the clerk in the Co-op said, "Oh, he's going to be with Miss Burn for the next two years. She'll whip him into shape." Poor Miss Burn, Miss Eva Burn, known around town as "Horsey" Burn, condemned by her looks to grow old in the home of her parents, on the shelf from the start, a born spinster. Although she was a tough disciplinarian, she was nothing like Mrs. Bottenheimer, the Grade One substitute teacher. When Miss Burns (no relation) was called away because of the death of her father in Kamloops, we had Mrs. Bottenheimer teaching us for a few days. She was absolutely frightening. She carried the strap around in her smock pocket. She would sneak up behind you and smack you across the back of your hands if she saw you doing something she didn't like.

Miss Burn was tough, but she was nothing like that. Besides, she seemed to like me; and if she whipped me into shape, she did it with kindness. Once, she picked me to dramatize a little play in front of the class, a scene from *Hansel and Gretel*, choosing as Gretel the prettiest girl in the class, Barbara Shamon, on whom I secretly had a crush. I was sure at the time that Miss Burn knew about my crush, and that made me shy. I survived the dramatization, though I never did let Barbara know that I thought she was wonderful. All of this, of course, was part of the wonderful world of puppy love. When we were in high school, she became the steady girl of my friend, Busher MacDonald.

FIRST STREET

Lena's, Mull's, the Dew Drop Inn, the Shojis and the "Y"

OFF MACKENZIE AVENUE, ON FIRST STREET, THERE WERE A NUMBER OF OTHER STORES, RESTAURANTS, AND HOTELS. ON THE EAST END[3] STOOD, SIDE BY SIDE, THE REGENT AND THE REVELSTOKE hotels (still in the Forties featuring spittoons in their lobbies). In the Revelstoke Hotel was Lena's Café (run by Lena Miller, a homely, small-sized, middle-aged woman, who walked with a forward bend. It was said—jokingly, and with a large measure of cruelty—that she had once won a beauty contest.) Across from Lena's was Mull's Pool Room, where Solo was played in the back rooms, and you could cash your CPR cheque out of banking hours—wives of men who drank and /or gambled would hang around the area on pay-days until their husbands came to cash their cheques, at which point they would confiscate the money and lead the sober and resentful husband home, almost, if not quite, by the ear. Next to Mull's was the Dew Drop Inn, a Chinese restaurant, where we teenage boys would wickedly order "Chicken Flied Lice."

Further to the south, in the next block, on the corner of Orton Avenue, was Rutherford's Transfer. From there, if you looked toward the railway line, you could see the Snow White Steam Laundry, owned and operated by the Shoji family, who, along with all of the other Japanese, had been scandalously forced away from the coast during the war. In Revelstoke, the Japanese who arrived as a result of this policy met some discrimination from the older residents—they were not, for example, allowed to join the golf club (a fact that my parents found disgusting)—but there was no discrimination among us younger people. Eddie and Yosh Shoji were a regular part of our gang of guys in high school.

Back on First Street, and further down the block from Rutherford's, on the other side of the street, was the former YWCA building, still run as a gym, bowling alley, and meeting area, and still called the "Y', though it was no longer run by the "Y."

Mackinnon and Colarch Cigar Store and Pool Room

On the west side of Mackenzie Avenue was the Mackinnon and Colarch Cigar Store and Pool Room, in which I spent far too much time as a teenager playing snooker and kelly pool. Usually, we'd play for the cost of the game, which was 25 cents. But there were variations. If one or both of us were short of money, we would split the cost 10/15; if we were really short of money, we would split 12/13. Speaking of money, in the early nineteen fifties, the Provincial Government brought in a 5% sales tax to cover hospital costs. The tax kicked in at 14 cents. Neil Colarch, the partner who was usually

---

[3] The town of Revelstoke is laid out on a north-west by south-east axis. The streets, however, running from Mackenzie Avenue as a centre line, are simply referred to as being "east" or "west." I have followed that system and extended it so that south-west becomes "south" and north-east becomes "north."

behind the counter, and who cared a great deal for the value of money, was much amused by the tax kicking in at this point. "Chocolate bars, 7 cents each," he would say. "Two for 15."

Neil called his partner, Joe Mackinnon, who was a fervent Catholic, "Holy Joe." Neil was a second-generation, raised-in-Canada, Italian-Catholic male in his attitude to the Church: that is, as the old saying goes, "he was carried in, married in, and buried in." Nothing more. Mackinnon, on the other hand, was a pillar of the parish. Among his many contributions, he rang the bell at St. Francis of Assisi, on the corner of Mackenzie Avenue and Fifth Street, every weekday morning at seven, summoning the faithful to 7:30 low Mass., which Father Jansen, probably to the relief of many, was able to mumble his way through in a little over twenty minutes.

Father Jansen Astounds the Bishop

WHEN I WAS A YOUNG BOY, DURING WORLD WAR II, THE PRIEST AT ST. FRANCIS WAS FATHER JANSEN. HE HAD ESCAPED THE TYRANNY of Nazi Germany in the Thirties, and somehow or other wound up in Revelstoke. He preached hair-raising sermons in an English that was thickly accented by his native German. His favourite topic, as I remember it, was married couples who fought with fury, throwing dishes and pots at one another. When people gathered at the back of the church on Saturday evening for confession, they often heard the good father's voice rising out of the middle of the confessionals, blasting their neighbours for some sin or other: "You did *vhat*? Vhy did you do *dhat*?"

> *They used to have confessions for children on Saturday mornings. I hated confessions. This sacrament seemed to me to be an exercise in humiliation rather than a vehicle of forgiveness. But my mother always insisted I go. So, I would head off to the area near the church, where I would hang around in the alley by Fifth Street, just south of Mackenzie Avenue, until enough time had passed. Then I would go home, cleansed of humiliation, if not of sins.*
>
> *Once, when I was eight or nine, the nuns lined us up in the parish hall to go to confession. I was caught, so I was undoubtedly not behaving well. Sister Mary Oliver accused me of kicking her in the shin. It wasn't me; I didn't do it; of that, I'm sure. The Mother Superior, horrid, fat Sister Mary Jean, when they'd got us all into the church, asked me to apologize in front of everyone. I refused. It wasn't me. I didn't do it. Afterwards, Sister Mary Oliver and Sister Mary Jean marched me to our house and showed my mother the bruise I supposedly caused. When my dad got home, the only time in my life, he beat me with his razor strop. I have hated people who think they have the truth ever since.*

Father Jansen was a hunter. Every fall he would shoot a deer or two. He canned the venison in quart bottles—nobody had freezing capacity in those days—providing him with much of the meat he would need throughout the winter. On one occasion, when Bishop Johnson was visiting the parish from the diocesan headquarters in Nelson, Father

Jansen took him into the basement and showed him the bottles of venison. The bishop was astounded. He accepted the fact that the priest had shot the deer, but he refused to believe that he had done the canning himself. When the war broke out, the police came to the rectory and took Father Jansen's rifle away from him, as they did from all other so-called enemy aliens. It wasn't long, however, before one of the lawyers in the congregation managed to have the rifle returned to him.

My Brief Career as a Singer

Next to Mackinnon and Colarch was Service Barber Shop, where Mr. Green (and later, Louis Sanservino) would cut your hair. Green, who had rigged up a bicycle seat on a swivelling bar attached to his chair so that he could sit while cutting your hair, also acted as the town veterinarian, in an odd way fulfilling the traditional role of the barber as medical man. I don't know how much he actually knew about animal medicine, but he was the best we had. The block was completed on that side by the Mac and Mac Hardware, a branch of a province-wide enterprise. Across from there was a popular café, the Sally Anne Coffee Shop, known simply as Sally's. It was run by Barney Evans and his grumpy wife, Bertha, and was very popular with the high-school crowd. We went there for coffee (10 cents), coke in those wonderful, twisted six-ounce bottles (10 cents), and plain hamburgers (20 cents).

In the next block, and across the street again, was the Credit Union office, run by George Patrick. George was a confirmed drinker, who took on the large puffiness of the alcoholic more and more as time went on. He was a joker. Once, in a quest which for him was one of patent absurdity, a Don Quixote fighting windmills, he had "written up the rules" for a job with the CPR, a process that had the candidate copy the rules out of the book of rules into a booklet designed for this purpose, a mind-numbing thing to have to do for anyone with a modicum of intelligence, and George had a lot more than that. His answers were creative: Question: "What is a Yard?" George's Answer: "Three feet." George's wife, a large woman I grew to know quite well, taught singing lessons from a piano in a room behind the credit union. After I had taken over the lead in the high school production of the operetta, "The Forest Prince," in Grade 11, and throughout my final year in high school, I took singing lessons from her—as did my girlfriend, Karen Abbott.

As part of the chorus of The Forest Prince, an operetta based on the music of Tchaikovsy, I was standing near the piano in the school gymnasium / auditorium as Dorothea "Dot" Lundell, the teacher responsible for putting on the operetta, was trying unsuccessfully to get the lead tenor, Bob Fisher, to reach the high notes in the aria, "Sweet to Remember," the lovely melody that makes up the andante cantabile of the Fifth Symphony. She splayed her hands and bent her head over the piano keys in a feminine gesture of despair. "Can I try that?" I said. She looked toward me grimly. "Why not?" she replied. And that's how, late in the production, I became the tenor lead and stage partner of Karen Abbott, the soprano lead. At the time, I had no idea that we would spend the next year and a half of our lives as the best of friends.

Karen carried on as a professional singer. I gave it up—apart from singing in choirs and quartets—when I went to college. Once when I went into the office for my back-room singing lesson, George said: "What's the difference between a camisole and a casserole?" I looked at him blankly. He continued: "It's a question of what kind of chicken you put in it." The joke made no sense to me. "What's a camisole?" I said. "Ask your girlfriend," said George. Ah, innocence!

After George Patrick had faded into the alcoholic woodwork, Raymond MacDonnell, the projectionist at the Avolie Theatre, who wasn't averse himself to a drink, opened Ray's Electric Shop in the credit union location, his store mainly dealing with radio sales and repairs. His son, Billy, was a friend of mine when I was little. One day, when we were seven or eight, he fell off a fence and broke his wrist. He came out of the hospital proudly wearing a cast. I was envious. About fifteen years' later, when I was teaching in England, Bill MacDonnell sent me an invitation (through his mother and my mother) to his wedding in Germany, where he was serving in the RCAF. It was impossible for me to get away from work, so I sent my regrets.

Dealing with the Mentally Ill, Revelstoke-Style

BESIDE RAY'S ELECTRIC WAS A DRY CLEANING ESTABLISHMENT OWNED BY GABY CAVA. IT WAS TO THE CHANGE ROOM AT CAVA'S THAT a mentally-ill patient of Dr. Armstrong, a popular young physician, fled after stabbing the doctor in the back of the neck as he reached into his lower mail box in the lobby at the post office. (There was no delivery in Revelstoke, so you had to go to the post office to pick up your mail.) The doctor, fortunately, was not badly hurt. The deranged patient was bound into a straight-jacket, escorted on to a train, and committed to the Essondale mental hospital. A decade or so earlier, it was a physician, Dr. A. L. Jones, rather than a patient, who was loaded on to a train in a straight-jacket. His problem was the surfeit of booze in his life, which eventually led to the courts taking away his driver's licence, and finally, to delirium tremens.

Paula's Beauty Parlour and the Town's Major Hoople

The last building on the south side of the block, right next to the railway spur that bisected the middle of the town, was Paula's Beauty Parlour, where the ladies of the town had their hair cut, shaped, and coloured. Paula Overhill's husband was a kind of Major Hoople character. (You will remember Hoople as the comic strip character who lived lazily on the proceeds of his wife's boarding house.) But Mr. Overhill was not a loser in the usual sense of the word. He was a well-read man of considerable intelligence, whose only real failing was his aversion to work. Only once that I know of did he have a job. During World War II, he was conscripted to be one of the guards on the railway bridge over the Columbia River. But the job didn't last long. He very quickly managed to fall off the bridge, injuring himself enough so that he was exempted from further duty, but not enough so that he was exempted from further free-loading.

The Pradolinis: Fall from Grace

On the corner, across the street from Paula's was Walter's Groceteria. At night there were cats behind the plate glass window in the lit-up front of the store, presumably there to keep rats and mice at bay. Next to Walter's was Sheedy's barber shop, where I was taken, screaming and yelling, for my first haircut. In the same block on that side of the street was Pradolini's store. The Pradolinis had been prominent Revelstokians since three brothers, Anselmo, Gaudenzio, and Achille, arrived in town at the beginning of the century and set up a construction business. They were hugely successful. Anselmo even served as mayor for a few years in the Thirties.

After the older generation died off, the firm was taken over by Anselmo's sons, Elio and Mario. Elio—known to everyone as "Al" or "Prad"—was a mountain of a man, a fine athlete, starring on both the football and baseball teams when he was at Gonzaga University and the star player of the Revelstoke Spikes baseball team during its glory days in the 1940s.

Mario had always been a bit strange, a factor which grew as he aged. He was a fine pianist, who might be heard at any time of the day or night pounding the ivories, alone, in the Pradolini warehouse near the edge of the Columbia River near Sawyer's Sawmill. (What was a piano doing in a warehouse?) In later years, he could be seen wandering about town talking to himself, or sitting in a booth in Manning's Restaurant holding a vivid conversation with the bench across from him. Elio, in the meantime, managed to run the firm into bankruptcy, at which point he cut his wrists in a minor sort of way and leapt out of the second floor of his store on First Street. He did not do himself much physical damage—but in the Revelstoke custom, he was bundled on to a train and sent to Essondale for treatment. He was soon released and returned home.

When I was a student, home for the summer of 1955 from Notre Dame College, I was hired by the people who had picked up the pieces of the Pradolini firm to empty a carload of bags of cement into a warehouse beside the spur that ran through the middle of the town. On the second of two days that I was doing this back-breaking job, I was joined by Elio, who had been given a chance to earn a little money doing the same thing. He said to me: "You should think about becoming a priest. It's the best way to go through life." I guess he felt that if he had done so, he would not have come down so far in the world. It was too late for him to escape that way, but, as he saw it, it was not too late for me. But it *was* too late for me. It had *always* been too late for me. I had other things in mind, involving such unpriestly things as travel and pretty women.

Revelstoke Motors

Further down First Street West was Revelstoke Motors, the GM and Shell Oil dealer, owned by the partnership of McGregor, Tomlinson, and Gerow. The sons of McGregor and Tomlinson, Garry McGregor, and Michael Tomlinson were both friends of mine in high school. Michael was nicknamed "Moe," short for "Motor," as his dad was in the car business. Gerow was one of the town drunks. Occasionally, late in the evening, when he was on one of his benders, Gerow would stop his car right in the middle of the street in front of the Revelstoke Grill, the greasy spoon across from Revelstoke Motors—there wasn't much traffic in the town after 6 p.m.—and go into the café for, one assumes, a sobering coffee. The single policeman who would be on duty at that time of the night would roust him out of the café, park his car on the curb, and drive him home. To my knowledge, he was never charged. The world was a gentler, saner, and emptier place in those days.

> *One winter evening during my year in Grade 11, I went to Garry McGregor's house on the corner of Third Street and Orton Avenue. "Come on up to my room," Garry said, glancing at his watch. "I want to show you something." We went in without Garry's turning on the light, which I thought odd. "Over here," he said from the window. We looked down to the kitchen of the house next door, where a woman was ironing clothes. "Her husband comes home every night at this time. The first thing he does when he arrives is feel her up." After a short time, the husband arrived. She appeared to greet him without turning around, remaining catatonically at the ironing board. The husband's hands reached around her and massaged her breasts. Then they disappeared into another part of the house. Was this a love game of some sort, planned ahead of time and agreed to? Or was the woman merely showing toleration for the situation?*

Boyle's Bakery and Mid-Century Dentistry

West of the greasy spoon, across one of the CPR's mid-block alleys, was Boyle's Bakery, where we bought candy as kids, paving the way for later trips to the dentist. I see short and rotund Mrs. Boyle (had she been into her own candy jar?), her brown, neck-length hair in tight curls, leaning down to me with my purchase of Cracker Jack (*A Prize in every Package*), gushing at little me. God! How I hated gushy women! Even then.

Dentists in those days were still using slow-grinding drills, the kind that had arms reaching out over the top of the chair, everything run by rope-like bands that transmitted the motor power, such as it was, to the drill-head. They were slow and painful and horrible to look at, the parts dangling above my head like the parts of a great praying mantis. Beside the chair stood a white porcelain bowl on a pedestal that you were told to spit into, water continuously swirling around within it and going out of its bottom, like a small, forever-flushing toilet. Strangely, I don't remember the pain itself. Perhaps one never does. Even more strangely, I remember a conversation totally unrelated to dentistry that took place between my white-coated sadist and his female chair-side assistant, in which they discussed the fact that the kilt-wearing, giggling, silly Scots singer, Harry Lauder, one of the greatest stars of the music halls, had just died. (So, this particular appointment was on or after February 26, 1950.) All recollection of the other appointments is gone. But thanks to Mrs. Boyle and my own bad cleaning habits, I had a string of meetings in that office above Paula's Beauty Parlour. I was thus, in some sense, faced with a Lauderish need to "keep right on till the end of the road," a dental road in this case—and I did.

Smythe's Pool Room and a Dickensian Loo

Next to Boyle's was Smythe's Pool Room. This venerable establishment (I use the term loosely) had no bathroom, and patrons, all male of course, went into a dark adjoining shed with a sandy, dirt floor and peed against the rubble wall. The odour of that Dickensian room comes back in spades every time I think of it. Not until I was in England in the late 1950s did I run across similar loos behind sleazy working class pubs. The place was run by Roy Smythe and his son, Jack. Jack's unmarried sister, Catherine, a minute hen of a woman, who, it was said about town, had been 39 for years, worked at Revelstoke Drugs on Mackenzie Avenue. Smythe's was the place you went to for a fishing licence. Near Christmas every year, the Rod and Gun Club held a turkey shoot in the Dickensian loo. They didn't actually shoot turkeys in there. What they did was put targets up against the rubble wall and you shot at them with a 22-calibre rifle. The best scores won the turkeys.

The Post Office and the Perpetual Mayor

At the end of that block, on the south side, was the Post Office, overseen by the postmaster, Walter Hardman, who was mayor of Revelstoke from 1937 to 1962, returned by acclamation year after year through all the years I was growing up and for nearly a decade after I had left the place. This short, cocky, bespectacled, expatriate Englishman seemed to me then to be as permanently in place as death, taxes, and Ottawa corruption. But he turned out to be a mortal man after all. During the 1960s, after he had retired from the mayor's job, he developed Alzheimer's disease and more and more frequently he became lost as he walked around the city he had been so much a part of for so many years.

> *Walter Hardman was the perfect escort for various members of the Royal Family during their brief visits to Revelstoke while their trains were being serviced: George VI and Queen Elizabeth in 1939, Princess Elizabeth and Philip in 1951, and Princess Margaret in 1958. He had dignity, and he treated them with the deference they expected, whether they deserved it or not. The visits always consisted of a walk down the long station platform and back, multitudes of Revelstokians cheering along the way. On October 19, 1951, in the midst of a snow flurry, I was a part of Air Cadet Squadron #324, which was inspected by the Princess on the road by the station platform. My friend, Jim Craig, as Flight Sergeant, got to shake the royal hand. For weeks afterwards, when he greeted anyone, he repeated that old line, "Shake the hand that shook the hand of the Queen." ("I danced with a man who danced with a girl who'd danced with the Prince of Wales.") She was not yet queen, but Jim Craig would never allow that fact to spoil a good line. In 1958, I was part of the crowd watching Margaret at the station, as she did the usual walk down the platform.*

Davidson Motors and the World of 408 Third Street West

The next two blocks of First Street West were made up of a combination of housing and empty lots. Beyond these was situated on the south side, where the road split the blocks—angling to Second Street, the High School, and Central School—the last business on this street, Davidson Motors, the Ford dealer. When my family lived at 408 Third Street West, the Davidsons of Davidson Garage were our next-door neighbours to the east. The year I was five, my mother and, no doubt, my four sisters— at that time, I inhabited a world largely made up of women—decided it was "cute" for me to send a valentine next door to Fern Davidson, who was also five. The valentine read: "Cross my heart and hope to die, / You're my little sweetie-pie." But it was not I who had launched "young Cupid's fiery shaft" at Fern. The thing was a put-up job! My brother certainly would not have been involved. And I'm sure my dad had nothing to do with it. He was a loner in a large family. Besides, he would not have been around. He would have had to hike through the snow that day to and from his teaching job at Begbie School.

> *Begbie School was a one-room school about three miles south of Revelstoke. Jack Keough taught there from 1927 until 1944, when he reached the age of 65 and retired. In the fall and spring he rode his heavy CCM bicycle from our house at 408 Third Street West, through the town, over the bridge on the Illecillewaet River, and along the dirt road to the school. In winter he walked, often laboriously through heavy snow along unploughed roads, often getting there early enough to light the pot-bellied stove to heat the place before the fifteen to twenty pupils in grades one to six arrived. The school consisted of a classroom and a cloakroom. The toilets were outhouses in the yard, one for girls, and one for boys. Water was pumped up from a well. Jack Keough loved teaching in this sort of school; he had done so all his life; he would never have been happy in a town school with many rooms and many teachers.*

On the vacant lot between our house and the Davidson's there were three horse chestnut trees, one of which as a youngster I used to like to climb. It was from these trees that I watched the funeral cortege of the woman at the end of our block, whom my mother called "Old Lady White," as it journeyed to Mountain View Cemetery some time around 1940. I remembered Old Lady White as a reliable purveyor of peppermints, so I was sorry to see her go. It was also in these trees that I sulked on the afternoon that all of the rest of the family—except my eldest sister, Kay, who was somehow deputed to baby-sit me—went to a matinee of the film, "Gone With the Wind." I was considered too young to go to it. But I whole-heartedly disagreed, and I was not pleased to be excluded from an event that had been much-talked about around the kitchen table during meals.

A couple of years' later, when my friend, Bob Graham, and I were in these trees, an unknown man began marching back and forth on the sidewalk. He was tall, and straight-backed and military, though he was not in uniform. Bob and I began counting his steps—"Left, right, left, right"—and he came over and started talking to us. My mother, seeing this happening from the house, came out and joined the conversation. The man claimed to be an American sailor who had been wounded somewhere in the Pacific. My mother asked him in for dinner—he said he'd join us as long as it wasn't one of my sisters who wanted him to (it wasn't)—and, as it turned out, he stayed the evening. I have no idea who he was, or what he was doing in front of 408 Third Street West in the middle of the war, or where he went when he left our house. But I was impressed to see a "real" sailor who had been wounded. My parents were sceptical about his wounds until he showed them an ugly scar that rippled across his chest.

The Cenotaph, My Paper Route, and the Legion

Armistice Day Parades

The Cenotaph, a small obelisk with bronze plaques embossed with the names of those who had died in the Boer War and WW I—and later those killed in WW II and Korea—was in the triangle formed where the road angled past Davidson Motors. There was always a parade of veterans and cadets to the Cenotaph on Armistice Day, November 11, later known as Remembrance Day. Also included in the parade were the boy scouts from the United and Anglican Churches. In the early days, there were a few marchers who were veterans of the Boer War, but most were veterans of World War I. Later, the parade was much enlarged by the return of World War II veterans. For a couple of years, when I was in my early teens, I was one of the air cadets in the parade. The air cadets had a bugle band, and I was made drum major. I was given a four-foot, decorated staff, like a mace, and taught how to point it and pump it in time with the music. I was not very good at it, being rhythmically-challenged. There was also in the parade the town band, with Mickey "Whisky" McMahon, who had been a drummer in WW I, banging on his snare drum and chewing an unlit cigar in his mouth as he marched along, spitting out the bits and the spittle, until, eventually, the cigar was gone, the parade was over, and Mickey and the other vets headed to the Legion to celebrate the day by getting plastered.

A Captured Cannon

Across from the Cenotaph, to the north, sat the two-storey Canadian Legion Building, in front of which was a cannon which had been captured from the Germans in WW I. During WW II, this cannon, in a flurry of wartime romantic silliness, was added to the war-effort scrap-pile of even greater silliness: pots and pans and cigarette wrappings, piled higgledy-piggledy next to the spur that ran across the town to the sheds in which coal was stored. Nothing was done with this scrap—it was, in fact, useless to the war effort, but the powers-that-be had decided that it would make people feel they were helping if they contributed something. It finally disappeared after the war was over, no doubt hauled away to be melted down or buried in a garbage dump somewhere. We youngsters loved to play war games on the cannon. It wasn't of much use for anything else, and it would have served the town better if it had stayed as a piece of decoration in its place on the grounds in front of the Legion.

> *Once, a liberator bomber flew over the town. God knows what this aircraft was doing over Revelstoke, but it was incredibly exciting to see. Then, one afternoon late in the war, a convoy of army trucks arrived from the west, on its way over the Big Bend Highway. They bivouacked in a field by the spur, at the end of Campbell Avenue, on top of the high banks of the river, just a few blocks from our house on Third Street. They lit bonfires in the evening, and all of us neighbourhood kids mingled excitedly with the uniformed guys as they sat around their fires. In the morning, they were gone.*

Paper Routes and Bowling Pins

In the basement of the Legion was a five-pin Bowling Alley. When I gave up my paper route, delivering 30 copies of the *Vancouver Sun* six days a week (subscribers paid, often reluctantly, a dollar a month, of which I got twenty-five cents), I took a job setting pins for five cents per person per game. So in one swoop, I was both relieved of my early morning delivery job and saw my finances take a turn for the better. The paper route money amounted to slave wages, even for paper boys, who are never paid very well. (Often, they are never paid at all; there are still people in Revelstoke who owe me money; unfortunately, most of them are by this time in Mountain View Cemetery.) We would meet Train No. 1 at 7:45 a.m. to pick up our papers. Old Andy Davidson of Davidson's Transfer, who was picking up the town's mail at the same time for delivery to the Post Office, would allow us to ride into town on top of the mail bags on the back of his half-ton truck. I would jump off at Mackenzie and First and walk to Fourth and Fifth Street East to deliver my route. We carried the papers in a large, white canvas sack, emblazoned on its side in black with *Vancouver Sun*, which hung over our young shoulders like a giant purse. In winter, pulling the bag over the snow banks as we crossed the streets was a daunting task. So I was mightily pleased to get my new job setting pins, even without considering the money angle.

The Queen Victoria Hospital

I Have My Ears Boxed

East of the Legion, just across the street, the three-storey, red brick Queen Victoria Hospital stood on fairly substantial grounds, its porte cochere centered like the head of a bird in between its two swept-back wings. On the grounds to the east of it was the cottage-like isolation hospital, no longer in use by the time I was growing-up. In fact, at some point in the Fifties, it was sold as a residence to Wentworth ("Wenty") Smythe, a teacher at Central School, who had in middle age married a girl in her late teens. The town was suitably shocked by this May/December affair, but it was said that the girl, who came from a large, poor, farming family, had a chance for a better life with Wenty than with her other prospects, which were apparently pretty meagre. It was not long before she produced a child, though I don't remember whether a full nine months had passed in the meantime. Not that it matters a damn.

But I do remember Wenty for personal reasons. In a class on health—funny I should remember that detail—in Grade 7, in which I was undoubtedly misbehaving and richly deserved what was about to happen, he slapped me across the head with the back of his hand. I stood up with creative indignation and walked out of the room, spending the rest of the period in the cloak room, one of which could be found at the front of each classroom. The health class met only once a week, and the next time it met, I did not go into the classroom but remained in the cloak room. After the class, Wenty called me into the empty room and apologized: "I'm sorry I boxed your ears," he said. And it was over. If I'd told my mother about the incident, which I didn't, she would have said that I no doubt deserved having my ears boxed. I can't imagine how this minor incident might have gotten blown out of proportion in today's world.

> *After a mid-winter Grade 10 phys-ed class in the Drill Hall—the school's gymnasium had not yet been built—late on a Friday afternoon, I was asked by the teacher, Peter Grauer, to come up to the library, as he wanted to show me something. The library at that time was a large closet-like area in behind the staff room. There was nobody else around, and the only light in the room was the winter light from the windows. Grauer brought out a bunch of photographs, taken, he said, during the war in Belgium. They were photographs of nude men, including himself, in homosexually-compromised positions. I was stunned. He wanted me to touch his penis. I backed away—and fled through the darkened staff room, into the hall, and out of the building. He called after me, "Don't tell anybody about this!" I was so astounded—and somehow ashamed—by this incident that I was never tempted to tell anyone about it until after Peter Grauer was dead, about ten years later. The incident did me no harm. In fact, it taught me a little more about what the real world is like. Peter Grauer, who was married and had a family, had for some reason or other let his real sexual preferences get out of hand. But why me? I kept asking myself. Why me?*

Getting My Head Dented

I experienced the Queen Victoria Hospital only once as a patient, if we exclude the fact that I was born there. When I was twelve, I was part of a group, organized by the ski club, which was night skiing on the slalom hill on Mt. Revelstoke, just east of the town. Illumination was provided by flairs, which were dark red sticks about a foot long and three-quarters of an inch in diameter, with a spike on the bottom to attach them to whatever. These flairs were exactly like the ones used by the CPR and were undoubtedly provided by the CPR, unbeknownst to the CPR. The flairs came with a cap that had an emery board on top. To light the flare, you removed the cap, struck the emery board across the top of the flair, and watched it burst into flame. I don't remember how long these flairs stayed alight, but one of them failed as I was reaching the bottom of the slalom course. Suddenly, everything turned black, and, as I couldn't see anything, I pulled over and stopped. Coming behind me was Billy Munro, who couldn't see anything either, including me, and he ploughed right into me, one of his skis hitting the top of my head.

From that point on, I remember nothing until early the next morning. While it was still dark, I woke up. I knew somehow that I was in a hospital ward; perhaps I knew this because someone was moaning off and on in the bed next to me. (The moaner turned out to be another young fellow, new in town, whom I didn't know. He had broken his leg.) The story is that I was knocked out by the collision, carried on a sled to the house of the Pletsch family, which was on the mountainside, where I remained for a couple of hours while the ambulance was rounded up and sent for me. I remember none of this, although they say I was unconscious for only a few minutes. The ski that hit my head caused a huge bump to grow, which, when it had subsided, turned into a two-inch-wide dent on the back of my not-yet-totally-hardened, twelve-year-old skull. It is shaped like a pock mark on the moon and has been with me all my life. I was kept under observation in hospital by Dr. Sutherland for four days and then released. I spent a few more days at home. After that, I went back to school, apparently none the worse for my adventure. (Some of you will say, "Ah Hah! So *that's* why he's the way he is! *Now* I understand!")

SECOND STREET

"There are no good eating places . . ." in Revelstoke

IN THE BLOCK JUST EAST OF MACKENZIE AVENUE ON THE EAST SIDE OF SECOND STREET, WAS ROGER'S LADIES' WEAR STORE ("STYLES OF TODAY WITH A TOUCH OF TOMORROW") AND THE HEATING AND plumbing firm of E. G. Burridge and Son. On the north side, in the back part of the City Hall, was the Fire Station, manned by volunteer firemen. Across the alley from the Fire Hall was the King Edward Hotel, an Edwardian pile with a turret, which purportedly had the best restaurant in town. When the writer George Woodcock visited the town in 1951, he stopped a man on the street he labelled as "an Italian" and asked him to recommend a good eating place. "There are no good eating-places," the man replied, "but there is one less bad than the rest just around the corner."[4] Woodcock found this puzzling, as he said the town "seemed rather cosmopolitan." But restaurants in small towns throughout North America in those days served food that was pretty mundane: a chop of some sort, mashed potatoes scooped on to the plate with an ice cream scooper and drowned in gravy, some over-cooked canned peas or mushy carrots. Revelstoke, in spite of its "cosmopolitan" aura, was no exception. But the fault lay with the cooking of the food rather than with the cooking ingredients. Especially available were good vegetables. Spring, summer, and fall, superb in quality and freshly-harvested, they were delivered throughout town by everyone's favourite farmer, Charley Sing.

---

[4] *Ravens and Prophets*, 131. I've always been puzzled by Woodcock's rant against Revelstoke food: ". . . the soup was inedible (though both our stomachs are tough and experienced), the meat was stringy and scanty, and the sweet an unidentifiable stodge." I should have thought that Woodcock, as an English expatriate, would have enjoyed his lousy meal, that it would have reminded him of home.

> *For many years, he drove his horse and wagon twice a week, spring, summer, and fall, up and down the alleys. Charlie Sing had a farm on the eastern edge of the town and delivered carrots, peas, beets, turnips, potatoes, and just about anything else. As a superb farmer, he had a real advantage: his crops were always ready even before even those of the best town gardeners. As children, we would run out to greet him when he arrived on our block. He was friendly and smiling and would give us carrots. Best of all, sometimes he would allow us to sit beside him on top of the wagon. In an era when the Chinese were generally looked down upon, everyone loved Charlie.*

Kate and Dolly and Toby's Ass

Davidson's Transfer occupied most of the block on Connaught Avenue, the next street west of Mackenzie Avenue, between Second Street and Third Street. As five-year-olds, Bob Graham and I sometimes showed up on winter days at Davidson's barn to watch their two huge Percheron work horses, Kate and Dolly, being backed into their traces. I thought at the time that the horses were named after my eldest sister, Kathleen, and Bob's eldest sister, Dolly. But apparently the names were coincidental. After the horses had been harnessed, we would hop on to the sleigh with the workmen and go along with them—the bells on the horses jingling merrily—as they picked up lump coal from the coal sheds and delivered it to the houses that had ordered it. From the back of the sleigh, a chain had been dangled (to remove static electricity?) Bob and I used to like to hold on to the sleigh there and ride the chain over the snow. When we came to the place where the coal was to be delivered, we marvelled at the strength of the great horses, their legs having largely disappeared into the snow bank, as they pulled the sleigh closer to the houses.

In the next block west was another transfer company, City Transfer, run by the Switzer family, which provided the same kind of service as Davidson's. In their yard, under open sheds, they had stored the town's old horse-drawn wagons (the stage coach, the hearse, etc.) that were no longer in use, except during town parades. These sheds of wagons were a great place for children to play. Unfortunately, in the 1950s, an arsonist set fire to the sheds and all of the wagons were lost. City Transfer had a man named Toby Belinski working for them; and, of course, as a man who was working with coal, he got very dirty. From this situation, the expression "Black as Toby's ass," was coined by some wag. To this was added the rather prurient response, "How do you know how black Toby's ass is?" The reply? "If it's anything like his face, it's mighty black."

Forges and Weigh Scales

Off Second Street, in the next block west of City Transfer, between Campbell Avenue and Boyle Avenue, there were two alleys, forming an east-west, north-south cross. Most of the block was taken up with houses, but on the south east corner was a blacksmith's shop. Even in the early 1940s, there were still quite a few horses being used to pull various wagons and carts, the garbage wagons of the Venuttis, and the winter sleighs of the transfer companies. Between the north and south crosses was a weigh scale, a sort of gabled drive-through house, where the transfer companies weighed the coal they were delivering.

> *What delight not two blocks from my house! In his warm, dark shop, the blacksmith blasted air into the forge, put in the horseshoe until it was bright red, pounded it into shape on the anvil, tempered it in water, lifted the compliant hoof of the horse, and nailed the new shoe on. And on my way home, perhaps, I would see a sleigh stopped on the weigh scale, the huge work horses moving their heads nervously where they stood off the scale at the front of the sleigh, anxious to get on with the job of delivering the coal.*

A BIT ABOUT THE KEOUGHS

JACK AND ESTHER KEOUGH WERE ORIGINALLY FROM THE IRISH CATHOLIC COMMUNITY OF BLACKVILLE, N. B. JACK'S FATHER, PATRICK OWNED A GENERAL STORE IN THAT COMMUNITY. AFTER graduating from Normal School (1900) and St. Francis Xavier University (1906), Jack headed to Western Canada, where he taught in one-room schools in Alberta and British Columbia. In 1917, while he was still employed in Coal Creek, near Fernie, B.C., he married Esther McCarthy in Medicine Hat, Alberta. He was thirty-eight and she was twenty-two. Neither family approved of the union. Thus, they were married in Nowhere, Alberta, with only the priest as witness.

The Keoughs arrived in Revelstoke in 1927 with four children in tow: Kathleen, Mary, John, and Joan. Josephine (Jo) and I were born in Revelstoke. I spent my first nine years in the little gingerbread-adorned house at 408 Third Street West. Across the road on the south side was an empty field in which there were some hazelnut bushes. My older siblings used to pick the nuts, put them in a gunny sack, and smash the sack against the sidewalk in front of our house to remove the prickly, green outer coverings from the nuts. On the corner to the west of the hazelnut bushes was the house of "Old Lady White," purveyor of peppermints—at least for awhile. On the corner to the east stood the simple, gabled building—the exterior boards unpainted, as I remember them—in which the town band practised. I recall strains of Sousa marches wafting across the road as we sat on our veranda on typical hot summer evenings.

On the corner of the next block east was the police station, a small, wooden building, not unlike the band hall. Out of this building, the B.C. Police operated.[5] Attached to the back of the station was a small holding cell that had a barred window.

---

[5] When the RCMP took over policing in British Columbia a few years later, they refused to use this ramshackle building and were headquartered instead in the lower regions of the fine Hooper Court House.

One morning as I was walking by there with my dad, the window behind the bars shot up and a face appeared. "Would you go to the post office and get my mail for me?" the face asked. "I'd be happy to," my dad said, getting the man's name, picking up a letter without difficulty from Mayor Walter Hardman, who as postmaster manned the general delivery wicket, which consisted of a barred hole in the post office interior wall, not unlike the one at the jailhouse. Security at both ends of this operation was a mile or so below maximum. But it was human.

> *My dad and I often went fishing for small trout on the Illecillewaet River, in Charlie Sing's irrigation ditch, at Greeley Creek, even as far into the bush as Canyon Creek. We rode our bikes to a trail, hid them in the bushes, and hiked into the fishing places. I used a cheap rod. Dad cut himself a pole, tied his line and hook on the end, and headed down the stream. He always made sure he went ahead of me. "It's safer that way," he said. "In case you fall in." Now, these mountain streams usually have only one small trout per pool. Dad, in spite of his primitive equipment, always caught far more fish than I did. It took me a long time to figure out why.*

I was seven years younger than my sister Jo, nine younger than Joan, eleven younger than John, twelve younger than Mary, and seventeen younger than Kathleen. So by the time I was ten, all of my siblings had flown the coop: Jo and Joan to Normal School and teaching; John to the Army and the war in Europe; Mary to a secretarial job in Nelson; and Kathleen to secretarial work in Montreal, and later, Whitehorse. In 1944, when I was nine, my father reached the age of sixty-five and retired. In order for my mother, who was fifteen years younger than my father, to receive survivor benefits, my father's pension had to be cut in half, to the princely sum of $75. So there was a need to find another source of revenue. My parents considered a number of possibilities. They were tempted by the small grocery story that was for sale in the part of town where most of the people were Italian. But they were concerned about how well they might be received there. Besides, there was the matter of their ages. Running a grocery store was something for younger people to do. (The store was eventually bought by the Cerolinis, who did very well there.) In the end they decided to buy the Hughes Apartments. Everything depended on what they could get for our house on Third Street. Mrs. Hughes wanted $4,500 for her place. My parents decided they would have to get $2,000 for their place to be able to close the deal. They were offered $1900. Mrs. Hughes agreed to come down $100 on her price. So the deal was made.

We Move to Fourth Street East

The Hughes Apartments at 317 Fourth Street East was really a large house: three apartments on the ground floor (we lived in the back one), two on the second floor, and one in the basement. There was also a room in the basement that my dad used for his study. This room served as a spare bedroom for our family; I found it spooky and was frightened to sleep in it. There was an octopus furnace, fed by small coal from an automatic stoker; I was in charge of filling the hopper and taking out the clinkers, which I removed with a pair of large tongs and put into great galvanized tubs, ready to be hauled out to the garbage, which was picked-up by Venutti Transfer once a week. The bathroom on the second floor was shared by everyone, an unthinkable situation today, but not uncommon then. There was also a universally-accessible toilet in a small room in the basement, which was used mainly by our family and the basement tenant—and by others in emergency situations, the less said about, the better. Everyone did laundry in the basement, each suite on its assigned day, using a wringer washing machine and hanging the clothes out to dry on the line at the back of the house.

The tenants were a mixed bunch. One of my high school teachers, Ernie Sones, and his wife, lived for awhile on the second floor. There was an oldish lady, whose name I have forgotten, living out her life on the first floor. When we were first in the building, there was a single man living in the basement flat, really one long room divided into a living-room-kitchen area. My mother was amused that even though he came to our back door at all other times when he had something to say—it was on his usual way out of the building—when he paid his rent, he came around to the front of the building , down the hall, and knocked on our front door. My mother called him "Roger the Lodger."

After Roger had gone, an interesting December / May couple took over the flat in the basement. The woman, who was *late* December, had spent much of her life as a missionary doctor in China; her husband, Howard, an electrician by trade, who must have been at least thirty years her junior, had married her on her return to Canada (or so the story goes) when her medical intervention had saved his life. From our apartment upstairs, in the summer days when the windows were open, we could hear her singing to herself as she went about whatever domestic tasks she was doing, always the same song, "You are My Sunshine." It was not long before she went to the hospital and died. This couple was new in town, and Howard had to do some significant scrounging to find six pallbearers to serve at her simple funeral.

As a consequence of my siblings all having moved away, I grew up as the only child of an aging couple in a post-war world that was nothing like the depression years that had been the background of my siblings' formative years. I was a new generation in what was in essence a new family. The town itself was also in many respects a new town. The post-war years were years of prosperity and years of change. But just as Revelstoke had been a good place for my older siblings to grow up in in the Thirties, it remained a good place for me to grow up in the Forties and early Fifties. I wouldn't have missed it for the world.

The End of the Beginning

I LEFT REVELSTOKE, TO GO TO NOTRE DAME COLLEGE IN NELSON AND BEGIN MY ADULT LIFE, EARLY IN SEPTEMBER 1953. I TRAVELLED ON the CPR branch line on a train with an old, old steam engine, used only on this line, to Arrowhead, at the head of the Arrow Lakes, some 28 miles south of Revelstoke. This branch line would soon be abandoned. There, I boarded the *S. S. Minto* for the journey to

Nakusp. The *Minto*, a paddle wheeler launched in 1898, would operate on the lakes for only another couple of years. The old train. The old boat. I was using old technology to take me into a new world. Karen surprised me by showing up at the station on her bicycle to see me off.

> We had—we said—said our farewells the night before. But she came to the station anyway, on her bicycle, just before the train was due to leave. I was happy to see her, but neither of us could think of anything much to say. Everything that young love could say had already been said: We love one another—We will be faithful.—We will be true—It will be hard, but it's not that long till we'll meet again at Christmas, when I'll return home for the holidays. Standing on the platform by the steps into the coach, we held hands and looked into each other's eyes. As the train was about to leave, we kissed chastely, as befitted this public scene, a scene that we had pledged to avoid the night before. I mounted the steps and went to my seat, where we waved and smiled. As the train pulled out, I watched her familiar back as she went to her bicycle, went away from me.
>
> To get on to the branch line south to Arrowhead, the train had to back up about half a mile to the road crossing that leads to the Big Bend Highway. We arrived there and stopped while the switch was being thrown. On the road by the crossing, she stood beside her bicycle waving. One last goodbye.
>
> I was anxious to head into the adult world, to get on with my life. I knew I would miss her. I didn't at that moment realize how much. Nor did I know that I would not be faithful and true in Nelson, and that when I came home for Christmas, she would begin the process of letting me go, gently, having found someone else. But that's another story, waiting for another time.

The opening bars of the Operetta, in which Karen sang the soprano part of Tatiana, and Terry sang the tenor part of Vaslav

Revelstoke in Mid-Century

Terry on the Slalom Hill

**Revelstoke Station Royal Visit in 1939
Hand-Coloured Photo**

Terry at the Pool Room

Queen Victoria Hospital

**Charlie Sing & Friends
(Earle Dickey Photo: RMA 1697)**

Mackenzie Avenue at 2nd St. E. ca. 1940

The Alley Behind 3rd Street
Bruce "Costello" Carlson, Bob Graham, Terry

Pedro

Jack and Esther Keough in the Raspberries ca. 1940

Terry & Bob Graham 1939

Mary & Terry on *S.S. Minto* 1943

Terry & John 1943

Jack Keough & Pupils at Begbie School Late 1930s

Jack Keough at Begbie School

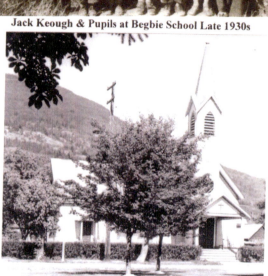
St. Francis of Assisi Church (Demolished 1960s)

408 Third Street W. in 1938
Top: Esther & Jack
Middle: Mary & Joan
Bottom: Jo, Terry, Leona Graham

Jack & Esther at 317 4th St. E. 1944

Terry, George Benson, Jim Craig
in the Old Rink

RHS Mountaineers & Peter Grauer:
Clockwise from Grauer: Busher MacDonald,
Jim Craig, Jim Tooley, Ray Beech, Moe
Tomlinson, Terry Keough, Morley Johnson;
Middle: Dale Marino

Beverley Rudd & Terry at the High School

Terry & Karen Abbott at Graduation Dance

"The Shadow of a Dream"
Terry 2nd from Right
Barbara Shamon 2nd from Left

The Forest Prince with Karen & Terry

Karen Abbott & Terry on Graduation Night

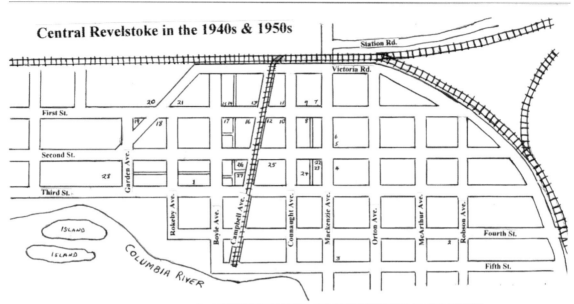

Central Revelstoke in the 1940s & 1950s

1. 408 3rd St. W.
2. 317 4th St. E.
3. St. Francis Church
4. Manning's
5. City Hall
6. Catlin's
7. Co-op
8. Mackinnon & Colarch
9. Sally Ann Cafe
10. Credit Union
11. Pradolini's
12. Paula's
13. Revelstoke Grill
14. Boyle's Bakery
15. Smythe's Pool Room
16. Revelstoke Garage
17. Post Office
18. Davidson Garage
19. Cenotaph
20. Legion
21. Queen Victoria Hospital
22. Brandon's
23. Hi-Lo
24. Davidson Transfer
25. City Transfer
26. Blacksmith
27. Weigh Scale
28. High School

Chapter 2: Wake up the Echoes[1]

NOTRE DAME NELSON (1953-55)

There are friends: other lives to brush against. But there will be no intimacies like the old ones. There will always be reservations, things one must leave out, events one can't explain without handing over a full map of one's life.
        Colm Toibín, ***The South***, 1991

How often the human race must bore God. I picture a cosmic yawn and His self-question, "Was it worth while creating them?"
        Charles Richie, ***Diplomatic Passport***, 1981

Da mihi castitatem et continentiam, sed noli modo. Give me chastity and continency—but not yet!
        St. Augustine, ***Confessions,*** Bk. VIII. 7

The Vision of Père Murray

IN 1927, IN THE DREARY PRAIRIE TOWN OF WILCOX, SASKATCHEWAN, A PRIEST FROM QUEBEC, PÈRE ATHOL MURRAY, ESTABLISHED A CO-OPERATIVE COLLEGE WHICH INITIALLY GAVE COURSES AT THE HIGH school level, and eventually, after affiliation with the University of Ottawa, at the undergraduate level. Murray had grown up in a well-off, English-speaking, Protestant family, a grand-nephew of Canada's first Prime Minister, John A. Macdonald. Murray's father, who was fluent in both French and English, had his son educated in French-speaking private schools in Quebec. It was while he was in this milieu that he converted to Catholicism and decided to become a priest.

    Père Murray was devoted to the classical bent that had been central to his own education—Latin, Greek, Philosophy, Theology, Literature—a type of education that can be given with minimal expenditures on buildings and equipment. All you really need is a

---

[1] This title is from the Notre Dame (Indiana) football song, which we shamelessly adopted as our own at our little Notre Dame.

room or two, a few good books, and teachers who are capable of teaching the content of the courses. Murray was able to scrape together these minimal requirements in his Wilcox parish. He had no hesitation in deciding on a name for his college. He was a devotee of the Blessed Virgin from a French background and a man of consummate faith, so he named his ramshackle college "Notre Dame." It's very likely that Our Lady never had a worse hair day than this one.

Against all odds, the college survived and grew in the midst of prairie poverty and the Great Depression. It became famous for its sports teams, which were given the name "Hounds." Especially good was its hockey team, which produced a number of future NHL players. It also became well-known for the co-operative system that made it possible. In this system, students were expected to help with the cooking and cleaning-up and provide janitorial and landscaping services on a rotating schedule. The fame of Notre Dame Wilcox, the little college that could, spread (more or less) throughout the land. "A magazine writer in the 1930's described Athol Murray as 'A Catholic priest with the soul of a saint, the mind of a Greek philosopher and the vocabulary of a dock worker.'"[2] A movie, *The Hounds of Notre Dame*, was made in 1980.[3]

> *More the story of the man who established it than the College of Notre Dame in Saskatchewan, this [movie] is the depiction of Father Athol Murray, a hard-drinking, chain-smoking man who believed that education and athletics were the way to success for young men in college. He was opinionated, but he managed to take a dump and make it into a well-respected college.*
>
> Tan Hobart, *All Movie Guide*

Notre Dame Nelson: *In Principio Erat Pignus*[4]

ABOUT A QUARTER OF A CENTURY AFTER PÈRE MURRAY ESTABLISHED HIS INSTITUTION, IN THE LATE SPRING OF 1950, TWO YOUNG MEN OF Irish stock from Massachusetts arrived in Revelstoke, accompanying the Bishop of Nelson, the Most Reverend Martin M. Johnson, D.D. The Bishop was on a tour of the diocese, raising money to establish a Wilcox-type Catholic university college in the diocesan capital. The two men were from a Boston fund-raising company. They brought with them the Massachusetts twang that ten years later would be made familiar to the whole world in the mouths of the Kennedy tribe. They also carried with them some far more important impedimenta: the paraphernalia necessary to sign up parishioners to a year-long pledge of monthly giving. They were organization men who had all the techniques and all the paperwork necessary for this type of campaign. They also had plenty of charm, a vital item when you are trying to pry money out of people.

---

[2] Jack Gorman, *Père Murray and the Hounds*, 1977, p. 97.
[3] The movie is based on Gorman's book.
[4] "In the beginning was the pledge," is my play on words on the opening of the Gospel of St. John: *In principio erat verbum*, "In the beginning was the Word."

In his sermon at each of the two Sunday Masses he attended in Revelstoke, the Bishop assured the congregation that rendering their money unto the Church rather than unto Caesar was in their best interests. Not only would the projected college provide an affordable place for their sons and daughters to pursue the first two years of university education, it would also put a pretty good down-payment on the saving of their immortal souls, warding them away from such godless institutions as the University of British Columbia—at least for a couple of years. Besides, and here was the kicker that would make giving irresistible, one half of the money collected would remain in the parish, to be used for whatever purposes the parish deemed worthy.

My parents, who had very little money to spare even in their best interests, pledged five dollars a month. "I wonder how much Mary Geoghegan is giving?" my mother asked my father. Mary Geoghegan was a middle-aged widow who lived with her sister and her sister's husband in a house directly across the street from us, one of the four people who made up my mother's bridge group, known to themselves as the "Owl's Club." Mary Geoghegan was said to have collected on a large insurance policy when her husband died a couple of decades earlier, shortly after she married him—taken away too soon for her to have produced a Catholic heir—and to have invested her nest egg in bonds and mortgages with considerable widowly acumen. But giving money to establish a college when she had no children of her own? Where was the interest in that?

At any rate, whatever Mary Geoghegan did, the pledges came in thicker than the clouds of locusts that pursued the Israelis across the Sinai, or whatever desert they were scrambling through, living on manna and matzo balls, in the days of the Pharaoh, who was distracted from pursuing them as he was coping with an unexpected water problem. These pledges made it possible for the co-operative university college of Notre Dame to open in a humble way (as suited a Christian institution in the mode of Athol Murray) down the street from the Cathedral of Mary Immaculate (1899) in a building that had once been a bakery. ("Not *another* bloody Notre Dame!" the lesser pious types were heard to remark—but the Bishop, who was a convert from Presbyterianism, or some graver form of Protestantism, was not a man with much imagination, and being the Bishop, and used to a plenipotentiary role, he gave himself exclusive permission to choose the name in emulation of the institution mentioned above.)

The city of Nelson, from which the bishop ruled his diocese, was in those days a railway and mining centre on the edge of Kootenay Lake with a population of something in the neighbourhood of ten thousand people. The flat area by the lake, potentially the prettiest part of town, was taken up largely by the C.P.R. railway yards. The use of the best land for industrial purposes was a common phenomenon all over North America. The town itself was built on the sides of the steep hill above yards. One needed a good heart to live there. The College began with twelve students, who were ensconced in two older houses that the Bishop had bought with money pledged by the faithful, two full-time lay faculty members, and a bevy of local priests who were able (more or less) to teach one thing or another, or so they claimed. In 1951, it was affiliated with the Gonzaga University in Spokane, Washington, run by the Jesuits, an institution whose greatest claim to fame was the fact that Bing Crosby had been a student there. Al Cartier,

M.A., was hired as Notre Dame Nelson's first President. Cartier was well-liked by the students and most of the faculty, but his tenure as president would be short, only one year, in fact, as he and the Bishop crossed swords over the way the college was to be run. Both, so to speak, wanted the power of the keys.

A Journey Further into the Interior

I DON'T REMEMBER WHEN OR HOW THE DECISION WAS MADE THAT I WOULD GO TO NOTRE DAME WHEN I GRADUATED FROM HIGH SCHOOL. I know I would have preferred at the time to go to U.B.C., as most of my friends were going there. Part of the reason may have been that my parents preferred that I get at least some of my tertiary education in a Catholic institution. But the primary reason was undoubtedly financial. Notre Dame was a lot cheaper than U.B.C. I couldn't earn enough in my summer job to pay for the year, even at Notre Dame, and the degree to which my parents could help me was limited.

My journey south to Nelson and Notre Dame in 1953 was by train, boat, and bus. The train on the branch line from Revelstoke to Arrowhead, 28 miles south along the Columbia River, ran twice a week—on Wednesdays and Saturdays. I had originally intended to go on Wednesday, September 9th, but when it was announced that Mart Kenney and his Western Gentlemen, Canada's foremost big band, was coming to town on Friday the 11th, I changed my plans and arranged instead to leave town on Saturday the 12th. The evening dancing to the Kenney orchestra in the high school gymnasium, the best dance floor in town, to the strains of "The West, A Nest, and You Dear," Kenney's theme song, gave my girlfriend Karen and me a wonderfully romantic last night together.

The train to Arrowhead was something of a toy. The steam engine that pulled it, which I had had to fire up numerous times when I worked in the CPR shops that summer, had been built in the early years of the century, was small, and didn't hold its steam very well. It was used only to pull this train, which ran a short distance over flat terrain that didn't challenge its capabilities. The train consisted of an express car, a freight car or two, and a passenger car, all of them old and about as decrepit as the engine.

Arrowhead was a small village at the north end of the widened area of the Columbia River known as the Arrow Lakes. There, I boarded the *S. S. Minto*, the rear paddle wheeler that had sailed on the lakes since 1898. The ship was a flat-bottomed river boat, a smaller version of the kind that plied the Mississippi. On its journeys on the river, it pulled into the few isolated, tiny communities, beaching its bow on the shore and delivering and collecting goods by way of a wooden plank that was run from the deck to the shore. Its sister ship, the *S. S. Moyie*, at that time still ran its circular route on Kaslo Lake. Once there had been many of these boats: the *Rossland*, the *Kootenay*, the *Nakusp*, and the *Revelstoke*, among others. The *Minto* was the last of the river boats on the

Columbia. She was retired in 1954 and beached at Nakusp. As there was no money available to preserve her, in 1968, she was set fire to and sunk near Galena Bay.[5]

At Nakusp, the only major town in the lake area (and I use the word "major" with a good deal of exaggeration), I left the boat and boarded a bus which took me through the sparsely-populated and wildly beautiful Slocan Valley to Nelson over mountain roads which were narrow, winding and unpaved. The area had still not received the attention of that road-builder extraordinaire, the Premier of British Columbia, then and for long afterwards, W.A.C. "Wacky" Bennett, and his Minister of Highways, "Flying" Phil Gagliardi, whose nickname arose from that fact that he got caught speeding so many times on the new highways that he spent years with his driver's licence in suspension.

> *Because of the condition of the road, the trip took many hours. At one point along the way, the driver announced that there were lots of huckleberries and blueberries in that area and he was going to stop for awhile to let us dozen or so passengers wander through the woods and pick them. In my naïveté, I did not realise that he was providing us with a bathroom (woodsroom?) break, which I was very much in need of. Everybody scattered every-which-way in the forest; in dense woods of this sort it was easy to find enough isolation to have a pee break as a first course, perhaps unsuitably followed by a berry feast as an entrée, and comfort as a dessert.*

Ex Nihilo . . . Out of Nothing the College Arises

I ARRIVED AT THE COLLEGE AT THE BEGINNING OF THE THIRD YEAR OF ITS EXISTENCE. THERE WERE 43 FULL-TIME STUDENTS, MOST OF THEM in residence, twenty-one night-class students, and eight professors. A site for a permanent campus, on the side of the mountain to the west of the city, had been donated to the diocese by a Nelson real estate broker and insurance agent with a thick Quebeçois accent, by the name of Jean Poulin. The Bishop and his wise men bought four prefabricated cabins, originally designed for erection in isolated mining camps, cleared a more or less level space in the forest, and erected them. ("What the hell!" one of the wise men might have remarked. "They'll do the job. Besides," he continued, working hard at being clever, "aren't students essentially miners of knowledge?") Three of the four were to serve as dormitories for males; the fourth, in the meantime, until the new college building was habitable, was to be used as a cook house and refectory. A rough trail was cut downhill through the coniferous forest to the rising college building, a trail that the male students would spend many a Saturday morning improving.

The female students remained, for the time being, in an old stick-gothic house on Mill Street, just down the street from the Cathedral, where they were close to the classroom area (at the beginning of that year in the basement of the Cathedral hall), and where, it was hoped, they would be safe from the ravages of the male students, who, even

---

[5] The *S.S. Moyie* was the only one of these boats to survive. It was beached in Kaslo, B.C., when it was taken out of service in 1957. It is now a National Historic Site.

though they were (for the most part) Catholic, were still deemed by their Catholic masters (though, certainly not from their own experience!) to be somewhat savage when it came to the pursuit of the opposite sex. Fortunately for both males and females, these masters had no control over the unlighted back porch of Mill Street, the back seats of borrowed cars, or the bushier areas of the new campus.

In the middle of the 1953-54 academic year, the new college building on the heavily forested campus, though far from finished, became useable. It was a two-storey, prefabricated school building, manufactured, I believe, in California. The building was erected by a contractor. While it was being assembled, the President of the College, Al Cartier, spent much of his time on the site, a couple of miles west of the Cathedral classrooms, not only keeping watch, but also pitching in himself to help with the erection. Often, he would arrive at the Cathedral basement from the campus at the last minute to teach his chemistry class, still wearing his carpenter's apron around his waist through the class, and afterwards returning immediately to the construction area. It was a classy bit of pretence.

Once the building was open, the women were moved from Mill Street to dormitories carved out of a couple of rooms on the second floor, originally designed as classroom spaces; the cookhouse-dining operation in the hut up the hill was moved to the lower level of the new building; and classes and laboratories in chemistry and physics were transferred from the basement of the Cathedral hall. Over the next year and a half, the students would finish the interior of the building during Saturday volunteer sessions. In 1955, the first dormitory building was erected in the same way. The College envisioned by Bishop Johnson was on its way.

The Idea of a Co-operative College

A CO-OPERATIVE COLLEGE IS BASED ON THE SIMPLE CONCEPT THAT THE COST OF RUNNING THE INSTITUTION CAN BE KEPT LOW, AND, as a result, tuition and board reduced to a minimum, if much of the work of running the college is taken on by the student body in time which would otherwise be free. At Notre Dame Nelson, the professors were on salary, though their remuneration was well below the norm. In this sense, they were also volunteers, giving up part of the salary they might legitimately have expected to be paid; they did so, because they believed in the vision. A local woman, Mrs. Thorbergson—known to one and all as "Mrs. T"—was hired to do the cooking and supervise the kitchen. All of the other jobs at the college were done by students on a voluntary basis. Students were assigned to a group and put on a rotation to do kitchen work and the cleaning of the buildings. Under the supervision of Mrs. T, when it was your group's turn to be on kitchen duty, you peeled potatoes and did other like chores, put the prepared food on the tables at mealtime, cleaned up the kitchen and dining room after each meal, and washed the dishes and pots and pans—there was no automatic dishwasher.

Saturday mornings were volunteer times for everybody. Not all Saturdays, but most Saturdays. A member of the Student Council, known as the Minister of Public

Works, who ascertained what needed to be done from the administration, was in charge. Until the middle of the year, when the new building was occupied, the women cleaned the Mill Street residence and the men worked on landscaping the campus. Once the building was open, jobs were designated, as one might expect at that time, on the basis of sex: the women did the cleaning of the interior of the one substantial building, which contained classrooms, kitchen, dining room, lounge, and the women's dormitory. The men worked on completing the building—painting, tiling, etc., especially when there was snow on the ground—and continued landscaping when the weather permitted, a job that consisted essentially of clearing brush from the forest floor with machetes and building pathways through the forest with shovels, grub hoes and rakes.

When I tell people these days about the volunteer work we did at Notre Dame, I often get a raised eyebrow and the question, "Didn't you resent having to use your Saturday mornings to do grunt work?" The answer is a resounding "No!" We were a group of young males from various parts of the province, anxious to get to know one another and make friends, and working as a group was a great aid to that process. Besides, doing hard work in a splendid forest is perhaps the perfect break from the week's student slog. There was good companionship, a lot of humour, a lot of fun, and the comfort of being a part of a group of people working toward similar goals. The general attitude toward volunteer work is obvious in one of the "About Notre Dame" columns (May 6, 1955) I wrote on a regular basis for the diocesan weekly newspaper, *The Prospector*. "Rocks! There are more rocks on the campus than anything else. Not that rocks aren't of some use, that is, the smaller ones; they certainly make a path or a roadway look neat when they are placed in long white rows on either side. But when they measure about five by five, standing like so many great tombstones scattered here and there on the campus, they present something of a problem. We work away at them with sledge hammers and bars. But when we can't move the mountain, we give up and take Mohammed around it!"

The Pseudo-Monastic . . . *Ora, Labora, et Studia*

IN SOME RESPECTS THE SITUATION AT NOTRE DAME IN THOSE EARLY YEARS WAS MONASTIC IN NATURE, INCORPORATING THE BENEDICTINE concepts of living a communal life: *ora, labora, et studia*: prayer, work, and studies.

Ora (Prayer)

Public prayer was a part of the life at the college. Father Mackenzie, known to all as "Father Mac," was a baby-faced, newly-ordained priest from Windsor, Ontario, who always began his classes with the Lord's Prayer. I was used to this sort of thing, as the school day in the home rooms of B.C. public schools in those days, by law, began with this Christian prayer and with a designated Bible reading.[6] None of the other professors began their classes this way. Some mornings in the first semester, Father Mac said a twenty-five-minute Tridentine low mass for the more devout among us, before breakfast

---

[6] This prayer regime still existed in the mid-1960s when I was teaching in a B.C. public school. I don't know when it was dispensed with. It certainly would not be tolerated today.

and classes, in the dormitory/cookhouse hut—in Latin, of course. I went once in a while. I liked the Latin. Still do. On Sundays, we hiked down the mountain and took the town bus in to the Cathedral. I was a member of the college choir, led by fellow student, Leo Moreau, who had come back to school in his early thirties. We sang masses in Gregorian Chant from the *Parish Kyriale*. We loved especially to sing the wonderful Gregorian *Missa Defuncta* at funerals in the Cathedral. People were happy to send their dearly departed souls to their reward surrounded by the simple beauty of this music. Word got around that we were highly affordable—we were free—so we sang at a lot of funerals.

> *Every once in awhile, Father Mac would decide to join us when we went into the Cathedral to sing at a funeral Mass. "Shit!" we would all say to ourselves in silent plain chant. He sang too loudly and he sang through his nose, with the result that the Dies Irae sounded as if a radio were buzzing off-station somewhere in the background. For the rest of us, it was a dies irae indeed when Father Mac joined us and spoiled the hard-gained unity of our singing.*

There were also occasional retreats. One that occurred in my second year was a three-day retreat preached by the Reverend W. N. Bischoff, S.J., from Gonzaga University. I liked the periods of silence, and the readings that were done at meals; I was less enthralled with the lectures on Marriage, the Value of the Soul, and the Supernatural Life, all of which seemed to me to be not only polemic but also of a highly speculative nature.

Labora et Studium (Work and Study)

Work at the college was of two types: academic study and co-op duties. It was during my two years there that I learned for the first time to work hard at my studies, and my marks steadily improved as time went by. My pose of pretending to lie down on the job at the Saturday morning landscaping sessions (ac*edia ficta* "fake sloth"?) was made fun of on a poster produced in the fall of my first year. I am shown at the bottom of the poster lying on my side, my head resting on my elbow, surrounded by hard-working volunteers. (See photo pages.) It was, of course, a joke; I worked as hard as any of the others. But it was satisfying to be made fun of in this way, as it seemed to mean that I was liked and appreciated by the group.

> *In the philosophy classes we studied selections from the Summa Theologica of Thomas Aquinas. I loved the rigid logic of his arguments, all of them constructed using the same patterns of thought. When we worked on the trails of a Saturday morning, we sometimes debated among ourselves the merits of his theses: How viable were his "proofs" for the existence of God? How true was his contention that a man has free choice to the extent that he is rational? On our trails the physical and the mental congealed.*

The Un-Monastic... *Acedia, Gula, et Luxuria*

IN OTHER RESPECTS, LIFE AT NOTRE DAME (I'M HAPPY TO SAY) WAS DECIDEDLY UNMONASTIC. LIKE MOST HEALTHY, NORMAL, YOUNG people, we contended from time to time with at least three of the traditional Seven Deadly Sins, bouts of *acedia* (sloth—in studies and volunteer work), *gula* (gluttony—drinking a bit too much beer and wine), and *luxuria* (lust—about which there is no need to comment, as everyone has enjoyed this least grievous of the Seven Deadly Sins[7]).

Acedia (Sloth)

I would have been less than human if at times when I woke up on a Saturday morning I didn't think, "Hell! I don't want to cut away at roots on the trail from the huts to the college building! I don't want to help with the varnishing of the walls in the upstairs halls!" And then there was the dreaded day when my group's week for kitchen duty arrived. But once the group had gathered and the task had been begun, the feeling of working on a common cause would take over and the initial feeling of reluctance to get involved would vanish. The same change of attitude would often happen in the getting down to one's studies, where laziness, as all students know, most often comes about as a result of procrastination. And the procrastination most often arises from a dislike of the course material. My greatest moments of sloth were in my first year, when I did my best to put off studying physics and mathematics, both of which I was disinterested in.

> *It was already 9:30. The evening was going by far too quickly. I knew I had to stop reading* War and Peace *and get to work on the optics section that would be on the morning's Physics exam. But Balashev has just been ushered into Napoleon's presence. How can I put this thing down now! What, I ask you, are the optics of that?*

Gula (Gluttony)

Gula is the sin of eating or drinking too much. There was a measure of guilt here from time to time. But I don't want to give the impression that we ate and drank too much on a regular basis. As far as eating is concerned, the college always provided enough to eat—this was not the world of Oliver Twist—but there certainly was never too much. We would also supplement the college food with our own snacks, as students always do. There were no machines dispensing soft drinks, chocolate bars and potato chips on campus, which was probably a good thing, but a few blocks down the hill from us was a neighbourhood corner store that was happy to fill the gaps in our appetites. In the late fall, the stores were full of mandarin oranges—in those unpolitical-correct days we called them "Jap Oranges," and we would buy a box of these and share them. So we were home

---

[7] The order of the sins, as promulgated by Pope Gregory the Great in the 6th Century, was eventually turned totally upside-down, so that the sins of the spirit *(Superbia,* Pride; *Invidia,* Envy; *Ira,* Anger; *Acedia,* Sloth; *Avaritia,* Greed) were seen as more grievous than the sins of the flesh *(Gula,* Gluttony; and *Luxuria,* Lust)—and rightly so, I say!

free in the food area. In the drinking area, we were at best moderate gluttons. There was never any alcohol on campus—it wasn't prohibited—it just wasn't a part of life there. I never saw anybody at any time in a totally drunken state. But that did not mean that some of us boys wouldn't head out on a weekend evening to have a few illicit beers.

> *Once a month or so on a Friday night, two or three of Ray Paris, Bill Oleski, Gene Godderis, Bud Godderis and I—the group varied—would walk boldly into the beer parlour at the old Hume Hotel, all of us underage—the drinking age in those days being 21. We would sit at one or more of their round tables and order 10 cent glasses of beer, delivered two at a time to each person at the table. One night, the server, suspecting we were underage, but never asking, and probably having us on for the hell of it, kept coming to us and whispering that there was a policeman on the street outside the hotel, so it might be a good idea for us to get out while the getting was good. We didn't budge. It would have been an admission. But I for one was nervous, and I expect the others were as well.*

Luxuria (Lust)

I have kept *luxuria*, the most interesting sin, for last. Not that there was a huge amount of this one either. But there was, of course, kissing and cuddling and some incipient petting. It would have been a strange world of young people if that had not been the case. For some reason or other, I was pegged in my first semester as a ladies' man. There was a poster, like the one mentioned above, which showed leisure activity around the college. On it there was a cartoon of me walking with a notebook in my hand, which I was looking at querulously. The caption beside it read, "Keough's List of Girls." I was, of course, flattered by the idea. But I was also puzzled by it. In the first couple of months I had had a fling with a couple of girls, first Donelda and later Shirley, both of whom were town girls. Neither relationship developed beyond the initial stages, and it was the girls who dumped me rather than the other way around. Some ladies' man! I asked the fellow who made the poster where this idea had come from. He said that a couple of the girls at the Mill Street residence had said I was "Kinda cute." Out of such molehills are mountains sometimes made.

Later in the year, I spent many hours playing cribbage with Lorette, who was a resident student at the College. I liked her, but saw her only as a friend, as I didn't think I had a hope in hell of taking her out. She had a fabulous singing voice, pure and clear, with perfect pitch; and she employed it with great success, performing with dance bands and various other groups throughout the year. When the conductor of the Gonzaga Glee club heard her, he offered her a scholarship to the university on the spot. But she had other plans, and at the end of the year she returned to her native Victoria to begin her teacher training at the Normal School. One day in the company of a couple of other female friends she said, "Terry will spend hours with you, but he never asks you out." Even then I didn't get the hint. Some ladies' man! In some respects, I think I was wary of getting into a relationship that would distract me too much from my studies. But there were occasions, few and far between, I'm sorry to say, in which my reputation for being a ladies' man was not entirely fraudulent, and I was able to circumvent for awhile the frustrations of being young and vigorous and without a girlfriend.

> *I had borrowed a car from somebody—I don't remember who—and taken Shirley to see Mario Lanza in The Great Caruso. Afterwards, we parked in the small gravel pit on the mountainside, not far from the campus. She gave me the pleasure of her small, pointed breasts, which stood out softly in the moonlight, as if tinged with silver, a vision of paradise. Luxuria, it seemed to me, was the least deadly of the bad ones.*

In the Classroom

IN MY FIRST YEAR AT NOTRE DAME, I CONTINUED TO TAKE COURSES IN PHYSICS AND MATHEMATICS, IN WHICH I WAS NOT INTERESTED, AS well as courses in English, history, Latin, and philosophy, in which I was interested, and the compulsory course in theology, in which I rolled along in neutral. Why I continued to take physics and mathematics is a mystery to me now; it probably had something to do with the fact that it had been drilled into me that if I ever stopped doing the sciences, I would never be able to pick them up again. I passed both physics and mathematics that year with grades in the "C" range. I never took another science course after that; and when I returned to the college the following year and signed up for classes in the Humanities only, it was as if a great burden had been removed from my academic shoulders.

As we had to write the British Columbia Grade 13 examinations at the end of the year as well as the exams that would give us credit at Gonzaga, we followed the B. C. curriculum in the core courses. This route was taken by the college as there was some anxiety as to whether the University of British Columbia (the only university in the province at that time and somewhat pompous in its authority—*superbia*?) would credit courses given at Notre Dame, as they had been asked about this situation and had refused to commit themselves. As things turned out, when students arrived at U.B.C., there was no problem with accreditation. The concern about it was all a man of straw.

English

The first-year English curriculum was a combination of literature and language. In the literature area, we did Ibsen's *A Doll's House*, Euripides' *Electra*, and Shakespeare's I *Henry IV*, some bits and pieces of poetry, and some formal and familiar essays. In the language area, we concentrated on methods of writing critical essays. The course was taught by Father Mac, who dropped the hail-fellow-well-met pose he affected around the huts and became a classroom martinet, who not only had all the answers, but all the questions as well. I could see a future for him in a reconstituted Spanish Inquisition. With each of the above-mentioned plays, for example, he first of all made us summarize the play in three pages of single-spaced writing; and after we had done that, he made us do it again in one page. But it was in the composition area that his fascist approach was most difficult (for me, at least) to stomach. He insisted that we begin all essays with the sentence—There are three reasons why (*Here state your thesis*): first, (*state reason one*); second, (*state reason two*); and third, (*state reason three*). There were to be three paragraphs following, each dealing in order with one of the reasons, followed by a conclusion, which mirrored the opening paragraph. Now, for exam purposes, there was some merit in this approach. It was deadly logical, should contain a plenitude of facts, and should thus be hard to mark down on anything except style. But I use the word "deadly" advisedly, for that's what this approach was: deadly. I hated it.

It will undoubtedly be clear by this time that I didn't much like Father Mac. I'm sure he was assigned to the College because the Bishop thought he was too immature to put in charge of a parish. He wore a cassock when he was teaching, something none of the other priests did. It was to me a symbol of his pretentiousness. I also didn't believe in his attitude outside of the classroom, where he played the part of the jolly priest, just one of the guys. He used to insist that a priest had the same qualifications as a Ph.D., which, of course, was absurd. Eventually he did go on to get his Ph.D., sent to the University of Ottawa for that purpose by the Bishop. Not too long after completing his degree, he left the priesthood, married, and took a job at the University of Lethbridge—not, I think, what the Bishop had in mind when he sent him away. When I heard of this development in the early-1970s, I began referring to him in letters to old Notre Dame friends as "Mr. Mac." He died in his seventies in 2003. It remains unknown whether he went to heaven in a cassock or to hell in a collection basket.

In my second year, I did courses with Martin Luther Brown in Shakespeare and Restoration Literature. Martin Brown, as his name decidedly indicates, was a young man who had transferred his credits from Lutheranism to Catholicism. His classes were for him (and for the amusement of us students) an exercise in exchanging his reading glasses back and forth with his distance glasses. He was likeable, a good teacher, and a master of his material, but he was also inscrutable. When I asked him why he didn't wear bifocals, he said, "Give me your hand." When he took it to shake it, he scratched my palm with his middle finger, one of the signals homosexuals used in those days to indicate their willingness to another person. But Martin Brown was not a homosexual. So what was he up to? For one thing, he was having fun. And he was not only avoiding answering the question, but also at the same time enjoying puzzling me.

Latin

I had studied Latin in Grades 10, 11, and 12, and in my first year at Notre Dame, where we followed the B.C. Grade 13 Curriculum, which consisted mainly of translating sections from Virgil's *Aeneid*, Books I and IV. For the final examinations, I did what students have done through the ages and chose passages I thought would be likely candidates for inclusion and memorized a translation of them. I was lucky, as parts of two of the three passages for translation on the exam were from sections I had worked on. This first-year Latin course was taught by Martin Brown. One day when he was absent,

Al Cartier, the college President, took over the class. He had obviously not prepared anything in particular and was not in a position to do whatever Brown had planned.

> *Cartier said he wanted to quiz us on some common Latin phrases. So, putting them on the blackboard one by one, he dredged up a world of Latin tags and sayings: Carthago delenda est (Carthage must be destroyed); facilis descensus averni (easy is the descent into hell); carpe diem, quam minimum credula postero (enjoy the day, trusting the morrow as little as possible); mutatis mutandi (things being changed that ought to be changed); and so on. He then wrote Cui bono? on the board and asked me to translate. Now, this is a very simple phrase used in criminal investigations, meaning literally "To whose good?"—i.e., "who had a motive to commit the crime?" But for some reason or other my mind went blank and I couldn't for the life of me translate the phrase. Cartier, who with reason assumed I would have no difficulty with it, thought I was having him on. It was not a pleasant experience.*

When I was tutored in Latin by Father Royce in my second year, he claimed he didn't know how I'd done so much Latin and knew so little of the language. But Father Royce, a young Jesuit from Seattle University, being a Jesuit, expected nothing less than academic excellence, and I think he was trying to motivate me by belittling my accomplishments. My Latin wasn't *that* bad. Royce was a no-nonsense man with a Ph.D. in Psychology, an odd area of study for a no-nonsense man, but the world is a weird and wonderful place. We met for our classes in his office on the second floor. In two of our weekly sessions we translated sections of St. Augustine's *Confessions*. I gained a great deal from this tuition. For the first time I was competent enough to be able to appreciate the beauty of the Latin I was reading. Our other weekly session was much more difficult and considerably less beautiful. I had to translate ten sentences a week from English into Latin from exercises in a book called *Latin Prose and Composition*. Compared to translating Latin into English, translating English into Latin is very difficult. I slogged my way through the exercises, usually ten compound sentences a week, each set of exercises based on some aspect of Latin grammar. I wasn't very good at it and I didn't enjoy it much, but I did my best to get them more or less right.

Everyday Life

In the Huts

THE HUTS WERE UNPAINTED, PLYWOOD STRUCTURES, WHICH WERE PUT TOGETHER ON A CONCRETE FOUNDATION. THEY HAD A SMALL, central foyer, off of which ran four bedrooms and a bathroom. The bedrooms had iron double bunks, two minute desks, and a small closet. There was one window. Everything was made from panels of fir plywood: ceiling, walls and floor, and there wasn't a drop of paint or a scrap of carpet anywhere. There were no laundry facilities. We washed our clothes in the foyer, using a bucket and a scrub board, and hung them to dry on makeshift lines outside of the cabins. Fr. Mac, as incipient Dean of Men, had a room to himself in one of the cabins. In second year, Mr. J. Coulson, a man who had finished his seminary training but whom the Bishop was apparently reluctant to ordain a priest, a weird little Englishman with round glasses and a bewildered look on his face, occupied a room by himself in one of the other huts. No doubt about it, we were roughing it in the bush. But we were young and enthusiastic and pliable, and I don't remember being at all appalled by these rustic quarters. We were surrounded by a beautiful forest; we took possession of our rooms, put posters on our walls, hung flags or other such items as curtains on the windows, and got on with getting an education.

> *Mrs. T. had Saturday and Sunday off, but we weren't left entirely to our own resources, as she would prepare food during the week which she would schedule for weekend meals. The students who were on duty were left to get out the cereals and make toast for breakfast, bang together some sandwiches for lunch, and heat up the stew or whatever she had prepared for dinner. One weekend, during the period when she was still cooking at the huts, Gordon Guidi and I decided we would deviate from Mrs. T.'s plan and make spaghetti bolognaise for the guys. I thought I had some idea of how to make spaghetti as my mother had made it often, and since Gordon Guidi came from an Italian background, I mean . . . how could we fail? The sauce we made wasn't too bad. But we didn't use enough water to cook the spaghetti and a lot of it stuck together in braids you could tie up a ship with. It was possible to eat it (just), but our fellow hut mates, and especially Fr. Mac, were not amused. We never ventured away from Mrs. T.'s plans again.*

The Notre Dame Quartet

Quartets were big in the 1950s. On top of the Canadian heap were the Four Lads, who had arisen out of the choir at St. Mike's in Toronto, with huge hits like *Istanbul* and *Moments to Remember*. Also Canadian were the Crew Cuts, with their big hit *Sh'Boom!* Jimmy Lynch, Eric Buckley, Ed Gaines, and I had no ambition to hit the big time, or, at least, no ambition we were willing to admit to. But we did want to sing at local dances and other get-togethers. It seems odd in today's world that a quartet would be in demand to sing at a dance put on for young people, but in demand we were.

Lynch was the best musician among us. He played the piano well and could arrange music. Later in life he would use his considerable skills in this area as a priest in the Okanagan valley to knit together a disparate congregation of local people and the eastern "frostbacks" who began invading the area in large numbers in the 1980s and '90s. In our case, Jimmy would write out our parts and we would practise them singly and then together under his direction. We sang up-beat spirituals like *Dry Bones*, barbershop favourites like *Seeing Nellie Home*, and sentimental Irish songs like *Danny Boy*. Jimmy Lynch wrote out each of the parts, like the bass part written below, which we were given to practise and memorize before we got together for a group practice.

We did nothing original. Once we were asked to sing at a sixtieth wedding anniversary celebration at Mt. St. Francis, an old-age home run by the Sisters of St. Anne, which was just down the road from the campus. The old man, tall and dignified-looking at 96, but blind, sat at a table in the lounge, dressed in his best suit, beside his active and petite wife, who was a mere 92. In front of them was a large anniversary cake. We sang *Just a Song at Twilight*:

> Just a song at twilight, when the lights are low,
> And the flick'ring shadows, softly come and go;
> Tho' the day be weary, sad the nights and long,
> Still to us at twilight comes love's sweet song,
> Comes love's old sweet song.

The nuns, his shepherds, stood watch near the table, the old man sat ramrod straight and unmoving in front of the anniversary cake he couldn't see, and as we sang, tears ran soundlessly in slow streams down his face. It was unforgettable.

Leisure Activities

We amused ourselves in simple ways. We borrowed trucks and had bottle drives to raise money for the basketball team (called—with a nod to Notre Dame Wilcox and the "Hounds," the "Pups"); we went to senior dances at the High School to look for likable girls; we ran contests to choose a Mardi Gras Queen, to be crowned at a Mardi Gras dance. We published on a mimeograph machine a few issues of a newspaper (called—with a nod to the *Ubyssey*, the *Odyssey*); we went to movies at the town cinema—once amusing us by advertising on its marquee, "Martin Luther with Selected Shorts"; we produced a yearbook—(called with a nod to our classical education, *Pillars*). Under the aegis of Professor of Speech and Drama, Miss Jane Stevenson, we rehearsed a play called *Once Before*, written by her cousin, David Scott, a Nelson resident, about the stand made against the Iroquois by Dollard at the Long Sault. The play began with a family in a shelter during the London Blitz of 1940, thus giving it the framework for its title. I had a minor part in the play, which we entered into the Dominion Drama Festival in Trail. We got clobbered in the judge's oral critique. Had there been television at the College, we would no doubt have watched it. But these were early days for television, and the College did not have a set. Instead we brought in movies and watched them on a fairly regular basis.

> *We used to have feature films on Saturday nights in the lounge. Involved were a 16mm projector, a portable screen, and a couple of large metal canisters of film. The projector ticked away as the film moved on the sprockets. The images flickered on the screen. Halfway through, the projectionist would have to change reels. When the movie was over, the reels would have to be rewound. Often these movies were followed by a sock hop, the music for dancing played on 78 or 45 rpm records. One night, as the projectionist was rewinding the films, and the students who were staying for the sock hop had just removed their shoes, a horrible smell arose in the room. Faces suddenly became rigid, noses twitched, eyes moved furtively around the room, all wondering whose feet smelled so badly, all hoping it was not their feet. Then, when it became clear that it was the projector's smouldering and burning some of the film (thankfully without flame), faces relaxed, heads began to move again, and eyes warmed up. The projectionist shut down the projector, windows were opened to let out the dirty-feet odour, and the sock hop went ahead as scheduled.*

Some Other Professors

I have already written about Father Mac, Father Royce, and Martin Luther Brown in some detail. But there were, of course, others:

Jane Stevenson: A tall, gaunt, rather masculine-looking middle-aged woman from England with degrees in the fine arts (LRAM, LGSM, ALAM), Miss Stevenson taught me in the second-year Survey of English Literature course. My sole memory of her is the fact that she taught all of the poems in our text of Cavalier poet Robert Herrick except his seminal "To the Virgins, to Make Much of Time." Poor woman. She had not gathered her rosebuds while she might.

Father Cullen: A young priest from a Toronto family famous more for producing NHL hockey players than priests, he was editor of the diocesan newspaper, *The Prospector*, and taught biology at the College. He was a great fan of the Walt Kelly comic-strip, *Pogo*, whose name he thus acquired as a nickname. I spent a fair amount of time working with him, as I wrote the College column for the newspaper, but I never got to know him very well. He was always affable, but he was shy and quiet and basically inaccessible on a human level.

John Thomas: A young man from St. John's University, famous as "The Book College," where education was conducted as much as possible using primary texts and every student was expected to be willing to tackle any area of knowledge, taught Physics at Notre Dame during my first year there. He was a good friend of Martin Brown.

> *For some reason or other, Professor Thomas washed all of his socks one spring weekend at the new college building and strewed them on bushes outside to dry, about twenty in all, if I remember rightly, all off-white, so any two socks could make up a pair. That struck me as a damn clever way to uncomplicate the pairing of the socks in your life, but I have never managed to follow his lead. (To those of you with a lascivious turn of mind, let me assure you that he was in no way related to Mellors' John Thomas in Lady Chatterley's Lover! There was no way you could refer to our John Thomas as a prick.)*

Al Cartier: In my first year at the College, as I have pointed out previously, Al Cartier was the President. He was a short, rather rotund individual who came from a French-Canadian background. He had a wonderful gift for relating to the students. Often on a Saturday-morning work session, he would join one of the groups, laughing and joking and working along with everybody else. He often pitched in in cleaning up the kitchen and dining area after a meal. Once on a College trip to Cranbrook with the basketball team when we took over an entire coach on the train, he borrowed the Newsie's cap and walked through the coach selling coffee and cigarettes. He was loved by all.

But as the year went on, rumours began to circulate that he and the Bishop were not getting along. Father Mac was increasingly hostile to him, even in public. When I reacted in surprise one day after he had been rude to Cartier in my presence, Father Mac said under his breath to me when Cartier had left: "A priest doesn't have to obey a layman." This remark said more about Father Mac's arrogance (*superbia*) than about any ecclesiastical dictum.

It became increasingly obvious that Cartier was on his way out. One sunny spring day near the end of term, I bumped into him on my way into the building, and he surprised me by saying: "It's a fine spring day. How'd you like to go for a walk?"

> *"What do you think has gone wrong here this year," he said. As far as I was concerned, nothing had gone wrong, and I said so. "Well," he said, "there must be something wrong"—and he chuckled at the idea, even though this was a serious conversation—"as I just told the Bishop to go to hell!" He explained that he had been working for practically nothing and that he had run into trouble paying his mortgage. After an argument, the Bishop had agreed to pay the mortgage off. But that hadn't solved the root problem, the fact that he wasn't being paid what he referred to as a living wage. "If you ever go to work for the Church," he said, "make sure you demand a salary that is commensurate with the work you are doing." The conversation was a remarkable confiding of a middle-aged man in a position of authority with a young man who was a pawn in his world. I was puzzled that he chose to confide in me—I am puzzled still—but I expect it is an example of the fact that it is sometimes easier to tell your troubles to a quasi-anonymous hearer than to someone who is an essential part of your life.*

My Future Plans

I'M NOT SURE WHEN I DECIDED TO DO THE FINAL TWO YEARS OF MY UNDERGRADUATE EDUCATION AT ST. FRANCIS XAVIER UNIVERSITY IN Antigonish, N.S., but the decision had been made before I left Notre Dame. One aspect of the place that attracted me was the fact that my father had graduated from there in 1906. I was also attracted by the romance and adventure of crossing from one coast of Canada to the other. But I think the final thrust came from the fact that a number of my fellow students—Tom Spring (my room mate at Notre Dame), Leo Smith, John Boucher, Leo Moreau, Leo Nimsick, and Pat Wilcox—had decided to head in that direction. So, as much as anything, it was friendship that was the impetus.

At any rate, when the exams were over, I headed once again to Revelstoke in reverse order of means of transportation—by bus to Nakusp, on the *Minto* for the last time to Arrowhead, and by toy train for the final lap of the journey. Throughout that summer I worked at a series of jobs, which included reading all the electric meters on houses throughout the town, as they were about to be replaced; bottling Fanta drinks on a machine that had no automatic pressure release and was always in danger of blowing up; and running a wagon drill boring holes into a cliff—fifteen miles west of town, beside Three Valley Lake—so the road in that area could be widened enough to allow two cars to pass one another the whole length of the lake. Later that summer, two men who were working the wagon drill were killed when a slide of large rocks suddenly roared down on them as they worked.

Post Res . . . Things That Came After

FOR SOME TIME, NOTRE DAME NELSON PROSPERED. IN 1961, IT SWITCHED ITS AFFILIATION FROM GONZAGA UNIVERSITY TO ST. Francis Xavier University—a strange coincidence since I and so many of my friends had headed in that direction almost a decade earlier—mainly because it was conceived to be better to be connected to a Canadian institution. In 1963, it was made an independent university by the province, which assumed most of the burden of its funding. At the height of its success, it had more than 2,000 students. But in the mid-1970s it ran into financial problems. The B.C. government took it over, gave it a charter, and renamed it David Thompson University. When the problems persisted, the government closed the Nelson operations and moved the College to the University of Victoria, where it was known as the David Thompson University Centre. In 1984, again for reasons of budget, it was closed. Bishop Johnson's vision of a Catholic college in the interior was over.

The campus in Nelson was taken over as a satellite of a newly-founded community college, Selkirk College, which has its headquarters in Castlegar, B.C., a few miles to the west of Nelson. The huts and most of the forest around them are gone, replaced largely by a road and a parking lot. The dormitories stand vacant, unheated, abandoned by an institution that has no use for them. But the prefabricated college building that all of those who were there in the early years worked so hard to build remains in use. The classrooms are still used as classrooms, and the downstairs area that contained the kitchen, the dining area, and the lounge, is now divided into cubicles where young music students practise on their various instruments, intent on dreams that are undoubtedly similar to those we had when we cooked and ate and played in the same area so many years ago. But I would be surprised if their experiences are as rich as ours were.

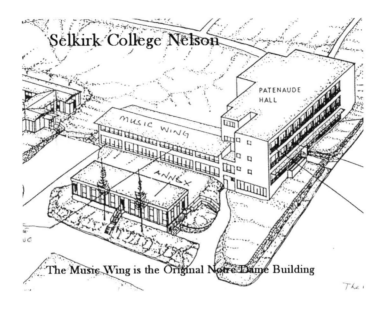

The Music Wing is the Original Notre Dame Building

A NOTRE DAME ALBUM

The New College Building in Winter (Yearbook Scan)

A Bunch of the Boys Ham it Up as the Birdwatcher's Club
(Terry is leaning on his hands Front Row left)

Bill Oleski Peels Potatoes

Faulty Table: Martin Brown, Al Cartier, John Thomas, Father Mac

Washing Up: Ray Paris Makes a Face

President Cartier Helps with the Dishes

Co-operation in the Classroom (Yearbook Scan)

Leo Smith Cleans a Furnace Part

Co-operation in the Lounge Area (Yearbook Scan)

Hut Dwellers: Leo Moreau is Second from the Right

Hut Student Room Frolics: Terry, Dennis Plamondon, Tom Spring

Heading into Town on a City Bus Terry is Fifth from the Right

Ping Pong Rounders

Lorette Sagmoen Sings

Singing the Doukhobor Song: Terry is on the Right

Poster on Notre Dame Life: Terry is lying down on the job, bottom centre

Varnishing the Hall Walls: Terry is Centre, Holding the Mirror

Choir Practice
John Boucher, Joe Giliotti, Bill Oleski, Ray Paris, Terry Keough,
Don Wilson, Dennis Plamondon, Joe Maksi, Gordon Guidi, Tom Spring

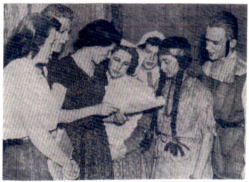

Cast of *Once Again*
Terry is Second from Left   (Yearbook Photo)

The Quartet
Ed Gaines, Jim Lynch, Terry, Eric Buckley

Heading that Appeared on My *Prospector* Columns

On Behalf of the Citizens of the Corporation of the City of Nelson

MAYOR JOSEPH KARRY

and the Aldermen

Dr. T. H. Bourgue	J. H. Coventry
G. Eckmier	A. Foster
W. S. Smith	Mrs. F. Wallach

Wish to Congratulate the Fifth Graduating Class of Notre Dame College

---

Wholesale

Fruit   Vegetables   Tobacco   Candy

Paper

Mac's Brand Vegetables

McDonald's Ginger Ale

McDONALD JAM CO. LTD.

FOR DRUG STORE SERVICE

MANN'S	MANN'S
Clinic Pharmacy	Drug Store
Phone 1505	Phone 81

MANN'S DRUGS LTD.

Nelson, B. C.

P. E. POULIN

GENERAL INSURANCE

AND REAL ESTATE

582 Ward St.   Nelson, B. C.

JACK BOYCE MEN'S SHOP

Your Sporting Headquarters
in Nelson

FRED WHITELEY, Prop.

514 Baker St.   Nelson, B. C.

Chapter 3: Hail and Health to Alma Mater[1]

ST. F. X. UNIVERSITY YEARS (1955-57)

Students would lounge and lie in the semi-dark with their brush-cuts and perms; the boys then wore white bucks and narrow rep ties, the Ivy look not yet yielded to the blue-jeaned geek look, and the girls wore single-strand pearls and pastel sweaters whose wool seemed to melt in the hand.
John Updike, Villages, 2004

"There is no man," Elstir began, "however wise, who has not at some period of his youth said things, or lived a life, the memory of which is so unpleasant to him that he would gladly expunge it. And yet he ought not entirely to regret it, because he cannot be certain that he has indeed become a wise man—so far as it is possible for any of us to be wise—unless he has passed through all the fatuous or unwholesome incarnations by which that ultimate stage must be preceded."
Marcel Proust, Remembrance of Things Past, "Within a Budding Grove," 1919

In Ages Past

MY FATHER GRADUATED FROM ST. F. X. IN 1906. HE NEVER ONCE TALKED TO ME ABOUT HIS TIME THERE, BUT THAT FACT IS NOT UNUSUAL, AS HE AND MY MOTHER RARELY TALKED ABOUT anything from their past lives. If one is to judge from the principal poem in the book of poetry he published in 1911, **Rhymes of a Rover**,[2] his experience at the university was not a happy one. "Echoes of St. F. X." is a satire of 1736 lines, written in heroic couplets in the style of Alexander Pope. In the poem he roundly castigates Dr. Alexander M. Thompson, the Rector (1898-1906), for his promotion of sport over academics:

---

[1] I have taken this title and a number of subtitles throughout this chapter from the St. F. X. football song, *Hail and Health*, which I have printed in full on page 85.

[2] This substantial book of poetry (223 pages), of which "Echoes of St. F. X." takes up fifty-three pages, was printed by J. & A. McMillan in St. John, N.B. The title may be inspired by the vagabondia works of well-known poet and fellow New Brunswicker, Bliss Carman (1861-1929). John Keough had travelled to Manitoba at the turn of the century to work on the harvest—a couple of poems in the book come out of that experience—but it's a bit of a stretch to refer to himself as a "rover". Keough's other book of poetry is *Thoughts of Happy Boyhood* (1902).

> *MA's, BA's, DD's and countless shams*
> *With just enough of wit to pass exams,*
> *Hockey and football graduates go their rounds,*
> *Whose sickly brains would scarcely weigh two pounds—*
> *Thy honoured graduates, Thompson! who if reft*
> *Of gown and parchment, nothing would be left.*
> *Too dense to learn, too indolent to think,*
> *They punt up for their sheepskin in the rink. (477-84)*[3]

He also has a go at the Reverend Jimmy Tompkins (1870-1953), who was vice-president and professor (1902-22) and, along with the Reverend Moses Coady, one of the founders of the Antigonish Movement, referring to him as "matchless James" (59), "Xavier's twisted saint" (285), "immortal James" (632), and "cankerous James" (661). He justifiably slams the Reverend Dugald Gillis, a professor of philosophy, who had a rule against discussion in class and considered questions impertinent. No one was spared among the professors and administrators. Even the Bishop of Antigonish (1877-1910), John Cameron, is drawn into the satire. Keough's general attitude toward the powers-that-be at the university is perhaps best expressed in the following lines, in which he pictures the priestly figures ranting at the students:

> *Preaching and prating, dunce succeeds to dunce,*
> *Ignorant of nothing save their ignorance—*
> *Perfect in imperfection, falsely true,*
> *The fools that Horace dreamed of but ne'er knew. (41-44)*

In the "Preface" to the poem, Keough refers to the ex-rector (Thompson retired in 1906) and "the terrific threats that he has made." One has to assume that Thompson had seen at least some of this poem, which, because it is very long and full of allusions, had to have been written over a considerable time. One of his threats was to have Keough excommunicated, a serious problem at that time for a Catholic of Irish roots. But in spite of this threat, Keough went ahead and published the book. Then all hell broke loose at home. Family lore has it that his father, Patrick Keough (1848-1939), being a good and obedient Irish Catholic, destroyed all of the books when they arrived at the Keough home in Blackville, N.B., ready to be sold by mail at one dollar apiece. Only one copy survived. It sits on my desk at this moment, yellow and crumbling.[4] As one might imagine, the relationship between father and son was never the same after that. The son went to Western Canada; and although he returned to Blackville briefly from time to time in the early years, and on one of those visits met again the woman who was to become my mother, he spent most of the rest of his life in the Interior of British Columbia. The

---

[3] My father was not at all anti-sports. He was a keen fullback on the university football team.

[4] A couple of decades ago, I made a dozen Xeroxed copies of the book. I sent one of these copies to each of my five siblings, and one to the St. F. X. Archives. When James D. Cameron, a professor of history at the university, produced his book, *For the People: A History of St. Francis Xavier University* (Montreal & Kingston: McGill-Queen's UP, 1996), I sent a copy to him. But when he complained in his thank-you letter that "most of us educated more recently are lost with the classical references," I replied that there are places where you can look these things up. For some reason or other, I never heard from him again.

relationship between father and son, never a very close one, was easier to handle when there were thousands of miles separating them.

Years to Come

MY OWN YEARS AT ST. F. X. WERE NOT AS UNCOMFORTABLE AS MY FATHER'S HAD APPARENTLY BEEN. I HAD NO QUARREL WITH the academic quality of the courses, which was, I believe, consistently high; and although sports were somewhat over-emphasized, and doing a course in religion was compulsory, I didn't care too much about that. The campus, with its splendid Georgian architecture, its quadrangles, and its restful landscaping, lent a profound element of peace to the academic challenges that are part and parcel of getting an education. The place felt the way one imagined a university should feel: beautiful, self-contained, exclusive, inclusive—all of these qualities presiding over the rumble of daily activity and the press of people in pursuit of important things. Whereas Notre Dame had been a ramshackle collection of wooden buildings, an experiment I was happy to be a part of, St. F. X. had a feel of permanence, the attitude of a place in which whatever experiments there were had been done long ago—it was established in 1853—and had been satisfactorily concluded.

But I found the hard-nosed, truth-holding, Celtic Catholicism of the administration, and (surprisingly) even of some of the students, excruciatingly difficult to adjust to. Whereas at Notre Dame we were surrounded by a Catholicism that was based on the more relaxed, southern European model—the sort of thing you would find in Italy, where the women go to church and pray for the men, who don't, with a perfect belief in the fact that their prayers will be answered by a fatherly God with a large handlebar moustache and a waggling finger—at St. F. X., the atmosphere was one in which the truth was held and harshly promulgated by the men in black, and there was the opportunity to be damned to hell (either here on earth, or later on in eternity) at every turn in the road. In this respect, as time went on, the satiric anger of my father's poem began to make a lot more sense to me than it had before.

Bugging our Way across the Country

I BEGAN MY TWO YEARS AT THE UNIVERSITY IN THE FALL OF 1955, FORTY-NINE YEARS AFTER MY FATHER HAD GRADUATED, WHEN Tom Spring, my Notre Dame roommate, and I arrived in Antigonish to begin our third year of undergraduate studies. We had agreed to meet in Medicine Hat, where the CPR main line meets the road from Cranbrook, on Saturday, September 10th, 1955. I took the Dominion train from Revelstoke at 10:05 on the morning of the 9th, and reached Medicine Hat at about 1 o'clock the next morning. Tom, who had the driven his new Volkswagen bug from his family home to our place of rendezvous, was waiting for me at the station when my train arrived.

We drove like mad over the next few days, getting snatches of sleep here and there, pulling off the road in entries to farmer's fields or on to side roads, inclining the seats back, and snoozing through a few hours at a time. Not once did we stay in a motel or even consider doing so, as neither of us had any money to spare. We got less than enough sleep, but we were young and able to manage perfectly well for a few days. And we were helped by the fact that driving the mostly two-lane highways of the 1950s was a lot easier than doing the same journey by car would be today. There was not much traffic, even in larger towns and cities, and as the railways were still carrying the bulk of the freight, there were practically none of the gigantic trucks that are such a menace on the roads today.

Keeping reasonably clean was a challenge. But when we stopped for gas or something to eat, we would slip into the bathroom, shave, brush our teeth, or give ourselves a quick rub-down with a face cloth. Every couple of days we changed our underwear and socks and put a clean T-Shirts. As a result of these forays into the realm of hygiene, we didn't smell too badly to those with whom we came into contact. At least, that's what we told ourselves at the time.

Our route from Medicine Hat took us through the Regina area, and as the Trans-Canada Highway had not been completed north of Lake Superior, where the road was little more than a gravel track, we went south to U. S. Highway 2 and drove on through Wisconsin to Duluth and Sault Ste.Marie. Back in Canada, we travelled through Sudbury to Ottawa, where we arrived on Tuesday, the 12th. After a brief visit with my sister, Joan, who was living in Ironside, Quebec, just outside of Ottawa, where we had morning coffee, we headed east through Montreal, past Quebec City on the south shore, through Maine to New Brunswick, and on to Nova Scotia. We arrived in Antigonish early on the morning of September 14th and caught forty winks by a farmer's field just outside of town. It was an incredibly fast trip across the country, but that's the way Tom wanted to do it, and it was Tom's car.[5]

Getting Started

WE PRESENTED OUTSELVES AT THE UNIVERSITY AND WENT THROUGH THE REGISTRATION REGIME TYPICAL OF UNIVERSITIES BEFORE THE computer revolution: line up here, line up there, line up everywhere. I paid my fees of $402 for the First Semester: Board $160, Tuition $100, Room $48, Laundry $16, Medical and Hospital $18. I was assigned a room—5 Xavier Hall—on the top floor of one of the older buildings on campus (1880). I was given a roommate—Paul Dugal of Worcester, Massachusetts. All of us students were given a medical: TB X-Ray, blood and urine samples (taken by Pre-Med students), and a cursory examination by a doctor. We were given a map of the campus. Student volunteers were available to show us how to get to where we needed to get to. We registered for courses. We moved into our rooms. We made new friends. We waited for classes to begin; and, most of all, we looked forward to getting into the rhythm of a daily routine.

---

[5] A year and a half later, during the 1956 Christmas vacation, Tom and his brother, Terry, who had joined him at St. F.X. in the fall of that year, drove home to Cranbrook, B.C., through the ice and snow of winter, and they did the trip even quicker than we had, cutting a whole day off the time. After Christmas, they drove back to Antigonish at the same pace. I thought they were crazy even to attempt it. I still do.

Here's a Toast to Merry Mockler

WELL, NOT *EXACTLY* TO "MOCKLER," ONE OF THE HALLS ON CAMPUS (WHICH, BY THE WAY, HOUSED BRIAN MULRONEY WHEN HE WAS first at St. F. X.), but in my case, a toast to old Xavier Hall. Room 5 had a floor-to-angled-ceiling window that overlooked the town of Antigonish. My father had lived in the same hall. In a letter to me in the fall of 1955, his only comment about the building was "How I remember the dormitory with its overabundance of rats." I never saw a rat (of the four-legged variety) in Xavier, so I assume that some Pied Piper had been by in the years since my father was in residence. (There was still a dormitory room in Xavier that housed twelve bright students from poor families who were on total scholarships provided by the university.) It goes without saying, that Xavier (unlike Mockler) was never described at "merry"—the alliteration didn't work. But like all student residences, merry it could be, and merry it often was.

Paul Dugal was one of quite a number of American students at the university, most of them recruited in the areas they came from by priests who in an earlier generation had done their undergraduate years at St. F. X. He was an easy-going fellow, and we got along well, but we never became close friends, and we travelled in different circles on campus. The arrangement proved good enough, nonetheless, that we continued sharing a room the following year in MacNeill Hall.

The room in Xavier was quite small; and because the building was old, it was a bit crooked in shape and slanty of floor. It was furnished with twin beds, little dressers, and minute desks. There was no wardrobe: a piece of wood at head height on the wall beside the dressers with dowels sticking out at intervals served that purpose. As there was no fire escape on the building, our means of getting out in case of fire was a coil of one-inch rope that was braided to a ring and bolted into the floor. It was assumed that, as we were young and healthy, we would be able to throw the rope out of the third-floor window and slide down it to somewhere near the ground. I'm happy to say that our agility in that respect was never tested. On each floor there was a bathroom with three sinks, two shower stalls, and two toilet cubicles.

Every day (except Sunday, of course) the beds were made and the rooms cleaned and tidied by General Purpose Maids. These maids, know from their descriptive title as "Jeeps," were girls in their teens and early twenties, with at best an elementary education, who were recruited from large country families, happy to have one less mouth to feed. They were provided with room and board in their own dormitories, paid a pittance, and supervised in all their activities by the Sisters of St. Martha,[6] who managed to recruit many of them into their order—I mean, what better prospects did they have? For us students, it was made ringingly clear that any kind of intercourse (and I use the term in its

---

[6] In the Bible, Martha prepares a meal for Jesus and his disciples. From the Middle Ages onward, she became the patron saint of housewives and the model of those who do the menial tasks that make life easier for others. The Antigonish congregation was established in 1900 to look after housekeeping tasks at St. F. X. The sisters later branched out into nursing and teaching, while retaining their role at the university.

broadest sense) with the Jeeps, on or off campus, was *verboten*. The penalty was instant dismissal from the university. It seemed to me at the time, since many of these girls were attractive, that in respect of the Jeeps the university was forgetting the line in the Lord's Prayer concerned with leading "us not into temptation." In fact, the warnings were largely superfluous, as we didn't see much of them. According to the Horarium in the Student Handbook (see p. 74 for my selections from this horrendous document), we were to be out of our rooms on ordinary days at 7:02 for chapel, morning prayers, Mass and breakfast. (I like the absurd exactness of the 7:02 bit!) In practice, the Jeeps did most of their work after 8:00 and were normally finished with the rooms by about 9 o'clock. So those of us who liked to dally about getting over to Morrison Hall for breakfast or getting ourselves together for the first class at 8:25, and who were not much interested in chapel, morning prayers, and Mass, had plenty of time to get ready to face the day.

The college provided three meals a day in the large refectory in Morrison Hall. We sat with our assigned group of eight at a designated table and were served by a student who was given the job of looking after two tables in exchange for free board. The food, which was prepared by the Sisters of St. Martha, was at best adequate, but it was plentiful enough. Two days a week, Wednesdays and Fridays, Nova Scotia being a seafaring province, and the fish stocks still being healthy and the fish cheap, we had codfish for dinner.

Our laundry was done by the Sisters of St. Martha. For this once-a-week service we paid $16 per semester. We were given a laundry bag, and designated a day for taking this bag, filled with dirty clothes, to the laundry. We were given a number and a pile of 1¼"x ⅜" tags with flexible pointed metal prongs at each end. We had to put our number on each tag in indelible ink. We attached one of these tags to the bag itself and one to each article of clothing. The sisters washed the clothes, ironed them where necessary, and re-sorted them into their appropriate bag. On a designated day, we picked up our bags and removed the tags, which were not immortal like our souls, but could be used over and over, like our bodies. One might think that this system would be fraught with problems, but it always worked fine for me. I never lost even a sock, which is more than I can say for the laundering in the rest of my life, even around my own home, where socks often entered into the washer or drier and were lost forever, eaten up, I expect, by some yet undiscovered laundry pair-a-site.

The Sisters of St. Martha were not just doers of menial jobs. They also ran the School of Nursing at the Antigonish hospital. And one of them ran the Infirmary on the top floor of Morrison Hall. I was admitted there once by Sister Mary Someone when I had picked up a virus and was running a fever. The large room was divided by curtains into a half dozen or so cubicles, each of them open toward one side of the room where there was a small altar, so that God could cure us of our ills even if Man failed to do so. The Reverend Moses Coady, founder of the Antigonish Movement and a fellow student of my father's back at the turn of the century, a giant of a man, but old and creaky now, had living quarters on the floor. Every morning he would speed his way through a low Latin Mass, which we were all able to watch and participate in from our beds of sickness. "*Dominus vobiscum*," he would say, turning towards us, and we would answer "*Et cum spiritu tuo.*" "*Sursum corda.*" "*Habemus a dominum.*" And so on. Father Coady remembered my father and asked about his life. When I mentioned this fact in a letter home, my father replied: "There was a Coady who graduated at the same time I did, 1906. He was a big, broad-shouldered, dark-complected chap and quite an athlete, taking part in all the campus games." That's the man, old and grey now, but still impressive.

> *"I'm feeling a lot better," I told the Sister. In fact, I was dying to leave the Infirmary to go to the big, all-party, political rally that was taking place in the auditorium that evening. I only made it to the half-way point of the rally. I just felt too awful to stay. I dragged myself back to the Infirmary. Sister was much amused and teased me about it until I left the place for good two days later.*

Here's a Health to MSB

AH, MSB! MOUNT ST. BERNARD! THE COLLEGE ON THE OTHER SIDE OF ST. NINIAN'S CATHEDRAL (SEAT OF THE BISHOP OF ANTIGONISH), WHERE the ladies were housed and taught and watched over by the Sisters of the Congregation of Notre Dame (CND) and kept safe from the devious manipulations of the devilish male students in the university proper. Because St. F. X., you see, wasn't exactly a co-educational university in those days. Sure, we shared classes with the ladies from the Mount, and it was permitted to date them for dances and other such things. Some of the CNDs, with their white wimples rising to a peak out of the black robes at the tops of their heads, making them appear to be animated church steeples as they glided along, even descended on a daily basis from the Mount and taught courses in the university proper. I was taught Spanish by Sister St. Carola, and History by Sister St. Veronica, who was, I believe, also a sister in a non-symbolic sense of long-time Nova Scotia premier (1930s, '40s, and '50s), Angus M. Macdonald, who died in office in 1954. Compared to the Marthas, the CNDs were the intellectuals of the church penguin parade. In general, I liked the Marthas better than the CNDs; they were more down-to-earth, more human, more motherly.

I never dated a girl from MSB. There were many of them that I admired from a distance, but I think I was intimidated by their patina of goodness and purity. On the other hand, none of them ever showed any interest in me. Perhaps they saw me as some creature that had crawled out of the Wild West. At any rate, the feeling—or lack of such—seemed to have been mutual. There was a kind of joke that had circulated—for decades apparently—regarding the ladies of MSB. It was said that upon arrival at the college, the girls were issued with a man-proof bra and a vaginal cork that had engraved on it the words that Dante had inscribed over the entry to hell, *Lasciate ogni speranza voi*, "Abandon hope, all ye who enter here."[7] When I dated, and I didn't have a chance to do that very often, not nearly as often as I would have liked to have done, it was with girls who were not directly connected to the university.

---

[7] *Inferno* III.9.

At the Engineers' Dance in November 1956, I hit it off with a girl I met there whom I shall call Theresa. She was a short, slip of a girl, blondish, moderately good-looking, who was in her final year of nursing at the Antigonish hospital. The nursing students were, of course, required to live in residence, but as this was Saturday, Theresa had leave to spend the weekend at her parents' home, a couple of miles outside the town. One of her girlfriends was going to drive her home after the dance, but Tom Spring, seeing the situation, offered to lend me his VW bug to take her home. At the ramshackle farm house with its higgledy-piggledy rooms, we settled into a couch in the dark off the kitchen to do some moderate necking. Suddenly, a door at the end of the long room flew open, light streamed into the room, and a tall, thin, fully-dressed, older man, with his back to us appeared. He had obviously been incapacitated to some extent by a stroke, and he appeared to be in some distress. Theresa ran to him and quietly calmed him down. When she came back to me, the spell was broken. It was time to go. The incident seemed to have destroyed any relationship we might have been building. I never took her out again. She married the brother of one of my friends the following summer. Apparently, they lived happily ever after.

Sing for Friends No Longer Near Us

WHEN TOM SPRING AND I ARRIVED AT ST. F.X., I WENT INTO RESIDENCE, BUT TOM, WHO, OF COURSE, HAD A CAR—CARS WERE prohibited to students in residence, if you can believe it!—found a trailer on the edge of town to rent; and he had to get permission to do so, as in the rule-bound atmosphere of the place, even to live off-campus required a *nihil obstat* from the powers-that-be. My own roommate, Paul Dugal, who also had a car, solved the problem by surreptitiously renting a garage in town in which to store it.

As a result of this separation, and in our second year at the university, of the arrival of his brother, Terry, Tom and I saw far less of each other than we had in the previous two years. But we still managed to get together from time to time, often in the company of other students from Notre Dame, Pat Wilcox, Leo Nimsick, John Boucher, and Leo Smith. Pat and I were both smokers, and as we could not afford to buy tailor-made cigarettes, we purchased as a partnership a hand-roller that would do five cigarettes at a time and shared the cost of the large tins of tobacco and the cigarette papers we used to make them. I often had coffee with Leo Nimsick at the Student Co-op Café, which was in the quadrangle that edged on Xavier Hall, or at the Brigadoon, a popular student hangout on Main Street in downtown Antigonish. Occasionally, all or some of us would get together on a weekend night at Tom's place or somewhere else in town and have a few beers, not many, though, as none of us had any extra money. It was a relief to get away from the rule-bound campus, which in time became less and less like a real world, and spend a little time among the great and lesser unwashed. But the beer, when I look back on it, was really horrible stuff.

> *The beer available in the 1950s, apart from the required water, hops and malt, was an incredible cocktail of up to 84 chemicals. Eventually, it began killing people, most famously in the case of the Dow Brewery of Montreal, whose product was proved to be a factor in the terminal heart attacks of a number of Quebecers. One weekend morning, Leo Nimsick and I decided to go to Chisholm House to see what John Boucher and Leo Smith were up to. When we opened the door to their room, we found them still in bed, with the windows shut tight. They had been somewhere in town drinking beer the night before—no alcohol was allowed on campus and drinking elsewhere was prohibited—and the smell of beer farts from that chemical beer was overwhelming. It was a smell that was instantly recognizable—you had to be there—and, I'm happy to say, is no longer with us. Leo and John survived. Dow Breweries did not.*

New Friends: Manly Hearts and True

Most of my new friends I met through campus activities. Des McGrath I first encountered in the Debating Society. He was a tall, gangly fellow from Cornerbrook, Newfoundland. He had a marvellous sense of humour and a great Irish capacity for underlining the absurd in every situation he found himself in. Our friendship ripened at the beginning of my senior year when the Debating Society held an extemporaneous speaking contest, which he badgered me into entering.

> *There were six of us who entered the contest, which was held in one of the classrooms in Aquinas Hall. Father Cyril H. Bauer, the Dean of Studies, and Father Vince MacLellan were judges. There was a small audience of about twenty people. I had expected Rick Cashin to be a contestant, as this grandson of a Newfoundland Prime Minister and scion of the Cashins, who had made their fortune in alcohol during the prohibition years, had a much-deserved reputation as an orator. But he wasn't there. My piece was not exactly extemporaneous, as it was a part of my baccalaureate essay, "What is a University," that I had put to memory, a rambling, creative piece, much influenced by Dylan Thomas. The judges granted me third place, pointing out, justifiably, that my speech, though wonderful, was not exactly extemporaneous. First place was taken by Russell Pellerin, Head of the Liberal Party on campus. Second place went to a sophomore, new on campus and unknown, by the name of Brian Mulroney.*

My association with the *Xaverian Weekly* began in the spring of 1956 with a column of quotations from other papers that were part of the Canadian University Press organization which I called "CUP Lines." The man with the grand title of Editor-in-Chief that year was Pat MacAdam, who later in life became an influential Conservative back-room man and friend of Brian Mulroney's. The Associate Editor was Lowell Murray, who decades later became well-known across the country as Mulroney's front man on the failed Meech Lake initiative. It was at the *Xaverian* that I met Dave Brophy, who took over as editor the following year. I still have a note Dave scrawled across a piece of yellow paper when we were delayed in getting the paper out by the inconvenient death of George Boyle,[8] a professor, journalist, and campus luminary, whose passing we felt we had to report at some length: "Terry: At 1:40 a.m. the Cog [Emmett Couglan] and I wish you Bon Voyage and safe passage during your trip to the *Casket*. We are now leaving for the Land of Nod. Brophy."

While I was working on the paper, I wrote a comic piece anonymously on the mega-rich New Brunswick capitalist and friend of Lord Beaverbrook, Sir James Dunn (1874-1956), referring to him as Sir James "Finished." Within an hour of the paper's distribution on campus, a group of us were herded into the office of Father John A. Rankin, an obstreperous priest who was Dean of Men. He demanded to know who had written the piece. No one was willing to give him that information (Thank God!—or Whoever!), which led him to rattle his symbolic, priestly sword in a fierce diatribe on the irresponsibility of students these days. The university, he said, expected to be left some money by Sir James; and if he were to see this sophomoric piece, he might cut the university out of his will. Consequently, no copies of this paper were to be allowed to leave the campus. Sir James died not long after this contretemps with Rankin. I don't know if the university profited from his will.

I felt very lucky to have escaped, because, given the relish with which these people kicked students who offended them out of the university, I think they probably would have turfed me out over this minor incident. As one might expect, I had researched Sir James Dunn's life before writing the piece, and once I had settled down in the wake of my escape, I was amused that these guardians of student morality, these holders of the truth, were willing to overlook the fact that Sir James had been twice divorced; and, at the same time, they were undoubtedly compounding their own sins, according to their own rules, by praying for a portion of the filthy lucre that he'd accumulated in what were at best morally dubious ways.

Dave and I represented St. F. X. at the Canadian University Press Conference in Toronto over the 1956 Christmas vacation. We stayed in the Ford Hotel, on the seventh floor. I had never been up that high in a building before and at first found it a bit frightening to look out the window. Also at that conference were Peter Gzoski, later a CBC radio icon, of the University of Toronto, and a fellow from UBC, whose name I don't remember, but whose fingernails bitten–to–the–quick I have never forgotten. Up for grabs was the award for the best university paper in the country that year. We did not have a hope of winning it. But Gzoski and Nail-Biter annoyed me considerably by playing a game of "You're going to win"—"No, You're going to win"—"No, You're going to win," *ad nauseam*! In the end, it was the University of Alberta paper that won.

"The Cog"—Emmett Couglan—when he took on the editorship of the Xaverian Annual for 1957 no longer had time to work on the *Xaverian Weekly*. But I still saw a lot of him, as I had agreed to be literary editor of the Annual. Besides that, Emmett lived on my floor of MacNeill House, so we often ran into one another there. Like all young

---

[8] George Boyle is best-known as the author of a biography of one of the two founders of the Antigonish Movement, *Father Tompkins of Nova Scotia,* New York: Kennedy and Sons, 1953.

people, we had dreams of utopia. We would gather in one of our rooms, Emmett and me, Charlie Murphy, Stu MacMillan, and others, and talk about how great it would be to rent a big house in the country and study all the things we didn't have time to study at the university. But, of course, reality had to triumph, and we all set out after graduation to hoe our own rows.

Memories of High Endeavour

Exekoi Society

ON THE BASIS OFF MY FIRST SEMESTER MARKS, I BECAME A MEMBER OF THE EXEKOI SOCIETY. THIS ELITE GROUP, LIMITED TO SIXTY-FIVE members derived its name from the Greek for "those having." Members were nominated by a faculty committee from those having an overall average above 80 percent (much harder to attain then than it is in these days of inflated marks), who had a "satisfactory disciplinary record," and who were in "possession of leadership qualities." My marks were good. At the end of the first semester, my overall average was 89 percent; at the end of the year, I passed second in a class of 66, and I retained an average above 85 percent for the rest of my time at the university, putting me in line for a B.A. *Summa Cum Laude*. Marks were given out at a scheduled interview with the priest who was in charge of the house one was living in. A copy was also sent home to one's parents.

> *It was my turn to go into Father Malcolm MacDonnell's office on the ground floor of MacNeill House to get my marks. MacDonnell sat behind his desk. Only the desk light was on. I was worried about my results this time around, as I felt I hadn't scored very well in Spanish or Religion. "How do you think you've done this term," Moose (his nickname among students) asked me. "Probably not as well as last semester," I said. "Well," said Moose, as he handed the sheet of marks to me, "either you're in the throes of a delusion or you're an unmitigated boaster." My fears were not realized. My average was 92 percent.*

Drama: The Part of Five Wits in *Everyman*

In my last semester at the university, I got involved again in acting, taking a part in the medieval morality play, *Everyman*, presented by the Xaverian Players on April 11 and 12 in the university auditorium. I played the part of Five Wits (i.e., the Five Senses). Young sophomore, Brian Mulroney, played the part of Fellowship, an appropriate role for him, as he played the same part for real throughout the rest of his life. When Mulroney was Prime Minister, he was often portrayed in cartoons as a man with a massive chin. At St. F. X., he was known by those who were put off by his arrogance as "Pea Mouth," as he seemed to have a mouth that was too small for the rest of his face. Perhaps his chin elongated as he grew older and ascended to the highest office in the land, where he became known as "Lyin' Brian," his chin a Canadian variation on Pinocchio's nose. The play was a hit with critics and audience alike.

Model Parliament

The various political parties on campus held a mock election in February 1957 to put together a Model Parliament. I campaigned and did a lot of the dog-work for the Liberal Party. I bought from the MacGillivray Press of Antigonish items advertising our campaign: "30 Posters, 12 x 19, 2 colors, $6.00; 1100 Blotters to give to potential voters—yes, we still used fountain pens in those days!--$11.00; and 50 Streamers, $2.25." The Liberal Party won the election, and we formed the government in the Model Parliament, which was held at MSB on March 9. I became, for a brief time, the Hon. Terrence Keough (Burnaby-Coquitlam), Minister of Citizenship and Immigration. Also on the Government side were Rick Cashin (who a few years' later actually became a Member of Parliament) and my friend, Stu MacMillan. Russell Pellerin, the head of the party on campus, was Prime Minister. On the other side of the House, Paul Creaghan was the Leader of the Opposition (later in life, for awhile, a Cabinet Minister in New Brunswick). Sitting with him as Conservatives were, among others, Brian Mulroney, Sam Wakim, and Fred Doucet. The rump of the C.C.F. included my friend, Leo Nimsick, whose father was at that time an actual C.C.F. member of the legislature—later a cabinet minister under Dave Barrett—in British Columbia. By far the best speeches were given by Rick Cashin, who was very much on top of his game. But it was Fred Doucet who brought the house down when he referred to Cashin as a "beached whale." (Cashin was often teased for being decidedly overweight, a situation that amused him and which he exploited by forming a group on campus that he dubbed "The Society of the Obese." He alone decided who was fat enough to become a member.)

The Literary Scene: A Metric Triumph

In the *Xaverian Annual* for 1957 is a section entitled "A Campus Who's Who." It consists of individual pictures and short write-ups of 33 students who were said to have made "more than an average contribution, both to their class and to the University." The section contained a few of my friends (Dave Brophy, Emmett Coughlan, Des McGrath, and Charlie Murphy), as well as a number of people I worked with in various activities, but who would better be described as acquaintances rather than friends (Pete Lesaux, Rick Cashin, Paul Creaghan, and Fred Doucet). In my own write-up, I am described, among other things, as "one of the foremost scholars and poets on campus." My status as the principle poet on campus resulted from my having won a couple of awards and from my having published in the national student magazine put out by NFCUS, the National Federation of Canadian University Students. Accompanying my picture among the B.A. graduates elsewhere in the Annual, I am described as one who "rose to campus fame by capturing the poetry award of the Engineering magazine 'Potential,'" and who was also a winner of a Literary "X," a certificate and pin given to those who made a significant contribution in that area. High praise, indeed! In this day and age, it's unlikely that one would rise to campus fame by capturing a poetry prize, but those were different times, in which the student body was made up of far more students in the liberal arts than it is today. There was also, by and large, a greater appreciation of the value of a liberal education; though, there were those, even then, who saw the liberal arts as peripheral.

> *Dave Brophy, Stu MacMillan, the Cog, and I were standing on Main Street outside the Brigadoon, a favourite student hangout in Antigonish, one warmish, late-winter afternoon, talking about putting together a piece on things cultural for the Xaverian Weekly. We were joined by Brian Mulroney, in his beige raincoat, collar turned up, wearing gabardine pants, and the white bucks that were so fashionable at the time, accompanied by his roommate, Sam Wakim. "Thank God for the CBC," I heard myself saying. "If I were Prime Minister," Mulroney chimed in in his basso profundo, "the first thing I'd do is dismantle the CBC." So it would appear to be true that the leopard does not change his spots, even though, in the face of reality, he may have to modify them.*

The Dean of Studies Requests an Interview

Early in the spring of my final semester, I received a note in my mail box in Morrison Hall one afternoon from the Dean of Studies, Father Bauer, asking me to call by his office, as he wanted to talk to me about something that could be of benefit to me. "You are one of the people we are thinking about recommending from the university as a candidate for a Rhodes Scholarship," he said. "How do you feel about that?" Needless to say, I was flattered by the idea. But the offer had appeared so suddenly and so unexpectedly that I asked if I could take a day or two to think it over. My problem was that I had spent nearly four years with practically no money for even the most basic items, and I was sick-to-death of being poor. I wanted to get out into the world where I could command a decent salary and finally buy a few of the things that I saw in the possession of other people and envied them for, basic things like a couple of good suits, some shirts that were not frayed at the collar from too many washes, leather shoes that didn't fall apart when they got wet. Besides, I told myself, there will be other candidates who will have better records than I have, and I may just be setting myself up for a terrible disappointment. So I told Father Bauer that I really didn't think I could present myself as a candidate. I have often wondered if I had put my name on the line whether I would have been given the scholarship. If so, my decision was one of the worst ones I have ever made. But who knows. It's a classic example of "the road not taken."

Rules and Regulations

If you ever wondered why the Church was moved to reform itself with Vatican II and the students of the Western World rose up against university administrations in the 1960s, not just in Catholic universities, but in all universities, you need look no further than the *St. F. X. Student Handbook* of 1957. The pettiness of the thinking behind most of the rules and regulations is amazing. Why did we put up with it? Out of the room at 7:02! (not 7:01 or 7:04); one 60-watt lamp in the ceiling! Permissions necessary to leave the campus after 5:40 p.m.! Students "a menace to the welfare of the community because of idleness, the use of profane or obscene language, dishonesty, gambling, the possession or use of intoxicating liquors, etc." subject to dismissal! Mark reports sent to parents!

Rubber heels on your footwear! "Deprivation of marks" for missing classes! Lights out at 11 p.m.! Penalties, penalties, penalties! But let us not omit one item on the good side. There is the health care that provides 21 days a year in hospital, and the cost of all ordinary drugs while in the hospital, for $6.00. Amazing!

Student Handbook

ST. FRANCIS XAVIER UNIVERSITY
Antigonish, Nova Scotia

Horarium

Class	Days	Sundays	Holidays
6.45	Rising	7.25	7.25
7.02	Chapel, morning prayers, Mass, breakfast	7.50	7.50
8.25 to 12.00	Class or study	10.30 to 12.00	
12.05	Dinner	12.05	12.05
	Free time		
1.15	Class or study		
3.55	Free time		
5.40	Chapel		5.40
6.05	Supper	6.05	6.05
	Free time		
	Chapel	7.00	
7.50	Study	8.00	7.50
11.00	Lights out	11.00	11.00

Rooms and common dormitories are to be vacated so that they can be made up at 7.02 a.m. on class days and at 7.50 a.m. on other days. Catholic students are expected to make Mass and Holy Communion the spiritualizing force through which all their activities are raised to the supernatural level. They are also expected to attend chapel for the late afternoon devotional period.

Permissions

1. Free morning periods are the most valuable part of the working day and should be used for serious study.
2. To be off the campus later than 5.40 p.m., students must register their names with their prefect or the Prefect of Discipline. On their return, they must register again in person. Overstaying of such permissions will be penalized.
3. The maximum number of evening permissions in any week is three. The better students rarely seek this maximum, and those whose standing is unsatisfactory will have the privilege restricted. On one night of the week designated by the Students Union, no permissions are granted.
This regulation applies to absences from rooms or study halls for more than one hour whether spent in rink, gymnasium, society rallies, or in any extra-curricular activity. Studying in the Library is the one exception admitted, in which case students sign a special Library sheet.
4. For special reasons, late permissions may be obtained in person from the Prefect. To overstay such permissions is a serious offence to be dealt with by the Committee on Discipline.
5. To be absent overnight, or to leave town, there is required a written permission of parents or guardians sent direct to the Prefect.

Examinations and Quizzes

Examinations on the matter covered during each semester in all subjects are held during the concluding days in January and in May.
Reports on the standing of all new students are sent to their parents after the October quizzes and at any other time that this is deemed desirable by the Committee on Studies.

Class Attendance

Students who miss class or laboratories must promptly account for their absence to the professor concerned. Failure to do this is penalized by deprivation of marks.
Absences on the days preceding or following all holidays including Christmas and Easter, no matter what the cause, are penalized by fining the student $1.00 for every class period and for every laboratory period missed. A fine of $5.00 is imposed for late registration.

Penalties

The chief penalties for infraction of the rules are withdrawal of privileges, suspension, and permanent dismissal from the University. A student who is guilty of a serious breach of conduct, or who habitually disregards the University regulations, becomes subject to dishonorable dismissal which will debar him from admission to other colleges.
When a student is considered to be a menace to the welfare of the community because of idleness, use of profane or obscene language, dishonesty, gambling, the possession or use of intoxicating liquors, etc., the Faculty Committee on Discipline takes up the question of his dismissal in consultation with the Student Committee on Discipline.

Hospitalization

A fee of $6.00 entitles students to hospitalization as bed patients in common wards for periods aggregating up to 21 days in one year. The cost of all ordinary services and ordinary drugs is included. X-rays are provided up to a cost of $10.00 for hospital patients.

Discipline

Quiet must be observed during class and study periods. Musical instruments may be played only during free time. Conscientious students refrain from anything that distracts their neighbors from serious work.
In so far as possible, students should have rubber heels on their footwear, and they should endeavor to walk quietly in all corridors. It is forbidden to wear football shoes in residence or classroom buildings, and army boots must not be worn in the dining room. Noisiness near buildings during class and study periods must be avoided.
A check is made at 10.45 p.m. to see that all are in their places. Everyone is required to be in bed at 11.00, when all lights are extinguished. Oil lamps and candles are fire hazards and are prohibited. For special reasons, the Committee on Discipline may authorize that lights be kept on until 12.00 p.m., but only on condition that absolute quiet prevail in the buildings.

Lights And Electrical Appliances

One 60-watt lamp is supplied in a ceiling socket of a student's room and each occupant is entitled to an additional 60-watt lamp, attached to the wall. Any other fixtures introduced will be confiscated. Electric irons may be used with caution in a room designated in each hall. The use of radios is permitted, but must be restricted to free time. All radios are subject to confiscation if they are a source of disturbance during study or class periods. Only one radio is permitted in a common dormitory.

University Property

All room decorations are subject to the approval of the Prefect and are to be attached to the moulding. Students will be fined for driving tacks in the plaster. A man of honor will personally report damage he has done to University property.

Health

A student who is so ill that it is not advisable for him to leave his residence to go to the dining room should obtain authorization from the Prefect to take a place in the Infirmary. Students who do not reside in the University halls are not admitted to the Infirmary.
Order and quiet must be observed at all times in the Infirmary. Students are expected to abide by the visiting hours which are posted. All lights in the Infirmary must be extinguished by 10.00 p.m.
All students are advised to spend at least an hour in the open air every afternoon, preferably taking part in some sport.

Courses: Forward Striving, Onward Driving

THE MOTTO OF THE UNIVERSITY, ***QUAECUMQUE SUNT VERA***, IS FROM PAUL'S EPISTLE TO THE PHILIPPIANS: *WHATSOEVER THINGS ARE TRUE, whatsoever things are honest, whatsoever things are just, whatsoever things are pure, whatsoever things are lovely, whatsoever things are known to be good*. It is not an easy motto to live up to, and I'm sorry to say that there were not many faculty who did so.

Father Bannon: Playing the Game

But in some classrooms, there were individuals who attempted to live up to the motto, especially in courses that were in the traditional liberal arts curriculum. My favourite professor was Father Richard Bannon, who had received his M.A. from Harvard under the tutelage of the great George Lyman Kittredge (1860-1941), whose editions of Shakespeare and Chaucer were standards until the 1950s and are still referred to by today's Shakespearian scholars. Father Bannon, a tall man with a totally bald pate, was a bit of a character in his own right. He sometimes drank a little more than he should have. If you were walking toward him on campus and he veered away from you and hid rather ineffectually behind a tree, you knew that he had probably been into the sauce. Once in a student / faculty golf tournament in which I was paired with him, he teed up on the first tee, swung, and missed the ball completely. "Why, you invisible bastard!" he said, sending our foursome into gales of laughter at this unpriestly outburst.

I did a number of courses with Father Bannon, including a survey of European literature in translation from the Greeks to the end of the Middle Ages, **English 22**, and a selection from *The Canterbury Tales*, **English 10**. The content of these courses was certainly true, honest, and lovely. It was the only time in my undergraduate career that I was exposed to sections of the great Greek epics, the medieval romances (*The Cid, The Song of Roland*), and works such as Dante's *Inferno* and Boccaccio's *Decameron*. But it was, at the same time, *pure* in the worst sense of the word. The texts we used had either been bowdlerised, so that any explicit references to things sexual had been removed from them, or sections considered offensive (e.g., Rabelais' conjectures on what makes the best material with which to wipe your bum[9]) were completely removed. Father Bannon apologized at the beginning of each of these classes for this situation, but he said that he was powerless to do anything about it except read in some of the missing bits from his own texts, which he did with great hilarity and amusement.[10] Clearly, no one in the class

---

[9] For those who have only read the family text: he concludes that the best thing to use for this operation is a goose's neck.
[10] Bowdlerization was not uncommon at all universities at that time. The term derives from the name of Thomas Bowdler (1754-1825), who published an edition of Shakespeare in 1818 that removed material he considered unsuitable for family reading, most of which was sexual in nature. When I taught a course for the University of Ottawa in Pembroke, Ontario, in 1970, I was sent copies of a bowdlerized text of *Othello* by the university bookstore. I did what Bannon did and read in lines such as "an old black ram is tupping your white ewe." Even prominent 20th century critics like Dover Wilson and Caroline Spurgeon either missed or tried agonizingly to ratiocinate many of the bawdy scenes in Shakespeare.

was harmed by these renditions of lines from the original texts. Even the young ladies from MSB, vulnerable to corruption, were spared.

Father MacSween: Manly Hearts and *Pure*

Another of the English teachers, and a minor poet in his own right, was the Reverend R. MacSween. With him, I did a survey of English prose writers, from the earliest time to the late 19th century, **English 14**, and a course on 20th-century American poets, **English 15**. I enjoyed both of these courses, which had few enough students in them so that MacSween was able to run them more or less as seminars. But I didn't like Father MacSween much. He had a big, round head, and he wore round, frameless glasses, through which he stared at you, frog-like, while you were talking to him, as if he were looking for a black mark on your soul. And he probably was. He was arrogant, prissy, and confident that he had a patent on whatsoever things are true. He certainly had a patent on whatsoever things are *pure*. Once during the course on English prose, he asked us to write a 500 word piece that would put forth a moral problem in a fictional setting. He was not pleased with the piece I gave him. It concerned a woman in a country setting, abandoned by her ne'er-do-well husband, who agreed to expose her breasts to a travelling salesman in return for the money she needed to feed her two young children. MacSween read everyone else's efforts to the class, commenting and leading a discussion on them. He said that my story, though well-written and concerned with an important moral dilemma, was not suitable for public discussion. The irony of the situation became clear after class, when a number of the students asked if they could read it.

Some of the Others

In my first year, I did **Spanish 1** with Sister St. Carola, a jolly creature, beaming from beneath her steeple-topped wimple, a course that I enjoyed immensely. I was taught **Economics 1**, by a Mr. J. W. Johnston, a Texan, who always sported a white Stetson as he walked around the campus. He did his best to convince me that I should major in Economics, as, he said, I was his best student and I had a real talent in that area. (Father Bauer, the Dean of Studies, who may have been proselytized by Johnston, also tried to veer me in that direction, but I stuck with my English major, as that was where I wanted to be.) I did the compulsory courses in **Religion,** one in each semester, but I remember only one incident from all four classes.

The Reverend R. MacDonald, in whose Religion 5C I was ensconced, was leading a discussion on the point at which a venial sin becomes a mortal sin. "If you mow your lawn for up to a half hour on a Sunday," he contended, "you have committed a venial sin. If you mow it for more than a half hour, that's a mortal sin." At this point of absurdity, equivalent to placing angels on the head of a pin, I took to staring out the window and dreaming of talking to some of the pretty girls I saw criss-crossing the quadrangle. Now . . . if I necked with one of these lovely creatures for less than half an hour . . .

In my first semester, I did **Political Science 1** with the Reverend Philip Mifflen. Father Mifflen, whose real area of academic excellence was philosophy, was one of the finest minds I have ever come across. But he was also a difficult man to get to know, as he constantly wore a mask of seriousness that was impossible to penetrate. In this course we were studying Canadian forms of government, both federal and provincial. Another member of this class was Brian Mulroney. In those days, the Social Credit government under W. A. C. Bennett in the province of British Columbia was relatively new, and since I was from British Columbia, in class discussions I was usually asked for my opinion regarding what was going on there, who this gang of weirdoes were, and how they ever managed to get themselves elected. I did my best to enlighten the locals on the situation in my far-away province, but if truth be told, I didn't know any more about the political world there than any of the other students in the class. Also of interest on the provincial scene was that other wayward group, the Union Nationale of Maurice Duplessis. This right-wing government, which historically had worked hand-in-hand with the Catholic Church to keep Quebec a peasant society, was now losing its grip in the face of the beginnings of what in the Sixties became known as the "Quiet Revolution." For local information on this situation, Father Mifflen took to calling on that other member of the class who was a native of *la belle province*, Brian Mulroney. Mulroney was much more confident in his assessment of the Quebec situation than I was of that in my home province. But I suppose, in hindsight, that was to be expected. Also in hindsight, I would guess that he was probably no more accurate than I was.

Education Courses: Play the Game!

BY THE TIME I RETURNED TO DO MY FINAL YEAR, I HAD DECIDED THAT I WANTED TO BE A TEACHER. IN COUNTING UP THE CREDITS NEEDED to complete my B.A., I found that I could finish it by taking only three full-year liberal arts courses, plus the compulsory Religion course. I chose **History 2** (History of Scotland), **Spanish 2** (Follow-up to Spanish 1), and **English 22** (Heritage of English Literature). According to the catalogue, if I added **Education 1** and **Education 10**, both full-year courses, and **Education 4** and **5**, which were semester courses, I would fulfil the requirements for a B.Ed degree as well.

On September 17, 1956, I signed up for the above regime and had my Course of Studies form initialled by the Registrar, Reverend W. X. Edwards. But a couple of days later, before courses had actually begun, I was called into the office of the Dean of Studies, where Father Bauer told me that it was against university policy to grant two degrees to a student in this way, and that if I wanted an education degree, I would have to return to the university for another year. As there wasn't much point in these circumstances in carrying an extra course, I dropped Education 10.

It wasn't until early in the second semester that I found out by accident that a student from Margaree Harbour (hometown—by the way—of the illustrious Reverend Dr. Moses Coady), who in the circumstances had better remain nameless, and who was noted among the men in black for the quality of his piety and snivelling obeisance to the rule-makers, that this Uriah Heap of Cape Breton Island had been given an exception to university policy and was to be granted both a B.A. and a B.Ed. in circumstances that—apart from his mediocre marks—exactly mirrored mine. I was furious at this hypocritical and unfair development. But what could I do? It was too late to pick up the extra course I would need to fulfill the requirement for the extra degree, and they wouldn't have allowed me to do it anyway.

This incident was the first of two that soured my feelings about the university. The second one follows.

Graduation: Life's the Goal that Gleams before Us

Interviews for the Job Market

IN THE 1950s THERE WAS A GENERAL BELIEF IN THE CORPORATE WORLD THAT A PERSON COMING OUT OF UNIVERSITY WITH A GOOD B.A. WOULD be capable of learning the particular skills needed in just about any job situation. Besides, it was felt that a background in the Liberal Arts was a decided asset in networking the boardrooms and dinner tables of the business milieu (not to mention the bedrooms—but this was the 1950s, after all), as a person with this sort of education should be able to converse intelligently on a wide variety of topics. Concomitantly, it was felt that to have an education that was too specialized could be a drawback, as the individual would have to unlearn certain approaches in order to master the particular way that the people who hired him wanted things to be done.

In these years there was also a drive in the corporate world to require that all of the new people hired to be officers of the company, to replace those who had gone from office boy to district manager, have a university education, as the old promotional system was no longer considered viable. A whole raft of companies arrived on campus and arranged interviews, looking for new blood. As my ambition to teach had been temporarily thwarted, I interviewed with a number of them. Very quickly, I was offered a job as a Junior Executive Trainee by the Hudson's Bay Company in their Vancouver store at a salary of $325 a month. I was pleased to find something immediately, and in my home province, and so I agreed to take the job. I was also influenced by the fact that they would send me a train ticket from Antigonish to Vancouver and pay for my expenses along the way.

A Celebration Leading to Horror

WITH THE EXAMS ALL FINISHED AND THE PRESSURE OF FOUR YEARS OF STUDY BEHIND US, A FEW OF US FROM MACNEILL HOUSE AND A couple of luminaries from other parts of the campus decided to go to the beach and have a celebration. Somebody managed to get his hands on two dozen bottles of beer, not enough when spread throughout the group to get anybody drunk, but at least a token of traditional celebration. Somebody else bought wieners, buns, and marshmallows. We each contributed a pittance to the cost. At the beach, we lit a bonfire and spent a couple of early evening hours celebrating our accomplishment.

Now, possession of alcohol, whether on or off campus, was strictly forbidden by university rules. I remember the President of the University, the Reverend Dr. Somers, raging on about booze in one of his sermons at Sunday Mass. "The Prime Minister of this country," he railed, "kept a cabinet post open for six months for a man, a graduate of St. F. X., who had great talent, but who could not control his drinking, so somebody else was given the job!"

Unluckily, on the way back through town, led by Pete Lesaux, who happened to be President of the Student Council and quarterback of the football team, a group of us were singing "Hail and Health" en route to the university. The town cop—only one was on duty at any given time—an officious creature of the type who becomes a righteous dragon as soon as you put him in a uniform, rounded a half dozen of us up and herded us to the police station. As soon as he got near to us, he could, of course, smell beer. We were not charged with anything. When he had us all in the station waiting room, he called the university to complain about our conduct.

As it was only about ten o'clock by this time, we were told to go straight to the office of the Dean of Men, the Reverend Father John Rankin, the large black Celt and unhappy priest, whom we have met before in this account in regard to Sir James Dunn and the *Xaverian Weekly*. Father Rankin fumed at us like a cheap cigar in the mouth of a capitalist exploiter. But he wasn't interested in our so-called misbehaviour. (It wasn't really worth being interested in.) What he wanted to know is where we'd got the beer. I mean, that was an offence against the university that could be given some legs. Unfortunately, after a long silence, one of our party blurted out that we had "found it." Now, the likelihood of "finding" twenty-four bottles of beer being next to nil, this was a stupid position to take. But with the loyalty to one another that comes from common oppression, we felt we had to fall into line with this explanation, in spite of the fact that we knew nobody was going to believe it.

Revelling in his power over us, Black Jack Rankin told us we would all most likely be sent down from the university without a degree. But, he said, he couldn't make that decision. The Committee of Discipline would have to be convened to hear our case. Happy that he'd frightened us as thoroughly as possible, he dismissed us. This interview was then—and remains still—one of the worst moments of my life.

The Committee of Discipline consisted of a dozen or so individuals, most of them priests, a few lay faculty members, and two student representatives. One of the students was Dave "Ticker" Whalen, the President of the Senior Class. The other was my good friend Des McGrath, who, ironically, had been at the beach party with us, but had been across the street with a couple of other party-goers. I remember him standing there, shaking his head in disbelief, as the town cop rounded us up.

For a day and a half, I lived in terror of what might happen to us. I couldn't sleep and I couldn't eat. One of my friends, I don't remember who, concerned for my welfare, contacted Father Donald Campbell, a professor of psychology, whom I didn't know, and asked him if he would talk to me. We met informally in the warm May weather outside of Chisholm House. It was obvious that he didn't like what was going on. It was also obvious that he had inside information. He told me I would be allowed to get my degree. "But," I said to him, "I'm expecting a *summa cum laude*." That he didn't know. He said he'd make enquiries. We ended the conversation by talking about Father James Royce, the Jesuit who had taught me Latin at Notre Dame. Campbell knew of him because he'd read his book, *Personality and Mental Health*, which had been published at Seattle University in 1954. It was a good ploy on Campbell's part to get the topic away from the horror of the Committee of Discipline. But even though I knew now that all was not lost, I still had to face the gathering of judges on the following day.

Auto da Fé in Morrison Hall

WE THE ACCUSED WERE GATHERED TOGETHER IN AN ANTIROOM IN MORRISON HALL AT ONE IN THE AFTERNOON AND WERE CALLED one at a time into the place of inquisition, one of the classrooms in the building. There were a dozen or so individuals in the room, most of them dressed in black and wearing Roman collars, though a couple were lay professors in jackets and ties, and the two student reps sat off to one side, as if of less importance than the others, which, of course, they were. The desk that usually sat at the front of the room had been pushed to one corner, and a kitchen-type chair had been placed front centre. The only thing missing from this place of inquisition was a naked light bulb hanging on a wire overhead and a strappado rope dangling against the blackboard.

We were asked to tell our side of the story. We had all agreed ahead of time that we had to stick to the absurd story that one of us (not to be named—which was easy, as nobody had done so) had found the beer. We also agreed to emphasize our belief that we had merely been engaging in legitimate student exhilaration on our way back to the university after going through a stress-laden examination period, and that the town cop had overreacted to the situation. I pointed out in my telling of the story to the assembled torturers that instead of rounding us up and taking us to the police station, if he had merely told us to quiet down, we would have done so. I could see support in a number of the faces in front of me. I said my piece. I was not asked any questions. I left. I was told later by Des McGrath that although he and "Ticker" Whelan had been excluded from the final reckoning, he'd been informed by one of the more reasonable members of the group that we had had more support than we might have expected in our argument that the town cop had overreacted, one of the priests even suggesting that the university had also overreacted.

I have always felt that one of the reasons we were not subjected to the capital punishment of being banished without a degree was the fact that we were all prominent members of the student body. I don't remember what happened to the other sinners—I don't even remember who they were—but Student Council President and football team quarterback, Peter Lesaux, had the Larkin Trophy, the highest honour given to a student by the university—granted for outstanding leadership in student affairs, sports, and academics—taken away from him. I had my degree reduced from a *summa* to a *magna cum laude*. Father Campbell, who spoke to me about it afterwards, said, "Don't worry about it. They can't take your marks away from you." I wasn't so sure.

Graduation

I HADN'T EXPECTED ANYONE FROM THE FAMILY TO BE ABLE TO ATTEND MY GRADUATION CEREMONY, BUT I WAS DELIGHTED TO HEAR in April that my brother, John, was planning to come to the event, which was to be held in the university auditorium on May 15. I received a letter from my dad, dated May 8, in which he wrote: "John has everything settled about the trip East. He's coming up on the bus to-morrow night and leaving Friday morning on the long trip East. I wish I could accompany him; but that is out of the question."

When graduation day came, I was puzzled, as I had not heard a word from John. It was not until I was in the line-up, all of us dressed in our caps, gowns, and hoods on our way into the auditorium to receive our degrees, on a May day that was overcast and threatening rain, that I found out why. I was near our class president, "Ticker" Whalen, who, as one of his duties in the confused world leading up to the ceremony, was to receive and pass on telegrams and messages from family and friends for graduating students. I mentioned that I was worried that I hadn't heard from my brother, who was on his way to the ceremony from British Columbia. A guilty look crossed Ticker's face. He reached into his pocket and pulled out a telegram with my name on it. "Oh, my God," he said. "I forgot about this telegram that came for you last evening. I'm *so* sorry."

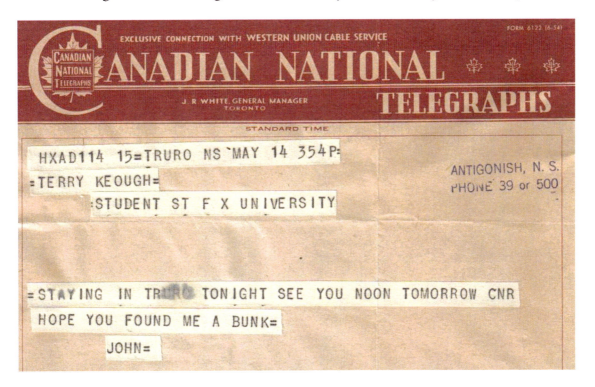

All through the ceremony I wondered if John had managed to make it. It seemed horrible that he might have come all this way and then missed the graduation ceremony because Ticker Whalen had forgotten to deliver the telegram to me. But as it turned out, he had arrived just in time.

John had kept a diary during his trip, which I will now mine for details I have largely forgotten. "I arrived at Antigonish at 2 pm, where it was raining cats and dogs. I was hungry, so I stopped at a small café near the train station where for $1.25 I had a most awful vegetable salad lunch. I took a taxi to the campus and got there just in time for the Graduation Ceremony. It was very impressive, and I was very proud of Terry as he received his Batchelor degree from the Bishop, as he reverently kissed the Bishop's ring."

I'm not sure that "reverently" is the right adverb here. The routine worked like this. You were lined up on the stairs to the stage in a prearranged order, and when your turn came, your name was called and your degree announced. You walked to centre stage, genuflected in front of the bishop and kissed his ring, the traditional rite before Vatican II when meeting a bishop.[11] He said, "Congratulations." Beside him, Father Bauer, the Dean of Studies, handed you a deep blue map case with your name printed on one end in white. Inside, nicely printed in Latin, and with your name on it, was your degree.

After the ceremony, we took pictures outside the auditorium (which was in the basement of the chapel). I had found my brother a "bunk," as he put it in his telegram, in the house in which Tom and Terry Spring had rented an apartment in their second year at St. F. X. My brother describes the rest of the day: "Terry and I celebrated by having a drink of rye, and I met many of his friends. We had a bite to eat at the 'Wheel.'[12] Terry got dressed for the Ball and had no suspenders, so I pinned his pants to his shirt with safety pins. He had trouble figuring out the black tie, but eventually he had it on more or less correctly."[13]

Tom Spring's sister had come from Cranbrook, B.C., for his graduation. I took her as my date to the ball. I suppose the ball was wonderful, though I don't remember a thing about it. I don't even remember Tom's sister's name. Afterwards, we went to Tom's place, where my brother was waiting for us. "Terry and Tom Spring came back about 12:30 a.m. and he, Tom, and I went to Tom's room." John had spent the evening in the guest room. "A lad who used to occupy a room above used to walk in his sleep and come down to this room. He was killed in Korea and his ghost was said to come to this

---

[11] In Nelson, Bishop Johnson, who was ahead of his time, banished the practice, insisting that people merely shake hands with him in the same way that they would do with anyone else. Undoubtedly, as we discovered later in the century, there were bishops who would have preferred that you kissed their bums, though I'm sure Canon Law must stipulate somewhere that that would be a ceremony that would have to be conducted in private.

[12] The Wagon Wheel was a café that was just off campus on the way into Antigonish.

[13] The tuxedo and related paraphernalia were rented from a student-run enterprise called the Tuxedo Club. I believe it's the only time in my life that I ever wore a tuxedo.

room at times. A spooky thought! Terry and I stayed in Tom's apartment until 2 a.m., then to the guest room for a long talk before going to sleep. No ghost walked."

And so ended my graduation from St. F. X., B.A. Magna Cum Laude, dressed in its accompanying robes of ceremony and celebration, on a rainy day that had been darkened by more than the weather. And so began my love / hate relationship with the institution that granted my first degree. Things have changed massively at the university, I'm happy to say, since those dark days of the Fifties. The black-suited priests with their white ring-around-the-collar are gone. Some of them literally left post-Vatican-II, when it became clear that the truths they were told were absolute turned out to be only relatively so. The supply of new priests dried up when enough talented young men to supply both parishes and university posts no longer wanted to enter the seminary. Nowadays, the church connection has become largely ceremonial—"Bring in the Bishop! It's time to give out the degrees!"—and the faculty consists of ordinary academics who have competed in the academic job market for the positions they hold. There has been much construction, many new and wonderful buildings. All residences are open to both sexes. The student body has quadrupled to over 4,000, about half of whom are in residence on campus. In the surveys of Canadian undergraduate universities (for what they're worth) conducted by *Maclean's*, St. F. X. is constantly in first place. So the grievances I harboured against the university have been corrected. In a six-page supplement to *The Globe and Mail* of February 19, 2008, the university advertised itself in the following manner: "Bring together top-calibre professors, highly engaged undergraduates, a diverse community connected to all corners of the world, and you've got a national-level, academic experience that is second to none. This is St. Francis Xavier University. University as it was meant to be." Amen, I say, unto that.

Home Again: By Train across the Continent

AS I REMEMBER PRACTICALLY NOTHING OF THE JOURNEY HOME TO REVELSTOKE, I WILL RELY, ONCE AGAIN, ON MY BROTHER'S DIARY. Our plan was to spend a couple of days in Blackville, N. B., where our parents had grown up, with our Aunt Van, who continued to live there in the Keough family home. We would then travel to Montreal, where we would spend a couple of days with our sister, Joan, and her husband Eric, who had moved there the year before from Ironside. Then we would head straight across the country to Revelstoke.

On the day following the graduation ceremonies, we caught a train at the Antigonish station at 2 p.m., arriving in Newcastle, New Brunswick at about midnight. We took a room for the rest of the night in the Hotel Miramichi, for which John paid $22. He didn't have very much money, but he had a lot more than I had. I had forgotten in my deal with the Hudson's Bay Company that even though they agreed to pay for my expenses on my journey to Vancouver, I would have to spend my own money along the way, money that I didn't have. We didn't suffer on our way home, but things would have been a lot more comfortable if I'd had the money to stick the Hudson's Bay Company for a few good meals in the dining car, for which they would have been glad to pay.

Blackville

The following morning [May 17th], we took a Budd Car on a 40 minute ride to Blackville to visit Aunt Evangeline—"Van" to one and all—who lived alone in the Keough family home there.[14] The Blackville station was a mile or so out of town and there were no taxis, so we weren't quite sure what to do. We were the only people who had got off the train. A man loading a station wagon with some boxes that had come in on the train asked us where we were going. We told him who we were and where we were going, and he announced that he was a cousin of ours by the name of Sam Underhill and that he would drive us to the Keough place. It seemed as if everyone we met was a relative of some sort.

Aunt Van met us at the back door and after a hearty greeting showed us our room. Later, we walked up town "to buy a film and visit Grampa and Gramma's graves."[15] As strangers in town, we were followed everywhere by curious eyes. John suggested that we drop into the local legion for a beer, but I vetoed the idea, as I knew Van would have a fit if we showed up back at the house smelling of beer. "At dinner time, Van had set the table as if we were in the Chateau Frontenac." We were asked to wear jackets and ties. (The Keough girls—Evangeline and Geraldine—as another cousin has pointed out recently, tended to be "uppity.") We looked at dad's paintings on the attic walls. "Van watched us like a hawk, so we weren't able to see inside the attic. Van clams up like dad and wouldn't show us any pictures of the old Keough family." There was no mention of getting into the store. We drove to Bartholomew River with Monica Donoghue (first cousin, once removed!), to look over what was the McCarthy farm, where mother had grown up. All of the buildings were gone. The next day, Monica drove us to Newcastle to catch the train. "Van is a nice person and a good cook. But our short visit was over and I was glad."

Montreal

We arrived in Montreal on Sunday the 19th, where we were met by our sister, Joan, and her husband, Eric Nielsen. We stayed a couple of days with them in their modern home in Ste. Therese de Blainville. Uncle "Mac" McCarthy [mother's brother], who was a barber in Montreal, his wife, Ella, and their lovely 15-year-old daughter, Pat, came out from Notre-Dame-de-Grace and spent an evening with us. The next day, "Joan washed and ironed our many shirts. We watched TV and played bridge."

---

[14] Evangeline Keough had married twice in her lifetime (1898-1970), both husbands dying within a year of their marriage. After her first husband, James Sweeney, died, she returned home from New York to "look after her aging parents." She married her second husband, Simon Dolan, in the late 1940s. Her sister, Geraldine (1896-1983), who never married, used to come home to live with her during the summer.

[15] Patrick Kehoe [later Keogh and Keough] 1848-1939 ran the store that John refers to. It stood next-door to the house. It was closed in 1914 with most of the remaining stock left in place and demolished, along with the house, in the 1990s, to make way for a new RCMP station. Patrick's wife was Bridget Jardine (1857-1942). Only four of their ten children survived them.

Revelstoke

John's account of the rest of the journey across Canada is severely truncated. I think he must have gotten bored with keeping the journal. "On the evening of the 22nd, we left Montreal, both of us sharing a first-class berth [courtesy of the Hudson's Bay Company]. Joan had given us a nice lunch. We drank some beer and ate our lunch in the club car. Dinner was too expensive to contemplate. [What did we eat for the rest of the two-and-a-half-day journey?] We arrived in Revelstoke on Saturday night. Marguerite [John's sister-in-law] met us with mom and dad. I had $4.25 left. Terry had 8 cents."

Hail and Health

Hail and health to Alma Mater,
  On for St. F. X.'s name;
Leading, trailing, vim unfailing,
  Play the game!
Life's the goal that gleams before us,
  Faith and honor free,
Swell the old Xaverian chorus,
  Sing for victory!

Sons of old St. Francis Xavier,
  Manly hearts and true,
Years may creep but still we'll keep
  Loyal to the white and blue.

Sing for friends no longer near us,
  Sing for happy days of yore,
Forward striving, onward driving,
  Get that score!
Memories of high endeavour,
  Stir our spirits still;
Here's to St. F. X. forever,
  Sing it with a will!

Here's a toast to merry Mockler,
  Here's a health to M.S.B.
Science, Arts men, play your parts, men,
  Faculty!
Strong Xaverian lights to guide us,
  Golden as we sing,
Whatsoever fates betide us,
  Let the old song ring!

ST. FRANCIS XAVIER UNIVERSITY
ANTIGONISH, NOVA SCOTIA
1955-56

Mr. J. Keough
517 Fourth Street East
Revelstoke
BRITISH COLUMBIA

EXAMINATION REPORT OF

Terence

I wish to inform you that the student named above obtained the following credits during the past scholastic year. University Pass is 60. Matriculation Pass is 50.

Religion 2A	82
Religion 5B	88
Economics 1	84
*English 15	95
*English 14	93
English 10	88
Philosophy 1B	85
Philosophy 2A	88
Pol. Science 1	86
Spanish 1	90
English 5B	92

This makes a total of 118 of the 130 semester hours required for graduation. This standing places the student 2nd in a class of 65.

Yours sincerely,
C. H. Bauer
DEAN OF STUDIES

Rehearsal schedule for "Everyman":   Place: The Auditorium
Monday March 25, 1957 to Saturday March 30, 1957 (inclusive)

6:45 ---- James Feeney
          Ronald MacKinnon
          Brian Mulrooney

7:15 ---- Terrence Tait
          Joseph Daybell
          Bill Morrissey

7:30 ---- Evelyn Mooney
          Estelle Dalton
          Bernard McGrath

7:45 ---- Donald Reilly
          Terry Keough
          Marty Robertson
          Katherine MacDonald

8:00 ---- Gene Newry
          Mike Skapa

Unless otherwise notified, the cast will follow this schedule for the rest of this week.

Rev. V. J. MacLellan

March 25, 1957

St. Francis Xavier Debating Society

This is to Certify that TERENCE F. KEOUGH has been awarded the Debating X for participation in Interclass Debates while a student at Saint Francis Xavier University, and according to the Constitution and By-Laws governing its Debating Society

Signed this 28TH day of APRIL 1957

Desmond T. McGrath
PRESIDENT DEBATING SOCIETY

Vincent MacLellan
FACULTY ADVISER

Brian Mulroney
SECRETARY-TREASURER DEBATING SOCIETY

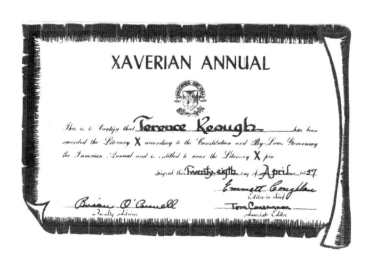

XAVERIAN ANNUAL

This is to Certify that Terence Keough has been awarded the Literary X according to the Constitution and By-Laws Governing the Xaverian Annual and is entitled to wear the Literary X pin.

Signed this Twenty-eighth day of April 1957

Emmett Coughlan
Editor-in-Chief

Brian O'Connell
Faculty Adviser

Tom Conseupan
Associate Editor

XAVERIAN WEEKLY

This is to Certify that Terrence Keough has been awarded the Literary X according to the Constitution and By-Laws Governing the Xaverian Weekly and is entitled to wear the Literary X pin.

Signed this Twenty-eighth day of April 1957

ST. F. X. UNIVERSITY ALBUM

Xavier Hall—My Room #5
3rd Floor, Right of Tower

Paul Dugal, Terry's Roommate

View of Antigonish from #5

Xavier Hall from Quadrangle

First Semester Fees

Morrison Hall: Refectory
Priests' Rooms, Infirmary

Sr. of St. Martha Working
in the Kitchen

My Dresser in No. 5

150th Anniversary Canada Stamp

Terry Spring, Terry, Tom Spring, Leo Nimsick

Pat Wilcox, Terry, Tom Spring, Anne Marie MacIntyre

Terry & MacNeill Hall

Mary Ellen MacGillivray, Leo Nimsick

John Keough, B.A. (1906)

Title Page

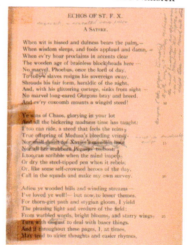

Opening Lines

Fifties Ladies & Mother St. Whoever, CND

Stu MacMillan & Emmett Coughlan

Terry & Des McGrath

Paul Dugal, Terry, Ed O'Hagan

Charlie Murphy, Stu MacMillan, Terry

Xaverian Weekly—Terry Writing

Debating Club: Brian Mulroney Des McGrath, Paul Creaghan

Xaverian Annual—Terry Back Right, P. Creaghan (sitting hat) Gerry Doucet (standing hat)

Terry Putting *Xaverian Weekly* to Bed at *The Casket*

Terry and MacNeill House

The Xaverian Players

Present

EVERYMAN

A Morality Play

University Auditorium

April 11 - 12, 1957

Cast of Characters
(in order of appearance)

Messenger	Eugene Newry
Death	Ronald McKinnon
Everyman	James Feeney
Fellowship	Brian Mulroney
Kindred	Joseph Daybell
Cousin	Terry Tait
Goods	William Morrissey
Good-Deeds	Evelyn Mooney
Knowledge	Estelle Dalton
Confession	Bernard McGrath
Beauty	Martin Robertson
Strength	Donald Kelly
Discretion	Katherine MacDonald
Five-Wits	Terrence Keough
Angel	Michael Skapa

Director .... Rev. V. J. MacLellan
Technical Adviser .... Rev. C. H. Bauer

Characters: Five Wits—Terry; Fellowship—Brian Mulroney

The Class of '58
cordially invites you to attend
the Graduation Promenade
at St. Francis Xavier University
in honor of
the Graduating Class of '57
to be held on
Wednesday, May 15, 1957, at 9 p.m.
at the Parish Center, Antigonish, N.S.
Formal Dress
Grand March: 9:30 p.m.

Terry after Graduation Ceremony in Front of the Chapel

CONVOCATION
Wednesday, May 15
1957

Bachelor of Arts
Magna cum laude

Donald Eugene Burgoyne	Glace Bay, N. S.
Frederick Albert Carrigan	Portland, Maine
John Sheldon Currie	Reserve, N. S.
Terence Frederick Keough	Revelstoke, B. C.
James Henry McDaniel	Margaree Forks, N. S.
Donald Aubrey MacDonald	Inverness, N. S.
William Fitzgerald Murphy	Antigonish, N. S.
Sister St. Arnold Marie, C.N.D.	Antigonish, N. S.
Sister St. Mary Stephen, C.N.D.	Antigonish, N. S.
Robert Colin Peter Westbury	Sydney, N. S.
Theresa Dawn Wolstenholme	Moncton, N. B.

The Graduate!

Terry and MacKinnon Hall

Brother John Keough, Who Crossed the Country to Attend

Chapter 4: It's Hard Not to Think of the Bay[1]

VANCOUVER 1957-58

So far we have not budged a step, and shall not unless Hitler pushes us out by the scruffs of our necks. In that case we shall certainly come to Canada, as we have a joint annuity there to die on. And Vancouver is the pick of Canada . . . .
      George Bernard Shaw, quoted by Eric Nicol, from a postcard
          received by Vancouver resident, Mrs. Fitz James,
          during the Battle of Britain.

People from the prairies, who have made their pile, spend their declining years in Vancouver on the road to heaven. [True then, true now, true always!]
      H. F. Gadsby, *Canadian Days*, 1911

I cannot say that I forgot the city, but I let the memory of it sleep. Yet, of course, it was *always* there, as *it always will be*, hanging in the mind like the mirage which travellers so often see.
      Lawrence Durrell, *Balthazar*, 1961

A City on the Cusp of Change

IN MANY WAYS, THE CITY IN THE LATE 1950s WAS A SMALL TOWN BEGINNING TO MORPH INTO A METROPOLIS, A PUPA ABOUT TO BECOME A BUTTERFLY. THE POPULATION OF GREATER VANCOUVER at that time was only about five to six hundred thousand. But getting from the downtown area—a peninsula between the Fraser River and the sea—to surrounding areas like North Vancouver and Surrey was often exceedingly difficult. Still, Rapid change was in the wind: the Oak Street Bridge, linking central Vancouver with Richmond and Sea Island Airport, opened July 1, 1957; work began on the ill-fated Second Narrows Bridge to

---

[1] This was the punch line of an HBC television advertisement in the 1980s. For a brief history of the Hudson's Bay Company, see p. 106.

North Vancouver;[2] in August, a system of one-way streets, reflecting a huge increase in traffic, was instituted in the downtown area; early in 1958, the last electric trams were taken off the roads and replaced by diesel buses; in April of that year, the Deas Island Tunnel was completed, replacing the ferry that had previously connected the city to Ladner; and on July 1, the Premier, W.A.C. "Wacky" Bennett, announced the establishment of a crown corporation, called B.C. Ferries, to run car ferries between Vancouver Island and the Mainland.

What was becoming true throughout North America was becoming true in Vancouver: for half a century at least, the car was to be the king-pin of governmental road-transportation decisions. The result: the development of suburbs as places to live, and of inner cities as primarily places to work; the building of roads with more and more lanes to accommodate more and more traffic, taking people to and from work; the neglect of public transportation; and eventually, crime in downtowns with too few residents, gridlock on the roads, carbon dioxide polluting the atmosphere, and global warming everywhere. I was an enthusiast for these changes, which were labelled everywhere as "Progress." I didn't own a car—the *sine qua* non passport into this new world—not because I didn't *want* a car—I did—but because I was saving money to go to Europe for a year or two or longer. As for the ultimate consequences of these changes, I was as blind to them as the rest of the world.

Architecturally, downtown Vancouver was beginning to evolve from a place of mainly small, one-to-three storey commercial buildings in a nineteenth-century style to a metropolis of skyscrapers, clad in concrete, metal, and glass. It was a time for "firsts." The B.C. Electric building, built in 1955, with its 23-storey façade of porcelain and glass, standing on Burrard Street like a beacon to the future—the lights left on 24 hours a day—was Vancouver's first modernist commercial building. The Georgia Towers, completed in 1958, had the city's first high-speed elevator. The first modern condominium-type apartments, overlooking English Bay, went on sale in 1957. (We said, "Who would want to pay $20,000 to own *an apartment!*") A new central library, already far too small before it opened, Vancouver's first "glass-curtain" building, was opened in 1958 at Burrard and Robson Streets. A block-square central post office, at the time the largest welded steel structure in the world, with a heliport on the roof for mail to be delivered from the airport, and a tunnel to the CPR Station to bring mail from the trains—both almost immediately abandoned as too expensive to use—began operation in 1958.

On a socio-cultural level, things were also changing rapidly. From the mezzanine windows of the Bay store in early June 1957, fellow workers and I watched the election entourage of John Diefenbaker wend its way down Granville Street, where his vassals had earlier stencilled, on the street and on walls, dozens of white footsteps and the words, "Follow John." He was elected Prime Minister on the 10th of the month, replacing the ageing Louis St. Laurent, who was a left-over from a gentler age, the last Prime Minister to walk alone to work on a daily basis from Sussex Drive to Parliament Hill. During that summer, Vancouver's Triple "A" baseball team, the Mounties, was fined, not only for

---

[2] The bridge collapsed during construction, killing 19 people and injuring 20 more. When I was told about this event, as it was happening, by someone in the HBC store, I thought it was the lead-in line to a joke.

playing on Sundays, but especially, for charging admission. The verdict was overturned the following year by the Supreme Court of Canada, much to the chagrin of the verbose supporters of the Lord's Day Act. (These zealots even objected to the use on Sundays of the telescopes in Stanley Park that you put a dime into, allowing you to scan the north-shore mountains for five minutes or so.) On October 4, 1957, much to the amazement of everyone everywhere, especially in the United States of America, the Soviet Union, boldly going where no man had gone before, sent the 19-pound Sputnik satellite into orbit around the earth. This was a rocket whose shot was heard around the world, opening up the space race of the 1960s. On a more earthly level, but perhaps in the end at least as significant, what would become Vancouver's biggest and best-known bookstore, Duthie's, opened in 1957 on the corner of Robson and Hornby. The old order was certainly changing, yielding place to new; though it seems that it was greed rather than God that was being fulfilled in many ways. Eventually, downtown Vancouver could be found only here and there in vacant lots and unimposing structures that seemed to be waiting eagerly for their transformation into building birds of paradise.

It was into this changing city, a wonder to a young lad who had never before lived anywhere but in small towns, that I found myself after graduating from university, eyes open to all things new, and head full of wonder at the new stage in my life that was about to begin.

Newfangled Beginnings

WHEN I ARRIVED IN THE CITY FROM REVELSTOKE BY TRAIN AT THE END OF MAY 1957, I FOUND MYSELF CONFUSED BY A TECHNO-logical innovation I had not up to that time encountered. In the station waiting room, I marched confidently to the pay telephones to call my high school friends, Garry MacGregor and Jim Craig, who I knew shared an apartment somewhere in the city. I put my dime into the slot. I looked at the dial. I had not encountered one of these before. The phones I had known were the kind where you lift the receiver, and a mellifluous female operator comes on and says "Number, please?" You say the number, and she connects you. At first, I tried to dial from the left side to the number. Nothing happened but recurring buzzes. Then I somehow connected with a nice lady somewhere out in telephone-land, to whom I explained my problem. She was amused at what I was doing, but helpful at the same time, explaining how the dial worked. With my newfound skill, courtesy of an anonymous woman, I dialled Garry's number. There was no answer. It was the middle of the morning. He and Jim would both be at work.

I considered crossing the street to the seedy St. Francis Hotel, where I had stayed once before on a brief trip to the city—and where, in the shared bathroom on the second floor I had read the immortal lines, "There's no use standing on the seat, / St. Francis's crabs jump forty feet"—but I decided it would be smarter to get a room for a week at the YMCA. So, I grabbed a taxi to Burrard Street, took out a temporary membership, and signed up for a room at the reduced weekly rate. That evening, I was able to get a hold of Garry, who suggested that I could sleep on the sofa in their living room once my week at the "Y" was over. In the meantime, on a couple of evenings that week, we got together at their garden-level apartment in an old house on the 3100 block of Oak Street, caught up on what we had been doing since high school, and reminisced about growing up in Revelstoke. While there, I encountered my second problem with new technology. Milk had always come to me in a glass bottle. When I went to the fridge to get some milk for my coffee, I was faced with a newfangled paper carton that I didn't know how to open. There were in those early days directions on the side of the carton that explained how to unfold the spout—but I, of course, opened it the first time at the wrong end.

When I moved in at the end of my week at the "Y," I became intimately acquainted with the chintz-covered, old green sofa I was to occupy for most of the month of June. My friends weren't charging me any rent for the rest of the month, which was a blessing, as I had only the $300 my mother had lent me to get me started. I paid my share of any food we bought in common, though most of the time our schedules didn't jibe and we prepared our own simple meals: pork chops or steak, baked or boiled potatoes, peas out of a can. I used a few dollars to buy a pillow, a blanket, and a pair of sheets and pillowcases on the employee card that gave me ten-percent off at the store. As it turned out, though, there was one huge drawback to my sleeping on the sofa in the living room of the apartment.

> *The third occupier of the apartment, John Hughes, a friend of Garry's, was out of work. As he didn't have to get up in the morning, he likewise didn't have to go to bed at night. Night after night he watched television in the living room where I lay on the sofa, trying to sleep. I got to know very well the patriotic "Oh, Canada" sign-off of whatever television station he was watching, the black and white red ensign blowing in the wind. I wasn't happy with the situation; but I didn't complain; I was an intruder into his life and a freeloader to boot.*

The Governor and Company of Adventurers[3]

ON MONDAY, JUNE 3, I BEGAN MY CAREER AS A JUNIOR EXECUTIVE TRAINEE AT THE HUDSON'S BAY COMPANY STORE ON THE CORNER of Granville and Georgia, one of a company of adventurers who were about to meet the governor. The seven of us "golden-haired boys" came from various universities across the country, including another St. F. X. person I had not known at the university, Colin MacInnes, whose shadow would cross my path regarding a love affair I had months later with a blonde in the Display Department. Curiously, in my year at the store, I never made friends with anyone in this group. In the last analysis, we had nothing in common.

---

[3] The Hudson's Bay Company (HBC) was incorporated by Charles II in 1670 as "The Governor and Company of Adventurers trading into Hudson's Bay." The initials HBC were in later centuries often interpreted to mean "Here Before Christ." The motto of the Company, *pro pelle cutem*, "skin for skin," was translated as "value for value," except by those who felt the Company was skinning them alive, who had a number of far more ironic translations. Some responded to the motto with humour. There's a great story told by Dr. Helmcken (1824-1920), a leading figure in 19th-century Victoria: "Mr. Douglas [HBC Governor at the time] asked the doctor why so many of the Hudson's Bay officers were bald. His answer was '*Pro pelle cutem*—they had sent their furs home.'" J. S. Helmcken, "A Reminiscence of 1850," *Victoria Daily Colonist*, December 1887.

We met as a group in what was known as the Training Room, next to the Personnel Office on the fourth floor, where the everyday training of new staff in such things as using cash registers and filling out daily tallies took place. The Personnel Superintendent, R. S. Carey, introduced the Store Manager, Mr. Howard, and a couple of senior executives who on that morning were able to attend—Merchandise Managers they were called—each of whom was in charge of a cluster of departments, or of a specialized area, such as Advertising. Mr. Howard, who had a wedge-shaped face, like a beaver—in the old days he might have been skinned in error and sent to England—wished us well in a few benign words of greeting and abruptly left the room, with the Merchandise Managers obediently at his heels, ready to whack their tails against the linoleum if any danger arose.[4]

At this point, Mr. Carey explained to us the regime we would be put through. The course would last six months. We would begin by being taught the basics of running a cash register by the store training officer, a charming woman who had emigrated from London to Canada. (I became quite a good friend of hers. When I told her nearly a year later that I was leaving the company and going to London, she gave me a letter of introduction to a friend there. "The good ones always leave," she said.) As we would often be responsible for having the register tally up the receipts for the day, a function it would do automatically if you pushed the right buttons, we were taught which buttons to push. Each machine would cough up a paper covered in figures, which had to be put in a special envelope and sent to the Accounts Office with the cash the register contained. Every couple of weeks, we would meet in the Training Room for a lecture from one of the store executives. He would give us an assignment on some aspect of the area in which he specialized; we would be required to write a short essay. The executive would read the papers and give us each a percentage grade.

> *I had a conspicuous success on one of these papers. The head of Advertising had lectured us on the effectiveness of advertising in various media. I wrote my paper on radio and television jingles. I used as one of my examples a jingle that was very popular at the time, "You'll wonder where the yellow went, / When you brush your teeth with Pepsident!" We picked up our marked papers from a box outside the Personnel area, so that all of the Trainees were able to look at any papers that had not been picked up. Word came to me that my paper had been glowingly praised and given a ninety. In this competitive world, my fellow Trainees were not pleased, though all of them, more or less reluctantly, congratulated me. As none of the other Trainees had graduated with a degree in English, this incident demonstrated more my ability to write a good paper than my acumen as an original thinker in the world of business.*

---

[4] Up until the Second World War, the managers of the six large HBC stores were treated as if they were royalty. They arrived at the store each morning and left each afternoon in chauffeured limousines. On the fender of the car flew the HBC flag: the Union Jack, top left, on a red field, "HB.C." in white at bottom right. This flag continued to fly on the top of the stores, even in my time. But the manager by then was a great man only to those who had to serve under him; and some of us, myself included, treated that greatness *cum grano salis*.

We began our immersion into department store retailing with a rotation through store areas not directly involved in selling: Shipping and Receiving, Advertising, Accounting, Display, and Personnel. When we had been through all of these ancillary departments, we would be rotated through a number of selling departments, after which we would be able to choose a department to work in from among those that needed extra help. At that point, we were just sales clerks, like the rest of the people in the department, but we were taught management processes by the manager and assistant manager, unlike the regular sales clerks, who were expected to know and keep their place as designated hewers of wood and drawers of water. Often, we were able to show our competence (and our position of privilege) by getting the cash register to spew out its totals at the end of the day. Eventually, our work having been satisfactory, when an opening occurred, we would become assistant managers, either in Vancouver or in one of the other large stores: Victoria, Calgary, Edmonton, Regina, or Saskatoon. Rumour had it that being sent to Saskatoon was the HBC equivalent of being sent to Siberia; managers who failed to make a profit and assistant managers of managers who failed to make a profit might find themselves there.

The Privilege of Being "On Contract"

Once we had completed a year at the store in a manner that was satisfactory to the company and had become assistant managers, we could apply to be put "On Contract." This "On Contract" business was a hold-over from the old HBC, from the days when factors were contracted to make a profit in whatever outpost or fort they were in charge of. If they made a profit, they were given a bonus. In the department stores, those "On Contract" were given a bonus equal to the percentage of the store's profit as a percentage of their year's salary, *provided that their particular department also made a profit.* So, both the store and your department had to make a profit for you to get the bonus. Needless to say, the opportunity to be put "On Contract" was available only to those who entered the company at the Junior Executive Trainee level or who were hired as Executives. This restriction led to a good deal of justifiable resentment on the part of loyal employees who had served the company well for many years. We golden-haired boys were not the most popular people in the store.

We were each given a schedule outlining our personal rotation. I began with a week in Shipping and Receiving in the sub-basement of the store. We were told to wear old clothes for this assignment. It was a psychological come-down to have to enter the store dressed as a labourer. Besides that, we were treated down there just as if we had been hired to hoist boxes around, open them up, if they had just arrived, or, if they were being sent somewhere, seal them. It was dirty in Shipping and Receiving, and I resented being forced to do labouring work. I was, after all, a golden-haired boy of the company and a university graduate. It's likely that the administrators who had devised this program to expose us to all aspects of retailing in the store, also wanted to make it clear that we were expected always to do the company's bidding. I survived my week and was able to don my regular jacket, tie, and old gabardine pants, the knees of which were shinier than they should have been, as I returned to the upper part of the store.

The Proper Dress for the Job

Dress was, in fact, a bit of a problem for me. I had enough shirts, socks and underwear to get by. But I had only one jacket, two pairs of pants, and one pair of dress shoes. Most of the other men wore suits most of the time. Suits were *de rigueur*. I would have to get myself at least one, if I were going to make what one might term a suitable impression on my bosses. I went to a small store on Hastings Street that was advertising tailor-made suits with two pairs of pants for $85. I got talked into buying two by a salesman who offered $10 off if I bought a pair; I chose a grey pepper and salt material for one, and a green material with a subdued black glen check for the other. I was measured up in the store by the salesman, who was as much tailor as I would get for my tailor-made suit. All through the following week, I worried about paying for two suits and metaphorically kicked myself for having bought two at once. When I returned to the store, I tried to get them to allow me to buy the suits over three payments, but they said I would have had to make those arrangements when I bought them. I had the money, and I paid, but my finances as a result were pretty tight for the next couple of months.

There was a strict dress code for all employees who worked in departments where the public was served. Men were required to wear jackets and ties, dress pants, and dress shoes. On very hot days in the summer, an announcement would be made over the public address system before the store opened to customers that men might remove their jackets if they so desired. But sleeves could not be rolled up, and short-sleeved shirts were not permitted. Women were required to wear dresses, blouses, sweaters, and skirts. Sleeveless tops of any sort were not allowed; customers might glimpse the horror of undergarments. The large display windows on Granville and Seymour Street had to be covered in sheets when the display staff were undressing and dressing the mannequins. If they neglected to do so, the phones would start ringing, as Jean Q. Public expressed indignation at the plastic nudity. Although some of these restrictions now seem absurd, at the time they were standard in the business world.

It wasn't until the sixties—just around the corner in these years of our lord, 1957-58—that the dress code began to break down and the jean generation to emerge, even to some extent in the business world, where women everywhere were allowed to wear pants, and men were in many areas no longer required to wear jackets and ties. In some work situations, bras could be doffed (solving the problem of glimpsing the horror of undergarments); and eventually, as doffing bras was not generally a good idea, straps could be shown proudly (form follows function). Dress-down Fridays became the rule. Even Lawyers and politicians, smilingly demonstrating their unity with the *hoi polloi*, were sometimes seen uncomfortably posing *sans* jackets and ties—just regular fellas when you get right down to it.

Establishing an Outpost among the Natives

ABOUT THE MIDDLE OF JUNE, GARRY MACGREGOR TOLD US THAT HIS BROTHER, KEN, WAS HAVING MARITAL PROBLEMS AND THAT THEY were going to share an apartment somewhere else in town, starting at the end of the month. John Hughes had got a job in Abbotsford and was leaving for that area. So, Jim Craig and I decided we would look for an apartment together; and when Bill Wood, my closest friend in my last year of high school, arrived in town to take up his desk job with New York Life, we decided to look for a place for the three of us.

We found a ground-floor unit in an old, unheated fourplex, slated for demolition later in the year, a place of all-night sirens, not far from Vancouver General Hospital. It was shabby, but it was cheap. The idea was that it would give us time to look around for something better. Across the hall, on the other side of paper-thin walls, were two dowdy women we referred to as "old maids," though they were probably thirty-something at most. They had one of those old-fashioned, foot-pedalled, small organs on which they played hymns, singing along with the music in a timid, mousy way. As young men, we found them absurd; and we mocked them by pretending to sing the hymns with them, blasting out whatever phrases we knew of *To Be a Pilgrim* and *Rock of Ages* with a gusto that would relegate the likes of Pavarotti to the operatic equivalent of a Burl Ives. The ladies were wise enough to ignore our adolescent silliness.

In August, we rented a two-bedroom flat in the upstairs area of a one-and-a-half storey house at 1815 West 11th Avenue, owned by an elderly lady we knew only as Mrs. Cooper. We had to go through the bottom hall and up the unenclosed stairway to get to our apartment. Poor old Mrs. Cooper. She tried her best to be good to us. She had a television set in her living room, and she was always happy to let us watch it on weekend afternoons and early in the evening. Sometimes, she would give us cookies or biscuits that she had made. Bill and I were kind to her. Jim, who had an arcane sense of humour that tended toward cruelty, was not. He made fun of her, referring to her to her face as "old lady," and berating her for being "past it." He thought he was being funny. He was not. It was a classic case of the Chaucerian caution that "a true jest is a bad jest." When I tried to point this out to him, he pooh-poohed my concern, making fun of me as well by saying I was reading too much into his remarks, as "eggheads" like me often did. ("Egghead" was a popular term for an intellectual following bald Adlai Stevenson's attempts to become President of the United States. He was too much of an egghead to win.) Jim had not gone to university, and I had; so I was an egghead. He just didn't get it.

The apartment was unfurnished; so as soon as we rented it, we began accumulating the stuff we would need to live in it: three twin beds for the bedrooms, a sofa and a couple of chairs for the living room, a kitchen table and four chairs, and all the little things you need to get by: cutlery, glasses, plates, cups, and so on, for the kitchen; sheets and blankets—which Jim and I already had—for the bedrooms; towels; and a rug for the living room floor. Buying new was expensive and out of the question, as we all knew these living arrangements were temporary. We bought beds and mattresses at a second-hand store. Our solution for obtaining the rest of what we needed was to haunt for a few weeks the frequent auctions that were held in a building on Broadway, not very far from where we lived. It was fun.

> *Before the auctions began, we would check over the lots. The big items were fairly easy. We would decide how much we were willing to spend on a chesterfield or a table and chairs. Most of the things that we could afford were essentially junk furniture, so the bidding was not very active, and we got them for a song. With the smaller items, such as cutlery, there was usually included in the lot strangely unconnected things, like a bread box or a bundle of books, things the auctioneers obviously wanted to get rid of. When you won a bid, you had to give the auctioneer your initials. One of them was amused at Jim's, which were "J.C." "You'll go a long way with initials like that," he said, "though you might come to a bad end." He got a good laugh out of that one.*

Sharing the burdens of running an apartment is always a problem for three young men, and we were no exception. When we first took possession, there was the question of who was to have a bedroom on his own. Our solution? We played a hand of five-card stud. I got better cards than the others, so I won. This method of deciding things around the flat became the norm. We gambled for who was going to cook dinner, wash the floor, do the dishes, and so on. This approach was in fact a good one, as a gambling debt is a debt of honour, and there is no question that it must be paid. But if you had a streak of bad luck—I once had to cook dinner five days in a row—it was wearying.

We enjoyed good times at 1815 West 11th. Often on the weekends we played bridge, needing only one other person to make up a foursome. That person was usually Bill's friend, Bill Lindsay; though sometimes we played with my old friend from Notre Dame years, Ray Paris, who was studying law at UBC.[5]

> *We often bought a bottle of sweet wine—Harvey's Shooting Sherry, or Emu 999—to sip as we played bridge. We were not drinkers, and the bottle would be no more than half gone at the end of the evening, enough left for the next time we played. We didn't carry on with the game terribly late, usually packing it in around eleven o'clock. But Mrs. Cooper would sometimes shout up from the bottom of the stairs something like, "Boys, don't you think it's getting kind of late?" and we would say "OK," and stop playing at the end of that rubber. Once Jim shouted down the stairs, "Go to bed, you silly old lady!"*

One of Jim's friends, Erwin Deary, who was a few years older than we were, was a frequent visitor. Erwin had contracted tuberculosis while he was in the navy, just after the end of the war, and he was as gaunt as a ghost. He did not work, apart from a little freelance accounting that he did from home. He was on a pension from the military, obtained for him through the good offices of John Diefenbaker—Irwin was originally from Saskatchewan—who had gone to bat for him when the bureaucrats had said there was no proof he had become infected while in the navy. When he was part of our group, the conversation somehow or other always seemed to turn to his health, with which he

---

[5] Ray, whose superb intellect I had always admired, making him, by the bye, a formidable bridge player, subsequently had a long career as a judge in the Supreme Court of British Columbia.

was rightly concerned. He sorted us out regarding the difference between his disease being "arrested," which it was, and "cured," which it was not. When I left Vancouver, Erwin seemed to be chugging along, so I was stunned to hear, in Spain a couple of years later in a letter from Jim, that he had died. He was about thirty years old.

Thinking Again of the Bay

ON THE WHOLE, I WAS UNHAPPY WORKING ON THE SELLING FLOOR AT THE BAY. SELLING IS NOT SOMETHING I LIKE TO DO, AND I WAS NOT very good at it. In my training rotation, I spent time in the China Department, in Men's Furnishings, in Sporting Goods, and in Men's Sport's Wear. Essentially, I was doing what everyone else in the department was doing—selling goods to people. I learned to keep a tally of my sales. I did not learn to be competitive regarding who had sold the most by the end of the day. Quite frankly, my dear—and anyone else who's reading this account—I didn't give a damn. I also did not like the fact that I had to work on Saturdays, when all my friends were doing interesting things around town, and having to take my day off in the middle of the week, when my friends were at work.

So, when the opportunity came to join the Display Department, I jumped at it. Some of my colleagues in the store advised me against it, as it was not a route toward promotion in the company, but I didn't care about promotion in the company. I had decided early on that I was going to leave as soon as I figured out something else to do. Besides, I had always had something of an artistic bent, and the setting up of in-store displays and the dressing of windows was something that appealed to me, even though I would be organizing the work rather than doing it. But more important than any of that, the entire Display Department had Saturdays off.

Mr. Michel was the Display Manager. There was some question as to whether his job was at the Merchandise Manager level, and the whole time I was there, he was fighting to keep his place as a member of the senior management team. The other senior managers would call meetings, for example, and "forget" to notify him. He was a decent man, always on his dignity, though short in stature, and with a wormy face, like Victor Mature. He strutted about the place as busily as the needles in the hands of an old woman knitting socks. Even though he worked very hard to gain it, by his very nature he did not command respect. It was not in his genes. Michel liked me and gave me the kind of support I needed as a result of my being parachuted into a department in which I was stepping on the feet of a couple of people who had been there for ten or fifteen years, Roy Weiss, the man in charge of interior displays, and Ray McFee, the supervisor of the windows. Both of these men had wanted to be put "On Contract"—and in a fairer world, both would have been. With their knowledge and experience they could run circles around me. But they were excluded by company policy. So, even though they always treated me fairly, I was uncomfortable in their presence. A couple of months after I had been on the job in the department, Mr. Michel showed his approval of me in an odd way. He tried to set me up with his daughter. Laura was about my age, kind, and intelligent; but she had her father's face, and she was not pretty enough for me to find her attractive. Every time I looked at her, I saw a Roman centurion.

Speaking of faces, Ron Grouhel, the Assistant Manager, had one that was covered with acne scars. And from this pitted visage, this war zone, he had a strange habit of talking out of one side of his mouth, as if the other side had been immobilized by a grenade. He was ambiguous in his relationship with me; at times, he seemed to be highly supportive; at other times, he seemed to be undermining me in subtle ways. He had had something of a chequered life, some of which he told me about one evening when I went to his apartment in the West End for dinner. One event remains in my memory. He told me he had been married a few years previously. He and his bride got on the train in Vancouver for the overnight journey to Banff, where they planned to honeymoon for a few days. As was common in those days, they had not had sexual relations before the event. When they got undressed in their compartment on the train, she took a jack knife out of her purse and tried to kill him. She had always been a bit high-strung, he said, but whether because of the stress of the wedding or for some other reason, she suddenly went mad. She was now in a mental hospital, he said. He had managed to divorce her, not an easy thing to do, when one considers the draconian divorce laws of the time. He was saved by the fact that the judge believed his contention that the marriage had not been consummated. The only other viable reason for a divorce was adultery. Usually, in order to prove adultery, you had to hire a male or female, as the case required—they advertised their services in the newspapers—have a picture taken of the two of you sitting on a hotel room bed, and have a detective agency attest to the fact that they had witnessed your entering the hotel together.[6]

Visiting Me in My Workplace

WHEN I WAS ON THE SELLING FLOOR, I WAS OFTEN VISITED BRIEFLY BY FRIENDS AND ACQUAINTANCES WHO HAD BEEN ADVISED BY others where to find me. In a world in which most of those I served were unknown to me, it was a pleasure suddenly to see a known face and a known smile. Often the faces belonged to people from Revelstoke on a visit to Vancouver, who had been told by my mother to be "sure to say hello to Terry if you go near the China Department in the Bay." Sometimes, the faces were of people who meant more to me. A few times during that year, my old girlfriend, Karen Abbott, then married and the mother of a young child, dropped by to say hello. Once, I was confronted by a girl I had taken out on one occasion only in Antigonish, whose name I was agonizingly, and embarrassingly, unable to remember.

Quite often, I had a far more distinguished visitor. When I was at Notre Dame, I had written a column about life at the college in the weekly diocesan newspaper, *The Prospector*. The Bishop of Nelson, Martin M. Johnson, was a devotee of the column and showered praise on me regarding it on a number of occasions. I was, of course, flattered. In 1955, Bishop Johnson was made Coadjutor Archbishop of Vancouver, as the incumbent, Archbishop Duke, was ailing. By the time I started work at the Bay, Archbishop Duke had died and Johnson had succeeded him. The seat of the

---

[6] This situation was wonderfully satirized by Evelyn Waugh in *A Handful of Dust*.

Archbishopric, Holy Rosary Cathedral, was just down the hill from the Bay, and Johnson, always dressed simply in clerical black, often came into the store. Sometimes he would merely give me a wave, but often he would stop and chat for a few minutes.

At Christmas, my mother and father visited me in the store a couple of times. They had come to the coast to spend the holiday in Ladner with my sister, Jo, her husband, Larry, and their new baby, Mark. I drove to Ladner on Christmas Eve, taking Jim Craig's Austen A40, which he'd left for me when he took the train to Revelstoke. He had forgotten to leave me the keys, so I had to bare the wires under the steering wheel and tape them together to get the car started. In those days to get to Ladner you had to take a flat-deck ferry at Woodward's Landing. I explained to the fellow lining up the cars that I couldn't turn off the motor, as I wasn't sure I'd be able to start it again. He just shrugged.

The Girls in the Department: Taking Stock

ON FEBRUARY 10, 1958, AFTER THE STORE CLOSED AT ITS REGULAR HOUR, ALL STAFF REMAINED BEHIND TO TAKE STOCK, AN EVENT that took place at least twice a year. Those of us in the Display Department were individually designated to specific areas of the selling floors to help with this process. When it was all done, some time around eight o'clock, as a thank you for making this extra effort (on top of the three hours' overtime we were paid), the store put on a party in the Seymour Room, the cafeteria on the fifth floor. There were sandwiches and canapés and fruit punch; there were raffles of various household goods; there was music, provided by a jazz trio. All in all, it was a good effort on the part of management.

Mr. Michel had the Display Department gather in our workroom, where complex displays were put together, screen printing done, etc., and offered us rye and ginger ale and gin and tonic. He also raffled off a half dozen bottles of Hudson's Bay Company Rum, none of which I won. Shortly after running the raffle, he said goodnight and left. The rest of us polished off the rye and gin and in the process got fairly tanked. First, one of the window dressers by the name of Wendy, a petite brown-haired bundle of pretty energy, led me in behind some of the stock shelves "to show me a project she was working on." She had something else in mind, and before I knew what was happening, we were having a fairly raucous necking session. But she broke it off, saying her fiancé was waiting for her outside the store.[7] I went back to where the others were gathered. There, Avril, the Department's interior designer, took my hand and led me to another area behind the stock shelves. Avril was a large young woman with an equine length to her face and a voluminous bosom. In no time at all, we also were having a fairly raucous necking session. We were, of course, about two sheets to the wind. In spite of that, I had the impression that though I had lost all of the earlier raffles, I had suddenly hit the jackpot. Apart from the booze, the reason for my popularity was the fact that I was really

---

[7] Wendy did marry her fiancé; but I heard three years later, when I contacted some of my old colleagues in the Display Department on my way through Vancouver to Castlegar, that the marriage had only lasted about six months; hardly surprising, given the level of commitment to him she exhibited with me in the workroom.

the only available young man in the department. The floor and window supervisors were in their forties and most of the guys who did the actual display work were not interested in women. But my dalliance with Avril didn't last. She suddenly announced that she had to go. I think she might have thought I would offer to accompany her. But I was not interested in starting anything there. So, once again, I returned to where the much-diminished group was still gathered.

I'm not sure why it happened—it wasn't my birthday or anything—but for the third time that evening, I found myself in the arms of one of our female staff. Margaret was the girl who worked the machine that punched out, laboriously, letter by letter, the printed signs that gave information and prices on the articles for sale in the store. She worked in a room next to the office I shared with Ron Grouhel, seated on a high stool beside her machine and next to an Austrian fellow by the name of Tony, who did the hand-painted artwork on the larger signs. I had often admired Margaret, who was a friendly, attractive, blonde girl with huge brown eyes, full lips, and a well-proportioned figure. But I had not moved beyond this distant admiration, as she was married, and therefore, I thought, out of reach.

But somehow or other on that boozy night, the last person was gone, the lights were out, and Margaret and I were in each other's arms in the back area of the workroom.

> *Time floated by, as it tends to do in these circumstances. We eventually made love, fully clothed, on the workroom floor. Afterwards, we went down through the dark silence of the deserted store, amazed that it was after midnight. At the locked employee exit door, we pushed the buzzer to call the security man to let us out. He was surprised to find us there. We were embarrassed at being caught out. Margaret had won some sheets in the store raffle, and he asked her about those. But he didn't question her story, and he opened the door and let us out on to Seymour Street. I hailed a taxi, dropped Margaret off in front of her apartment building on Pine Street, and went on to 1815 West 11th. It had been quite a night.*

At work the next morning, it seemed that everyone in the department was determined to tease us both about our romantic evening, and, in the circumstances, we were both happy that they didn't know the half of it. In one of the windows being dressed—as always, behind sheets that screened it from the street—Earl, one of the few heterosexual guys in the department, said, as he fondled the plastic tit on a mannequin, an action which mystified me, "Let them talk. In a couple of days they'll have forgotten all about it."

What I didn't know, until I took her to the Georgia Hotel after work for a drink that day, was that Margaret had left her husband a couple of weeks before and was living on the sofa at Wendy's. This situation went a long way to explain why she had been so available. But I was loath to get involved in any serious way with her. She was not right for me. She had left high school after Grade 10. She thought her job as a punch operator was challenging. At the same time, she was a beautiful woman and difficult to resist. She asked for nothing from me but my company, from time to time, and my love-making.

During the following months, I understood that she had also made friends with Colin MacInnes, the other fellow from St. F. X. who was a Trainee. One day in June, after work, I asked her out for a drink. She said that she was supposed to meet Colin, but she would tell him she had to go home. "You know," she said later, as we sat across from each other in the bar at the Georgia, "Colin is a strange guy. He hangs around me, but he never lays a hand on me." Strange indeed.

B.C. Centennial Celebrations

IN 1958, BRITISH COLUMBIA CELEBRATED THE CENTENERY OF ITS ESTABLISHMENT AS A CROWN COLONY. I WAS PUT IN CHARGE OF organizing the window displays for the store. After a number of meetings between Mr. Michel, Ron Grouhel and me, and after having received the authorization of the senior management, we decided to cover the back walls of the windows with huge enlargements of pictures from Vancouver's history. We also set out to borrow or buy historical artefacts to use as props for the items we would be displaying in the windows. We were cautioned not to forget that it was the selling of the merchandise that mattered most in the putting together of the windows; the HBC never lost sight of the main game of skinning the public—*pro pelle cutem*!

In order to get the pictures, and, hopefully, a few artefacts, I made an appointment to see Major Matthews (1878-1970), the City Archivist, in his cramped and crowded bailiwick in the upper regions of Vancouver City Hall. Major Matthews had a reputation for being a difficult man to deal with. Born in Wales and brought up in Australia, he arrived in Vancouver in 1898 and fell in love with the city. He served in the Canadian army in the First World War, rising to the rank of major, a title he used throughout the rest of his life. He was a natural archivist and had begun the accumulation of materials on Vancouver history early in the century—photographs, civic records, personal accounts—when nobody else seemed to care. After he retired from his business as scow-owner and tug operator in 1924, he devised his own system of cataloguing the nearly 500,000 items he had gathered in his home over the years. In the late 1920s, he was allowed to move his collection into the dank and dirty attic of the old city hall and was given an honorarium of $30 a month to look after it. When the city insisted that they now owned the collection, the major moved it back to his house. After some protracted negotiations, the city agreed to make him City Archivist and he agreed to move the collection back to city hall. When the new city hall was built, the archives was given a home of its own on one of the upper floors. It was here that I first encountered Major Matthews.

Mr. Michel had warned me that the Major was a difficult man. So, on each of the three occasions I went to negotiate with him for permission to enlarge some of his historical photographs and to borrow irreplaceable artefacts, Michel armed me with a gift for the Major: first, a tin of HBC pipe tobacco; then, a small hamper of snack foods, some with HBC labels; and finally, a bottle of HBC rum. Contrary to all the warnings I had been given about the Major's irascibility, I found him charming, gracious, and co-operative. "The Hudson's Bay Company is a good organization," he told me. "They do a wonderful job of looking after their own massive archives in Winnipeg." So, he led me to a selection of likely photographs, some of which were eventually copied, blown up and installed in the store windows. As for artefacts, he was more selective in what he would let us have, as most of them were one-of-a-kind and irreplaceable. But he did lend us a few items, after I had assured him that I would be personally responsible for their return. The people at the store were amazed at how well I had done with the Major, but I think it was simply a matter of my treating him and his collection with the respect that they both deserved.

As it turned out, I never saw the completed windows, as I left the company before they were installed, but before I left I made Ron Grouhel promise to look after the artefacts, telling him I would personally come back and assassinate him if anything happened to them. True to his word—and mine—he made sure they were all returned to the archives and the safe-keeping of the irascible major.

Planning My Escape

IN MY TEENS, I HAD HEARD A LOT ABOUT EUROPE. MY BROTHER HAD SPENT HIS LAST YEAR IN THE CANADIAN ARMY IN LONDON, AFTER being wounded in World War II and sent back to Blighty for repairs. My sister, Joan, had sharpened her French at the Chateau Frontenac, in Quebec City, before embarking on a two-year stint, studying at the Sorbonne in Paris. My sister, Jo, had lived in England for a couple of years in the early 1950s. So, I was anxious to see Europe for myself.

Early in the spring of 1958, Bill Wood and I decided that we would quit our jobs and go to Europe together. By June of that year, I had saved about $1,000 out of a salary of $3,900. At the end of May, I went to see Mr. Carey, the Personnel Manager, and told him I would be leaving at the end of June. He asked me why. I said it was because I didn't like the job. He was visibly taken aback by this assertion. After all, he had spent his life in this business, *and I didn't like it!* I could see a flash of anger cross his face. But quickly recovering his calm, he asked me what I intended to do. I did not like to say that I was heading off on an extended trip to Europe, so I told him I wanted to go back to university, to UBC, to do an MA in medieval studies, specifically to study Chaucer. He seemed pleased that this was the reason I was leaving, and he said the company would be happy to give me part-time work in the evenings and on weekends. I was almost tempted to chuck the Europe plans and enrol at the university.

On June 23 Bill and I booked passage on the *S. S. Homeric*, sailing out of Montreal on August 18, at Lloyd's World Travel Service on South Granville Street in Vancouver, paying $190 each for the voyage from Montreal to Southampton. A couple of weeks earlier, we had made a booking on the dowager CPR liner, *Empress of France*; but after talking it over among friends and between ourselves, we decided to change to a newer ship that had a reputation for appealing to a younger crowd. The travel agent, a dour man with rimless glasses, was not pleased at the extra paperwork, but he made the change in silent rancor. What choice did he have?

Toward the end of the month, we had the problem of what to do with our furniture. Mrs. Cooper said she would take all of it for $50, as she had found a couple of girls who wanted to rent the apartment furnished. But she refused to take—or even let us leave in the apartment—our ragged old chesterfield. So, we thought, what are we going to do with it? Jim solved the problem by borrowing a small truck from a friend of his, and the night before we left, we dumped it on one of the boulevards out by the university. Good citizens to the end.

Jim remained in Vancouver, moving into an apartment with a friend of his. Bill and I, and Bill's perennial Revelstoke girlfriend, Beverley, drove to Revelstoke in his slope-backed 1950 Dodge. Beverley had quit her job and was going home to be with Bill until we went to Europe. A couple of years later, she finally convinced him to marry her—"She *sure* pursued him a long time before she got him," my mother said. (They had been an item, on and off, since 1952.)

Our plan was to hitchhike across Canada to Montreal later in the summer to board the *Homeric* for Southampton. And that's exactly what we did.

The Royal Charter of the Hudson's Bay Company

Text of Royal Charter

Granted by King Charles II of England, May 2nd, 1670, the Royal Charter gave an exclusive trading monopoly over the entire Hudson Bay drainage basin to "the Governor and Company of Adventurers of England trading into Hudson Bay." The Charter comprises seven thousand words of hand-lettered text on five pages of vellum - sheepskin - each one 31"x 25". Its clauses outline the rights and obligations of the Company of Adventurers over their new domain, including the right to exploit mineral resources and the obligation to search for the Northwest Passage.

At the time the chartering of monopolistic companies by England, as well as other European powers, had been an established method of trade and territorial expansion for over a hundred years. Serving as the original articles of incorporation of Hudson's Bay Company the Royal Charter also sets forth the framework of the company's governance - by a Committee of seven, headed by the Governor and Deputy Governor - as well as the frequency of elections and meetings. In it the King names his "dear and entirely beloved cousin" Prince Rupert as the Company's first Governor of the territory which shall henceforth be known as "Rupert's Land."

First page of the Hbc Charter
HBCA 1987/363-C-25/6

The Charter states that the Company was to control all lands whose rivers and streams drain into Hudson Bay - all told an area comprising over 1.5 million square miles, stretching from Labrador in the east as far west as the Canadian Rocky Mountains and well south of the present U.S/Canada border. It represented over 40% of modern day Canada.

Hotly contested over the years, particularly by the North West Company, Hbc's main fur-trading rival, the Charter's terms were finally confirmed upon the merger of the two companies in 1821. At that time the government conceded to the Company not only "the powers vested in them by the Charter," but added the licence to trade over the whole of British North America. This licence was renewed in 1838 for a further twenty-one years.

In 1868, the *Rupert's Land Act* paved the way for the surrender of most of Hudson's Bay Company's lands to the British Crown and their subsequent transfer to Canada. The *Deed of Surrender* outlined the terms Hbc was to receive from the Canadian government in return. It was signed in November 1869 and the transfer to Canada followed on July 15, 1870 - effectively ending the Charter's monopoly almost exactly 200 years after the initial grant.

Entry in Hbc Grand Ledger for 28 May 1670 showing the cost of obtaining the Charter

The original Royal Charter is preserved in the Company's Corporate Head Office in Toronto and is both the premier artefact and primary record of the Company.

VANCOUVER

The Bay Building and Birk's

View from Roof of Bay Building

View from Little Mountain

1815 W. 11th Avenue

View of Street from Our Flat

Jim Craig, Erwin Deary, Bill Wood

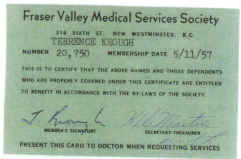
Health Insurance Pre-Medicare

Living Room

Kitchen Table

Bridge at 1815 W. 11th

Captain Wonderful

Chapter 5: Hitching Canada to Sail on the *Homeric*

OFF TO EUROPE: AUGUST 1958

What happened is a wonder, though memory is always incomplete, like a map with places missing. But it's all right, it's entered the imagination and nothing is ever the same.
                      Dermot Healy, **The Bend for Home**, 1998

They say that in old age the long-term memory becomes vivid, punches its fists through the skin of the present, insists on being heard and seen and felt. . . . But how crowded and unfocused this looking back is . . .. I scarcely know which images are mine and which have been taken by me, fully developed, from the others, or whether there is in the final analysis, any difference.
                      Jane Urquhart, **The Underpainter**, 1997

A Freight Train through the Rockies

BILL WOOD AND I LEFT REVELSTOKE ON WEDNESDAY, AUGUST 6, 1958, AT ONE IN THE MORNING, BOUND FOR EUROPE. BILL HAD ARRANGED FOR US TO RIDE THE REAR ENGINE UNIT OF A CPR freight pulled by diesel No. 8447 as far as Field, about 125 miles to the east. An older friend of his, Ken O'Rourke, was the engineer. We were twenty-three years old. We had grown up together, gone to school together, and graduated at the same time from different universities.

     A few days before we left, a Revelstoke insurance agent had given Bill a couple of day journals. We both began keeping them as soon as we set off on our adventure, writing about our experiences every two or three days, sometimes in great detail, at other times, sparingly. My journal is both appealingly innocent and embarrassingly naïve, but it has given me in most cases enough information to jog my memory into details that I had otherwise forgotten. The result is that this account is a palimpsest, a layered manuscript, a rendering on many levels, some on the surface, some under the surface, some hidden. In this way the journey of a lifetime is written on top of the simple account put on the pages of an insurance agent's journal half a century ago.

On that warm, moonless night, we moved through the dark of the railway yards toward the bright lights of the interior of the roundhouse where we had both worked five years before, in the summer of 1953, as hostler's helpers. We were well-known there, so we veered around the outside and approached the shop track where our engine waited in the dark. We did not want to get O'Rourke and his crew in trouble for giving us an illegal free ride.

The rear section of a four-unit diesel engine was, in those days, a duplicate of the front section coupled backwards; so we had seats to sit on which were exactly like those used by O'Rourke, his fireman, and his brakeman. The smell of the engine, of the diesel oil and steel, was familiar from our summer jobs in the roundhouse, where we had learned to put fuel and traction sand into these machines and run them here and there around the yards. But riding backwards took a little getting used to. Symbolically, there was a cultural cordillera to overcome. Forwards in Canadian history and literature seems always a matter of going from east to west, as if in obedience to the 19th century invocation to American youth—"Go West, Young Man!" a phrase attributed to Horace Greeley, though the attribution is much disputed—and not the other way around. So our riding backwards, facing west rather than east, is not entirely antithetical to traditional accounts of crossing the country, although we were in fact going in the opposite direction. This backwards riding, also, in a sense—as I write in another present—provides an image for memory; for what else is memory but a facing backwards, a journey from west to east, a riding against the flow of time into the past.

Incredible Dawn in the Rockies

WHEN O'ROURKE'S FREIGHT WAS UNDERWAY, WE TRIED TO SLEEP ON THE FLOOR, WHERE WE COULD STRETCH OUT; BUT THE ENGINE noise and the incessant shaking, combined with the hardness of the metal floor, made sleeping difficult. So we spent most of the night trying to sleep on the padded chairs that were provided for the three men of the engine crew: the engineer, or "hogger," as he was known to those in the railway business, the fireman, who on coal-burners would have spent his trip shovelling coal but had nothing much to do on these modern engines except relieve the engineer, and the brakeman, who threw the switches at sidings. Besides, we were excited with the prospect of setting out on our trip and would probably have found it difficult to sleep even in our own beds. And here we were, rocking backward through the dark, past one-room mountain stations, the telegraph operators staring out at us, glad of our temporary company. Past Beavermouth—the mosquito capital of the world—where I'd worked briefly on an extra gang when I was fifteen, in that summer when in another part of the world the Korean conflict was heating up; and Golden, where, on the same summer job, I'd seen a brakeman injured when he fell from the top of a moving freight car, on his way back to the engine from the caboose.

> *He'd fallen off the outfit car we were riding in. The engineer had accidentally put on the car brakes instead of the engine brakes, so the brakeman did not hear the train stopping one car at a time from the front, as he would have if the engine brakes had been applied,. The conductor had seen him fall and pulled the emergency lever to stop the train. The brakeman had not fallen under the train, but on to the ground beside the track, so he had not been run over. Hurricane lamps appeared all around him where he lay on his back on the ground. "Mosquitoes!" he said. "Mosquitoes!" He was unable to lift his arms to wipe them off his face. The Swede with the Irish accent who worked with us said, "He's a goner." But the man proved only to have broken bones and bruises and survived to walk on top of many more trains.*

We moved on into the Kicking Horse Pass, with the still-remembered and always-raging Kicking Horse River thrashing beside us, so close that it sometimes seemed to be right under the track. It was a scene out of E. J. Pratt's book-length poem, *Towards the Last Spike (1952)*:

> The rivers out there did not flow: they tumbled.
> The cataracts were fed by glaciers;
> Eddies were thought as whirlpools in Gorges
> And gradients had paws that tore up tracks.

It became light around five o'clock as we were reaching Field, the next divisional point. The day was beginning with a sunny magnificence that could also only be expressed adequately in poetry, as in Earle Birney's *David* (1942), where he describes the two young men awaking in the morning:

> We rose . . . while the stars went out, and the quiet heather
> Flushed, and the skyline pulsed with the surging bloom
> Of incredible dawn in the Rockies.

We rose—Bill and I—where there was no heather to inspire us. Only smelly steel. But the mountains loomed above us, and the skyline pulsed with beauty, and we were glad to be on our way.

We piled out of the diesel cab with our bags awkwardly in tow. Bill asked O'Rourke if he would speak to the new crew to see if they would let us continue to Calgary. He said he would. So while we waited, we walked to the station, where the lunchroom was just opening. We had coffee and a typical CPR ham sandwich, modelled on those served at Ladies' teas in Edwardian England, two slices of crustless, soft, white bread enclosing the thinnest piece of ham in the British empire (which was by this time almost as insubstantial), a wonderful coalescing of good taste and greed.

A Surprise Visit Enroute from Field to Calgary

ONCE AGAIN WE SLIPPED INTO THE CAB OF THE DIESEL, CONFIDENT THAT O'ROURKE HAD SPOKEN TO THE NEW CREW. BUT AS WE approached the Spiral Tunnels, an engineering marvel that reduces the grade by running the track through the mountain in loops, the fireman, who had come back to do a routine check of the units, clacked through the metal door, and visibly startled to find us sitting there, hitched up his striped bib overalls and blasted us.

> *"What the hell are you guys doing here?"*
>
> *We explained. He listened. He was not pleased. "You know," he said, shaking his balding head sadly and looking out the window, "a friend of mine just walked the streets for a month for allowing this sort of thing."*
>
> *It was upsetting for us to be caught out this way, but even more upsetting was the chance that they would make us get off the train in this wilderness, void of roads—even of trails—and make us walk the tracks many miles back to the Palliser station. But as I was contemplating this awful prospect, I remembered that a conductor had said exactly the same thing when I jumped on a caboose with a couple of friends to go home for the weekend when we were working on a CPR paint gang near Kamloops in the summer of 1951. On that occasion, the engineer, who was the father of one of my friends, slowed the train down so we could get on. Things like that happened around Revelstoke.*

As the fireman turned to go again to the front unit, shaking his head, hot with news for his colleagues that there were two modern hobos on board, I said to his back, "It'd be easier for all of us if you haven't seen us here."

Perhaps he took my advice not to say anything to the rest of the crew, though that is unlikely. Probably they all decided it was better just to leave things alone. They knew that there wasn't much chance of their getting caught as long as we hopped off the train at the yard switch in Calgary, which anyone with a knowledge of how the railway ran would do automatically, thus avoiding a confrontation with the railway yard cop. That is what we intended to do, and that is what we did. We understood the system.

A Night in a Calgary Flophouse

WE WALKED THROUGH THE YARDS TOWARD TOWN AND FOUND A RUNDOWN HOTEL, THE *ALEXANDRIA*, THE FIRST OF THE dilapidated, Edwardian-built places we would stay in, all of them named in colonial fashion after British upper-class twits and twitesses. It was typical of the three and four storey, wooden, walk-up hotels that were built all over the country in the early part of the century, with their ground-floor beer parlours and their paneled lounges, complete with worn and cracking leather-seated chairs and floor lamps with flouncy shades. In the fifties, they were nearing the end of their usefulness as hotels. At the dark-oak, bar-shaped desk in the minute lobby, about the size of a large closet, we signed up for a room under the gaze of a reticent, middle-aged man with a hooked nose, who was wearing a black Stetson. Indoors. I was reminded of the old expression of derision, "Big hat, no cows." But we were, after all, in Calgary, otherwise known as "Cow Town."

Our hotel room, like most of our cruddy rooms across the country, had on its worn, hardwood floor, a dresser, a freestanding, rectangular porcelain sink, and a double bed. There would not have been room for twin beds in any of the rooms we stayed in, but that didn't matter, as it never occurred to us to mind sharing. We were old friends, our sexual proclivities were not in doubt, and in that more innocent age, friends of the same sex shared beds because that's the way things were. Although it was only five o'clock in the afternoon, we were exhausted after a night without sleep. We dragged ourselves into a greasy spoon across the street, where we had hamburgers and milkshakes. Back in the hotel, we hit the sack right away, and neither of us woke until six o'clock the next morning. Ah, youth!

After breakfasting in the hotel coffee shop—a waitress in a pink uniform, walking on sensible, flat, white shoes, an arborite counter with a screwed-on aluminum edge, chrome-like overstuffed napkin dispensers, bacon and eggs on oval plates with butter-soaked toast on the side—we inquired of the man with the hooked nose and the black hat the best way to hitchhike out of town to the east. He told us there was a bus that went from just down the block all the way to the other end of town. By eight o'clock we were on it, dragging our bags. It took us, as the man had said it would, all the way to the eastern edge of Calgary, which was then a much smaller city than it is today.

Thumbing Our Way East

IN THE LATE 1960s, WHEN HITCHHIKING ACROSS THE COUNTRY BECAME ENORMOUSLY POPULAR AMONG YOUNG PEOPLE, HITCHHIKERS donned packsacks and wore T-Shirts and jeans. In the fifties, when hitchhiking wasn't popular, especially among the middle classes—it seemed to indicate a lack of money, which was shameful—it was standard wisdom that if you dressed respectably, drivers would see you as non-threatening and be more likely to pick you up. We both wore the clothes we had worn to work in Vancouver: white dress shirts, ties, grey herringbone sports jackets that were similar but not identical (that year's fashion), and well-pressed gabardine dress pants. (We kept them well-pressed by putting them under the mattress overnight, an old bachelor's trick.) With our new, cheap, blonde, pigskin Gladstone bags in tow—at that time packsacks were unthinkably low class, like travelling with your clothes in a shopping bag—we must have looked very nearly ridiculous standing by the side of the road, as if in some kind of uniform, well-washed thumbs jerking enthusiastically as each car sped by. Ridiculous, perhaps, but we were certainly ridiculously *respectable*.

We were picked up for the first time by a travelling salesman. I got into the back seat with the two bags. Bill got into the front. The salesman was a slight, nervous man of indeterminate age (late thirties, early forties) with square glasses in the heavy brown plastic popular at the time, dressed in a cheap, wrinkled, powder-blue gabardine suit that shone at the knees. For a couple of minutes, he said nothing to us, as he accelerated to highway speed. He was obviously a reticent sort of character when it came to dealing with strangers, an odd characteristic for one who made his living selling things to other people. Though, in a way, the travelling salesmen of that era were really men with catalogues who wrote down orders from the stores they serviced in the small towns on their routes.

> "Where ya headed?" he asked, expecting us to say, maybe, Regina, or at the extreme, Toronto."
> "Europe," Bill replied.
> "Europe, eh." Pause. "Guess I can't take you that far. I'm only going as far as Strathmore." Chuckle. Chuckle. "That's fine," I said, stupidly, anxious to be supportive. Strathmore was only thirty miles or so down the road. But it was a start. We certainly hadn't expected to get a ride all the way to Europe. All other things considered, there was the little matter of the ocean.

We both tried to start a regular conversation with our salesman, but after his initial attempt at humour, he for the most part replied with grunts. It's hard to have a conversation with a grunter. Occasionally, he would murmur, "Europe, eh," as if he couldn't believe that anyone would want to go that far. Was he jealous? Probably. Did he resent our being young, footloose, and fancy-free? Almost certainly. But who could blame him? At this distance, as I write this episode, I'm even a little jealous myself.

Outside, the level prairie flashed by with a monotony that was only matched by the monotony of our non-conversation. We had been picked up by a local whose range as a travelling salesman was profoundly limited. In fact, in macro terms, he remained essentially in place while on the move, like a lengthy field of wheat waving in unison from Calgary to Strathmore, Strathmore to Calgary, maturing only in growing old, waiting like those around it to be cut and harvested when its time is right.

Our reticent salesman dropped us off at a gas station in Strathmore; and, as unlikely as it may seem, we were picked up by another after only about thirty minutes. The country was alive with travelling salesmen in those days—before there were shopping malls in every village, before every town had the same chain stores as every other town—taking orders for manufacturers and distributors from stores within their territories. Legend had it that salesman were the most likely people to pick up hitchhikers, as they travelled alone and were in need of company. So far, legend seemed to have it right.

Unlike our previous benefactor, this man was gregarious. He was large: potbelly bulging under the end of his red tie, a round face with a double chin, sparkling brown eyes.

> "Hi. I'm George," he said as we got into the car. "Where ya goin'?"
> We replied inadvertently in chorus, a little timorously this time, "Europe."
> "Europe!" he shouted, throwing his head back. Then he softly said, as if to himself, "Well, I'll be damned." But he added, addressing us with a twinkle in his eye, "I'm only going as far as Medicine Hat."
> Not a bible-puncher, this guy. A lot of Calgary red-eye—draught beer laced with tomato juice, popular at the time in that city—had gurgled in George's belly and settled in George's double chin. "What in hell you goin' to Europe for?"

The 1950s in Canada—Culture Was Elsewhere

IN THE 1950s, GEORGE'S QUESTION WAS NOT AT ALL UNUSUAL. WE HAD MET IT A NUMBER OF TIMES BEFORE. AND THE ANSWER, THOUGH simple, sounds pompous and snobbish, even (God help us!) anti-Canadian. From a moral perspective, if the whole western world was beginning to struggle, finally, against Victorian puritanism and hypocrisy, Canada was still on the whole happily conforming. Perhaps, Mordecai Richler, who had fled to Europe a few years before we left, put it best when he described Canada in the 1950s as "a Presbyterian twat." Decades later, he was, in the voice of one of his characters, he was even more damning:

> Canada is not so much a country as a holding tank filled with the disgruntled progeny of defeated people. French-Canadians consumed by self-pity; the descendents of Scots who fled the Duke of Cumberland; Irish the famine; and Jews the Black Hundreds. Then there are the peasants from the Ukraine, Poland, Italy and Greece, convenient to grow wheat and dig out the ore and swing the hammers and run the restaurants, but otherwise to be kept in their place.
> **Solomon Gursky Was Here**, 1989

Richler, for whatever reason, left out the plethora of English twits and twitesses who, not able to make it at home, came to Canada to try to rule over those who in the Empire were seen to be of lesser value.

The country was, in fact, a cultural and intellectual desert. There was no professional theatre outside of Stratford, and Stratford was in its infancy. The big hit of 1957 was a college review from McGill, *Spring Thaw*, which toured the country and was marvelled at. Whatever contemporary painters we had were under-appreciated, and those who continued to be praised (the Group of Seven, Emily Carr, and a few others) belonged to the past. Writers—with the notable exception of Morley Callaghan, who had done his stint in Europe with Hemingway and Fitzgerald—were part-time, starving, or expatriates like Richler. There was no classical music to speak of outside of Toronto and Montreal. We produced no movies except the documentaries cranked out by the National Film Board—though we were justly proud of our accomplishments in that area, especially lauding the work of Norman McLaren and his film, *Neighbors*. We wrote no songs. If you exclude "It's a Long Way to Tipperary" (only half written by a Canadian) and some of the temporary hits of the Dumbells, who entertained during and after the First World War, you could count the Canadian hits on one hand. There was a rumbling of popular music in the 1950s with songs by the quartets, The Four Lads, and the Crewcuts. There was "The World is Waiting for the Sunrise," which, in a very Canadian way, Ernest Seitz was ashamed of having written because it was too low-brow. There was "When You and I Were Young [Maggie]," words written by George Washington Johnson, published in *Maple Leaves* in 1864, and set to music in Chicago two years later by an expatriate English composer by the name of J. A. Butterfield. The woman to whom the poem was addressed, Maggie Clark, married Johnson in the year the poem was published and died in the year it was set to music. It all seems so *Canadian*! The poet is named after an American president, the composer of the music is an Englishman, and the woman for whom the poem was written died tragically young. It was this kind of situation, in our literature, that Margaret Atwood is having fun with in *Survival* (1972): "What happens in Canadian literature when boy meets girl? . . . She gets cancer and he gets hit by a meteorite."

We were going to Europe because it was an oasis to which we could travel from the desert of our culture, by default European, but weakened by the pragmatism necessary to build a new country. We knew that as an oasis Europe would not in the end do, because it was to us a mirage that would hold its reality only while we were a part of it. We would have to return to our particular Canadian desert and work at our own mirages until they became solid and real. Some of our artists had gone to Europe— painter James William Morrice early in the century and Joe Plaskett in the mid-century, writer Mavis Gallant in the early 1950s, for example—and would never return to Canada on a permanent basis; though their work would never lose a certain Canadian flavour. Others would stay in Europe for years, principally in England, before returning: Mordecai Richler, Norman Levine, Margaret Lawrence, and Mario Bernardi, for example.

. Those of us who came back sooner—and there were thousands—did not as individuals bring back the mirage *in toto*, but we brought it back in bits and pieces and built our own oases and our own mirages right across the country; and like many John the Baptists, prepared the way for our own cultural redeemers, who appeared in the 1960s and thereafter. (None of them, I'm glad to say were Christs, though some of them had inclinations in that direction.)

I have, of course, overstated the case. Many fine artists had been at work in Canada over the years. There are the so-called Confederation Poets: Charles G. D. Roberts, Bliss Carman, Archibald Lampman, Duncan Campbell Scott; the Montreal Group: F. R. Scott, A. M. Klein, A. J. M. Smith, and Leo Kennedy.

> *It was 1982. I was at a small conference at the Chateau Laurier in Ottawa, celebrating the work of Morley Callaghan, who had come up from Toronto for the occasion. ("This is weird," a robust old Callaghan said. "On the plane up here today, I had the feeling that if you guys are celebrating my work, I must already be dead!") As we were standing around with drinks in our hands before the first session of the conference, an old man limped into the room, leaning heavily on his cane. "I'm Leo Kennedy," he said. Kennedy, who had not written anything substantial since the 1930s and had spent most of his life selling insurance in the United States, looked as if he had very little time left on this earth. His visit was a surprise to everyone. He and Callaghan ignored one another.*

There were, of course, others who were not part of a group, like Charles Sangster, Pauline Johnson, E. J. Pratt and Earle Birney. There are many painters: William Krieghoff, Paul Kane, Lucius O'Brien, William Brymner, Emily Carr, Tom Thompson, Jean Paul Riopelle, to name but a few; there are some fine novelists: John Richardson, William Kirby, Sara Jeannette Duncan, Ralph Connor, Martha Ostenso, Mazo de la Roche, Frederick P. Grove, Hugh MacLennan, Robertson Davies; there are the humorists: Thomas Chandler Haliburton and Stephen Leacock. And so on. But even where there was in Canada an appreciation of things Canadian, it was for the most part an appreciation of things which had been produced by Canadians who were safely dead, or those whose careers had blossomed before the Second World War. Living artists were on the whole ignored. Culture was elsewhere.

I would like to think that I was pondering these things at the time, but I was not. Much of the erudition I display above, such as it is, was learned subsequent to our journey. I was not a snob about things cultural. But I did know that I was leaving Canada because I was in a world that wasn't satisfying to me. There was a hole in my life that needed filling, and I felt that it might be at least partially filled by a sojourn in Europe, if only for a time. Anyway, whatever the circumstances of my leaving, the question remains: How do you say these things to a man peddling goods throughout southern Alberta for the food firm of Kelly Douglas when he asks you what in hell you're going to Europe for?

We Take an Unexpected Detour

ABOUT FORTY MILES AWAY FROM MEDICINE HAT, GEORGE DECIDED TO TAKE A SHORTCUT THROUGH DUSTY AND DESERTED SIDE ROADS. As we moved further and further into nowhere, George's frown indicated there might be a problem, but he drove on in silence. When we eventually came around a corner and the road stopped at a small river, he had to admit he was lost.

"I'm lost," he said.

Beside the river was a tattered frame house that leaned eastward and was in need of paint. On the river was a two-car ferry, of the sort that is powered by the current in the water. A girl of eight or so watched us from the steps of the house. She wore a gingham dress in a faded floral pattern, the left waist pocket of which was torn. There was not here the smell of ripening wheat, but the dry odour of sand and sagebrush. We were in the desert area known as the Palliser Triangle.

George went over to the girl, habitually tugging up the waist of his pants as he got out of the car. It was a gesture of authority—and insecurity.

"The ferry runnin'?" he said to the girl.

"Yep."

"Your father runnin' it?"

"Yep."

"Sadie," we heard from the leaning house.

"Yes, pop?" Sadie yelled back, never taking her eyes off George, who stood with his hands on his hips.

"You tell them fellers I'm at my dinner."

"Pop's at his dinner," repeated Sadie to George.

"Tell 'em I'll take 'em over when I'm done."

Sadie again repeated what her father had said. "He'll take you over when he's done."

There was nothing to do but wait. So we did, lounging around the car in our city clothes while the ferry man finished his dinner. He came out of the house, a tall, lean man in ironman pants and a faded cowboy shirt with pearl buttons, wiping his lips with a blue spotted handkerchief. We boarded the car on the ferry, Sadie's pop released us into the current, and we drifted along the overhead cable to the other side of the river.

We eventually arrived at about two o'clock in Medicine Hat. The locals had wanted to get rid of this odd and wonderful name in 1910 and change it to something "more suitable." No less a luminary than the poet of colonialism, Rudyard Kipling, stepped into the controversy, praising the name's "uniqueness, individuality, assertion and power,' and suggesting that anyone who would change a name as good as this one would have to rechristen the city "Judasville." The locals, good Christians and colonials all, dropped their campaign.

George dropped us off at a café near the eastern end of town. We were hungry and tired, but after having a late lunch we felt better and decided we should press on.

Weird Names Country: Medicine Hat to Moose Jaw

AT FIVE O'CLOCK, WE WERE STILL STATIONED BESIDE THE ROAD AT THE EAST END OF TOWN. THE PLAN WAS THAT IF WE DIDN'T GET A ride by seven, we would go back to Medicine Hat for the night. One quality you need in spades if you are to be a good hitchhiker is patience. Standing by the side of the road offering your thumb to every car that goes by is a boring business. You know that most cars are going to ignore your digital plea, but you can't afford to pick and choose among the cars that go by, as you never know which one of them will stop and pick you up. As most people do when they're hitchhiking in pairs, we used to take turns holding out the thumb, giving each of us a chance to sit on our bags when we weren't on duty. Bill and I spent half an hour thumbing and half an hour sitting. Sometimes, we would place a small bet (a quarter) on who would manage to get a car to stop.

So far, we had been incredibly lucky in getting rides. But in those days, hitchhikers were few and far between. We did not, in fact, see anyone else hitching throughout our entire trip on the road. There was not as well the fear that drivers would develop when hitchhiking became the rage among young people a decade later and a number of ugly incidents made the practice of picking up strangers at the side of the road a dubious thing to do. Our being well-dressed helped, and we were obviously donning good clothes to give drivers some assurance that we were decent young men. But I'm not sure that it was really necessary for us to do so in order to be given rides, especially by travelling salesmen, who were known to pick up hitchhikers in order to give their lonely lives on the road a bit of spark.

Whatever the circumstances, we had so far had lucky thumbs. We had covered a lot of miles in an incredibly short time. And our good luck continued. Shortly before six, an oil salesman, driving one of those incredibly large 1950's American cars, a young man with a decidedly upper-middle-class English accent, picked us up.

> "Europe," we replied to the inevitable question.
> "England?"
> "We're going there first," Bill said. (I was once more in the back seat with the bags.)
> "I'm from England myself. [We had noticed the accent.] Chichester. Ever heard of it?" [We had.]
> "We're hoping to spend the winter in Spain," I said. I had wanted to go to Spain for a long time, an urge that was essentially romantic and had arisen during my two years studying Spanish at St. F. X. and from my reading of Hemingway's Spanish novels. I had not yet become acquainted with Gerald Brennan's adventures south of Granada; but had I been, I would have been even keener.
> "Wogs," said the Englishman, whose name was Brian.
> He was tall and very thin and about our age. He had a shock of curly hair of an indiscriminate brown that rose in tight waves to the centre of his head and dropped in waves to the other side, a wedge. He drove his finned DeSoto—which rode as softly as a living room sofa—like a European: fast, and with the seeming expertise of a race driver. He passed everything on the road, and in the process, scared the hell out of both of us.
> Bill asked him why he had come to Canada.
> "Money," he said. "No money in England. Country's going to rack and ruin. Too may wogs." He spoke in half sentences. "Empire's finished. Country's filling up with Pakis and blackies. Rhymes that. Sit around doing nothing. Collect welfare. English see the wogs on the dole doing nothing. So, they think, 'Why should I work?' So they quit and collect the dole like the wogs. Now the whole country's full of wogs: black wogs and white wogs. All on wog-fare!" He grinned in pleasure at his play on words. But we were merely a new audience. It was a speech he'd made many times before.

In this way, we were entertained by Brian all the way to Moose Jaw. "Moose Jaw! Moose Jaw!" he said. "Wouldn't that be an odd name for a college town?" We said nothing, but later when we discussed this remark, we laughed at the fact that we had both at the time thought of "Oxford," an equally odd name from the animal kingdom. Brian dropped us off at a cheap hotel, much like the one we'd stayed in in Calgary. We had dinner in the Chinese restaurant across the street, returned to the hotel, and went to bed.

More Brian: From Moose Jaw to Regina

IN THE MORNING, WE WERE UP AND OUT SHORTLY AFTER SIX, AS BRIAN HAD TOLD US HE WOULD PICK US UP AGAIN IF WE WERE ON THE ROAD early enough. "Always away by seven," he said. As there was no public transport in Moose Jaw, we walked the two miles to the edge of town through the empty streets in the early sunlight. All towns, no matter how dirty—or in the case of prairie towns, dusty—in summer look fresh and clean at this time of day. Even Moose Jaw. When we reached the highway, the morning was already getting hot. My collar had begun to chafe my neck and I had looped my jacket through one of the straps of my bag.

Brian, who was always away by seven, came by about a quarter past eight. There had been no more than a dozen or so cars in over an hour, most of them local. So we were glad to see the finned DeSoto (two-tone, salmon pink on top and grey around the belly) pull over and stop.

> "Late start," said Brian, running a hand through his wedge-hat hair as we sped east at what seemed like a hundred and fifty miles an hour. "Donna—that's my Moose Jaw crumpet—didn't want to let me go. Had a helluva night. Hump, hump, hump. Can't have had more than two hour's kip. How'd you fellows make out?"
> "Fine," we both said together, nearly in unison. I whispered "Hump, hump, hump" to myself, without realizing I had whispered a little too loudly.
> "What's that?" Brian said.
> "Dump, dump, dump," I said.
> "Moose Jaw?"
> "Yeah."
> "You're right about that. Nothing but wogs in Moose Jaw."

Brian dropped us off where the highway skirted the road going into Regina. It was high morning by this time and the heat was blasting down on us. There was no wind. Not a murmur. Not enough to stir the feathers on a prairie chicken's ass. There are no trees on this part of the prairies, except where they have been planted by man—and man hadn't planted any near enough to be of any use to us. There was no shade. None. The traffic was sporadic, and as none of it seemed to be ready to pick us up, we stood in our shirtsleeves at the edge of the road and fried. Two respectable, if sweaty, young hitchhikers.

In the distance, perhaps a mile of flat prairie away, we could see Regina rising out of the wheat fields like a mirage. The city's original name was Pile O' Bones, much to be preferred to the colonial name chosen by the CPR. Once the capital of the North West Territories, it was originally the centre of operations of the Royal Canadian Mounted Police—RCMP—at that time, the Royal North West Mounted Police—RNWMP. It remains an important training facility for the Mounties to this day. Regina also gave its name to the Depression-spawned *Regina Manifesto*, written for the most part by poet Frank Scott, which was the founding document of the socialist party, the Commonwealth Co-operative Federation—CCF, which in 1961, morphed into the New Democratic Party—NDP.

That Regina existed at all seemed something of a miracle. Or perhaps the miracle was that it was placed exactly where it is. How did they (whoever *they* were) decide to put it *there*? Why not a mile west? Or a mile east? Or, best of all, as we grew hotter and thirstier, a mile south, right where we were now? All of the prairies were the same anyway, so what did it matter? I had visions of Victoria Regina, after whom the city is named, old and fat and leaning over a map at Windsor, a veritable Michelin tire woman, taking a pin out of her bonnet and puncturing the map with great gusto and saying to Disraeli, "We will have our capital here." But all of this is pure fantasy, as Disraeli was not only out of power but also dead by the time Regina was founded in 1882.

In the heat of this summer day in 1958, we were beginning to feel a little dead ourselves. By 11:30, hunger and thirst and heat exhaustion had driven us to lug ourselves and our Gladstone bags into a café on the outskirts of Regina, where we ordered two plain hamburgers and drank four bottles of Coke each. The Cokes were only six ounces in those days of hedonistic restraint—none of that two-litre stuff in the Fifties, by God! It was a mental struggle to lug ourselves and our bags back to the highway and the heat, but what choice did we have? The alternative was a day and night in Pile O' Bones.

Scouting Our Way to Winnipeg

AFTER ABOUT AN HOUR AT THE ROADSIDE, WE WERE PICKED UP BY A JOLLY, PEAR-SHAPED SCOUTMASTER IN FULL SCOUT UNIFORM—green shirt covered in badges, neck scarf cinched by a leather loop, short pants held up by a wide leather belt with a scout-crest buckle, knee-high socks with tabs, a whistle—who responded to the inevitable answer to the inevitable question about where we were going with the banal statement that he had been brought up in Nova Scotia. He meant by that that he had himself lived on the edge of Europe for many years.

> *Geoffrey—for that was his name—was one of those people who are always shifting position as they drive. "Just let me adjust the seat," he'd say, reaching under it for the lever. I was in the front this time, where Geoffrey and I shared a bench seat. Bucket seats would not arrive until the Sixties. "When I count three, push forward with me. One—two—three-ee!"*
>
> *Forward went the seat.*
> *"Too much!" said Geoffrey. "One—two—three-ee!"*
> *Back went the seat.*
> *"Too far!" said Geoffrey.*
> *Eventually, we got it in place to Geoffrey's satisfaction. "Ah, that's better," said Geoffrey. But now that the car's seat was in the right place, his own personal one was not (haemorrhoids?), and every few minutes he would make a minor adjustment of the large end of the pear, either forward, backward, or to the side.*
>
> *Bill, in the relative obscurity of the back seat, was having difficulty suppressing a laugh. It wasn't only the Geoffrey-shift that amused him. Every time Geoffrey moved, his whistle, which hung from a ring near his waist, clanked against the metal buckle of his belt, so that between shifts, both of us waited for the sound which would indicate the next shift.*
>
> *But Geoffrey was more aware of our silent mocking than we thought. "Something amusing you, Bill?" he said, frowning into the rear-view mirror.*
>
> *"Not really," Bill replied. "I just found the back-and-forthing kinda funny."*

Geoffrey, who drove slowly at the best of times, had really slowed down during this exchange. The silence that precedes a blow-up hung heavily over the three of us. I felt like the Indian girl, Keejigo, in D. C. Scott's "At Gull Lake: August 1810," waiting for the horrendous wrath of her elders:

> A storm-cloud was marching
> Vast on the prairie,
> Scared with livid ropes of hail,
> Quick with nervous vines of lightning—

I fully expected Geoffrey was going to stop and tell us to get out. He was going that slowly. But the car suddenly picked up speed; and Geoffrey, having for reasons unknown dropped the confrontation, became visibly more relaxed. He began to question us as to whether we had ever been scouts. We hadn't. "That's too bad," he said. "Scouting is about helping other people, about doing things that make everyone happy. About accepting one's fellow man for what he is, not what we want him to be." (Was this sermon the reason for his change of mood? He was going to instruct us?) "I always tell my Prairie Dogs—that's the name of my troop—I'm off to rally them now—that a good prairie dog rejoices in other people's happiness."

A Pit Stop in Virden

As Geoffrey wanted to see some scouting friends in Virden, he dropped us at the hotel there, promising to pick us up again later. It was one of those common three-storey buildings with a veranda running across its entire front. We had a sandwich in the hotel coffee shop and sat on the edge of the veranda while we waited for Geoffrey. The town was compact, unusual for a western town, almost as if it had been designed as a set for a cowboy movie. The main street ran for a couple of blocks, one-storey buildings with false fronts, containing the usual small-town assortment of stores. Mature cottonwoods shaded the sidewalks. It was a market day, busy for a small town on a Friday afternoon. Nobody seemed to be paying any attention to us, two city-dressed young fellows on the hotel veranda, but it's likely that we were being assessed carefully and surreptitiously. You can't be too careful with strangers, especially city strangers.

It was in a town such as this that Robert Stead's novel, *Grain* (1926), comes to life; and on streets like this that Gander Stake, Stead's anti-hero, suffers the scorn of those who think he ought to be in the trenches in Europe during World War I rather than on the farm producing food for the troops:

> The first year of the war was the hardest for Gander. Before another season's crop was being threshed the world—the Allies' world, at any rate—had awakened to the quite obvious fact that the war must be won by wheat. Growing wheat became a patriotic duty into which Gander fitted like a cylinder nut into a socket wrench. He could grow wheat, and none of that "form fours" nonsense about it.

And it was on streets like this that Sinclair Ross set *As For Me and My House* (1941), where Philip Bentley, uncomfortable in his clerical collar, regrets his life amid dust storms and hypocrisy:

> Another little Main Street. In the foreground there's an old horse and buggy hitched outside one of the stores. A broken old horse, legs set stolid, head down dull and spent. But still you feel it belongs to the earth, the earth it stands on, the prairie that continues

> where the town breaks off. . . . But the town in contrast has an upstart, mean
> complacency. The false fronts haven't seen the prairie. Instead they stare at each other
> across the street as into mirrors of themselves, absorbed in their own reflections.

On the surface, these prairie towns appear to be neighbourly and unjudgemental, but scratch that surface and all the maggots of anger, jealousy, and greed will emerge.

On the Road Again

Geoffrey drove us through to Portage la Prairie, where we had hamburgers at a drive-in. What a Fifties thing drive-ins were! You cruised the main drag looking for girls, showing off your car's elaborate fins, if you were lucky enough to have a car that had them. You pulled into the A&W for a burger, fries, and a root beer, served by a girl in a skimpy skirt, who took your order and brought it out to you on roller skates, attaching the tray to your partly rolled down window. You went to the drive-in theatre with your date, and, as the old joke goes, took swimming lessons, learning the breaststroke. It was a time when cars had plenty of room, when a compact was a thing a girl carried around in her purse rather than a small automobile. Before McDonald's, with its emphasis on relationships that are social and familial rather than private and romantic. Before experience was talked about. Before letting it all hang out was a good thing. Before the Sixties.

When we arrived in Winnipeg, we said goodbye to Geoffrey, good scout to the end, at the corner of Portage and Main. In our short acquaintance, we had become rather fond of this big prairie dog. He was a little too naïve, perhaps, but not nearly as innocent as he at first seemed to be, or as we at first wanted him to be. It never occurred to us that we were arrogant and insensitive and lacked any real understanding of the human condition, seeing ourselves in the omniscience of ignorance as somehow privileged to be different from the common herd. The blindness of arrogance is total.

Winnipeg: It's Not Paris[1]

SO—WE HAD MADE IT TO WINNIPEG, THE LARGEST CITY ON THE PRAIRIES. IT WAS CLEAN AND BORING AND HAD BEEN THAT WAY FOR more than half a century. But in its beginnings, more than a hundred years before that, it was a place of mud and excitement—the two often go together—and at the turn of the twentieth century, it was a boomtown. James Reaney, in the poem, "A Message to Winnipeg" (1962), asks: "Winnipeg, what once were you?" And the question seems to be answered in John Newlove's poem, "Crazy Riel" (1968):

> Poundmaker. Big Bear. Wandering Spirit,
> Those miserable men.
> Riel. Crazy Riel.[2]

---

[1] This remark was made by Bob Edwards (1859-1922), about his arriving in Winnipeg on September 12, 1894. He was an acerbic Scot who settled in Calgary, where he wrote and published the *Calgary Eye Opener*.
[2] Poundmaker, Big Bear, and Wandering Spirit were Indian leaders on the Prairies who took part in the two Riel Rebellions against federal rule in the last quarter of the 19th century. They were led by the Métis mystic, Louis Riel (1844-85), who was hanged for treason.

But there was no excitement for us in Winnipeg on that summer evening in 1958. A few blocks down Main Street, in a seedy neighbourhood, we found an acceptably seedy hotel, the King Edward, whose entrance and lobby were flush with, and opened right on to, the street. Many of the smaller hotels, those not grand enough to have a veranda, were built in this way in the west in the era before the First World War, the era in which Edward was king. It was an era in which Canada had been a land of hope and promise. "The twentieth century belongs to Canada," the Prime Minister, Wilfrid Laurier, had boasted at its beginning. He was spectacularly wrong about that. Only the first decade or so belonged to Canada, a time of huge immigration, rapid growth, and massive building. After the First World War, the country went into a profound period of stagnation, from which it did not begin to emerge until the 1960s. In many ways, the 1950's Canada we were hitchhiking across was an Edwardian Canada gone to seed, a country in which the worn-out Edwardian hotels still featured spittoons in their lobbies, even though nobody much was in the habit of chewing tobacco and spitting anymore.

Our King Edward hotel was typical. Everything was decrepit and minimal. But it had the merit of being cheap, four dollars a night for both of us, plus a refundable one-dollar deposit on the key. The man who took our money when we registered was missing his right hand (the war?); the light bulbs in the halls were forty watts and naked, dangling on their cords as if they had been torn down from the ceiling; the paint on the walls, replete with stains and spatters, was an ancient, uneven, charcoal green. The venetian blind on our room window was void of two of its slats, through which the neon hotel sign, missing its "*g Ed*," blinked *Kin- --ward*"; the brown-painted metal bed had a straw mattress which was covered with canvas stripped in grey; the pillows were pancake thick. After settling into our palace for the night, we walked down Main to the Hudson's Bay Company store, outside of which I felt a kind of nostalgia, after my year in Vancouver, almost as if I were at home there. We had dinner at a little restaurant called *Child's* and returned to the Kin- --ward Hotel and the luxury of a four-dollar night on a straw mattress. We had had a long day since leaving Moose Jaw and had come a long way, and we slept on that straw like dead men till eleven the following morning.

The Lonely Land Along Lake Superior

AFTER CHECKING OUT OF THE HOTEL, WE FOUND A BUS THAT TOOK US TO THE EASTERN EDGE OF THE CITY. IN NO TIME, WE WERE PICKED up by a tire salesman who was going all the way to Port Arthur, a good long ride. Another salesman. This one was a husky, somewhat rough-looking man—in a down-homey way—who looked to be about thirty-five years old. He wore a wide, thick moustache, unpopular at the time. (This type of moustache would be resurrected from the past in the 1960s and become for a time the thing to have.) He was not a very talkative man, except in regard to hockey, which he obviously loved. Our luck as hitchhikers had so far been phenomenal. We were beginning to think we couldn't miss, that all we had to do was stand by the roadside in our sports jackets, thumbs out, and wait to be picked up. It was a pleasant illusion while it lasted. What we didn't know was that our luck was running out and that our string of pick-ups by travelling salesmen who would take us over long distances would soon come to an end.

We were travelling through a wilderness of lakes, and on our right, for many miles, the oceanic hugeness of Lake Superior lapped at the shore. This is the land that A. J. M. Smith refers to in his poem, "The Lonely Land" (1936):

> This is a beauty
> of dissonance,
> this resonance
> of stony strand,
> this smoky cry
> curled over a black pine.

And much beauty there is. But it is the *same* beauty, mile after mile. In the end, it's boring. This fact is reflected in my journal for this leg of the journey; it is sparse to the point of being non-existent. It contains only the following entry: "To Port Arthur with a tire salesman." Not much information there to take us through these many miles of repeating beauty. But there is a novel, set in this area, Frederick Philip Grove's great *Master of the Mill* (1946), that will keep us amused as we roll along. It concerns a town in the future that is deserted except for an enormous, totally-automated, flour mill and the huge mansion of the mill owner, Senator Samuel Clark, who as an old man looks back over his life and the life of the town. Contrary to his wishes, and unable to prevent the incessant take-over of people's jobs by machines, he has watched the mill and the town go from a hive of workers and their families to the emptiness of a few maintenance people, as his world is caught up in the final stages of the industrial revolution.

> To many people, as the old man was aware, that mill stood as a symbol and monument of the world-order, which, by-and-large, was still dominant; of a ruthless capitalism which had once been an exploiter of human labor, making itself independent, ruling the country by its sheer power of producing wealth. . . . The amazing thing—incomprehensible to one who had seen different methods of production—was that that monstrous edifice was filled with machines only which had come to be by a logic of their own and which did man's bidding without man's help.

Grove sees here the end result of processes that have come to pass in many areas of industrialization in the sixty years since the novel was published. It is a fine novel and a much more interesting read than my journal for the day we travelled through that country featured in it. My journal for that day, in fact, remained unwritten, not only because there is not much to be said about the area we went through, but also because we found ourselves in a far more interesting situation when we arrived in Port Arthur at 10 p.m., and I abandoned an account of the "lonely land" and went right on to an account of the "sleazy land."

We Bottom Out in Sleaziness

THE TIRE SALESMAN LEFT US AT THE PORT ARTHUR GREYHOUND BUS DEPOT, WHICH CONSISTED OF A WAITING ROOM THAT WAS NEARLY deserted, a small café with a half dozen mushroom stools up against an arborite counter and a waitress in a modified maid's uniform with the name "Joan" embroidered over her left breast (Fifties joke: "What'd'ya call the other one"?), and a ticket office in which sat a tiny, dark-haired, middle-aged man who was countering his boredom by reading a copy of the *Toronto Star Weekly* and flipping a toothpick over and over, expertly, with his lips. He was consciously ignoring us.

> "You know where there's a cheap hotel," Bill asked.
>   The ticket man looked up from his paper, over his square reading glasses, a Harry Truman face, and the toothpick came to a stop, sticking vertically out of his lower lip like a scanty, over-grown incisor.
>   He shook his head. "Not much available. Fair's on." He returned his eyes to his paper and the toothpick resumed its rotation.
>   "Fair?" Bill asked.
>   "Town fair. Happens every year at this time."
>   "Anything'll do," Bill said, "s'long as it's cheap."
>   "Well," said the ticket man, taking the toothpick in his hand and pointing it over his shoulder, "if you're not too fussy about where you stay, you might try the Cozy Rooms, a block and a half that way."

We went in the direction he had pointed, out the door and around the back of the building, burdened as always by our suitcases. In the distance we could see the light dome made by the fair and hear the rumble of the rides and the noise of the fairgoers. At the back of the building, where it was dark, we disturbed two pairs of lovers. The first was a man and a woman making love up against the back wall. When we surprised them, she scrambled out of her panties, which were down over one ankle, and ran, her lover pursuing her, pulling with fumbling dexterity at the zipper of his trousers. The second pair of lovers was a couple of cats, who apparently considered their lovemaking an innocent enough occupation, and continuing their caterwauling, ignored us.

A block and a half down a summer street of dilapidated buildings, with widely-spaced streetlights, we came upon the Cozy Rooms, housed in a two-storey brick building with two stores at the street level, one a junk store, the other what seemed to be a kind of hardware-variety store, both with low-wattage night lights in their windows. Over the central door between the two stores was a light under a green, upside-down-basin-like shade; on the glass window of the door was painted in an amateur hand, *The Cozy Rooms*. Behind the glass we could see a small foyer, exactly the width of the worn wooden stairway with a railing on either side that climbed in twilight to the second floor.

We pushed open the squealing door with some trepidation, and climbing the stairs, found ourselves on a kind of landing. There was a small table, the surface of which was covered in stains from coffee mugs (and God knows what else!), and a dark green wooden kitchen chair, above which hung a single light bulb. The light, which was too high up to be reached from the floor, was operated by a chain which was made accessible by a piece of dirty white cord tied to the bottom of it. To the left and to the right, the hallway ran by the dark doors of the rooms, four or five at each end. The place felt as if it was completely deserted, like a warehouse that has been abandoned even by the rats and mice. There was not a sound to be heard from within the building. From a distance the rumble of the fair seeped into the dark hallway. We stood in silence, both of us feeling that we were perhaps making a mistake in staying in this place. But what choice did we have? It was already quite late, and the chance of finding somewhere else in a city we didn't know while a fair was in progress was pretty remote.

Outside, we could hear the muffled sounds of the town at play. We stood silently under the light, waiting for a reaction to our entry.

"Hello!" I said in something less than a shout. "Is there anybody here?"

Silence.

"Hello?" Bill shouted.

More silence.

Then: "Who the fuck's that?" from the room directly behind the table. We both looked up at the painted glass transept over the door, which opened inward at forty-five degrees.

"We're looking for a room," I shouted at the transept, trying to show more courage than I was feeling.

"Don't have any," the voice said.

"Anything'll do," Bill said.

"There ain't none."

"We'll pay double," I said, somewhat recklessly, though we were desperate, and double could not be much in a place like this.

Silence.

Bill and I grimaced at one another.

The door opened. A huge, balding man came out, wearing only his pants and an undershirt. His unfashionable handlebar moustache was grey at the edges, like his hair. He had neglected to do up his fly. He looked at us suspiciously. We were too classy to be in a place like this.

"How much can you pay?"

"How much are the rooms," I said.

"Regular eight dollars."

That had to be inflated. At least doubled.

"We'll give you ten," Bill said.

"Twelve."

"Eleven," Bill said.

"Twelve's as low as I can go. Take it or fuckin' leave it."

Bill and I nodded at each other. "We'll take it," we said together. The man put out his hand for the money, and we crossed his palm with twelve dollars.

"It's number three," he said, preceding us down the hallway. He opened the door, reached in and flicked on the naked ceiling light. Then he noticed his fly was open and reached down and zipped it up. "Coffin's open," he said, grinning. "Must have a stiff in there." Both of his incisors were gold.

The room contained two metal double beds. There was no other furniture. On the floor by one of them were a half dozen or so empty beer bottles and a cheap carpetbag out of which hung the sleeve of a shirt.

"Whose is that?" I said.

"It's the guy who rented that bed," the huge man said.

"You mean we're *sharing* the room!"

"Wha'd ya want for six bucks—the Ritz?"

"Twelve," Bill said.

"Yeah. Six each."

As soon as the man had gone, we went to bed; and in spite of this slough of seediness into which we had wandered, as usual, we fell asleep immediately, both of us once more exhausted. But in what seemed to be no time (it was, in fact, ten to three), I was awakened by noises in the hall. "This is some dump," I heard a woman slur, drunkenly. "It's better than the fuckin' bush," a male voice responded. "Not much," the woman said, giggling. Our roommates.

In they came. They turned on the 40-watt bulb, but only briefly, to remove their shoes and outer clothing. I watched secretly. They were both blind drunk. They paid no attention to us, as if they had expected the room to be shared. The man was short and slight and had out of control, balding, blonde hair. In his forties. In cowboy clothes. The woman was native, short, and fat, also in cowboy clothes, round everywhere: face, thorax, posterior. They put out the light and stumbled into bed. I heard their grunts and groans as they made love, or whatever it was they were doing.

In the morning, the room had the unmistakable Fifties beer-fart smell. A unique, awful smell: something like sulphur mixed with cabbage that has been boiled up in the skin of a skunk. It was a smell like no other.

Bill and I were both anxious to get out of this horrible olfactory factory. This feeling was compounded when I noticed with horror an old blood stain on the bottom sheet of the bed we had slept in. It was elliptical in shape, about a foot long. We both froze for a moment at the horror of having slept with it, and then we rushed like madmen to get out of there and away from it.

We washed in a hurry in the common bathroom down the hall: a single chipped and stained porcelain sink, a piece of broken mirror leaning on the back of it, a hook and eye lock on the door. We packed our bags and headed out. Neither of our roommates showed any sign of being awake, though the Indian woman—I could see now that she was probably still in her teens—rolled over and hugged the pillow, exposing a pudding-shaped breast as she did so, its gravity shifting like a rock in a sock. I felt no twinge of lechery: only sorrow, pain, and an enormous urge to get the hell out of this horror.

Stuck in the Bush on a Puritan Ontario Sunday

SUNDAY IN THE FIFTIES. THE LORD'S DAY ACT. YOU HAD TO HAVE LIVED THOSE SUNDAYS TO UNDERSTAND THEM. EVERYTHING WAS closed up as tight as a miser's pocketbook. All day. Even at amateur sports events, such as hockey or baseball games, admission could not be charged, so a "silver collection" was taken up—you'd have a hard time doing *that* with our debased modern coins—usually with a "suggested donation" of 25 or 50 cents. Hard-line Christians went looking for violations. (What else was there to do on Sunday?) The trouble with these Sundays for hitchhikers was that nobody was going anywhere, and those who were going somewhere already had company with them. Families tended to "go for a drive" on Sundays. (What else was there to do?) Worst of all for hitchhikers, there were no travelling salesmen travelling on Sundays.

So, you had to be ultra naïve to try to hitchhike on a Sunday, particularly to try to hitchhike from Fort William Montreal-ward in the vast emptiness of Northern Ontario in the summer of 1958. We were not only *naïve*, but we were also stupid, ignorant, and arrogant. We did not consider that there would be no commercial traffic on the roads. We did not think about the fact that everything in puritanical, Protestant Ontario would be shut. We did not know L. A. Mackay's verse, "Frankie Went Down to the Corner":

> Ontario's such a respectable place;
> Drinking's no crime, but it's still a disgrace,
> So hide us away behind curtain and screen
> While we stealthily go through the motions obscene
> In a manner genteel, correctly genteel,
> Secret and stuffy, but always genteel.

This piece of doggerel was written in 1936, but not much had changed by the Fifties. In the bliss of our ignorance of how things were, we headed out on to the highway once more. And at first our luck seemed to be continuing. We got an early ride of a few miles—fifteen or twenty—and throughout the day a couple more of about the same distance.

But by four o'clock, we were stranded at a crossroads in the middle of this vast Ontario wilderness, beside a general store and gas station which was allowed to open for a few hours on Sunday afternoon, presumably to take care of families who needed gas for their Sunday drives. There we were told that the CPR mainline was only a couple of miles from the crossroads corner, that there was a station there, and that an eastbound passenger train went through every evening. We were tired and depressed and afraid we might get stranded on the roadside overnight, so we decided to take the train as far as Sudbury, where we could continue hitchhiking the next day, Monday, a business day.

We discussed this plan and agreed upon it, as we hauled ourselves and our bags along the country road to the station. But when we got to the station, the chance to go all the way to Montreal by train and give up the hitchhiking became overwhelmingly attractive. So we bought tickets to Montreal, spending the night in the relative comfort of the day coach (no roommates, no fart smell, no blood), and arrived in Montreal the following morning.

"If cities have gender," Hugh MacLennan wrote in his essay, "City of Two Souls," in 1954, "then Montreal, the second-largest French speaking city in the world, is masculine in every one of the innumerable ways in which a self-confident and self-satisfied man can display his maleness." A few years later, the Quiet Revolution would occur in Quebec and all of that would change. The male confidence and self-satisfaction would be gone, replaced by a changing and changeable romantic French-speaking chauvinism. MacLennan seems to express the difference in his 1967 novel, *Return of the Sphinx*, in which one of the characters says, "Don't forget—*la belle province* is a woman." Male or female, our Montreal was merely a waiting place for the coming in of our ship. Our minds were on Europe, and the voyage to get there, and although we did some of the tourist things the city had to offer, I didn't bother to write about them in my journal. Our hearts and minds were on the future.

ACROSS THE ATLANTIC ON THE SS HOMERIC

WHEN WE WENT ABOARD THE *HOMERIC* ON AUGUST 18, WE WERE EXCITED AND IMPRESSED, NEITHER OF US HAVING PREVIOUSLY BEEN ON ANYTHING MUCH LARGER THAN A ROWBOAT. BOUND for Southampton and Calais on a regular eight-day Atlantic crossing, the *Homeric* seemed huge to us, though she was for the time more or less mid-sized, about 26,000 tons. She was the flagship of the Home Lines, and although she was owned in Greece and had an Italian crew, she was, like a lot of other vessels both then and now, registered in Panama, where the regulations are looser than they are in Europe or the Americas.[3]

Waiting for me inside Cabin A-84, which was located about half-way into the bowels of the ship, was a letter from Walter Grant, one of my fellow workers in the Display Department at the Bay in Vancouver. It begins with the incredible sentence: "Utter utter blissikins to hear from you, old thing." I'm not sure what prompted this letter, let alone its incredible opening. I must have sent Walter one of the half-dozen or so postcards I mailed to friends at the Bay as Bill and I crossed Canada. Walter, as even a casual glance would tell you, could not have been anything but "gay" (though the word was not then used in this context); but like most of his "kind" (*pace* Christopher Isherwood), he remained firmly in the closet, as did the rest of his colleagues in the Department, a smart thing to do in the repressive Fifties. He never made any kind of a pass at me. My interest in the girls in the Department was obvious. In his letter, Walter even refers to my Departmental love-interest—"Margaret sends her love."—so I can only think he somehow hoped that I was bisexual. I did not respond to Walter's letter. Not for any negative reason. I just never got around to it, busily exploring a new world. As is the case in so many other short-term acquaintanceships and friendships, the glue that bonded us together had not set enough for it to matter. I never heard from him again.

> *We threw our bags inside our cabin—there was plenty of time to deal with those later—and immediately went off to explore our Second Class section: the decks, the lounges, the dining room, the gymnasium, the swimming pool, the movie theatre, the nightclub—the whole wonderful world. It was almost beyond excitement to be aboard this ship, as if we were the principle actors in our own personal movie, an intriguingly unscripted one, with the future a blur of delicious anticipation.*
>
> *Just after 11 a.m., two tugs pulled us away from the dock at Shed #6, at the foot of St. François Xavier Street. We joined the crowds at the rails, some of whom shot out the traditional coloured streamers, the final tactile connection between friends and relatives. This celebrating was as it should be. But we were disappointed that there was no band playing on the dock. There was always a band in Hollywood ship departures.*

---

[3] The *Homeric* was launched by the Matson Line in 1931 as the *Mariposa*. She sailed on a Pacific route until the war, when she was used as a troop transport. The Home Lines rebuilt her in 1953 for use on the North Atlantic. In 1964, she became a Caribbean cruise ship. After a fire in 1973, she was scrapped.

We did not know that we were participants in a scene from the end of an era. Earlier in the summer, Bill and I had gone to Sea Island Airport (now Vancouver International) to have a look at a new jet airliner, the Boeing 707, which was on display there for a few hours. This aircraft marked the beginning-of-the-end of regular-service ocean liners on the Atlantic between North America and Europe. I would travel twice more to Europe by sea on regular-scheduled liners, the *Empress of England* and the *Empress of Britain*, both new Canadian Pacific ships. Their tenure would be short-lived. From 1965 onward, only seven years after sailing on the *Homeric*, when I went to Europe, I flew. By then, most of the liners had been rerouted to cruising, or scrapped. Only a few—like the *Queen Elizabeth II*, which developed a clientele on snob-appeal that kept it going for awhile on the North Atlantic, and the Polish *Stefan Batory*, which catered to those for whom snob-appeal was too expensive—struggled on more or less in the old way.

For the first two days, as we sailed along the sheltered St. Lawrence and its gulf, crowds of passengers took part in the onboard activities. In the mornings, on the open decks, there was trap shooting (aft) and shuffleboard (fore). In the afternoons, at 2:15, there was a movie: the eminently forgettable *The Law and Jake Wade* played on the 21st. Contract Bridge get-togethers began at 2:30. Bill and I played most days, and lost every single day, not because we played badly, but because we had terrible cards, day after day, incessantly. There were prizes, but, unfortunately, no booby prize, which we certainly would have won.

At 4:15, there was high tea in the main lounge, with the Corradi-Rosignoli Orchestra providing a background of light classics. This was followed by a horseracing game that was played with dice and toy horses that were moved along a canvas racetrack by a white-coated steward. Each night, beginning at 9:30, there was a costume dance in the main lounge, arranged around a theme that changed every day. For Apache Night, for example, the daily program gave the following hints for dressing up: "Men: turtle necks—check your guns and chewing gum—Girls: short skirts, blouses, pullovers, berets, caps." Help with costumes was available at the Purser's. But we ignored the costume shtick, as did many others, and donned our usual jackets and ties. I mean, what had all this to do with Apaches? At midnight, part of the Corradi-Rosignoli band moved to the "Taverna," the tiny nightclub tucked into the bowels of the ship, where the dance continued for the small number who still wanted to party. In all of these venues the drinks were cheap—genuinely duty-free in those more honest times—fifteen cents, for example, for a rum and coke.

On the third day out, the atmosphere aboard ship suddenly changed. When Bill and I went into the dining room for breakfast that morning, it was largely empty. During the night, we had left the sheltered waters of the Gulf of St. Lawrence and entered the North Atlantic. The ship had begun to roll and pitch, gently, but perceptibly. For the next few days, many passengers were seasick. Numbers entering the dining room for meals waxed and waned, but they were usually pretty light. Some arrived for a meal, took a jaundiced look at the food, and abruptly ran for the door. But as the days went by, there was a steady improvement. Attendance at meals increased from about one-third to two-thirds as people's systems got used to the movement of the ship and they got their sea-legs. Bill and I were both good sailors—you don't get a choice: you are or you aren't.

The Possibility of an Onboard Romance

ONE OF THE CLICHES OF TRAVELLING ON AN OCEAN LINER, NEVER ABSENT IN CINEMATIC VERSIONS, IS THE SHIPBOARD ROMANCE. Although one always hoped to be lucky enough to find a partner to dance with and kiss and cuddle on the after-deck, one did not expect there would be more than this preliminary peripheral sex involved in the relationship. Romance was a bud that usually flowered in the short time available at sea, and then wilted and died when land was reached. Girls guarded their reputations, as public norms of sexual conduct were still highly restrictive in the Fifties. But it wasn't only a matter of reputation. Their attitude was not as prudish as it may seem today to be. It is easy to look back on that decade from the distance of a half century, as John Banville does in *The Untouchable* (1997) and get things not quite right:

> Everyone nowadays disparages the 1950s, saying what a dreary decade it was—and they are right, if you think of McCarthyism, and Korea, the Hungarian rebellion, all that serious historical stuff; I suspect, however, that it is not public but private affairs that people are complaining of. Quite simply, I think they did not get enough sex.

But getting enough sex was a perilous situation. These were pre-pill times, when choosing "to go all the way" mechanically unprotected was fraught with peril. Condoms, usually called "French safes," or just "safes," were, of course available. (Joke from the Fifties: *Question*: How do they know that Napoleon was in the army?' *Answer*: "They found his discharge in an old French safe.") But the world of condoms was veiled in the same fog of hypocrisy that surrounded everything else of a sexual nature.

Besides, condoms, as anyone who has used them knows, are pretty unsatisfactory, diminishers rather than enhancers of pleasure. So there was a tendency (still among us, even in our own enlightened days) to avoid their use and "take a chance"—to play a game of sexual roulette with a gun loaded in all six chambers. Yet in spite of the many drawbacks and the theories put forth by John Banville and others, those of us who lived the decade know that there was plenty of sex in the Fifties. There always is. Most girls were eventually willing, in a sustained relationship, to go along with anything short of penetration. And those that broke that rule, often found themselves standing at the altar rail (if they were lucky) with a thickening waist, going forward into marriage as the only socially acceptable option. If they were unlucky, and they couldn't or wouldn't marry their partner (or someone else who was willing), they went off to a relative in a distant city to "work" or "study": i.e., to have the baby and give it up for adoption. Keeping and raising the baby as a single mother was not an option. A backroom abortion, the other alternative, was not only highly dangerous, but also difficult to arrange, though it was chosen by some. Any of these alternatives could, and often did, lead to life-long trauma.

It is a fact that is often ignored that without the invention of the birth-control pill the sexual revolution of the Sixties would never have happened. The pill was developed by a conservative American Catholic, John Rock, who saw it as a "natural" method of birth control that the Church could adopt. When Pope Paul VI's 1968 encyclical, *Humanae Vitae*, banned its use, Rock, who had for years been a daily attendant at Mass, left the Church. Unlike St. Peter, he was not a rock upon which the Church was built.

My Shipboard Romance: Denise Duval

BILL AND I KNEW THAT LEGEND HAD IT THAT THE NORMS OF SEXUAL CONDUCT ARE MUCH RELAXED IN A SHIPBOARD ROMANCE. IT IS, after all, an unreal, temporary world and a good opportunity for an adventure that should not affect the rest of one's life. We were lusty young men who wanted to believe the legend, and we were looking forward with eagerness to the possibility of a whirlwind romance. For awhile, it looked as if we were not going to have any luck. You can't really create a romance; it either happens or it doesn't. So it was with great relief that on our third day out we met two girls from La Sarre, Quebec, Denise Duval, who became my shipboard romance, and Lise Baril, who was Bill's. Denise, at 24, was accompanying Lise, she said, as a kind of older and wiser guardian. Lise was a mere 21. More to the point, I think, was the fact that Lise was so gorgeous that she attracted men as honey attracts bees, and the wisdom in La Sarre was that she needed a chaperone. This sort of arrangement was not that unusual in the thoroughly Catholic Quebec of the time. And these were thoroughly Catholic girls.

Bill was a kind of male counterpart to Lise, exceptionally handsome in a Richard Chamberlain sort of way. Women vied for his attention. The best-looking girl was always his for the taking. That left me with the other one. Denise was not gorgeous, but she was pretty enough; and as the days went by and Lise revealed the ditzy side of her nature, I was glad I had a companion I could talk to, especially through the long night when we sat up in the lounge (as they do in the movies) waiting for the dawn. A cold and foggy disappointment, as it turned out, on the North Atlantic. (I'm rationalizing. If I'd had a chance to be with Lise instead of Denise, in spite of her ditzyness, I'd have taken the young man's route and jumped at it. And her!) When we said our good-byes at Southampton, Denise and I vowed to meet again in a few weeks in Barcelona, even though we both knew it probably wouldn't happen.

It didn't. But we kept in sporadic contact at American Express offices around Europe, and we did meet again for a few days in London the following January, when Denise contacted me at the hostel in which I was living and came to stay there for a few days on her way back to Canada. But that is another story that will be told in another chapter.

OFF TO EUROPE

Hitchhiking Across
    Canada
        by Rail & Road

Incredible Dawn in the Rockies

The Prairies

The Lonely Land

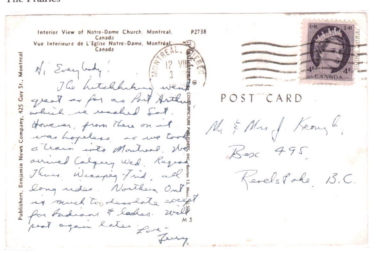

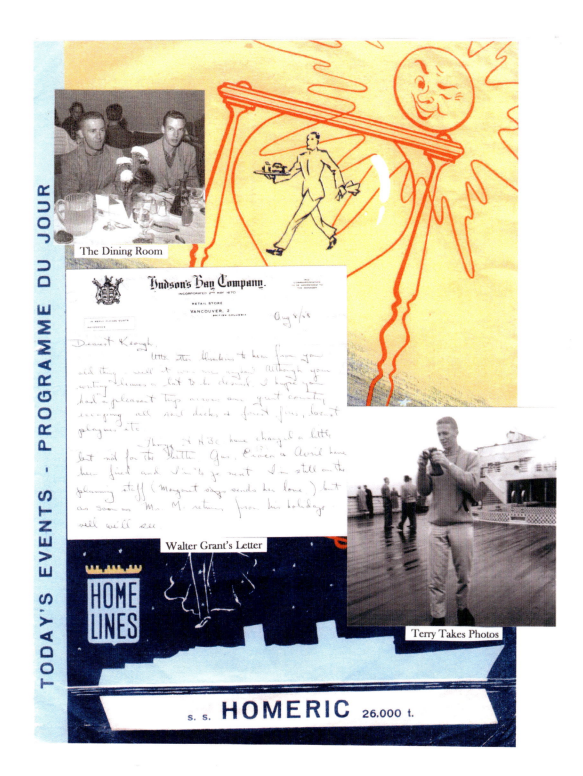

S.S. Homeric

Tugging Out in Montreal

The Stern on the St. Laurence

Terry and Bill at Lunch

Lunch Menu

Terry and Bill relax in Cabin A-84

Denise and Terry: outside the Taverna and sailing by the Isle of Wight

First Night in London

Has Earth any thing to show more fair?

Chapter 6: Europe on a Moto Guzzi Cardellino

A CONTINENTAL JOURNEY

"It's a beautiful thing to refuse to forget," she said after a few moments.
He made a helpless gesture, implying that no one can choose his memories.
"I'm not sure that *beautiful* is the right word," he said, indicating the walls covered with works. "Sometimes I feel as if I were a cemetery. It's a very similar feeling, all symbols and silence." He considered what he had just said and smiled sadly. "The silence of all the ghosts that you've left behind you. Like Aeneas fleeing Troy."
Arturo Pérez-Reverte, **The Fencing Master** [Maestro de esgrima, 1988] Trans. by Margaret Jull Costa, 1999

"When I came to this great city," an African traveler wrote, "I looked this way and that way; there is no beginning and no end."
Peter Ackroyd, **London: The Biography**, 2000

London: You Rub Your Eyes and Wonder[1]

AT SOUTHAMPTON WE LEFT THE *HOMERIC*, WHICH WAS GOING ON TO CALAIS WITH OUR TWO TEMPORARY QUEBEÇOISE GIRLFRIENDS, AND took the boat train to London. I was fascinated by the hundreds of chimneys, sticking up in multiples on the roofs of the red brick row houses that sprouted like clusters of urban mushrooms along the route. And by the profound green of the rolling Sussex countryside. It was 10 p.m. by the time we arrived at Waterloo Station. We walked out of the station into a warm, still-light summer night, into the capital of the quickly-diminishing empire under which we'd grown up, bags in hand, with no reservations, no plan as to where we were to spend the night, no guide books, no maps. Only the young and the foolish would have arrived that way. And we were both.

---

[1] Walter Bell wrote these words in a report for the London Topographical Society in 1928: "You rub your eyes and wonder. Can this really be the City—this hidden place, where people live their lives, and tend their flowers, and die?"

A middle-aged man, seeing us standing bewildered on the steps under the large Doric pillars in front of the main entrance to the station, came over and kindly asked if we needed any help. It never occurred to us to question his motives, which may have been just as well, as he had none other than to offer some help. We asked if there was a hotel in the area, and he offered to take us to The York, a small, run-down, but respectable-enough place on Waterloo road. "If you cross the river," he said, "it'll cost each of you at least thirty bob for the night." (About $5—at that time the pound was worth around three Canadian dollars.) At the York, room with a bath was eighteen shillings apiece. The hotel was old, dark and Dickensian—in other words, perfect. When we entered Room 16, one floor up, we looked for the promised bath. Not there. We returned to the desk and inquired. "Your bath will be brought to you in the morning at seven," the clerk said. And so it was: a jug of hot water and two white towels. It was the first and last time in my life that I used a Victorian bedroom wash stand. I considered it a great beginning to my time in London.

Even this early in our excursion, however, I was beginning to be concerned about my money supply. In my year at the Hudson's Bay store I had saved about $1,000. Passage on the *Homeric* had cost $190. Then there was the month in Revelstoke, where, even though I was living at home for nothing, I went through about $60 on incidentals. The journey across Canada had cost another $50 or so; and on the ship I had spent about $40. So when we arrived in London, I had about $650 left. I had always planned to tour at the beginning of my time in Europe, and when the money supply got low, to look for a job. I thought I could probably find work teaching English as a Second Language in Spain, and I planned to canvass the language schools when I arrived in Madrid. If that didn't work out, I expected I could find a teaching job in England, where at that time there was a growing shortage of teachers and there were no bars against Commonwealth citizens working. At the rate I was going through my stash of money, I began to realize that I would have to look for work sooner than I had expected. In the meantime, I would have to be very careful in my spending.

The Hostel at 19 Cross Street, Islington

ONE OF THE WAYS IN WHICH WE PLANNED TO ECONOMIZE WAS TO STAY IN YOUTH HOSTELS. SO WE JOINED THE INTERNATIONAL Youth Hostel association, and bought sleeping bags and the sheet sleeping bags one was required to use to enclose them. We tried (heavy Gladstone bags in hand, and on the buses, of course) to get into the George VI hostel in Kensington, but it was full. There they told us about a place in Islington called the Student Society Hostel, where we could stay for more than the four days allowed at association hostels. It cost seven shillings a night. Bags in hand (what a burden they were!), we boarded the Number 15 bus, and got off, as instructed, at the Angel. The Angel was once a pub which stood for hundreds of years in a y-split between Essex Road and Upper Street in Islington, just north-east of the centre of London. It has been there a long time, since before the Great Plague, in fact. Dickens mentioned it in *Oliver Twist*, and Anthony Trollope referred to it in his 1882 novel, *Marion Fay*: "They had a little more whisky and water at the Angel in Islington before they got into the cab which was to take them down to the Paphian Music Hall."

George Orwell in 1945 described the area around the Angel as one of "vague, brown-coloured slums . . . a cobbled street of two-storey houses with battered doorways which gave straight on the pavement and which were somehow curiously suggestive of rat-holes." Not much had changed when Bill and I arrived there in August 1958. The building that had housed the Angel still stood, but had become a Lyons Corner House, about the only place in the area that served an acceptable cup of coffee.[2]

Bill and I walked along Upper Street to Cross Street, which bridges the short distance between Upper Street and Essex Road. The Student Society Hostel, at Number 19, was part of a three-storey terrace along the south side of the street. There, we shared a room with two Germans, an English fellow, and a diminutive, weird American from New York, who spent a couple of hours each afternoon pacing on Cross Street in a black, ankle-reaching raincoat, reading Jaroslav Hasek's *The Good Soldier Schwiek*. He was going up to Cambridge in September. I had never heard of this wonderful spoof of war. I did read and enjoy it when I returned to London later that year. And when eventually I got around to reading its Canadian equivalent, Earle Birney's comic war-novel, *Turvey*, it was immediately obvious how Birney owed to it. Too much, perhaps. If you wonder why this literature is relevant to my story, read on.

> *Flash ahead two months. I'm back in London and back at the Cross Street Hostel, alone and lonely, after having toured the continent. Just about every day, I go to either a play or a concert. One afternoon, while I was sitting in the "gods" at the Apollo on Shaftsbury Avenue at a performance of Christopher Fry's translation of Jean Giraudoux's Duel of Angels, starring Vivien Leigh and Claire Bloom, a young woman sat beside me. We both instantly realized that we recognized one another. It turned out that she had also worked in the Bay store in Vancouver, though we had not known one another there. "Do you know Earle Birney's novel, Turvey?" she asked. "It's our name he used. He and my dad both taught at UBC." I was ashamed to tell her that I had not read the novel, but I didn't feel under the circumstances that I could pretend to have read it and get away with it. I would have liked to have asked her to go for an after-theatre coffee, but I felt too much intimidated by her even to try. So I watched Liz Turvey walk out of the theatre ahead of me, never to be seen again. I returned to my room in Islington, a room shared with strangers, with a heavy spirit.*

We Sample 1950s British Cuisine

IN THE MORNINGS, WE HAD BREAKFAST AROUND THE CORNER AT THE ESSEX CAFÉ, JUST OFF ESSEX STREET, BY THE BUS STOP FROM THE

---

[2] The building now has a Co-operative Bank where the pub used to be. A modern pub, which calls itself The Angel, is in a building next door to the original. The area is vastly changed since Bill and I arrived there in 1958. Islington began to be desirable once again in the 1960s. Returning there in 2007, I found the whole area massively gentrified, the houses tarted up and expensive, and Upper Street and Essex Road probably having more bars and restaurants than any part of London outside the West End.

West End, the only café or restaurant in the area. It was typical of lower-class English cafés of the period: grubby, cheap, dirty-looking and dirty. It was small, a hole in the wall, really, with room for no more than half a dozen people. The furnishings were rudimentary—crude wooden chairs placed around three tables covered in garishly-patterned oilcloth. Breakfasts weren't too bad, if you like fried eggs dripping in grease. But the lunch and dinner food was awful: meat and two veg; greasy steak (i.e., a small piece of leather-like material that might have been cut from the saddle); greasy chips; "processed" peas—out of a can, like washed-out pellets of green dough, indescribable to anyone who has not tasted them—and so on. British cuisine was living up to its reputation. The tea was good, but always served by the cup (usually chipped), and always having added to it two heaping teaspoons of sugar and what seemed to be a gallon of milk. We learned quickly in establishments like the Essex Café to say, "No sugar, please, and only a little milk," but often we were not fast enough, especially in the Lyon's Tea Houses that were all over London at that time—one at the corner by The Angel tube station—where they could bang out a cup of tea from a great steaming urn before you could say, "No sugar, please, and . . . damn! Too late!" (Whatever happened to the Lyon's Tea Houses?)

At the Essex Café there was no coffee. When you asked for coffee, they served you a cup of brown liquid called "Camp Coffee," which was made from a syrup that came in a Worcester-sauce-size bottle and consisted mainly of chicory essence.[3] It tastes like brown bricks dissolved in Buckley's Mixture, and it looks like the juice excreted by grasshoppers when you hold them in your hand and say, "Spit tobacco!" I'm not sure which end of the grasshopper spits.

Ladies Fair and Foul

AFTER GETTING ESTABLISHED AT THE CROSS STREET HOSTEL AND GETTING OUR VISAS FOR SPAIN, WE BEGAN TO VISIT THE USUAL LONDON tourist sites: Westminster Abbey, the Tower of London, Oxford Street, Harrods, and the main museums and galleries. In the evenings we went to the theatre. The first piece we saw was a revival of *Where's Charley*, with Norman Wisdom splayed romantically on the floor, picked out by a spotlight on an otherwise darkened stage, belting out "Once in Love with Amy,"—I was greatly impressed. But the highlight of our theatre-going was *My Fair Lady*, with Rex Harrison and Julie Andrews, at Drury Lane in Holborn, a part of London that I would work in daily four years later. We bought scalper's tickets for this show, paying, for seats in the "gods," 15 shillings for 5-shilling tickets. What you did was go to the entrance to the theatre, where people shook a purse full of money to indicate that they had tickets to sell. Later, we learned that there were counterfeit tickets being scalped for this immensely popular musical. We were lucky to get the genuine item.

---

[3] Even today, you can buy a bottle of this stuff. I understand, amazing as it may seem, that there are people who *like* it. It apparently originated with the British army in India, a fact that is reflected on its label design. It remains another vestige of the empire on which the sun never set.

One evening, we ran into a couple of hookers, who tried to pick us up at the Wimpey's hamburger place on Shaftsbury Avenue, right next to Piccadilly Circus. In those days hookers hung out in a highly visible way on the streets of Soho, confidently and openly displaying their charms. Occasionally, they were arrested, appeared in court the following morning, and paid a standard fine of two pounds. This happened often enough that the magistrates knew many of them by their first names. (At least, that was the reason the *magistrates* gave. The fact that some of the girls knew the magistrates by their first names might lead one to more insidious conclusions.) The system worked well and was probably safer for the girls than it would become a couple of years later when new laws were passed, driving them underground. The girls approached us because we were obviously tourists, wearing silver maple leaf pins on our lapels—mainly to show we were not Americans, who, we had been told, were generally disliked in Europe. (The fact that we had to wear a pin to show we were not Americans is telling.) One of the girls had a nasty-looking sore on her chin. The security man at the Wimpey's shooed us away. The girls tried to convince us to go with them to a "neat club" off Shaftsbury Avenue. The situation looked dangerous, so we decided not to go. Later, we felt a trifle disappointed at being so timid. We rationalized our timidity by agreeing that we would have gone with the girls if only one of them hadn't had a sore on her chin. But I think Bill would have gone with them if I hadn't been there. I was the stick in the mud.

Brussels and the 1958 World's Fair

ON AUGUST 29, WE BOARDED A TRAIN AT VICTORIA STATION FOR DOVER, WHERE WE WENT ABOARD A FERRY FOR OSTEND, EN ROUTE to Brussels and the World's Fair. It was a warm summer night, so we stayed out on deck. It was crowded, and neither of us managed to get one of the many chaise longue chairs that were scattered here and there about the deck to stretch out on. These chairs were almost as good as having a bed, and the experienced cross-channel travelers had occupied them as soon as they got on board. The alternative was to try to get comfortable on the deck. Pillowed against our luggage, we soon discovered how hard a deck can be. . Around midnight, we put our heads together as to what we could do to get through what remained of the night more comfortably. We decided to hop over the ribbon of rope that was the only barrier separating the peasants from the First Class section, where it was not crowded, and spent the rest of the night comfortably dozing on first-class lounge chairs, which had the advantage of being padded. We put our plan into operation. Stealthily, we wound our way around sleeping bodies, luggage raised high to avoid a collision with those privileged to be in deck chairs, careful not to cause a ruckus by bumping into somebody in the semi-dark and draw the attention of the crew. As it turned out, nobody challenged us, and we spent the rest of the night in relative comfort. Early in the morning, before the ship docked, we returned to our rightful area.

As the train to Brussels, third class, had slatted, wooden seats, which were horribly uncomfortable, we were glad it was not a long journey. In Brussels, we found out that the youth hostel didn't open until 4 p.m., so we left our bags in lockers at the station. Before going to the Fair, we paid five francs to shave and clean up in the station bathroom.

> *The bathroom for hommes was a fairly large, rectangular room, with toilet stalls on one side, a row of sinks at one end, and a bank of urinals on a raised platform at the other. We were surprised and somewhat disconcerted to see a middle-aged woman seated at a small table near the door, only about ten feet from the urinals, knitting. She was responsible for keeping the place clean. As we washed up at the other end of the room, we kept glancing in the mirror as her regulars strode in with a "Bonjour, Madame!" unbuttoned their trousers and fired away at the urinal. Often they would chat with the woman as they peed. On the way out, they would drop a coin into the ceramic dish on her table. We knew we could avoid this scene by going into a stall to pee, but that would be a cowardly thing to do. "Let's have a go," I said to Bill, when we had finished washing up. So, holding our shaving kits in one hand and unzipping our trousers with the other, we strolled nonchalantly up to the urinals, and—admittedly, after some hesitation—managed to do the deed. On the way out, we each, like regulars, dropped a coin with a satisfying clink into the woman's ceramic dish.*

On the way to the Fair, we passed the world-famous Mannekinpis fountain. (There was no woman knitting beside *him*!) In his red coat and hat, and black trousers, this statue of a young boy looked ever so much like a redcap peeing on the front entrance of a hotel. It's interesting to recall that in the regressively enlightened world of the 1950s, cards sent to Canada depicting this fountain were confiscated by the Post Office as obscene.

At the Fair, we walked and walked and walked. That's what you do at world's fairs. (I went to another one in Montreal in 1967, so see myself as something of an expert in this area.) We visited the Canadian, American, and Russian pavilions. We put coins in a machine that massaged your feet for two or three minutes, a blesséd but very temporary relief. We looked in awe at the Atomium, whose silver balls and struts hung in the air as symbols of the nuclear age, harbingers of what was seen in those days as a new beginning for mankind, a misguided beginning, as it turned out. This molecular model seemed to me to be not so much a futuristic structure as the kind of meaningless "thing" I used to build when I played with tinker-toys.

With no sleep to speak of the night before, and no rest all this day, we were exhausted. We were discovering what hard work this touring business can be. And, with the World's Fair on, Brussels was *so* expensive. So, when we went to the station to retrieve our bags, we decided to take the train, which was leaving at 11 p.m., to Milan, where we would be able to buy Vespas or Lambrettas, or some other kind of motorcycle. Anything to cut down on the walking! Our third-class rail tickets on the overnight train cost 817 francs each. The train was crowded, but we did manage to find space in one of the compartments on the typical straight-up, padded bench seats in European trains of that era, which seated four people in a row on each side. Everyone did his best to sleep sitting up, but heads all around inevitably fell on to the shoulders of strangers, accompanied (if the head woke up) by profuse apologies—in what was probably a foreign language.

We changed trains in Basel and arrived in Milan at 2 p.m. We went to the youth hostel, which opened at four, and when we got in, went straight to bed. After two virtually sleepless nights (not to mention a day of hard sightseeing at the World's Fair), both of us slept solidly for twelve hours. We woke up to a sleepy Sunday in this northern Italian industrial city. We spent the morning at or near the Duomo, and the rest of the day orienting ourselves to the main business district. Late in the afternoon, we returned to the youth hostel with sausage, bread, and bottles of sterilized milk (which we disliked); and after supper, we went to bed for another long night's sleep.

Milan and the World of Moto Guzzi

IT WAS MONDAY, SEPTEMBER 1—LABOUR DAY AND A HOLIDAY AT HOME—AND IN MILAN, THE BUSINESS WORLD WAS HUMMING. WE went forth in search of motor scooters, but the cheapest, the Lambretta, was at $300 beyond our price range. So we settled on the Moto Guzzi "Cardellino", named for its dashing red color, as brilliant as a Prince of the Church, but, unfortunately, much less powerful, which cost the more affordable lira equivalent of $113. These bikes were shaped like motorcycles rather than scooters, but with engines that produced only 73 cc, they were designed for short trips in an urban setting rather than for touring around Europe. We knew this. But they were all we could afford.

> *V. S. Naipaul, that inveterate 20th-century traveler, in Finding the Centre, wrote, "I travel to discover other states of mind." While perusing other people's ways of thinking may be part of the reason for all journeys into areas unknown to the individual, it does not take into account a far more important reason to travel: to discover one's own state of mind. By the time Bill and I had arrived in Milan and checked out the motor scooter world, I had reached two conclusions vis-à-vis my own mental condition. First, that travel was hard work and unremittingly tiring; and second, that it led to an inevitable series of disappointments. As we were young and full of energy, the hard work and fatigue were easily dealt with—a good night's sleep always refreshed us. But it was more difficult to put aside the disappointments: the known sites we had looked forward to which seemed mundane in the flesh; the places we had wanted to see, but for whatever reason were not able to get to; the difficulties involved in trying to stretch out limited money, such as having to buy underpowered motorcycles; and the problems of choice in everyday eating and sleeping, of the weather not co-operating, and of loneliness. But on looking back on this venture, I realize that the disappointments were what made me a stronger person in the long run and gave me a legacy I was able to carry with me throughout life.*

Buying the bikes, we soon discovered, was not going to be easy. First of all, we had to go to a police station and get a three-month resident permit. Then we had to join the Automobile Club d'Italia, Milano branch. After that, we had to get permission from our consulate to make the purchase. As there was no Canadian consulate in Milan, we went to the British consulate, as our passports directed us to do in these circumstances. (The passports in those days still contained the statement: "A Canadian citizen is a British Subject.") There, a bored and arrogant male secretary listened to us colonials in a condescending way before providing us with the necessary form.

On Wednesday, forms in hand, we went back to Moto Guzzi and bought the bikes. The young, chunky, Italian girl we were dealing with, who spoke excellent English, said the bikes would not be available till the following Monday, so she suggested that in the meantime we might like to go to Como, in the lake district north of the city. We took the train there, stayed at the youth hostel, and tried to keep busy as tourists, though we were distracted by the delicious prospect of finally getting our motorcycles and heading out on our tour of Europe.

> *I bought a copy of H. E. Bates' Fair Stood the Wind for France, a propaganda novel from the Second World War, the only light novel in English I could find in a local bookstore. I enjoyed its exciting story of the Résistance. It was a perfect time-waster. When we were not reading, we walked by the lake. One day, we were strolling in a park that contains the Volta Museum (Count Alessandro 1745-1847, inventor of the electric battery, from whose name the word "volt" was coined). Near a building where there were public toilets, we were pursued by a middle-aged woman in the black dress of a widow, with a roll of toilet paper in her outstretched hand, shouting "Gabinetto! Gabinetto!" What a way to make a living! We didn't need a Gabinetto, but she may have been desperate for some money, and if we had been more sensitive, we would have given her some.*

The Last Supper and the Italian Gran Prix

ON SATURDAY, WE RETURNED TO MILAN, WHERE WE WENT TO THE REFECTORY OF STA MARIA DELLE GRAZIE TO SEE LEONARDO DA Vinci's ultra-famous mural, *The Last Supper* (1495-98), which had been restored (apparently badly—but we didn't know that) after being extensively damaged in a bombing raid in 1943. It was the beginning of my interest in the history of art, an interest I pursued in an amateurish way in the various cities I visited throughout Europe over the next couple of years.

The Italian Grand Prix was being run on that Sunday at Monza, a village not far from Milan, and we went to it with some keen Australians we had met in the hostel. I found it a crushing (not *crashing*) bore. Zoom, zoom, went the cars. Zoom, zoom. Afterwards, we lined up to get a bus back to Milan. Eventually, an articulated bus arrived, two buses joined in the middle, like a two-car train. It was the first of these I'd seen. The line of people waiting for the bus, which up to that time had been polite and orderly, dissolved into a rabble of noisy Italians trying to get on to the bus ahead of other noisy Italians. The line disintegrated, as everyone broke for the doors. Elbows flew. It was every man for himself. For a moment we stood back in amazement. Then, like everybody else, we made a dash for it, pushing our way aboard in our own leg-race version of the Italian Grand Prix. When in Rome, do as the Romans do.

We were disappointed when we returned to Moto Guzzi to pick up our bikes on Monday morning, when they told us they would not be ready until Wednesday. We were beginning to learn about the way things happened (and didn't happen) in Italy, so we were not at all confident that they'd be ready even then. But they were. A couple of mechanics took us to a park, where they showed us how to ride the bikes. We practiced for awhile, amid hurricanes of mechanical laughter (so to speak), and then returned on our bikes, through the traffic of Milan, to the hostel to pick up our bags. There was no way that we could tie our pigskin Gladstone bags on the carriers at the back of our bikes, so we bought canvas duffel bags, transferred our things into them, and threw the Gladstones behind a bush in the park. (Goodbye Gladstones!) In the early afternoon, we headed for Genoa, essentially unpracticed, totally unprotected (no riding gear, no helmets, no gloves, no boots), and completely incapable at twenty-three of considering that we could wind up with broken bones in the middle of an Italian road.

Along the Riviera at 50 kms Per Hour

Bill Disappears Briefly

AFTER TRAVELLING FOR SOME TIME ON THE AUTOSTRADA, WHICH IN THOSE DAYS WAS NOT VERY BUSY, BUT STILL NOT SUITED TO vehicles that hummed along at a minuscule 50 kms per hour, we branched off on to a secondary road and stopped to consult our maps. We were in rolling countryside. At the spot we stopped and pulled off, there were two or three houses that hugged the narrow, deserted road. Out of these came a half dozen or so curious locals, adults, kids, and dogs, who hung around looking at us. We smiled at them and they smiled at us, but as we had no language in common, that was as far as our communications could go.

> *When Bill and I had worked out where we were going, he started off ahead of me. I was busy trying to stuff my map into my duffel bag, so I didn't see what happened next. Suddenly, the locals were rushing at me, exclaiming and pointing down the road. I looked in the direction of the waving hands. Bill was nowhere to be seen. There was nothing in the direction he had gone but the road. Then, on the left-hand side, a head with a massive grin appeared over the edge of the embankment. Bill had hit the accelerator when he had meant to hit the brakes, lost control, roared across the road, and shot over the bank. As the grin indicated, he had not hurt himself. Nor had his bike been damaged. The area he fell into was, luckily, soft country soil. All of us by this time were having a good laugh, Bill, me, the locals, and the dogs. I didn't know then that the next day it would be my turn to make the same mistake—with not such a happy outcome.*

That night we slept in a field at the side of the road, and I rolled over on my sunglasses and shattered them. I didn't feel I could afford to replace them. This was the first of many problems I would encounter over the next few weeks.

I Come a Cropper in Genoa

IN GENOA, WE STAYED AT THE YOUTH HOSTEL, A FINE OLD CASTLE-LIKE BUILDING ON THE EASTERN EDGE OF THE CITY, ACROSS A BUSY STREET from the sea. There was a good beach that was surrounded by large rocks. The water was clear and vibrantly blue. We were told that pollution was a major problem in the whole of the Mediterranean, but the water here appeared to be crystal clear.

To get to the hostel, you had to climb a short road with a hairpin turn halfway up. It was on this turn that I came a cropper, making exactly the same accelerator / brake mistake that had sent Bill flying the day before. I didn't fall very far, perhaps six or seven feet on a 45-degree angle, but I landed on large rocks, so the damage was greater than it had been in Bill's case. Both my hands and knees lost some skin and were slightly bruised. Having injured hands was a problem in driving a motorcycle which had the accelerator and brake controls on the handlebars. I could still drive, though not very comfortably.

The bike had also suffered some damage. Part of the frame had been bent, as well as the leg rests. These would have to be repaired before we could hit the road again. I drove gingerly to the Moto Guzzi dealer the next day. My hands and knees were less than happy, and the bike felt decidedly wonky. While it was being repaired, I attended to my cuts and scrapes by applying some spirits I bought at a *farmacia*. Then, to pass the time, I got my hair cut at a little barbershop. The barber spoke some English. During the Second World War, he had been a prisoner of war in Canada.

From Nice to Marvelous Les Baux

ON SATURDAY, WE DROVE TO NICE, WHERE WE SPENT A COUPLE OF NIGHTS IN THE YOUTH HOSTEL. WE SWAM AT THE PUBLIC BEACHES along the ocean and ogled the girls. But looking at the girls was at the same time enjoyable and frustrating. The problem was money. The girls were too rich for us. Nice was too rich for us, too *nice* for us. Bill took a slide of me with *my* camera, sitting on my Moto Guzzi Cardellino, across from one of the posh hotels on the esplanade, as if that were the place we were staying. It was a trifle more splendid than the youth hostel. But were we envious? Not on your life.

We headed west from Nice with no regrets. After traveling for some time on the main road, we decided to continue west on a quieter secondary road and arrived by accident at Les Baux (local population in tourist season at that time, about 500). Neither of us had heard of this splendid elevated rock, which rises 650 feet or so out of the Chaîne des Alpilles. We were greatly impressed, as many people have been in the past, including the English painter, Augustus John, who wrote about it with his usual humor in a letter to his wife, Dorolea, in January, 1910:

> —an extraordinary place, built among billows of rocks rather like Palestine as far as I remember. The people of Les Baux are simple folk—a little inclined to apologize for their ridiculous situation. We could have a fine apartment there cheap. There are plenty of precipices for the boys to fall over.

The road approaches Les Baux from the southeast, passing by vineyards and plantations of olive trees, and then spirals to the top through extensive rock cuts. (Here's an oddity: Bauxite, which was first discovered near here, is named after it.) The site was once a medieval village owned by the Baux family, though it had been inhabited more or less continuously from at least Roman times. Today, a half century after Bill and I arrived there, it is a tourist trap, as thick with sightseers as Venice's St. Mark's piazza on a Saturday afternoon in July. Cars fill the lots and park on both sides of the road below the village, as if this were some kind of disorganized French Disneyland, which, in a way, it is. But when we were there, in the pre-jet fifties, it was not particularly crowded.

The ruined walls of a castle rise up at one end of this giant rock. Underneath it, in rooms carved out of solid stone many centuries ago, was the youth hostel. It was a splendid place to stay: rock walls, beamed supports and ceilings, and, here and there, windows, carved out of the outer-wall, that opened on to cascading cliffs and spectacular Provençal views. The beds were the usual crowded bunks. In the late evening, just as the sun was setting, two German girls sat on the rock wall outside the castle and entertained us with Mozart on their flutes.

At Les Baux, Bill and I decided to go our own ways. There was no quarrel. Bill was not much interested in Spain, and I didn't want to go to Yugoslavia and Greece. So in the morning, just before 9 o'clock, we drove our Moto Guzzis down the spiral road, shook hands, and headed in opposite directions. We planned to meet later that fall in London, and we did. I was in some respects happy to be on my own. At the time, I had no idea how lonely and isolated I would feel just a few days later.

Motorcycling in the Rain

ONE OF THE THINGS YOU NEVER CONSIDER WHEN YOU ARE A YOUNG PERSON PLANNING A TRIP ALONG THE RIVIERA IS THAT IT MIGHT rain. I mean, isn't the Riviera a sort of European California? And we all know it never rains there. The morning Bill and I went our separate ways, the clouds were threatening; and by the time I reached Arles, 24 kms from Les Baux, at about 11 o'clock, the rain had begun to come down hard. I had no rain gear, apart from a cheap plastic raincoat that lived in a cheap, plastic pouch. I found temporary shelter under the canopy of a filling station and prepared to wait out the storm. But an hour later it was still pouring, so I decided to leave, even though I knew I would get soaked. This happened more quickly than I had expected it would. The raincoat was next to useless on a motorbike in rain this intense. The snaps that held the front together would unsnap moments after I snapped them shut, leaving my front totally exposed.

> *So once again I decided to try to wait it out. I stopped for another hour or so under a railway overpass, this time wet and cold. When it became obvious that the rains were going to keep coming down, I headed out again. By the time I reached St. Gilles, 16 kms west of Arles, not only was I dripping wet, but my duffel bag and everything in it was saturated. I found the local youth hostel, which luckily was open during the day, and proceeded to deal with my situation. I had nothing dry to change into. So I put on my less-wet things and spent a miserable afternoon and evening trying to dry out some of my clothes by wearing them on my body or spreading them around my bunk. I had no interest in making friends with the other people in the hostel, nor in seeing the town's fine abbey. Nor did I care that St. Gilles was once a pilgrim stop on the route to Compostela. I was too wet and miserable to care about things like that.*

In the morning, I bought a tarp to cover my bag and a hat to cover my head. It was a start. I set out for Perpignan under cloudy skies, and as noon approached, I stopped at a roadside restaurant along the way for a lunch that cost 450francs (C$1.50)—an extravagance (if you can believe it)—but I was feeling a bit sorry for myself after the rain-soaked previous day and needed to give myself a present. When I arrived at the hostel in Perpignan, about 4 o'clock, I discovered that I had lost my hostel card, probably in the process of trying to dry everything out the day before. The warden refused to let me stay unless I bought a new one for 1,000 francs, which made me regret my spendthrift lunch. The hostel was crowded. Next to my bunk were two English fellows who talked through the night, and in the room next door, a group of German girls sang, so I didn't get much sleep. In the morning, to compensate for my expenses of the day before, and to assuage my guilty conscience for overspending, I bought a jar of Nescafe instant coffee, a sweet bun, and a liter of sterilized milk and made my own breakfast

The Land of Don Quixote

IT WAS ON THURSDAY, SEPTEMBER 18, 1958, THAT I ENTERED SPAIN FOR THE FIRST TIME. IT WAS THE FULFILMENT OF MANY DREAMS, THE END, in a sense, of my quest for the land of Don Quixote. I had the same sensation that Ted Hughes (*Birthday Letters*) had on arriving there:

>   Spain
> Where I felt at home. The blood-raw light,
> The oiled anchovy faces. The African
> Black edges to everything.

And, unlike Hughes, I was lucky not to have Sylvia Plath, who hated the country, along with me. Even the weather had cleared up, miraculously, as I crossed the border. I luxuriated in the sun, driving along the narrow, twisting roads that in those days ran high above the blue Mediterranean from the border to Barcelona.

There was next to no motor traffic. But there were a number of two-wheeled carts pulled by mules, some by donkeys, many of them carrying faggots piled incredibly high. Apart from the restrained menace of the Guardias Civiles, who stood at the sides of the road every twenty miles or so, in their green woollen uniforms and flat-backed patent-leather hats, the highway was largely empty. The joke was that these hats were designed so these policemen could lean against walls without tipping them off. The Spain I was travelling through was as beautiful as a medieval world. I loved it. And, curiously, given my profoundly different background, I felt at home. It was as if I had somehow existed here in an earlier life. As if one of my ancestors had dallied with a Spanish sailor from the wrecked Spanish Armada on the wild shores of 16th Century Ireland, a sailor who had deposited his genes among my branch of the Kehoes.

Barcelona's Drunken Warden

APPROACHING BARCELONA, I LEFT THE WORLD OF THE MIDDLE AGES AND ENTERED ONCE MORE THE TWENTIETH CENTURY. HERE WAS A city whose essential beauty, the beauty of the Spain I loved and yearned for, was suffering from the effects of industry and smog. At the hostel, a group of workmen were building a gate, moving at half-speed or less, a scene that I was to witness many times in the Spain of that era, the lassitude that seems automatically to arise in the repressed world of dictatorship. (I was to see the same kind of thing thirty years later in Yugoslavia.) The warden, a nervous, middle-aged, thin man with a balding problem, was fruity, grumpy, and drunk, a rather bad combination. He was insolent, rude, and abrupt in signing me in, but luckily a busload of Germans arrived, distracting the warden and allowing me to flee to my bunk. I went to bed early, writing in my journal that I was, "well-bitten by mosquitoes." It had never occurred to me that there would be mosquitoes along the Mediterranean.

The next day, Friday, September 19, I had the bike greased while I visited a tourist-driven "Spanish Village," walked along the wonderful Rambla boulevard as a counterfoil to that, and strolled through and around the unfinished Sagrada Familia cathedral of Antoni Gaudí. The building had been begun in 1893, but work had more or less stopped after Gaudí was run over by a streetcar and killed in 1926. Its strange and appealing mixture of gothic and art nouveau seemed to me to have an affinity with an imaginary garden of helter-skelter giant asparagus.

That night at dinner there was a nasty scene when the warden, who was drunk again (still?), accosted two English fellows, Dave and Merv, who were unable to produce their dinner tickets and claimed to have lost them. "Billete! Billete! Tee-ket!" he shouted at them, as they sat down at the long communal table to eat the cooked meal provided by the hostel for those who had paid the full-board charge of 60 pesetas (C$1.00) and were issued tickets for meals. Since they had paid full board less than an hour previously, they thought he should remember. The warden pulled a pocketknife and began fiddling with it drunkenly.

At this, the boys stood up and headed to the other side of the table, where the warden stood. Now, Dave and Merv were big young men, who I earlier learned, had served their National Service in the paratroops and had been among those dropped on Suez in 1956, so they were not to be taken lightly. The warden, who knew none of this, but could appreciate their size, decided, like Falstaff, that the better part of valor was discretion. As the boys approached him, he made a hasty retreat to his office, barking his shins on a chair along the way and sending it flying with a clatter and a clash. He didn't bother to stop and pick it up. Dave and Merv returned to the table and were served their dinner like the rest of us. Later, Dave gave me his address in Chiswick and asked me to look him up when I got to London. I did so more than a month later, when I was in a difficult situation. I had returned to London from Scotland on a Saturday and had underestimated the amount of money I would need to get me through to Monday. The banks, of course were closed for the weekend, and in those days, there were no ATMs, and only the very rich had credit cards. After a horrible night in Liverpool Street Station, I called Dave, and he agreed immediately to put me up and feed me at his parent's home in Chelsea. It was an enormous relief to me not to have to spend another day and night on the streets with no money for food or lodging.

The Road to Monserrat

ON THE ROAD ABOUT TEN O'CLOCK, AND OUT OF BARCELONA, I BEGAN MY JOURNEY TO MADRID. A FEW MILES INTO THE COUNTRYSIDE, I got tangled up in a bicycle race in this mountainous country, up, up, up—it seemed forever—leaving the sea behind, a strip of blue in the distance. With my 73 cc power plant, I not only sometimes passed them, but they also sometimes passed me. A bit embarrassing, leg power overcoming motor power, but they laughed as they went by, and I laughed back. It was in and out, as we blanket-stitched our way into the mountains, and after a time I became annoyed with it. Besides, the wind was blowing hard and occasionally raising uncomfortable swirls of dust that spiraled across the road and into my face. So I decided to detour to the hilltop monastery of Monserrat, which I remembered reading about in connection with St. Ignatius of Loyola, the founder of the Jesuits, in E. J. Pratt's *Brébeuf and His Brethren*:

> Loyola, soldier-priest, staggering with wounds,
> At Pampeluna, guided by a voice,
> Had travelled to the Montserrata Abbey
> To leave his sword and dagger on an altar
> That he might lead the *Company of Jesus*.

I parked the bike amid a group of cars and buses at the base of a perpendicular cliff that rose hundreds of feet and was capped by what appeared to be large stone buildings. There was a funicular railway scarring the scene, and I was happy to take its swaying cable car to the top, instead of lugging myself up on the footpath. The views from the top were the first things that occupied my interest, fantastic vistas, stretching over rolling hills and forests of olives and fields of grapes all the way to the Mediterranean. Reluctantly turning my attention from these to the fortress-like buildings, I headed (with a group of other tourists) into the large cathedral, carved out of rock and very richly, almost garishly, appointed, as, I would discover, is common in Spain: statues covered in gold and blood and gore are the rule rather than the exception. In an enclosure at the top of the altar, accessible by stairs at the back, was the small statue of the Virgin that was the reason for this shrine's having been built, the miraculous Black Madonna.

> *I left the cathedral and went to a bar I had seen on my way in—from the sacred to the profane—where I met an American sailor, one of many I had seen wandering around the complex. Apparently, the American Seventh Fleet was paying a visit to Barcelona. The sailor was from "Salem, Mass.", he said, and had been in the navy seventeen years. He was fairly drunk. He told me "I'm not married," at least ten times, said he hated his mother and father, had slept with the admiral's wife, and lived in a fen in Florida. After one beer I retreated from the sailor's tale of woe and bravura, took the cable car back to my bike, and hit the road again.*

As it was getting to be late in the day, I stopped at a village called Cervera, near Lérida. Here there was a charming old hotel, comfortable and cheap. A good dinner, bed, and breakfast was a mere 42 pesetas. Outside my room was a lovely village square. As I strolled around it after dinner, a shepherd, his dogs, and his flock ambled lazily through the square. The shepherd, dressed in a dark grey poncho and a black hat with a round brim, stopped in the middle of the square, and the flock circled around him in clouds of dust, as the sheep and dogs went ahead of him out of the village. It was a scene from another century and seemed at the time to be all I had come to Spain to be a part of. Fifteen years later, in the 1970s, recognizing the charm of this place, the great teacher of the classical Spanish guitar, Emilio Pujol, established a guitar school in the village, and innumerable aspirants to be the next Segovia began to beat a path to his door. But in 1958, it was simply a charming small town, quiet and unpretentious, and I exulted in my short stay there. "Why did I not stay longer?" I ask myself now. Why?

Dave and Merv Again

SUNDAY, SEPTEMBER 21st. OUT EARLY AND RIDING THROUGH MILES OF FAIRLY FLAT, ALMOST DESERT-LIKE COUNTRYSIDE, WITH SMALL towns that were poor and decrepit. Farmers, looking like Sancho Panza, rode mules to their parched fields, their stubby legs splaying out like pegs on either side of the animals. Here and there were two-wheeled carts, pilled high with faggots and pulled by scrawny-looking donkeys. It was obvious, in spite of the song from *My Fair Lady*, that the rain in Spain didn't fall mainly on the plain. At least not on this part of the plain. But in these near-drought conditions, the Franco government for the previous twenty years has been busy planting trees, oak trees, and they were prospering; and in some areas they stretched in all directions right to the horizon. Later, on my way north from Madrid, I would see the same phenomenon in a more westerly part of the plain. The story was that the government was replacing the oak forests that were cut down in the sixteenth century to build the ships of the Spanish Armada. The trees would eventually rehabilitate the land, stopping and reversing its creeping tendency to become a desert. It takes a great deal of patience to rehabilitate in this way, but the Spanish, in those days, were a patient people.

Outside of Zaragoza I ran out of gas, and chastised myself, in words that were unprintable at that time and would be vulgar now, for being so stupid. But I was in luck and had to push the bike a mere two kilometers to a roadside service station. Gassed up again, I went through Zaragoza and on to the village of La Alumnia, where I decided to call it a day. My miniature *fonda* (pension) had no running water, but jugs of hot water were available on request. A pretty young girl, probably no more than fifteen or sixteen, in the black dress, white lace-fringed apron and bob cap that was the universal dress for maids in Spain at that time, delivered a jug to my miniature room, so I was able to get cleaned up. There was a chamber pot in the cupboard. I wondered if this was the extent of the bathroom facilities. The suggestibility of this device, the likes of which I had never before used, might have been the reason for my sudden desire to have a crap. Whatever the reason, I employed the chamber pot and stowed it back in the cupboard. I wasn't sure what was the right routine in using one of these things, but I thought probably one just put the pot out of sight and the maid would empty it in the morning. Afterwards, looking around the place, I discovered that there were two outhouses attached to the high wall of the courtyard at the back of the building, and I felt a bit guilty about leaving my deposit in the chamber pot. I intended to take it out later and dump it, but I forgot.

When I went down to the miniature dining room to have supper, I once again encountered Merv and Dave, who were with Wendy, an American girl who was staying in the hotel. She had a small Seat (the Spanish Fiat), and was giving Merv and Dave, whom she had met in Barcelona, a ride to Madrid. She was in her early- to mid-twenties, not very attractive, pudgy and short of chin, though she had lovely blonde hair, cut on one side daringly on the bias. She was from California and spoke Spanish fluently. She appeared to have plenty of money and exuded the confidence that money creates. As the meal progressed, she showed a good sense of humor and a sharp mind. She told me she would be happy to take me to Madrid along with Merv and Dave, if she could find some way to attach my motorcycle to her car. (Impossible, of course—but I appreciated the sentiment.)

After we had eaten, I went outside with Dave and Merv, who were going to sleep in the fields on the edge of the village. If I was travelling as cheaply as I possibly could, staying in *fondas* and third- and forth-class hotels, Dave and Merv were totally roughing it. I was willing to make sacrifices, but not of the sort that they were making. In the village square there were numerous chickens and dogs and people. The evening was alive, as it always is in the summer in Spain, when the heat of the day has passed and it is pleasant to mingle with friends and neighbors in the village square. In a building opposite the fonda, teenagers danced to recordings of American music. Bill Haley's "Rock Around the Clock" blasted out from loudspeakers through the wide open windows. Even in this remote village, the American globalization of their culture was beginning to make inroads. The old Spain was meeting the new. I didn't like it.

When I returned indoors, I waved goodnight to Wendy, who was the only other guest in this four-room fonda, as she was just heading up to her room. Later, it occurred to me that she might have been waiting for me to talk to her when I came in. But I was too shy even to start a conversation. When I did not see her in the morning, I kicked myself for not trying to find a way to meet her in Madrid. Already, I was lonely and experiencing the world of those who travel solo. I was in great need of the company of others. I wanted to talk about what I was seeing and experiencing. But in the case of Wendy, I had missed my chance.

On the Road to Madrid

> Madrid is a strange place, anyway. I do not believe anyone likes it much when he first goes there. It has none of the look that you expect in Spain . . . Yet when you get to know it, it is the most Spanish of all cities, the best place to live in, the finest people, and month in and month out the finest climate. **Ernest Hemingway**

A Flat Tire in the Middle of Nowhere

OUT BY 8 A.M. I MET DAVE AND MERV ON THE ROAD AT THE SIDE OF THE FIELD WHERE THEY'D SPENT THE NIGHT. THEY WERE WAITING for Wendy to pick them up. We agreed to meet at the hostel in Madrid, but in fact we met for coffee a couple of hours later at a roadside restaurant, where I recognized Wendy's car as I was driving by. They must have passed me without either of us noticing it. Once again I was too shy to ask Wendy if we could get together in Madrid. She and the boys left before I did. As it turned out, that was unfortunate. It would have been better if I had not joined them in the restaurant and had gone ahead of them. My problems started when I had a flat tire in the middle of nowhere, forty-two kilometers from Guadelajara. I took off the tire and looked for a hole in the inner tube, but all I could find was a loose valve core. I put the tire back on again and attached the hand pump to fill it with air. But, just as I was about to do so, the bike fell over and the pump broke into two pieces.

> *It was midday and the torrid Spanish sun was blasting down on me, here at the side of a largely traffic-less highway. A quarter of a mile or so down the road from which I'd come was a roadside hovel. I decided to go there and try to get help. This was a silly idea, as the peasants who lived in it had yet to enter the twentieth century and had no understanding of motor bikes and pumps, let alone the convenience of running water and electricity, or telephone contact with the rest of the world. But a sun-wrinkled middle-aged man responded to my knocking and my bad Spanish and came to the bike with me to have a look. A look was all he could do for me. As we couldn't communicate much with each other, I went to work on the pump to assess the damage, something I should have done in the first place. I discovered that all that had happened was that the rubber hose that goes from the pump to the tire had pulled off a metal nipple. So I fixed that by reattaching it to the pump. When I pumped away, to my surprise, the tire held air. So I threw a relief-inspired "Muchas gracias" at the peasant, who seemed almost as delighted as I was, and took off down the road.*

In Guadelajara I gassed up, but the gas was bad, and the bike coughed and farted off and on all the way to Madrid. But it did get me there, and about that I was grateful. It was nearly five o'clock when I found my way to the large youth hostel in the Casa de Campo, built in the middle of what was once, like Hyde Park in London, a royal hunting area. It had been a trying day. But the prices at the hostel were as usual in my comfort range: nine pesetas for a bed (*cama*), and 42 pesetas for full board (*completo*). I'm not sure, at these prices, why I didn't stay much longer in Madrid. Perhaps forever!

The Most Spanish of All Cities

IN THE FEW DAYS I SPENT IN MADRID, I PURSUED THE PATH OF THE CONVENTIONAL TOURIST. I PUT IN MANY HOURS AT THE PRADO, systematically visiting many of the galleries, guide book in hand, carefully reading, as a student might, what it had to say about the various paintings. And how I loved those paintings: Velázquez and *Las meninas*; Goya and *La maja vestida* and *La maja desnuda*; and all of the wonderful El Greco's, the Murillo's, The Titian's, the Raphael's, the Bosch's and the Breughel's. In following this self-imposed course in the history of art, I was avoiding the task I should have been pursuing: checking the language schools to see if I could find a job teaching English. I wasn't strong enough to do this yet, not roughened up enough by travel to bull my way into difficult situations. Instead, I avoided doing it, immersed myself in art, wandered through the past, read the only English paperback I could find, a copy of Shaw's *Back to Methusela*, of all things. At the hostel, I met a tense American, Bob, coiled up like a spring, getting near the end of a round-the-world tour which had apparently been prescribed by his psychiatrist. Judging from his mental state at this point, he must have been a helluva mess when he started his trip.

Bob had a car, so he took us into Madrid in the late evenings to go to the cheap restaurants in the back streets that lead from the Puerta del Sol to the Castellana. Always dressed in black pants for practical reasons, Bob said in Rome people kept asking him if he was a priest. Also accompanying us on these evenings in town was Jorge, who came from Costa Rico and claimed to be a communist. He told the story of being in love with a girl from Vienna, with whom he'd spent a month in Mallorca. She, like Chopin, was a pianist. (Jorge was not at all like Georges Sand!) At the end of their Mallorcan adventure, she was upset because she thought she was pregnant. Then, when she went to a doctor and found out that she wasn't pregnant, she was upset about that. "Either way you lose," said Jorge.

El Escorial and the *Vale de Los Caidos*

ONE DAY, I RODE MY MOTORCYCLE TO *EL ESCORIAL* AND THE *VALE DE LOS CAIDOS*, BOTH OF WHICH ARE IN THE SAME AREA, ABOUT 45 KMS north-west of Madrid. *El Escorial* is an enormous complex (224m x 153m), built by Philip II in the 16th Century, which contains a monastery, an art gallery with many old-master paintings, a royal palace, a mausoleum in which most of Spain's monarchs are buried, and a fine library of medieval manuscripts and *incunabulae*. It is claimed (apparently on precarious grounds) that one of the manuscripts is in the hand of St. Augustine of Hippo. (I took a picture of it through the glass in the display case.) I have been told that the Augustinian monks who live in *El Escorial* were asked by *El Caudillo* ("The Leader") Generalissimo Francisco Franco to look after his Valley of the Fallen, which is right next door. They refused on the grounds that the monastery built to serve it was too luxurious a place for them. The real reason—that they did not wish to be associated with this monument to Franco—would have been dangerously unmentionable.

The *Vale* was constructed on the orders of Franco as a monument to the dead of both sides in the Civil War. The original idea was that all of those who had fallen, on either side, would be reburied in this valley, forty kilometers from Madrid, uniting in death those who had been bitterly opposed in life. At a time when the economy of Spain needed every peseta to lift the country out of the Middle Ages, Franco embarked on this venture in fascist architecture, using money on it that would better have been spent elsewhere. The Spanish people were not fooled, knowing all along that *El Caudillo* was building a monument to himself. It is a huge cathedral, cut out of a mountain, on top of which is erected an enormous cross, which, it is claimed, can be seen from Madrid's tallest buildings on a clear day. When I was there, in the fall of 1958, the *Vale* was still not quite complete, and the exterior of the entrance to the Cathedral was surrounded by scaffolding. I had to admit, in spite of wanting to feel otherwise, that it *was* impressive. Plans to move the dead of the Civil War into the valley came to nothing. Even the idea of piping out the sound of High Mass on Sundays and amplifying it throughout the valley was not put into operation. Eventually, Franco himself would be buried in the cathedral, near the high altar. One is reminded of the words of the son of Christopher Wren, written on his father's tomb in another great monument, one genuinely designed for other purposes than self-agrandization: *Si monumentum requiris, circumspice.*[4] To this day, the Church in Spain has refused to designate the structure officially as a cathedral; and plans to bury other prominent Spaniards near the man who referred to himself as *El Caudillo*, have come to nothing. *Sic transit Gloria mundi.*

Heading for England

My Shoes Go Missing

IT WAS ON SUNDAY MORNING, SEPTEMBER 28, HAVING GOT UP AND HAD BREAKFAST IN THE HOSTEL IN THE *CASA DE CAMPO*, THAT I SUDDENLY decided it was time to leave Madrid and head to England once again. My decision was entirely an emotional one. I had been wasting time for days, avoiding finding a job in Madrid, and I no longer felt up to pursuing that course. But I was not anxious to get on my motorcycle and head north after the trouble I had been having with it, so I checked at the railway station about shipping it to San Sebastián. But that turned out to be too expensive. So I left Madrid aboard the motorcycle about noon, heading north. At one point along the way I thought the air in one of the tires seemed a little low, so I stopped and took out the pump to blow it up. Once again, the bike fell over and the hose separated from the pump. But this time I knew how to fix it. My worry about the level of air in the tire was, in any case, paranoid. The air in the tire was fine.

Early in the evening I arrived in Burgos. I booked into the third-class Hotel Norte y Londres and sat through dinner with a dauntingly boring middle-aged English couple,

---

[4] If it's a monument you want, look around you.

obviously tired of each other, and of life, and both a little drunk. They no longer seemed even to have the energy to fight with each other, though in every sentence they were on the verge of doing so. Barbs were thrown from both sides and from both sides ignored. They were, like the world in the fifties, in a state of cold war. They knew that if they responded to the barbs, they would destroy each another. So they continued with their lives in a state of armed stand-off.

When I went up to my room and unpacked my bag, I found my wonderful Hartt shoes were gone. I had owned these expensive shoes for only a short time, having bought them for my European trip as a exceptional treat to myself, after my months of austerity, in my last days at the Bay. I had forgotten them under my bunk in the hostel in Madrid. It was a depressing discovery, one of those horrors about which nothing can be done. But in the morning, my depression about the shoes was somewhat relieved when I learned that the bill for dinner, bed and breakfast was a mere 175 pesetas.

My Tire Goes Flat Again

MY PLAN WAS TO HEAD THROUGH VITORIA TO IRUN AND ACROSS THE BORDER TO FRANCE, A DISTANCE OF ABOUT 300 KMS. BUT MY best-laid schemes, like those of the mouse in Burns' poem, were about to gang a-gley. After traveling about a hundred kilometers, and approaching the city of Vitoria, I once again had a flat tire, the same tire as before. What to do? I took the wheel off and removed the inner tube. But I couldn't test for a leak without water, so it seemed impossible to make a repair. Then I saw, perhaps a hundred yards ahead of me, a small stone bridge. As small bridges often span small streams, I walked to the bridge to have a look. Sure enough, there was a stream, one that was nearly, but not quite, dry. It certainly contained enough water for my purposes. I found the leak, put a patch on it, and put the bike back together. I was pleased with myself. I had solved, I thought, the problem. But there was another problem, the cause of the puncture, which I had not solved, and which would return to give me a great deal of grief.

What I should have done, and did not do, was to go to a bike shop in Vitoria and have a proper vulcanized patch put on the inner tube. In making the repair, they would have discovered the other problem. Instead, I sailed through Vitoria around noon, in those days a sleepy hamlet, today, the bustling capital of the Basque region. I was unaware that it was here in 1813 that Wellington won the decisive battle of the Peninsular War. It was also from here that Sir John Moore retreated toward his death in Corunna (*La Coruña*) in 1809. I would have been interested had I known, as Charles Wolfe's poem "The Burial of Sir John Moore at Corunna" was taught in the schools of British Columbia when I was a student, one of the late vestiges of empire propaganda:
>Slowly and sadly we laid him down,
>From the field of his fame fresh and gory;
>We carved not a line, and we raised not a stone,
>But we left him alone with his glory.

This passage, if one can believe it, was also used in grammar lessons to teach the "-ly" form of the adverb.

About 17 kms north of Vitoria, nearly halfway to San Sebastián, the tire went flat again. I tried to pump it up, but the pump refused to work. The hose that connects the pump to the valve had developed a leak. I took it apart and put it back together, but it was no good. After nearly two hours had passed, I flagged down a car and asked in my rudimentary Spanish for help. A balding, middle-aged man emerged from the car, opened his trunk, took out a pump (it amazes me now that he had a pump in his trunk!), helped me to re-inflate the tire, and drove off. I started back to Vitoria to get some profession help, but about a kilometer later, the tire went flat again. So I parked the bike at the side of the road, leaving my duffel bag with all my possessions, except my document case, tied to the back—such was the honesty of the rural Spaniards in those days that I was not fundamentally worried that anything would be stolen—hitch-hiked into town, found the Moto Guzzi dealer, and bought a new hose. I tried to buy an inner tube, but they told me that tubes of that size were not available in Spain. I kicked myself for not bringing the tube into town with me to have it repaired. But at the time that I decided to go to Vitoria I couldn't face again taking the tire off the bike and wrestling with my tire iron to remove the tube.

I Go for Help in the Middle of the Night

SO I TOOK A TAXI BACK TO THE BIKE (140 PESETAS), PUMPED UP THE TIRE, AND STARTED OFF AGAIN FOR VITORIA. BY THIS TIME IT WAS almost dark, and it had begun to rain heavily. About five kilometers out of Vitoria, the tire went flat again. I waited beside the road in the rain for awhile, tired, upset, and unsure what I should do. Across the road from me there was a large deciduous tree that I thought should offer some shelter from the rain, so I rolled the bike across to it, took out my sleeping bag, and prepared to spend the night. But as the hours went by and the rain continued to fall, my sleeping bag became wet through and I was decidedly uncomfortable. At 11:30, I decided to go for help.

I walked toward the lighted windows of a building I had seen across the field. The door was opened by a maid in the traditional black dress and white apron. I said, "Does anyone speak English here?" both in English and no doubt horrible Spanish. The maid closed the door and came back with a rotund man with a fringe of hair around his head and a kind-looking face. "What's the problem?" he said, beckoning me to come into the entrance hall. It's hard to express the relief I felt that I had found an English-speaking person. In retrospect it seems almost miraculous. I explained my situation to him. "Let's have a look," he said, putting on his raincoat and leading me to his Seat. We drove over to where I had told him I had left the bike. It wasn't very far, no more than a hundred yards or so from his place; so he drove back, and I pushed the bike behind him.

As it turned out, I had gone for help to a small agricultural college. The man who came to my aid was the director of the college. He had been a student in New York, which explained his English. He introduced himself as José Manzano. His family, his wife, a fine-looking blonde daughter in her late teens, and a younger teen-aged son, were all just finishing a late Spanish dinner. In spite of my bedraggled state, I was plunked down at the family table, and the maid was instructed to bring me bread, sausage, milk, wine, and coñac. The daughter asked me if I was a bachelor, which pleased me, though I'm sure her question was purely social in nature, and I'm not at all sure her father accurately translated her meaning. But it flattered me that she had expressed interest in my availability. After my meal, I was taken up to a room in the student dormitory area of the college. I had a shower, cleaned up my clothes as best I could and laid out to dry those that were wet. I was comfortable, warm, fed, protected and secure. My appreciation of what these good people had done for me, a stranger in distress, was boundless. I fell asleep immediately and slept soundly throughout the night.

I Discover That My Troubles Are Not Over

I WAS UP AT 8:30, AND AFTER HAVING BREAKFAST WITH THE FAMILY, I WENT BACK TO MY ROOM TO PACK. IT WAS THEN I DISCOVERED THAT I did not have the fold-over document case containing my passport and the *carne* for the bike. I went outside to the bike, hoping I had left it there, but I hadn't. This was a great worry. When I told José the problem, I said I thought I must have left the case in the taxi I had taken out to the bike the day before. He asked me to describe the taxi. I remembered that it was black and had a distinct wine stripe along the sides. We went right away into Vitoria and searched for the taxi. As Vitoria was in those days not a very large place, José had a pretty good idea which taxi we were looking for, and we found it almost immediately. We were in luck. The driver still had the case. He said he had planned to turn it into the police later that morning, but in the meantime was hoping that I would come back for it. You didn't mess with the police in Spain in those days, so I was greatly relieved. Taking the case into my hands, I felt almost as if I were in the middle of another miracle.

José and I then took the wheel from the bike, which we had brought with us, to the Moto Guzzi place to get the tube repaired properly. The mechanic also installed a new lining in the rim—the old lining had been damaged in my repair attempts, so that the rivets that ran up its middle were puncturing the tube. This was the problem I had not recognized and had not solved. All of the repairs were done under José's direction. He took charge, as one might expect a college director to do. But it was his kindness rather than his decisiveness that impressed me. I felt enormously in his debt. As Hemingway's hero, Robert Jordan, muses in *For Whom the Bell Tolls* about the people of Spain: "They are wonderful when they are good and when they go bad there is no people that is worse." I had seen them at their best; and in the many contacts I have had with the Spanish in subsequent years, I have never seen them at their worst. Of course, Hemingway's book is set during the Civil War, and no people are civilized in civil wars, which might better be called "uncivil" wars.

We returned to the agricultural college, put the bike back together, and had lunch. After that, we toured the barns and other outbuildings. At 3:30, as I left for San Sebastián and the border, José gave me his final bit of advice: "Don't drive at night." "I won't," I said. In fact, I hadn't been driving at night when I'd run into trouble, but he would not have believed that. As I got away from these wonderful people, who had been so generous to me when I most needed them, I felt a heavy emotional let-down and was overtaken with a great weariness. So when I spied a pleasant-looking *fonda* on the main street of the village of Tolosa, a few kilometers from San Sebastián, I stopped there for the night, instead of going into the city itself. I did not wish to face the greater pressures of the urban world. It was a good decision. After an emotionally draining few days, I had a relaxing evening and a good night's sleep.

Fair Stood the Wind for France

I HAD BREAKFAST IN THE *FONDA* WITH A DUTCH SEAMAN AND WAS ON THE ROAD BY NINE O'CLOCK. AT ELEVEN, I WENT THROUGH THE French-Spanish border at Irún, unaware (not being John the Baptist), that I would be coming through this border point again in the other direction in less than a year. As it was raining a little, I stopped for coffee. But the rain didn't let up in that short time, so I took off again. This was a mistake, exactly the same mistake I had made just before leaving France for Spain a few weeks earlier. By three o'clock I was soaked through, and frigidly cold. It was *déjà vu* all over again, as the joke goes. I entered Labouheyre, a town south of Bordeaux, in Gascogne, in the middle of the spindly, closely-planted trees of Europe's largest area of forest, and found a hotel. I took a room without even asking the price, as I was so cold and miserable that I had to find shelter. In my room, I stripped and went to bed, where I remained for an hour and a half. Still cold, I got up with a blanket wrapped around me and stuffed my shoes with the paper lining the dresser drawers to try to dry them out. I had no other shoes now. I dressed in the driest clothes I had and went down to the bar, where, still cold, I had two cognacs, which went a long way toward warming me up. I had dinner at 7:30 and went to bed, finally reasonably warm, hoping for better weather in the morning.

All Alone in a Hostel Barn in St. Julien

MY HOTEL BILL WAS 2,740 FRANCS (C$8)! OUCH! YESTERDAY IT HAD SEEMED WORTH IT. TODAY, IT WAS A LOT OF MONEY. I DECIDED, however, that I was going to have to spend even more money before I left this market town, purchasing a pair of rubber Wellington boots for 1,000 francs to keep my feet dry. I cashed a traveller's cheque for $10, not much money in France, and left about 9:30 in light rain. All day, off and on, there were showers, but as I approached St. Junien, not far from Limoges, about 5 o'clock, it had cleared, so I decided to stop while the going was good and hope that tomorrow would be rainless.

I asked directions to the *auberge* of a group of pre-teens, who were leaning on their bicycles and examining me as if I had come from outer space. They were, like all young boys, most interested in my motorcycle, my red Moto Guzzi that was giving me so much trouble. They didn't understand me when I asked directions, so I got out my Youth Hostel booklet and pointed to the address, at which they led me to the edge of the village and a farmyard. When I was checking in with a woman I assumed to be the farmer's wife, a wan teenage girl, who looked very ill with something or other, stared at me constantly, making me feel uncomfortable. When I went into the barn and selected a bunk, she followed me at a distance, her shocking white face staring at me, like a full moon on a cloudless night. She seemed to be (to use a contemporary term) brain-damaged in some way.

The hostel was a converted barn, a huge place on two levels, open in the middle to a high roof, the second floor of dormitories having been constructed in a square around the edges, like a medieval inn. Because I was the only one there, the place seemed to be even larger than it was. One part of the building was still being used as a barn, and throughout the night I heard the thumping sound of shuffling cows. Chickens wandered freely in the yard. There was no indoor plumbing, and the outhouse lavatories were rife with spider webs. Everywhere the place was dirty, unused, as if no one had stayed there for a long time.

When I had settled in, I went to work on the bike, once again decarboning it. Throughout the day, I had had a lot of trouble with it. The problem was caused simply by the fact that it was too small a machine for long-distance travel, which, of course, was not news to me. The plug would carbon up and it would begin to short. I would stop, remove the top of the cylinder and clean off the carbon. The bike would then go reasonably well for a while. What it needed was to be taken apart and cleaned properly, but I was unable to do that, and I didn't want to pay to have it done. On top of my problems with the bike, I had ripped my plastic raincoat, which, though still useable, had become pretty porous along the back. As I was tired and all alone, I bedded down early, after eating bread, sausage, and cheese that I had bought in the village. I fell asleep quickly, considering that I was a little frightened to be all alone in this monster barn in the middle of nowhere, with the cattle stomping beyond the wall, and a nagging concern about the white-faced girl who had been watching me in such a strange way.

Money Problems in Blois

AT ABOUT NINE O'CLOCK, I LEFT THE BARNYARD UNDER THE GAZE OF THE WHITE-FACED GIRL AND HEADED TO BLOIS. I WAS LOW IN CASH, but also low in gas, so I used what money I had to fill up the tank. I knew I would not make it to Blois before the banks closed, so stopped in a small village where I saw a bank to cash a couple of traveler's cheques. The bank refused to cash them, making me understand that they'd never seen them before, and that they'd have to verify the bank signatures (printed, of course) on the cheques. All of this negotiating was done in fractured French and a bit of English, and I may not have understood exactly what their arguments were; but they were adamant, and I left the bank with no money. I found the hostel at Blois, five kilometers out of town, and checked in. It had been a wonderful, sunny day, a chateau in every village, the grape harvest in full swing. But it was October-cold. The bike had continued to be erratic, the carbon building up and needing to be removed every couple of hours, but I was not held up for long by that and was happy that I could keep going. My immediate problem was that I didn't have enough money for a hostel dinner. As I had had no lunch, I was starving; so I spent what money I had buying a loaf of bread, and an egg to be boiled at the hostel, and with my instant coffee made this my supper. All I had in my pocket for money after this purchase was a

100 franc coin from Monaco that someone had slipped into my change the day before and that nobody else seemed to be willing to take.

The Blois hostel had a rule that they didn't open the dormitories until 9 p.m.; so, tired and dirty, I had to wait till then in the lounge. The waiting time was relieved by the antics of a damaged local man, probably in his mid-twenties, who kept coming up to me and producing an envelope in which he had a live butterfly. He would open the top of the envelope, the butterfly would spread its wings as far as it could (but not far enough to fly out), and the man would look me in the eyes and laugh. He did this with the others who were in the hostel (two teenage Spaniards), repeatedly, without apparently remembering that he had shown his treasure to us immediately before. I was relieved when the dorm was opened and I was finally able to get cleaned up. I went to bed shortly afterward and fell asleep right away, even though I was worried that I didn't have the 100 francs I needed to pay for my night's accommodation.

In the morning, I tried to pay the hostel with a 100 franc Monaco coin, but the warden refused to take it. So I left my gear as hostage, went into town, cashed a $20 traveler's cheque, returned to the hostel, paid, and headed north once again. The weather was sunny but unsettled, a few drops of rain now and then, but on the whole it was dry—and cold. I had lunch at Chartres, at 835 francs expensive for me. As I left the city (without even taking a peak at the cathedral!—too anxious to get to England), I resolved to stay out of restaurants in future. In the afternoon it rained for awhile, but I sat it out in a café over a long cup of coffee, so I didn't get wet. Was I finally getting smart? Perhaps. Back on the road again, the weather was getting really threatening, so I stopped earlier than I had intended, at the hostel in Louviers, where I changed the oil and once again dealt with the buildup of carbon in the motorcycle.

On to England at Last

EARLY IN THE MORNING, SUNDAY, OCTOBER 5, I LEFT LOUVIERS, PUTT-PUTTING NORTH, THROUGH ROUEN. MY PLAN WAS TO STOP FOR THE night in Arques. But for reasons unknown to me, the gendarmes had closed the hostel, so I headed for Calais. As it happened, I was just in time to catch the evening ferry to England.

At Dover, I went through Customs, paid the required insurance on the bike, and got a room at the Hotel Continental (18/6 for the night). In the morning, I opened the curtain in my room and looked out on the white cliffs of Dover, jutting up from the sea in brilliant, October sunshine. It was great to be in England once again.

A CONTINENTAL JOURNEY

Student Hostel at 19 Cross St., Islington

No. 10 Downing St. When You Could Still Get Near It

Brussels's World Fair: The Atomium

Milan: View from the Duomo Roof

Italian Officialdom re Motorcycles

Youth Hostel in Genoa
Where I Came a Cropper

The Beautiful Riviera Near Genoa

The Hilltop Structures of Les Baux

Dinner Ticket Like the One Lost
By Dave and Merv

Plains in Spain Near Lérida Where I Had the First Flat Tire

Prado Entrance

The Monserrat Monastery

Franco's Oak Reforestation

TUESDAY — Sept 3°
Up at 8³⁰ & breakfast with family — discovered lost passport, came, etc. — worried such — looked in town with José and found finally in taxi where had left it — had tube repaired and new lining for tire — returned in car to agricult college where put bike back together — had lunch with people and after toured barns and what not — at 3ᵖᵐ left for San Sebast, but stopped in Tuñon for the night (128 pts - sup, bed, break) — never met such

Chapter 7: Dark Night of the Soul

ENGLAND AGAIN

The Twilight

> We carry our past with us, trailing it like refugees who load what possessions they can collect on a cart and drag it along the endless road, in flight to a future somewhere else. But we carry our future too, pushing it in front—the hopes and fears that might be useful wherever we are going.
>   Nicholas Wollaston, ***Tilting at Don Quixote***, 1990

> Man needs memory as a tree needs roots.
>   Ilya Ehrenburg, qtd. in W. Stanley Moss, ***Ill Met by Moonlight***, 1950

Back to the Cross Street Hostel

ON THE CHANNEL FERRY, I MET A SOUTH AFRICAN COUPLE WHO RECOMMENDED THE HOTEL CONTINENTAL IN DOVER—ROOM AND BREAKFAST, 18/6. THEY WERE HAPPY TO BE RETURNING TO England once again. I—who felt more foreign than they, having spent only six days in the country—was ecstatic, rolling over and over in my mind Robert Browning's homesick call from Florence, "Oh to be in England, now that April's there." My crie de coeur arose not from homesickness, but from a yearning to connect with the culture that my educational system had raised me on. It was, of course, October rather than April, but that did not seem to matter, as the lines rolled relentlessly, like a tune one cannot stop playing, through the caverns of my mind.

    As I boarded the ferry in Calais, there was one of those dramatic, late-afternoon shafts of sunlight, low-angled in the sky, piercing black and ominous-looking rain clouds that hung, heavily, over the islands to the west. If the gods had been just, and the pathetic fallacy in operation—and I could put it into operation now if I wished to lie—the evening of my arrival in Dover would have been calm, clear, and welcoming. It was not. Instead, a rain storm, accompanied by strong winds, lashed me as I pushed my bike off the ferry and into the custom's hall. But the storm had a positive effect as well. Later, the sound of the rain and the wind was to comfort me as I fell asleep, cocooned in the warmth of my English room.

> *The following morning, I awoke to cerulean skies and the sun shining on the white cliffs of Dover, which I could see from my room standing in splendid chalk-white, a hundred yards away, across an indentation in the land. The gulls cried as they swept past my window, and some of them hung motionless as they rode the air currents, like gliders. Watching them in the early-morning sunlight, I was filled with a feeling of calm and balance. I had a large, greasy, English breakfast and checked out of the hotel. If it had not been for the October cold that blasted my face when I hit the road once more on the Moto Guzzi—perhaps, I hoped, for the last time—the day would have been perfect. But this minor discomfort did not matter. I was back in England, and that was perfect enough.*

As I approached London, even the cloud of pollution that hung over the city like a toque, isolating it from the countryside, did not disconcert me. The journey from Dover to London took about two hours. Arriving at B.C. House in Lower Regent Street around one o'clock, I checked for mail. I was disappointed that there was nothing for me, and my mood immediately and precipitously reversed from comfortably happy to profoundly lonely. The young man who checked for mail gave me a *Guide & Map for Visitors from British Columbia*. I knew I would need to contact the London County Council (LCC) to set up a teaching job, so I asked him for the address. He gave it to me and I wrote it down on the front of the *Guide*, where it remains still, reading like something out of an Oscar Wilde play: The County Hall, Westminster Bridge, SE 1 (WA 5000).

I went into the tiny reading room, where the B.C. papers were displayed on wooden spines. There was nobody else there. B.C. House was a mausoleum, and I was the only visitor. Here I was in this huge city with no reasonable prospects of settling in and settling down without a great deal of nerve-wracking effort. After looking at the most recent copies of the *Revelstoke Review* and discovering that I had read them before leaving home only a couple of months earlier, I drove to the student hostel at 19 Cross Street in Islington, where Bill and I had stayed in August. There, in the quiet of a sunny October afternoon, I found myself sharing an eight-bed room with only one other person, a middle-aged German, who had coke-bottle glasses and limited English. As I was tired and cold, I had a shower, lolled around for the rest of the afternoon, had a bite to eat at the greasy café on the corner, and went to bed early, pretty thoroughly depressed.

A Feast of Theatre

FOR THE NEXT TWO WEEKS, I LIVED IN A WORLD OF AVOIDANCE. I AVOIDED LOOKING FOR A CHEAPER AND MORE PERMANENT PLACE TO stay; I avoided trying to find a teaching job. Instead, I spent my mornings seeing the sights of London, and my afternoons and evenings at the theatre or the concert hall. Apart from a natural tendency to procrastinate in areas I have a gut feeling I want to avoid, I think I was also to some extent basking in the relief of being in a country whose language was mine and whose culture was partly mine. Escape, for sure. But if I had to be into avoiding the reality of my situation, it was a wonderful way to do it.

In those days, if you took a seat in the "gods," as I almost always did, the theatre was not expensive.[1] A pound would stretch a long way. So nearly every day I went to at least one performance: October 7: Lyric Theatre, *Irma La Douce* (7/6). October 8: (Afternoon) Cambridge Theatre, T. S. Eliot's *The Elder Statesman* (8/6); (Evening) Royal Festival Hall, Hepsibah Menuhin, Bartok Piano Concerto (12/6—no cheaper tickets—ouch!). October 9: Royal Festival Hall, Yehudi Menuhin, Elgar Violin Concerto (21/-)—cheapest ticket available—ouch! ouch!). October 11: (Afternoon) Vivien Leigh in *Duel of Angels*; (Evening) Bridget Bardot in the film, *Love is My Profession*. October 13: Royal Festival Hall, Alan Loveday, Beethoven Violin Concerto. October 14: (Afternoon) Comedy Theatre, Peter Shaffer's first play, *Five Finger Exercise* (5/-). October 15: (5:55 p.m. Concert Series) Royal Festival Hall, Piet Kee Organ Concert (4/-). October 17: Film *Cat on a Hot Tin Roof*. October 20: Royal Festival Hall concert. And so on.

This rash of theatre-going was not a total exercise in avoidance. I was living in a dormitory room in a hostel where there was nobody to strike up a friendship with. In all that mighty heart, I knew no one. So I was feeding my soul on the best that London had to offer, dealing with my loneliness by burying myself in the theatre. While the plays were in progress, I could identify with a character and become a part of his dilemma. The theatre provides an oblique but real experience in human interaction, something I needed badly at the time. But in the end, since my money would not last forever, I had to come to terms with my situation.

A First Foray into Getting Established

I STARTED OFF WITH AN EASY TASK, THINKING THAT IF I SUCCEEDED AT ONE THING IT WOULD SPUR ME ON TO TACKLE OTHER THINGS IN THE areas I was avoiding. On October 10, I went to the Customs Office to fill out the forms to make it possible to sell the motorbike in England. A man there told me that I first had to get a form filled out by officials at the Canadian Embassy, confirming I was who I claimed to be and that they had no objections to the importation of the vehicle from a Canadian point of view. I was reminded of the red tape involved in buying the motorcycles in Italy. But I managed it all in a morning, and congratulated myself in taking this step in the right direction. I also went to the British Museum to try to get a ticket for the Reading Room, thinking I might emulate Colin Wilson, whose book, *The Outsider*, tells the story of his arriving on his bicycle at the Reading Room in the early 1950s, day after day, and writing what turned out, unexpectedly for a book of literary criticism, to be a smash popular hit. But there was no way I was going to get a ticket without references. So it was a win-one, lose-one situation.

---

[1] In those pre-decimal days, the pound was made up of 20 shillings, and the shilling was made up of 12 pence. So, the numbers £12/9/8 meant 12 pounds, 9 shillings, and 8 pence; 7/6 meant 7 shillings and six pence; and so on.

> *Three years later, my tutor at the University of London Institute of Education, Mrs. Moore, suggested, after reading some of my poetry, that I might like to work on it in the Reading Room and wrote me a note that got me a ticket immediately. I went only once. It was an impressive place to work, but it was far too slow for my liking, taking up to an hour to have a book delivered to my carrel. Besides, I couldn't see that anything I was writing needed this library. The unrationalised truth, of course, was that I was not made of the same stuff as Colin Wilson. If I had anything to say, I had no idea how to say it. I had not developed my art. I was lazy and had not worked at it, and I had been too shy to seek competent and professional help by taking a creative writing course.*

When I was at the afternoon performance of *Duel of Angels* on October 11, I made an acquaintance, referred to in a previous chapter, in the interval between the acts, who might have helped me establish a circle of friends. Liz Turvey had been in the advertising office of the Hudson's Bay store in Vancouver when I worked there as an executive trainee. We had not known each other at the time; but sitting beside each other in the theatre that afternoon, we knew that we recognized each other. It was a classic "Haven't I met you somewhere before?" situation. She told me she was supply teaching in London. It was an erratic way to earn money, but it left her with a lot of free time to explore the city. I was interested in how she had gone about getting her job, and she gave me some advice on how to get hired as a supply teacher. We also discussed, as I have pointed out before, Earle Birney's humorous World War II novel, *Turvey*, which I knew of but had not read. I would have liked to have seen her again, but I left the theatre without suggesting a coffee or even getting her telephone number. Everything seemed wrong about our getting to know each other, even as friends. We were both from British Columbia, but we came from different worlds.

I did nothing more for a few days about searching for a teaching job. I used a chance discovery on October 12, when leafing through my journal, to continue procrastinating in that area. There, I came across the address and phone number of Dave Harley, one of the two ex-paratroopers I had met in the hostel in Barcelona. I was dying for some congenial company, *any* congenial company; and, at the same time, happy to be distracted from the task of finding a job. I phoned him at Chiswick 5350 (don't you just love those old phone numbers!), and he asked me to come to lunch at his parent's house at 81 Park Road the following day. So I spent the next day with him and his family. It was a warming experience to be involved with a family again. But there is a drawback to temporary happiness. When I left the Harley house and faced again the loneliness of London, I found that the experience had made me more depressed than ever.

It was obvious, however, that I really had no choice but to make a concerted effort to find work, as my money was steadily dribbling away. So on October 15, buoyed by Liz's account of her supply teaching, I went to Burton's, on the corner of Oxford Street and Tottenham Court Road in Holborn, and bought a greenish-brown wool suit. It had a button fly, which amused me. On the other hand, the news that the minor alterations (cuffing) were going to take four days annoyed me, as the delay could do nothing but dampen the momentum I was trying to build. To go with the suit, I bought a pair of cheap oxfords. I couldn't show up for a job interview in my rubber Wellingtons, or in my battered, bike-scared oxfords, and they were all I had.

First Attempts at Getting a Teaching Job

THE SUIT WAS NOT READY FOUR DAYS LATER, AS PROMISED—THE TAILOR HAD BEEN, I WAS TOLD, ILL. I WAS ASSURED IT WOULD BE there the next day. And it was. So, dressed to the nines (or, at least, to the eights and a bit), I went to the London County Council in Lambeth, on the south side of Westminster Bridge, to find out what I had to do to begin teaching. I was told that I had first to get "permission to teach" from the Ministry of Education, across the city in Hampstead. So I crossed the city to the Ministry. There, they told me I could not be given permission to teach unless the LCC had a specific job for me. While there, I filled out a number of application forms, including one to send to St. F. X. for my qualifications. I was told by the bureaucratic twit I was dealing with that when they heard from the university, the Ministry would "decide whether my degree would be recognized." The next day I returned to the LCC with what the Ministry had told me about a specific job. But *their* bureaucratic twit still insisted that *they* couldn't give me a job without Ministry approval. I felt like a tennis ball, batted back and forth in a kind of Wimbledon.

Darkness Falls

A foggy day, in London town, / It had me low and it had me down,
I viewed the morning with due alarm / The British Museum had lost its charm.
George and Ira Gershwin, "A Foggy Day (In London Town)," 1937

I Decide on Impulse to Go Home

THE NEXT COUPLE OF DAYS I WAS TOO DEPRESSED TO DO ANYTHING BUT WANDER THE STREETS. IT ALL SEEMED SO HOPELESS. ON THE 22nd, as I was passing through Trafalgar Square in my aimless wandering, on impulse I went into the offices of Canadian Pacific, which were then in a large building on the south side of the square, and booked a passage to Montreal on the *Empress of France*, the ship that Bill and I had rejected in favour of the *Homeric* on our voyage to Europe.

> *I walked out of the office into the square, sat by one of Landseer's magnificent lions, meek as a mouse, and tried to convince myself that this was the right decision, that there was no way out of this mess but to head for home, taking the Moto Guzzi with me, as I could not legally leave it in England. My audience, the pigeons in the square, seemed to concur. But I found it difficult to keep buried in my subconscious the feeling that I was taking the coward's way out.*

On October 23, I took the train (bike in the baggage car) to Liverpool, where I arranged to have the Cardellino made ready to be put aboard ship. The man I left it with was to drain the gas out of its tank, the full extent of the preparation. It would remain in the shed on the dock, joining other material being made ready to be loaded on board. As there were about ten days before the ship was to leave for Canada, I decided to take a train to Edinburgh and do a last bit of touring. Keeping myself busy was one way of avoiding the argument continually raging in my mind between the forces that wanted me to stay in London until I prevailed, and those that felt it was better to give up and go home with my tail between my legs.

False Dawn

> She [Madame Merle] declared that in England the pleasures of smell were great—that in this inimitable island there was a certain mixture of fog and beer and soot which, however odd it might sound, was the national aroma, and was most agreeable to the nostril; and she used to lift the sleeve of her British overcoat and bury her nose in it, inhaling the clear, fine scent of the wool.
> Henry James, *The Portrait of a Lady*, 1880

Once More unto the Breach

CURIOUSLY ENOUGH, IT WAS IN THE OCTOBER FOGS OF EDINBURGH, SO THICK THAT AT TIMES I COULD NOT SEE THE CASTLE FROM Princess Street, and perhaps as a result of the aroma emanating from a thousand kilts (into which I definitely did not bury my nose), that I began to emerge from this dark night of the soul. For this change of attitude, this lightening of my spirit, this renewal of my will to tackle once again the London teaching world, I have no explanation. It may have been my innate stubbornness pushing up through the gloom. I was damn well going to tackle this problem and win!

It may also have been the jolly, late-middle-aged warden of the youth hostel who roused us in the morning, Billy-Butlin-like, with a stentorian "Wakey! Wakey!"—his handlebar moustache flaring and his leather sporran flapping from side to side as he tramped through the dormitories in his voluminous kilt—who contributed to my change of mind. He was an admirer of Major Douglas, the founder of the Social Credit Movement, and since we had two nominally Social Credit governments in Canada, in Alberta and British Columbia, he was full of questions about what they were accomplishing. His singling me out and listening to my crude explanations made me feel important, wanted, almost needed.

Whatever the reason, I changed my mind about returning to Canada, and on Saturday the 25th I took the train to Liverpool. There, I retrieved my motorbike from the docks. The man who turned the bike over to me spewed out a torrent of well-chosen swear words as he pointed out to me that the person who had prepared the bike for placing in the ship's cargo had broken the nut that held the gas line to the tank, making it necessary for me to tape it up, not very successfully, but well enough so I could run the bike as far as the railway station. It was far too cold now to consider riding the bike to London. I put myself and the Moto Guzzi on a slow train (cheaper than a fast one, and quite without a plan, but enervated by my decision to stay the course in Europe, I returned early on Saturday evening to Liverpool Street Station.

Down and Out in London's East End

I WAS SHORT OF CASH, A SERIOUS PROBLEM ON A SATURDAY EVENING IN THOSE PRE-CREDIT-CARD, PRE-ATM DAYS, HAVING LESS THAN A pound in my pocket. But I wasn't too worried, as I had ninety dollars in traveller's cheques. But when I tried to cash one in the cafeteria at the station, where I had a sandwich and tea, I was told they "didn't do traveller's cheques." This setback made matters worse, as I had to use about half of my cash to pay for the food I'd eaten.

On a Saturday evening in 1950's London, the banks were, of course, closed. And so was just everything else; so there was really nowhere I could get any money. I could have gone to an expensive hotel, where, as a guest, they would have cashed my traveller's cheques, but my overall shortage of funds made that a bad idea. I could have gone to Cross Street—probably *should* have, as they knew me there and might have listened to my story and given me credit—but as they had in the past insisted on getting cash on the barrelhead on arrival, I was reluctant to go there and ask. So I made the decision to park my bike on a side street near the station, spend the two nights there, and use what little money I had left to buy food. It was one of the dumbest decisions I ever made.

I had not reckoned on how long a night can be, sitting on a hard bench under the bright lights of a huge station waiting room. Nor had I expected to have a policeman come round every hour and throw me, my duffel bag, and everyone else who did not have a train ticket out into the cold. And it *was* cold out there in the middle of the night, dressed as I was in summer clothes, the only clothes I had with me. Eventually, the cop left me alone—I'm not sure why, as he continued to kick out the others—and I lay back on a bench, duffel bag for a pillow, and managed to get some intermittent sleep.

But it was a long night, one of the longest I have ever experienced, before or since, and in the cold of the dawn I realized that I couldn't face doing it again.

So about ten o'clock in the morning I called Dave Harley again and explained my problem. He graciously said (after checking with his mother) I could stay at his place overnight. And why didn't I come over now and have lunch and dinner with them. As you can imagine, I was not reluctant to take up his offer.

When I got to Park Road, I began to take off my rubber wellies at the front door, but stopped when I realized my feet smelt so rank that it would be more of an embarrassment to permeate the house with an offensive odour than to walk on their clean floors in my dirty boots. The hostel in Edinburgh had had only cold-water showers, a bad idea in October, so it had been a few days since I had got properly clean. It's likely that more of me than my feet smelt. So when I was shown to my room, I asked Mrs. Harley if she would mind if I had a bath. Mind? She was delighted.

We had lunch and dinner, and in the evening, Dave took me to the local Conservative Club, a small meeting room over a shop, where we had a couple of pints of beer. I was pleased to be able to use most of the rest of my money to pay for my round.

In the morning, I rode the Cardellino to Trafalgar Square to cash in my ticket at the Canadian Pacific travel offices, where I had bought it less than a week before. I thought I would need a good excuse to do so, so I was prepared to tell them I was a serious Catholic and wanted to go to Rome for the election of the new pope, Pius XII having just died. But they were not interested in excuses. They were happy to give me a full refund, eighty-four pounds and change. Until I found work, that and my remaining traveller's cheques were all I had to live on. Although the total amounted to a lot more money than it might appear to be today, it would not last more than a couple of months, so the situation would become drastic if I didn't find some way to earn a living. I had burnt my CPR boat. When I returned to the square, the pigeons seemed a bit nervous about my decision, though Landseer's lions might have been holding their heads a little higher.

I returned to Cross Street, and the next day, with renewed energy, I tried once again the London County Council / Ministry of Education route, but I continued to be batted back and forth between the two bureaucracies. In the meantime, on the steps of the National Gallery, I met a Jewish American, Adam Crane, who was staying at the King George VI Youth Hostel in Kensington. He had been on a Master's scholarship to Exeter University but had decided he couldn't face another academic year and had left soon after the term began. When he suggested we ride my bike to Israel, I agreed to think about it. But the idea of the two of us riding the Moto Guzzi that distance, given the size of the bike and its minimal horse power, was absurd. Besides, he was an emotional basket case. Not the type of person I needed to have around me at the time. So when I met Adam a few days later, once again on the steps of the National Gallery, this time by arrangement, I backed out. Desperate as my situation was, it was not *that* desperate.

Now that that idea was out of the way, it was crucial that I find cheaper, more permanent accommodation if I were to make my remaining money go as far as possible. Always in the back of my mind, of course, was the increasing realization that I would very soon have to find work, or I would be in dire straits indeed, cheap accommodation or no.

Real Dawn

This is the land of lost content,
I see it shining plain,
The happy highways where I went
And cannot come again.
A. E. Housman, ***A Shropshire Lad***, 1896

O N SUNDAY, NOVEMBER 2, I WENT TO MASS FOR THE FIRST TIME AT WESTMINSTER CATHEDRAL. IN SPITE OF ITS SIZE, I HAD SOME trouble finding it. Designed by John Francis Bentley (1839-1902), it was built between

1895 and 1903. It spurred on the revival of the Byzantine style of architecture in England, though it is not by any means pure Byzantine and is in many respects eclectic in its design. The exterior is largely red brick, broken up by horizontal bands of a grey stone, which also predominates in and defines the entranceway. In the 1950s it was, in spite of its size, still hidden behind a row of Victoria Street shops, some of which have subsequently been removed, providing it today with an esplanade and a vista. Even in its unfinished state, the interior, sheathed in green- and red-toned marbles, is impressive. I immediately fell in love with it, so much so that I went back in the evening for Benediction, not a service that I had ever been very much attached to, though I loved the old Latin hymns, *Tantum Ergo* and *O Salutaris*. But if truth be told, it was probably more loneliness and a need for spiritual consolation that took me back to the Cathedral, to the comfort and familiarity of the Catholic rituals, which in those days were the same all over the world. But I was quick to realize that all of this was an exercise in avoidance, and I was in danger again of rationalizing my avoiding of my central problem: finding a job and a place to live.

Early on the following Tuesday evening, I again went to the Cathedral, although there was no service, and sat quietly in its largely empty magnificence, pondering what should be my next move now that I had been thoroughly frustrated by the Ministry of Education and the London County Council. I had first to solve the accommodation problem. The Cross Street hostel was not at all suitable for the long term. On my way to the Cathedral that evening, I had explored the adjacent streets, and had noticed the Cathedral rectory just around the corner. As I sat in a pew, listening to a choir, probably in rehearsal, singing Mozart's fabulous *Ave Verum*, a hymn we used to sing when I was in the choir at Notre Dame, I decided to go to the rectory and see if they could recommend a more permanent place for me to stay.

After talking to me for a few minutes to find out what I wanted, the woman in the rectory picked up the phone and made a call to a hostel that provided long-term room and board. She asked them if they had room for a young male. They did. She asked me, her hand cradling the speaker, if I wanted to go there right away, that evening. I said I did.

I took the address and the directions the rectory woman had written down, and caught the No.15 bus to Cross Street, where I picked up my bag. I left the bike on the elevated sidewalk in front of the hostel, saying that I would pick it up the next day and drive it in daylight to Acton. The directions sent me on the underground's Central Line to West Acton station, south on Noel Road to Lynton Road, left to Creswick Road, and right on Creswick to Pierrepoint.

> On the corner, at 3 Creswick Road, lights blazing on this cool October night stood an imposing, late-Victorian brick building, etched like a romantic castle against the night sky. It was, I later learned, called Peace Haven. Standing on the corner contemplating it, I had no idea that in crossing its threshold, I was about to enter one of the happiest years of my life.

ENGLAND AGAIN

HOTEL CONTINENTAL
DOVER

M _____ Room No. 9

Date Oct 5/58

		£	s.	d.
Residence				
Room and Breakfast	1 @ 18/6		18	6
Early Morning Teas				
Afternoon Teas				
Luncheons				
Dinners				
~~Tea~~, Coffee	1 @ 1/-		1	0
Light Refreshments				
Bedroom Fires				
Telephone Calls				
Garage				
Sundries				
			19	6
5% Service charge			1	0
Less Deposit				
Amount Due £		1	0	6

PAID WITH THANKS

HOTEL CONTINENTAL, EAST CLIFF, DOVER

Cross Street Hostel

A Landseer Lion

The White Cliffs of Dover

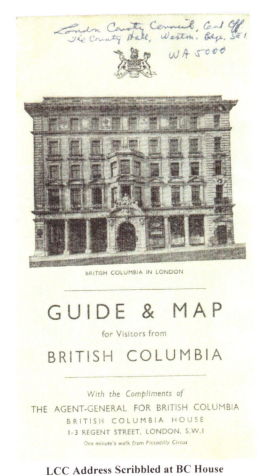

LCC Address Scribbled at BC House

Parking Permit in Liverpool

1950s Liverpool Street Station

Westminster Cathedral

David Harley's Address with Directions on Top Right

Chapter 8: A Young Man's Fancy

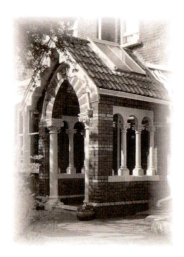

PEACE HAVEN 1958-59

> No, Sir, when a man is tired of London, he is tired of life; for there is in London all that life can afford.
> Samuel Johnson, **Letter to Boswell**, 20 Sept., 1777

> The rising birth rate and accelerating prosperity of London in the 1950s helped to create a younger society which wished to divest itself of the limitations and restrictions of the postwar capital. There was no sudden transition, in other words, to the "Swinging Sixties." There were cafés and coffee bars and jazz-clubs in Soho; there were clothes-shops and small bistros in Chelsea some years before the efflorescence of boutiques and discothèques.
> Peter Ackroyd, **London: The Biography**, 2001

> There was so much I ought to have recorded,
> So many lives that have vanished—
> Families, neighbours; people whose pockets
> Were worn thin by hope. They were
> The loose change history spent without caring.
> Now they have become the air I breathe,
> Not to have marked their passing seems such a betrayal.
> Brian Patten, **The Betrayal**

MOST YEARS GO BY UNNOTICED. THEY ARE ORDINARY, BLAND, HARD TO REMEMBER. LOOKING BACK ON THEM, THEY SEEM ALMOST UNLIVED. THEY OFFER NOTHING PARTICULARLY memorable, no gears shifted in the race of living, no turns into roads undriven, no new friends, new loves, new hates. And then there are those years—not many, and often unrecognized at the time—that are seminal, their pattern and detail remembered forever, even when their influence over the rest of life has been shunted off to a periphery of the mind. My year at Peace Haven was such a year, happy in the living, most happy in the memory.

Peace Haven is the name of a late-Victorian private home (1892) turned into a hostel, located at 3 Creswick Road in North Acton, a borough to the west of London. It was built by a banker as his family home. No expense was spared in its design and construction. It is in many respects the chief character in my story of that year, and of all my loves—with the exception of Jenny, whom I found there—the one I loved the most.

The exterior is red brick, patterned with stripes and crosses of yellow brick, in the manner of the great Victorian architect, William Butterfield. At the front, which faces south, there is a four-sided turret on the east end, which is attached to the house by a wider fifth side. In the centre, there is an impressive pillared entranceway. Between the turret and the entrance are windows that are bayed through two storeys, right up to the bottom of the gables. On the other side of the entrance are boxed bay windows on the ground level, and above these, a flat façade that rises to a gable roof end. Along the gables and over the entranceway is some heavy ginger breading.

At the back of the house, there is a large garden area, most of which is lawn. If you stand on the lawn, facing the house, you will be immediately impressed by the square bowed-out windows of the second floor, behind which is the area that in the 1950s we called the Games Room, later named the Noel Ede Hall. This room rises up through a steep-pitched attic storey to a square rooftop cupola with clerestory windows on all four sides.

> *There was a ping pong table in the Games Room, where Jennifer and I used to play. She was a fine athlete and a strong competitor, having been a teenage tennis champion in Dorset. I can still see her reaching for an impossible ball, her arm stretched to its limit, her blonde hair flying off her shoulders, as she returned a bullet of a shot that I, in turn, often missed. She usually beat me. I blamed her dominance on the fact that she was left-handed. But the truth is that she was just the better player. And I loved her for her playing hard and not just letting me win, as many girls would have done.*

The west side of the house, facing Pierrepoint Road, has two boxed bay windows on the main floor, one on the library, the other on what is now a dormitory, and as is the case on the front, a flat façade above and ginger breading on the gable. On the east side, the only distinguishing feature is the stained-glass window in the office area. Across from the east side, in what was once the mews, there is the one-storey kitchen, not part of the original buildings and probably added when the house was turned into a hostel. Next to that is the dining room, also a later addition, above which is the Warden's apartment. Behind that is a two-storey building with a pitched roof, probably the original stables, which in the 1950s had an office on the ground floor and accommodation for the live-in domestic staff above. Around the entire property is a substantial, capped brick wall, five to six feet high.

The house was bought in 1946 by the International Friendship League (IFL), an organization founded by Noel Ede in 1931. (Ede was the brother of Chuter Ede, who was

Home Secretary in the 1945 Labour Government.) The plan was to use it as a hostel where people from all parts of the world could intermingle and become friends with one another. The name "Peace Haven" comes from the south-coast town of Peacehaven, where in the early 1930s Ede first brought together a group of young people from Germany and England as an experiment in creating friendship among nations on an individual level, a strangely ominous concurrence, considering the way the next fifteen years in Europe were to evolve. The aims of the IFL were: "to promote contact, friendship, tolerance, and understanding among people of disparate backgrounds, and thus contribute to the peace of the world."

The organization continues to exist and has branches in many parts of the British Isles as well as in a number of other countries. When I came to the hostel in 1958, it was thriving, with a dozen or so longer-term residents (British, Irish, Spanish, French) and a constant stream of visitors from all over Europe, Africa, and Asia. I was the only North American long-term resident. The hostel was home to both males and females, a fact not lost on the neighbours, who jokingly referred to the IFL as the "International Free-Love League." Need I state, as an insider, that this attribution was a bit of an exaggeration?

The House Felt Warm and Welcoming

I ARRIVED AT PEACE HAVEN ON THE NIGHT OF TUESDAY, NOVEMBER 4, 1958. STANDING IN THE OAK-PANELLED HALLWAY, I LOOKED INTO THE, office of Miss Devitt, the Warden, which was a splendid square room, curiously a couple of steps down from the hall. It was brightly lit, with night-time unreadable stained glass windows across its back. The house felt warm and welcoming, and I was immediately pleased to be there. My feelings were no doubt influenced by the fact that I was moving into a more permanent world than the cold land of itinerant hostels. For whatever reason, I felt at home, a feeling that across the intervening years has never left me.

Miss Devitt was a plain, Irish-Catholic spinster, medium height, with tightly-permed, greying hair and square, rimless glasses. She was probably in her early forties at the time, but to me, at twenty-three, she was ancient. Every morning, she went to early Mass at Our Lady of Lourdes Church on the High Street, no more than a ten-minute walk from the hostel. Apart from that, her Catholicism was not obtrusive. Although her spinsterly morality may have been the source of her considerable annoyance when she caught me in the library late one evening, early in my tenure at the hostel, at a time when all good Christians should have been in bed, with a girl from Germany whose name I have forgotten. We were not in a particularly compromised position, but as all the lights were out, it was clear that we were not reading.

She often projected a no-nonsense attitude that was discomfiting, though I was soon to learn that this superficial sternness belied a heart that was soft and generous. She was in that sense the old spinster equivalent of the traditional old whore. But there was a surprise in store for us residents regarding Miss Devitt. A couple of months after I arrived at Peace Haven she departed hurriedly, without even a cursory farewell to the long-term residents. One day when I came home from my school-teaching job, she was gone. Totally wiped out, erased. As if she had never been there. Word among the residents was that she had been fired. Nobody knew why. I expect the job was too much for her, and that she hadn't been doing it very well.[1]

The hostel had three dormitory rooms, used to house itinerants, each with eight to ten single beds accommodating males or females (never both together), as the need arose. I was placed in one of these rooms when I arrived. At first there were two others sharing it with me. As the weeks went by, people came and went and the numbers varied. As it was winter, and few groups were seeking accommodation, I often had the large room to myself. There was no central heating, and the electric heaters, which demanded shillings at an alarming rate, were inadequate in such a large room. England, in spite of rumours to the contrary, can be cold and damp in winter. In bed, however, I was able to make myself comfortable, as I slept in my sleeping bag, wearing a heavy wool sweater. There were, besides these large dormitories, a number of smaller rooms, each housing two or three longer-term residents, referred to by everyone as "permanent" residents.

When one of the regulars moved out at the end of the month, I was invited by Peter Rafell, a youngish "permanent" resident, who in some mysterious way represented the IFL, to become one of them. Peter gave the impression of being a bit of a slick operator. He almost always wore a lounge suit, even on weekends, which I understood as either a sign of his feelings of inferiority, or an expression of his exalted status, whatever that was, within the IFL. On top of this, he was outspokenly puritanical regarding the inevitable love affairs that blossomed among the residents. Since this was the 1950s, these affairs tended to be absolutely respectable in their public face, and whatever intermingling occurred in private was done as surreptitiously as possible. There was nothing Peter could do about these affairs, of course, but he made it clear he disapproved of them.

> *After I was gone from Peace Haven, I heard that Peter had been involved in his own surreptitious affair, carrying international friendship a bit too far. The result was that he got the Italian maid—a voluptuous creature in her late twenties by the name of Ida, after whom all of us male residents lusted from a regrettable distance—pregnant. So much for his "holier- than-thou" attitude! And, with one of the domestic staff, if you can believe it! I have to admit that I was pleased he'd got caught out in this way. Nevertheless, in his response to the situation, he proved to be not such a bad guy. He "did the right thing," as we used to say in those days, and married her.*

Settling in as a Permanent Resident

I MOVED INTO ROOM 10, AT THE TOP OF THE HOUSE, SHARING IT WITH ITS TWO OTHER OCCUPANTS. ONE WAS "MAC" MACGREGOR, A YOUNG

---

[1] Eighteen years later, in the summer of 1977, when Barbara and I were on vacation in England and staying at the run-down Hotel Ivanhoe in Bloomsbury, there was an older woman supervising the breakfast room. It was Miss Devitt. She did not recognize me and I did not introduce myself. I'm sorry about that now.

man from Scotland, who worked as an apprentice in an Acton engineering firm. The other was Leslie Dunkling, a native of Acton, who had just set a course toward complete independence by moving out of his paternal home on Bollo Lane. Next to us on the top floor, in Room 9, were Frisco, a Spaniard, and his roommate, Paddy, who was (as one might expect) an Irishman. Across the hall, in Room 8, were three young girls, Rosemary Edwards, from Wales, Danielle Raffaitin, from France, and Jennifer Sharp, from the English coastal town of Weymouth.

In those days, television was not as intrusive in people's lives as it was later to become. There wasn't a set at Peace Haven. So there was more social interaction than would be the case a few years later, when the tube became both entertainer of and mediator among people gathered together in groups. Throughout the winter, on weekend afternoons and in the evenings, there was often a crowd of people in the lounge. It was a most attractive room, panelled in oak, with a bay window on its long side and the four-sided alcove of the turret at the end farthest from the door. On the wall opposite the window was a fireplace, topped by a glassed-in landscape and ornamented by an elaborately-carved mantelpiece. The residents mixed with whatever itinerants were staying at the hostel. We played cards together—*Oh Hell!* and *Hearts* were favourites—chatted, flirted, and in the course of things planned visits to pubs, the theatre, and the cinema. We males were always on the outlook for romance, checking out any girls that might have arrived during the day—from France, Germany, Brighton, or wherever.

Mieke Roodenburg, who was from Amsterdam, will do as an example of a short-stay girl I dated. She spent only three or four days with us over a weekend in late November. She was physically solid without being large and had a square face of a type that is not uncommon among the Dutch. She had a way of flaring out her deep brown, shoulder-length hair as she flashed her cerulean blue eyes in my direction. I was captivated, to say the least, and I made the effort to ask her out before one of the other young males got in ahead of me. You had to move in quickly, or it was too late.

> *On a Saturday afternoon, I took Mieke to a matinee at the Odeon Cinema on the High Street, where we did more kissing and petting than watching the movie. That evening, we went to the theatre in Richmond, where there was a good repertory company whose plays I often attended. I have forgotten the name of the play we saw. After the play, I was hoping to advance our afternoon of kissing and petting, but when we got back to Peace Haven, Mieke was interested only in a couple of brief kisses before she went off to bed. I was disappointed. But I realized that in her head she was probably already on her way home and had marked down our passion in the cinema as her fling for this trip. I had been written off. Our brief relationship was over. Forever. And, quite frankly, it didn't matter. Our short time together had been fun. It was all that either of us asked. And there would be other times, for both of us, with other people.*

One of the things I discovered on my dates with Mieke, a discovery whose universal nature would be underscored throughout the following couple of years, was that

English and European girls did not wear the horrid rubber girdles that were *de rigueur*—what a wonderful pun!—among North American girls. It was nice to be relieved of the impression that you were feeling up a hot water bottle.

Christmas Days with Loralie

OVER THE CHRISTMAS HOLIDAYS, THERE WAS LORALIE. SHE HAD COME TO PEACE HAVEN FROM HER HOME IN MANSFIELD, BECAUSE she did not get along with her step-father and his first family, with whom Christmas that year was to be spent. She was nineteen. She had strong blonde hair, which she wore pulled back into a French roll. Her ancestors might have been Vikings, as her eyes of greyish-blue were set in a face that was roundish and Nordic. She was quite tall without being the least bit willowy. I found her very attractive.

> *A few days after we began going out, we were enjoying a sunny wintry afternoon in Springfield Park, just down the road from Peace Haven. I took pictures, using black and white film. She was wearing a light blue, home-knit dress that showed her eyes and hair to advantage. But the dress was calf length, and as the fashion for skirt-length had recently changed, up to the middle of the knee, she kept pulling up her dress to that length when she sat down. We had the park to ourselves on this winter's day. While we sat side by side on a park bench, she showed me a photograph of her biological father sitting on a camel in a light khaki uniform. He had been killed in Egypt during the war. She can't have remembered him very well, but it was clear he remained important to her, at least in some kind of mythical sense. (How life would have been different had he lived!) After she had showed me the photograph, she kissed me, and while doing so, took my hand and placed it on her breast.*

Loralie had a friend, Marge, who had come with her from Mansfield. They worked in the same office, doing I don't remember what, but they were probably employed as stenographers—takers of dictation in Pitman shorthand on small, wire-bound pads, typers of what was taken down, lickers of envelopes and stamps, mailers. Marge was a shortish brunette, not unattractive, with twinkling eyes. But she had a loud, voluble laugh that could overwhelm a room. I found her embarrassing. She immediately teamed up with Charles, who was also visiting over the holidays, I think from Birmingham or Manchester. Loralie told me that she and Marge had made a pact (as young girls are wont to do) to have a good time on this holiday and not "to gooseberry" one another. (I had not heard this expression before and had to have it explained. "To gooseberry" was to hang around a friend who was trying to make out with a new partner.) So, for the most part, we did our thing and Marge and Charles did theirs. We didn't gooseberry each other.

On Christmas Eve, an Irish ex-merchant-navy sailor by the name of Mick Gaul, like myself a recently-installed, permanent resident of Peace Haven, received an unexpected bonus at work and brought home a collection of booze he'd bought at the

Duke of York, a pub that was only a short walk from Peace Haven: scotch, gin, rum, etc.[2] He organized a party, for which we offered Room 10. Everybody in the hostel was invited, except a group of a dozen or so Ghanaian fellows, proud of their recent independence, and dressed in the colourful flowing robes that were their national dress. Earlier that week, Mick had been roundly criticised by their leader for calling them "Ghanese". It was an innocent mistake, often made at the time, on the analogy of China/Chinese. But the Ghanaians were in the sort of arrogant mood that overtakes people who have recently triumphed over their masters, in this case, the British; and they corrected the mercurial Mick a bit too sharply. While the party was on, they complained to Miss Devitt that they had not been invited to it. She mentioned their displeasure to Mick. But he held his ground. "I invited my friends," he said. "They are not my friends." Everybody else in Peace Haven was: residents, itinerants, maids, Adolf the cook—even Miss Devitt, though she had enough diplomacy not to attend.

There wasn't all that much booze for a crowd as large as this one, so the party remained civilized. After a couple of hours, people began to disperse. Loralie and I and Marge and Charles went into Paddy and Frisco's room next door. None of us in those more innocent times locked our rooms. (The innocence was in fact forced on us, as there were no locks on the doors.) At any rate, we four turned out the lights, and each couple hopped on to one of the two single beds. We kept our clothes on, more or less, but things were nonetheless getting hot and heavy when the door burst open and Paddy, flicking on the light switch, walked in. He was not amused. Looking back on it, no longer possessing the arrogance of youth, I sympathize totally with his annoyance. No one wants someone else making out on their bed. But at the time, I was young and foolish and merely shrugged off his anger. Silly old bugger.

Loralie and I had come close to "going all the way," as we so quaintly put it in those days. But close doesn't count when it comes to losing your virginity. She was still *virgo intacta*. Later, as we sat together on our own downstairs in the library, she pondered on the mixture of pain and pleasure she had felt. She was obviously proud of herself in adventuring so far. And, I think, if truth be told, relieved that she had been saved by Paddy's sudden arrival. While we were making love, she kept saying "No," but she did not pull away or struggle. At that magic moment, she was certainly willing. But the magic moment did not come again. In a few days she was gone. After that, there may have been one or two letters exchanged. I don't remember.[3]

I don't want to give the impression that all of my relationships with itinerant women were romantic in a physical sense, that I was some kind of prowling Don Juan.

---

[2] The Duke of York was the pub we most often went to. It was run at that time by a middle-aged man who had been a bodyguard of the Aga Khan. When he left that job, he had been set up in the pub as a retirement gift. He and his wife ran the bar, along with a pair of German shepherds who were stationed behind it. Although the dogs were as friendly as could be when they were on the customer side of the bar, when they were on the landlord's side, they were most unhappy with anyone who ventured even a hand over the bar. The pub still exists. I don't know what happened to the landlord and his dogs.

[3] Another girl who was important that year visited for a few days in February. I had met Denise Duval on the *Homeric* the previous summer on the crossing from Canada. I tell the story of her visit to Peace Haven in *Europe on a Moto Guzzi Cardellino*.

Once Jennifer and I had become a couple, I was no longer interested in itinerant girls. I cared too much for her to play around on her. And there were many times before Jennie when I asked girls to go out with me and they refused. There were other times when I hit it off with a visiting girl, and we would spend enjoyable time together in the public rooms at the hostel, sometimes with other people present, sometimes alone, getting to know one another a little bit. There's no doubt that in some cases, if circumstances had been different, our relationship would have progressed to another level. One of these girls, who came from Sweden, had spent a long evening talking with me in the library the day before she left for home. We were very much attracted to one another, but there was nothing to be done about it. I was staying, and she was leaving, and anything else was too complicated even to consider. To turn a well-worn phrase upside down: we were ships that passed in the day. When I arrived at the hostel after work the next day, February 21, I found a note lying on top of my bed: *"This is not the right way to say good bye, but anyhow I must say it to you, mustn't I? Life is worth living, isn't it? Even if you have to say good bye. Ingrid."*

I Get a Teaching Position at Harlington School

A COUPLE OF NIGHTS AFTER I ARRIVED AT PEACE HAVEN, I GOT THE INFORMATION I NEEDED TO LEAD ME TO A TEACHING JOB. THERE were two elementary school teachers who happened to be staying in the hostel. I'm not sure why they were there; perhaps, they'd been kicked out by their wives, or maybe they had left their homes in a huff. Neither seemed to be connected to the other in any way—they taught in different schools—and when the autumn term ended, they were both gone.

> *Sometimes it so happened that I walked to Acton Mainline station on my way to work with one of them, also on his way to work. He had the kind of dark-complected face that looks as if it has been carved in granite. On his nose sat a pair of round National Health glasses. But it was his mind that got to me. It was replete with the kind of pettiness that we used to associate with a certain type of man who taught at the elementary level, especially in his attitude toward those better-educated than himself. He knew I had a university degree. He would try to catch me out on silly things. One morning, he asked me how I spelt "paid." "P-A-I-D," I said. "A lot of people think it's P-A-Y-E-D," he said. "I thought maybe it was an Americanism."*

It was the other teacher, an ordinary, amiable chap, who gave me the information that led to my teaching job. A crowd of people, perhaps fifteen or so, had gathered in the lounge on the second evening after my arrival at Peace Haven, talking in groups of three or four. I didn't really know anybody yet. I was standing awkwardly by a group that was sitting in the alcove, trying to become a part of things, when I was approached by a middle-aged man with wavy, greying hair, wearing a light yellow open-necked dress shirt, tie-less. We shook hands as we introduced ourselves. He asked me what I was doing in England, and I said I was looking for a teaching job and had had a royal run-around in dealing with the London County Council. He asked me if I had tried the

Middlesex County Council (MCC), the jurisdiction under which he taught. I did not then understand the county divisions in England, did not know that London was both surrounded and penetrated by counties that were not London. It was a revelation, perhaps not quite on the scale of Paul's on the road to Damascus, but at the time it felt near that. He told me that the headquarters was on Great Russell Street in Westminster. It surprised me that it was not in Middlesex, but in central London, just across the river from the LCC, where I had had such a frustrating experience. Sometimes things really are better on the other side of the river.

The next morning, I took the underground to Westminster Station, found the MCC headquarters, and was ushered into an office where people like me were looked after. After a desultory conversation with an unsmiling bureaucrat in which I talked about my qualifications, the unsmiling one asked me when I could start. I said, "Right away." "Today?" he said. "Today," I said. After shuffling through some papers, he told me there was a job available at a secondary modern school, Harlington County Secondary School, in Hayes. If I was interested, he'd call the headmaster. I was amazed at the speed at which things were happening. After having experienced so much frustration in dealing with the LCC, I had expected something the same from the MCC. I had no idea what a secondary modern school was, or where Hayes was situated; but I immediately said I'd take the job. At that point I would have taken a job on the outskirts of hell! During his telephone conversation with the headmaster, the bureaucrat put his hand over the mouthpiece and asked me if I could get to the school that afternoon by one o'clock. I said I could. It appeared that the school was as desperate to hire someone as I was desperate to be hired.

The unsmiling bureaucrat wrote the address on a piece of paper and gave it to me. He took out a map of Middlesex and pointed out the location of the school, sketching a map of its location on the same paper. The map, of course, was largely meaningless to me, and it could have been a map of Rawalpindi or the moon and been of as much value. He said I could get to Hayes on public transport, but he did not tell me how.

When I left the office, I sat down with my underground and railway maps, and worked out a route. But I did not realize how much the maps were stylized. Consequently, I took an incredibly circuitous route that involved an hour and a half of riding on and changing trains. When I eventually reached Hayes Station (British Rail), I had to take a bus and walk a couple of blocks to get to the school. But I *did* find it, and congratulated myself in doing so.[4] The school building itself turned out to be a surprise. Apart from the use of considerable brick in its construction, it was a modern building, quite similar in design to schools that had been built all over North America after the Second World War, the California design that made schools look like factories. I'm not at all sure why I was surprised. I mean, what was I expecting? Something out of *Goodbye Mr Chips*?

---

[4] The school was close to Heathrow Airport. I later found that when planes were taking off from the nearest runway, I often had to pause in my teaching until the noise had passed.

> *The headmaster had an unfortunate surname, "Pead"—he signed himself R. G. (Reginald) Pead. When I entered his office, he struggled out from behind his desk and came to the door to meet me, a big man, near retirement, with steely grey hair, glasses, a strong chin, prodigious false teeth, and a heavy limp. One of his legs was considerably shorter than the other, the result of some horrible wounding in the Great War, and he wore a substantial-looking boot on that leg, the sole about an inch and a half thick from toe to heel. After we had exchanged pleasantries and had a laugh about the convoluted route I'd taken to the school, he gave me a timetable and turned me over to one of the teachers, an East Indian, who introduced himself as Mr. Vera. He took me to my home-room class of thirteen-year-olds. As he left, he said to the class: "Anyone misbehaves, they'll have me to deal with." Pause. "Got that?" (I later learned that the students referred to him as "Mr Varmint"—but they respected him nonetheless, and I had no trouble with my class that day.)*

Teaching in a Secondary Modern School

THE ENGLISH SCHOOL SYSTEM OF THE 1950s WAS CREATED BY THE BEVERIDGE REPORT OF 1944, IN ANTICIPATION OF THE BRAVE NEW world that would come with the peace. It provided for the establishment of two types of schools, grammar schools and secondary modern schools. Students were placed in one or the other on the basis of an examination, the Eleven Plus, that it was claimed measured their intelligence. As its name implies, the exam was taken at the end of elementary school education, when students were eleven years of age or thereabouts. Roughly the top fifteen percent of those writing the examination went to grammar schools, where they followed a rich, traditional academic program. They had been singled out as the middle-level societal leaders of the future. (The *real* leaders were, of course, expected to come out of the great public schools like Eton and Harrow, beyond the imagination and ambition of the *hoi polloi*.) The remaining eighty-five percent went to the less-demanding secondary modern schools, where they followed a simplified academic program and received some training in manual and clerical areas. They had been singled out to be the hewers of wood and the drawers of water of the future. Harlington County Secondary School was this type of school.

On that first afternoon in the school, as a Canadian, I was exotic enough to keep their interest without much effort. A lucky thing, when you consider that I was totally untrained and had never before stood in front of a class as a teacher. But I recalled the wisdom of a crotchety old teacher I once heard say to my father, who was also in the profession, "The secret of teaching is to keep the kids busy, keep 'em happy." My timetable for the rest of that day was made up of two geography classes and one English class. Neither geography class seemed to know what they had been doing in previous classes—not much, I suspect, though claiming ignorance is a common student ploy—so I took an atlas and drew a map of Canada on the blackboard. "We're going to learn the rivers of Canada today," I said. I had them copy the outline map, and when they'd done that with some semblance of accuracy, I had them draw in and label the great rivers, one by one, and put a name alongside the snake of each of them. In the English class, I did "reading around the class," to find out how well they read. I was astounded at how bad they were at this basic skill. I was beginning already to get a sense of the academic level.

> *It was not until a couple of months had gone by, and I was seen to be thriving in the job, that I was told by one of my colleagues about the teacher I had replaced. She was a Miss Thompson, a neophyte in the profession, though unlike me, a trained neophyte. Her problems, though they were apparent from the beginning, gradually developed throughout the autumn term to a crisis level. She could not keep discipline in the classroom. She took to trying to dampen down the din by using a whistle, which was effective only for a day or two. After that, the students just ignored it. A week or so before I took over her job, in the middle of a class, Miss Thompson went into the storeroom cupboard, which was off the front of the room, to get some supplies, leaving her key in the lock. One of the students ran to the door, closed it, and turned the key. After ten minutes or so, they let her out. But that was the end for Miss Thompson. She went on permanent leave, taking her nervous breakdown with her.*

As the days went by, I became more confident in what I was doing. In spite of the fact that I was untrained, I was not without experience in the broadest sense. Like everybody else who has ever stood in front of a classroom for the first time, I had only to reach back in memory to my own student days to work out ways of doing things. Besides, I come from a family of teachers (grandmother, father, two sisters), so it could be argued that teaching is in my blood. I "kept the kids busy, kept 'em happy." It didn't matter much what they did, as long as the work was within their capabilities. I did not try to push them beyond what they could do. That way meant trouble, and trouble I didn't need. But at the same time, I did not put up with any nonsense. I quickly became known as a good disciplinarian, so much so that in March, when the Board of Governors of the school came for a visit, Mr. Pead adjusted the time table so that I was teaching the toughest group in the school.

Every morning, school began with an assembly, which according to law had to be religious in nature (i.e., in the non-Roman-Catholic system, based on the Christianity of the 'established' Anglican church).[5] This tradition was brand new to me. In the beginning, I thought it was a huge waste of time, especially when Mr. Pead got windy and went beyond the allotted time with his daily "sermon," with the result that the first class of the day was shortened. But after I had experienced the assemblies for some months, I changed my mind about their usefulness. They had the effect of bringing the whole society of the school together, with the result that a cohesiveness was created among the various parts of the group that made up Harlington County Secondary School: administration, teachers, separate classes, individual students, all brought together and mixed up, as it were, in one great pot.

---

[5] In *Autumn at the Institute*, I discuss a compromise that was reached regarding the religious assembly in the school in which I did my teaching practice, Central Foundation School, in the east end of London, whose student body was about half-Jewish.

> *The students were marched into the gymnasium/auditorium by the on-duty teaching staff. Once they were standing in their assigned areas, the teaching staff entered the room and stood in front of their chairs on the stage, and then Mr. Pead, dressed in academic gown and mortar board, limped to the podium in front of the teachers. The religious part of the assembly was dispensed with first. We said the Our Father—the "For thine is the kingdom" part added on the end and heads bowed in the Protestant fashion. We then had one of the better "scholars"—Mr. Pead always referred to the students as "scholars," a superb example of inflated language—read the Lesson for that day, usually a passage from the Bible. After that, we sang a rousing hymn or two, To Be a Pilgrim, For Those in Peril on the Sea, and such like. We were then permitted to sit down, the staff on chairs, the students on the floor. At this point, Mr. Pead in a booming voice (he was a good amateur singer in his other life) would deliver a secular kind of sermon, in which he would either praise or harangue the "scholars" and make any quotidian announcements that needed to be made. After that, standing for Mr. Pead's limping retreat, we left the room in reverse order from our entry and began classes.*

It was quite a performance, and, as time went by, I found myself looking forward to and thoroughly enjoying this daily ritual.

Another ritual at the school which I never really learned to like was supervising the hot lunchtime meal. As a teacher, one did not have to do this duty, but I choose to do it in order to save money and the hassle of bringing a lunch. Lunch was free for teachers if they sat with and supervised a table of students. These lunches had been set up by the educational authorities, remembering the poverty of the lower classes in the days of the great depression and the suspicion that many children did not get one decent meal every day. They were really dinners rather than lunches: a stew or a chop of some sort, potatoes, a couple of vegetables, some artificial gravy, bread, and a pudding and custard for dessert. The food was pretty awful, the smell of the overcooked vegetables alone often turning me off. But a free lunch was a free lunch, and I ate my wan pork chop, my lumpy mashed potatoes, and my smelly cabbage with a will.

The Day My Money Ran Out

> Money is the most important thing in the world. It represents health, strength, honour, generosity, and beauty as conspicuously as the want of it represents illness, weakness, disgrace, meanness, and ugliness.
> George Bernard Shaw, **Man and Superman**, 1903

BUT MY HAPPINESS IN FINDING A PLACE TO LIVE AND A JOB WAS SOON COMPROMISED BY A PRESSING FINANCIAL PROBLEM. ONE DAY I found myself—having used the last of my money to pay for my week's room and board at Peace Haven and my one-way fare to the school—literally out of money. And I mean *literally*. I didn't have a single penny to my name. Not one. It was a Wednesday, sometime in November. For a moment, after I had reached the school, it appeared almost miraculously that the crisis had been solved. It was pay day, and there at the school was my first pay cheque from the Middlesex County Council. At the end of the day, as I did not have any money for the fare home, and with my cheque warm in my pocket, I walked the considerable distance from Hayes to Acton (ca. 8 miles), trying to figure out how I was going to handle things. What I should have done, of course, was explain my situation to Mr. Pead and ask for a short-term loan until I could get my cheque cashed. But I didn't want to appear to be the sort who manages his finances so badly that he has to borrow money from people he hardly knows.

The crux of the problem was that I would be working while the banks were open on Thursday and Friday, so I wouldn't be able to get any money until Saturday morning. A simple solution would have been to phone the school in the morning and claim I had the flu or something of that sort. But I didn't have the four pennies I needed to make the phone call. I surely could have borrowed four pennies from someone at Peace Haven. But as was the case at the school, I didn't want to ask for a loan—even of a measly four pennies—from people I hardly knew. So I decided to take the day off, go to the Barclay's Bank in Acton, open an account, get some money, and then phone the school. The earliest I could do so would be after 10 o'clock, when the bank opened for business. I would just have to be AWOL for my first couple of classes. It was a stupid way to handle things, and I am embarrassed about my stupidity to this day.

> *I was waiting on the steps of the bank when it opened in the morning, worried to death about not phoning the school to explain my absence. When I presented my cheque to the teller, I explained that I wanted to open an account, deposit the cheque, and take out five pounds to get me through the next few days. He told me it would take four days to clear the cheque and I couldn't have any money till then. This scenario was impossible for me. I had to have some money. I explained my situation to him. I pointed out that if a cheque from the Middlesex County Council was no good, he might as well close his bank. He appeared to be unmoved. I thrust my passport through the hole at the bottom of his brass wicket and said: "Keep this till the cheque clears. I can't go anywhere without it." He screwed up his face as if he were considering my offer. "All right," he said. "I'll give you your five pounds. You can keep the passport."*

Having set up the account, been given a passbook and five pounds (including four of the enormous pennies that were still current in those days), I rushed out of the bank and hurried back to Peace Haven. There was a pay phone in the vestibule inside the front door. I put in my four pennies, and when the school answered, I pushed Button "A," listened to the pennies drop, and heard the voice of "P.M." Holbrow, the Assistant Head. "Where are you?" she said. "What happened?" I figured the truth was my best option at that point, so I told her my story. She was understanding. But beneath her empathy I could sense a wonder at how I could have handled this thing so badly. "You should have *told* us. *Anyone* would have lent you some money." I was suitably apologetic, downright grovelling, in fact. And so I should have been. I had acted in an undeniably stupid way. I offered to head straight for the school, but she said arrangements had been made to cover my classes for the day and I should come back in the morning. I am happy to say that my pay was not docked. They must have recorded my absence as due to illness. An unexpected kindness.

A Mixed Bag of Colleagues

"P. M." Holbrow, the Duchess, and "Lance Corporal" Hopkinson

A WIDOW IN HER EARLY FIFTIES, "P. M." HOLBROW, WAS TALL AND THIN, WITH TIGHTLY-PERMANENTED HAIR THAT WAS DYED A DARK brown. She wore the stern business suits typically deemed appropriate to women administrators in that era. She was popular with everyone on staff, quite a feat for an Assistant Head. Although I never got to know her very well, she made one memorable remark to me in the staff room that has stayed with me over the years. On a school trip to Arundel, after warning the students not to, I came out of the wrong exit from the castle and got lost, holding up the bus that was taking us to Littlehampton. My students insisted that the bus could not go without me. P. M. said of this incident: "I remember when I was young, how the students loved *me* in that way. Now it's your turn." As I grew older in the teaching business, I experienced the same kind of shift of affection from me to the younger teachers, and only then really appreciated what she was saying, and felt what she must have felt.

A well-preserved woman, whose name was Mrs. I. A. Hazell, but whom we young bucks called "The Duchess," told us at every opportunity how good she looked for her age. She was forty-seven. And apart from a certain thickness through the middle that comes to us all as we grow older, she did look good for her age. But to us young people, all of this was irrelevant. She was ancient. The Duchess had a soft spot for another teacher to whom we also gave a nickname, a tall, narrow, sixty-year-old man with a pencil-thin moustache and a military bearing, whom we called "Lance Corporal" Hopkinson. He was the sort of teacher that the following scenario captures precisely:

> *Mr. Hopkinson let his head slide upwards and backwards and closed his eyes . . .*
> *"Where's your football shirt?"*
> *"Haven't got one, Sir."*
> *"Gym shirt?"*
> *"Haven't brought it, Sir"*
> *"Why not?"*
> *"'Tisn't gym, Sir."*
> *"Are you trying to be funny?"*
> *"No, Sir."*
> *Mr. Hopkinson took a deep breath. "Why haven't you got a football shirt?"*
> *"Forgot it, Sir."*
> *"Brakespeare, you're hopeless . . . What are you?"*
> *"Hopeless."*

"Hopeless, what?"
"Hopeless, Sir!"[6]

When the students lined up by form on the playground at the sound of the bell, Hopkinson would stand in front of them, rigidly at attention, and call each form to march into the school, row by row. The lining-up-by-form routine was normal, but when Hopkinson was in charge, the occasion was turned into a parade ground scene. He not only *stood* ramrod stiff when he was barking orders at the students, but also *sat* ramrod stiff when he was at his desk. "He's a *real* gentleman," the Duchess used to say, "a real gentleman." With his staff-sergeant ways, we thought him an idiot.

I have only a passing recollection of most of the other men on the teaching staff. They ranged from the robotic Mr. Gamage, who taught science and was never seen wearing anything other than a white lab coat, to Mr. Williams, who taught English and arrived every day on his no-speed bicycle, his pant legs clipped at the calves. Also on staff was someone I remember only as Mr. J. Cleasby, a man with dyed black hair, slicked back as flat as a wig, which it may well have been. As you chatted with him in the staff room, he stared at you, silently and impassively, as if he were on a balcony at Buckingham Palace. His position in the greater world outside of Harlington School was impressive. Every afternoon, promptly at four, a uniformed chauffer would arrive in a large Rolls Royce to pick him up. In his other life, he was that year's Mayor of Lambeth.

Diane, Tess, Brenda, and Gerry

THE MEN ON THE STAFF—WITH A COUPLE OF EXCEPTIONS—WERE AT BEST UNINTERESTING, RANGING FROM THE RIDICULOUS TO THE barely conscious. In that sense, they were a good complement to the women, hardly an interesting one, certainly not a good-looking one, among them. Diane Pratt was a bouncy, slightly-built blonde, who was far too enthusiastic about everything. Talking to her was like talking to a Jill-in-the-Box. Tess Jones, who, like a lot of teachers in England in those days, was from Wales, was willowy and had natural, tightly-curled hair that was almost negroid in its texture. She was calm and friendly, and I enjoyed chatting with her. I often discussed with her the cost of renting a cottage in her part of Wales, where I fancied, away from the turmoil of life, that I might be able to write a masterpiece. Rents were cheap, she said, as little as eight pounds a month. Brenda Peers, a large creature, with a don't-hit-me, dog-like expression on her face, tried to be prim and lady-like, not an easy thing for a woman her size to pull off. She was highly aware, she pointed out to me a number of times—I don't know why now that she did so—that she should keep her ankles together when she was sitting. It was advice that was apparently generally given to young women in those days.[7]

---

[6] With apologies to Pat Barker, *The Man Who Wasn't There*, from whom I've borrowed the basis of this scenario. Though, the overall situation is familiar to anyone who taught in or went to a school a generation or two ago.
[7] A few years later, when I was teaching at Kingsway Day College in Holborn, I overheard in the staff room one of the other teachers, an enormous female creature by the name of Gaynor Something-or-Other, remark to one of the other female teachers (daringly, she felt, I'm sure) that a woman only opened her legs

There were two women who were reasonably attractive. One was Clare Ramsey, a cute, blonde biology teacher I would like to have got to know. The other was Gerry Street. She was medium-height, with dark, straight, shoulder-length hair, and a slight but well-proportioned figure. The floral, shirt-waisted dresses she wore at school in deference to female pedagogical respectability did not do her justice. At the staff party at the end of the summer term, which was held at the Castle in Richmond, Gerry and I slipped away into the park after having had a few drinks. For awhile she responded to me with enthusiasm, and I thought I'd won the lottery, but then she turned morose. She was planning to get married in the fall and was not happy about it. "Why are you marrying a man you don't love?" I asked. "What choice do I have?" she said. "I'm twenty-nine. I've been going out with him for over a year, and nobody else is likely to come along." The next morning, the last day of the term, I went to her home room to say goodbye. I was surprised when she treated me like some kind of pariah. People had apparently been talking about our disappearance into the park the night before. She was publicly embarrassed. I understood. But I was still a little hurt. When I visited the school a couple of years later, she was no longer there. They said she had got married and quit teaching when she had a baby. So maybe things worked out all right for her in the end.

John Davison

I MADE ONE GOOD FRIEND AT THE SCHOOL, THE ART TEACHER, JOHN DAVISON. HE WAS TALL AND BEARDED AND DRESSED WITH A CASUAL flair in corduroy jackets and hopsack pants. For reasons that are not at all clear to me, he reminded me of Errol Flynn playing Robin Hood. He introduced me to his artsy friends, the girls, Jenine and Evelyn, his beautiful, blonde girlfriend, Christine, and his fellow painter, Brian. They had been students together at the Ealing Art School. This friendship expanded my world outside of school and Peace Haven. At Whitsun, we borrowed the caravan of P. M. Holbrow, which was parked permanently on the south coast at Burton Bradstock in Dorset. John, Christine, and I drove there in John's Sunbeam Rapier convertible. The next day, we were joined by the others. We spent the week doing what people do at the coast in England: exploring the pebbled beach that in that area rests at the bottom of fairly substantial brown clay cliffs, lying fully-clothed in the cool May sunshine, going out for meals, going to the movies (*Seven Brides for Seven Brothers*, for example, on May 18, at the Palace and Lyric in Bridport).[8]

The Wonderful World of Jennifer Sharp

> Say I'm weary, say I'm sad,
> Say that health and wealth have missed me,
> Say I'm growing old, but add,
> Jenny kissed me.
>   Leigh Hunt, **Rondeau**, 1835

---

for one reason. Looking for fun, I asked her pseudo-seriously what that reason was. She let out a roar and threw a chalk brush at me. Fortunately, my wound was slight—and in a mentionable place.

[8] I have written much more about John Davison in *Living in Franco's Spain*.

AT THE END OF OUR WEEK IN BURTON BRADSTOCK, BRIAN DROVE THE GIRLS BACK TO LONDON, AND JOHN AND I DROPPED IN ON JENNIFER Sharp, who was home from London for the holidays at 10 Ullswater Crescent, in Weymouth. Jennifer was my girlfriend. We had met at Peace Haven. She was just eighteen at the time, medium height, solid-looking, athletic, with a well-proportioned figure. Her most attractive physical qualities were her blonde hair, which she wore neck-length, simple and straight, and her full upper and lower lips, which called out to be kissed. She was beautiful in the Ingrid Bergman / Julie Christie mode. When we had finally become a couple, I felt very lucky to have her as a girl friend. Our relationship began, Jenny told me, though I didn't know it at the time, when a group of us were going into the West End to a play, shortly after I had arrived at Peace Haven, and she resolved to stand beside me whenever possible to attract my attention. Being a male, I failed to notice her. We laughed about that later on.

For a long time, we were just good friends. When we went somewhere together, we were always part of a group. The first time I went out with her alone, I asked her to (of all things) an ice hockey game at the Empire Pool and Sports Arena in Wembley, on March 21, 1959. Canada was playing the Wembley Lions. The old federal Tory leader and former Ontario premier, George Drew, dropped the opening puck. It wasn't meant to be a *date*, in the usual sense of the word. I was merely looking for someone to go to the game with me. When we got back to Peace Haven, I didn't even kiss her good night. Some Lothario! But the idea was building.

> *A couple of evening's later, an odd thing happened. When Jennifer came into the lounge, she walked a couple of steps toward me, and without warning, almost in slow motion, she sank to the floor in a faint. I went to her side, as did a couple of other people. She immediately began to try to get up. "I'm all right," she said, and began to slip away again. I held on to her and more or less carried her up to her room. Danielle Raffaitin and Mac MacGregor came with me. She was totally alert and embarrassed by that time. We made her lie back on the bed. We pulled a blanket over her and smoothed out the bumps. "Have to be careful not to smooth out those bumps," I said, referring to her breasts. She laughed. Even then I did not realize what was happening, that we were moving inexorably toward one another. In a few minutes, we left her to rest. "She's only trying to get your attention," Danielle said to me, as we walked down the stairs toward the lounge. I found it odd that Danielle was being so mean about Jennifer. The reason would become evident much later, on my last night as a permanent resident at Peace Haven, just before I left for Spain.*

Nevertheless, it was in the midst of the drama of this evening, I think, that I decided to pursue Jennifer with some seriousness. We did the usual things together: movies, plays, concerts, dinners, pubs, walks in the park. Many times in the evening we would have a drink at the Duke of York. We always returned home via Rosemont Road instead of Creswick Road, because it was dark and good for love-making. Often, we would spend some time in the shadowy garden behind the hostel before going into the house. Finding places to be alone in the 1950s was not easy.

> *One evening, we took the tube to Knightsbridge to go to my favourite restaurant, Luba's Bistro,[9] just down the street from Harrods and the Brompton Oratory, on Yeoman's Row. I had been introduced to it by John Davison. We bought cheap Beaujolais at the Bunch of Grapes, the pub on the corner, as the restaurant didn't charge a corkage fee. We enjoyed Luba's Russian dishes: things like stuffed green peppers, galubtzy (cabbage rolls), and stroganoff.[10] When we got back to Acton Town station, Jennifer announced that she'd left her handbag in the restaurant. So we had to do the trip all over again. I was beginning my adult lessons in dealing with what was then known as the "fair sex." But it was worth it. Later, in the library at Peace Haven, I held her from behind and for the first time put my hands on her breasts. She snuggled her back up against me. The library would become our favourite trysting place, late at night, lights out, after everyone else had gone to bed.*

But, you may ask, how did couples like us avoid an unwanted pregnancy in this era before the advent of the birth control pill? The options were condoms (not very satisfying),[11] an intrauterine device (IUDs had been known to fail), a vaginal spermicide (not very romantic, and possibly deleterious), *coitus interruptus* (dangerous—leave a dab of sperm in the vagina and you might be leaving 100,000 or so of the little buggers, even though you've withdrawn 2,000,000, and only one errant homunculus was needed to make it to an egg and it was game-over), and the frustrating regime which allowed everything but penetration. We chose the latter. Perhaps a passage from John Updike's novel, *Villages*, set in the 1950s, will make our attitude clear: "Not that he and Elsie ever—in a word they never used between them—fucked. He was too smart for that, too anxious to avoid wasting his one life. He knew that fucking led to marriage and he was not ready for that." In our case, we were both in total agreement on this point. So when we parted forever, she remained (technically-speaking) a virgin. Over the long term, it was too frustrating a method to sustain, but we were not looking at the long term. It wasn't that we didn't love one another. We did. But Jennifer was only in her late teens

---

[9] Luba's Bistro occupied this site for more than thirty years, from the mid-fifties to the late eighties. The story of the bistro is charmingly told in Luba's fractured English in *Luba Gurdjieff: A Memoir with Recipes*, by Luba Gurdjieff Everitt (1993; Berkeley: SLG Books, 1997.) In 2004, I checked out the site of Luba's, which is now occupied by an upscale Italian restaurant. The Bunch of Grapes is still on the corner. It now had a sign promoting a First Floor restaurant of its own.

[11] When my friend, John Davison, married Janet Tubb, a couple of years after this time, her father, who owned a barber shop (barbers were among the main purveyors of condoms in England), amusingly gave them a gross of condoms as a wedding present. Current at the time was the following joke. A man buys a gross of condoms on a Friday afternoon. On Monday morning, when the barber arrives to open his shop, the man is standing there looking disconsolate. "You know that gross of condoms you sold me on Friday?" he says. "There were only 142 in the package." "Sorry I spoiled your weekend," replies the barber. Also current at the time, this joke: A man buys a dozen condoms. "That'll be $4.95, plus tax," says the clerk. "Never mind the tacks," says the man. "I'll tie them on."

and had things to do; and I was dabbling in teaching, wandering about Europe and had no plan for the future. Marriage would have been a disaster for both of us.

By the time summer came, we had both made plans for the next year. We made them separately, selfishly, and totally amicably. Jennifer was bound and determined to become a stewardess with BOAC. I wasn't sure where I was headed, but I knew that I was not then headed toward marriage. Curiously, given the circumstances, Jennifer and I both found ourselves going to Spain. She was off to Bilbao to spend a few months teaching English and improving her Spanish at a language school there, in order to give her a better chance of being hired by BOAC.[12] I was going to Madrid to teach English at the Instituto Garrett. We did not plan this together. She was not going to Spain because I was going to Spain, nor was I going to Spain because she was going to be there. It just happened that way.

Before going to Spain, Jennifer took a job for a couple of months in Paris as a companion to a French woman who wanted to practise her English. Jennifer's French was already quite good, but she wanted to brush it up. She stayed with this woman at her Paris apartment. She wasn't paid much, but she had free room and board. She and her host spent most days playing either golf or tennis, switching every hour or so from one language to the other. So it was a good situation for both of them. On our way to Spain, Dick Whitehead and I stayed overnight in Paris and I was able to spend a few fun-filled hours with Jennifer in the area around Boul. Ste. Michele[13]

The Residents at Peace Haven

Harold, the Man of Culture

WHAT OTHER INTERESTING PEOPLE WERE AT PEACE HAVEN AT THAT TIME? MOST OF THE RESIDENTS WERE YOUNG, LATE TEENS OR early- to mid-twenties. Among this group was Harold, whose home was in Yorkshire. He had not lost his rural dialect's subject/verb agreement system, which seemed strange to my ear with it's "he were's," and other peculiarities. Like Leonard Bast in *Howards End*, he was desperate to prove that he was cultured. Every few evenings he would come into the lounge with a brand new copy of a paperback tome, *The Story of Jazz, The Penguin Dictionary of . . .* Something-or-Other, Bede's *Ecclesiastical History*, and so on. All of these books turned out to be stolen, and Harold was eventually caught and given the option of being prosecuted or going home to Yorkshire. He went home. But not before he stole the flash attachment for my camera and my university ring. Poor Harold. He was obviously a died-in-the-wool kleptomaniac.

---

[12] Jennifer was rejected by BOAC because they said she was "too vivacious," if you can believe it! It seems they wanted frumpy women from the horsey set. She was soon thereafter hired by TWA, which apparently preferred vivaciousness to horseyness. We kept in touch for the better part of ten years. In the mid-1960s, in Kansas City, Mo., she married a lawyer, Francis Xavier Waterman. He was a Catholic, and Jennifer converted to his church. But in a letter, she attributed her conversion to Catholicism partly to me. The last I heard from her, about 1969, she was the happy mother of two young daughters.

[13] See *That Summer in Jaca*.

Petite Danielle

Danielle Raffaitin was a pretty brunette from St. Maur, France. She was a miniature woman, perfectly proportioned, but tiny all round. Like a doll. She was in London to perfect her English, which was good but heavily accented. Her favourite expression of annoyance or frustration was the then-fashionable Parisian expletive, "Zoot!" In many ways she was a little firecracker, proud and explosive.

> When I came home late on my last night in London, after having had dinner at Luba's Bistro with Leslie Dunkling and Dick Whitehead,[14] she was waiting up for me. She astounded me by declaring that she loved me. How could I have been so mean, she said, as to think about leaving without saying goodbye to her? I was responsive in a guarded way. I didn't want to hurt her further. We continued to correspond off and on for a couple of years. The last I heard from her was a postcard from Santiago de Compostela, the great pilgrimage site in Galicia, the end of a road not taken. But there was never really any chance that we would make life's pilgrimage together.

Irish Paddy and Spinster Sybil

Paddy and Sybil were two older residents, both of whom in their late forties or early fifties. They were not connected to one another in any personal way, and I deal with them together only because, as they were older, they were a kind of anomaly at Peace Haven. The rest of us young people thought they were ancient. Sybil was tall and solid, wore pinkish plastic glasses, and had obviously never been much to look at. She had greying blonde hair. She was a great smoker, cigarettes seeming to sprout from the ends of her fingers. In the summer, she did romantic watercolours in the garden. Behind her back, often literally, we laughed at her efforts, thinking in our youthful arrogance what a silly old Victorian she was. Paddy was a short, pudgy, and mostly bald Irishman. He was quieter and much less sociable than Sybil. Both of these individuals had jobs, but I don't remember what they did for a living. We thought that they were sad cases, that life had passed them by.

Frisco and Rosemary

There were other residents I didn't know very well. Frisco, a pencil-shaped bundle of energy in his late twenties, came from Spain and shared a room with Paddy. Rosemary was a homely Welsh girl with a kind of jack-o-lantern face. She was large of frame, though not fat. She had a reputation in the hostel of being very religious. When I kissed her, among others, at midnight on New Year's Eve, as was the custom, she stunned me by shoving her tongue deep into my mouth. There was obviously more to this girl than there appeared to be. Perhaps, it crossed my mind, I'm not a member of the right church.

---

[14] See *That Summer in Jaca*

The Peace Haven Staff

Ida, Mathilda, and Adolf

AMONG THE STAFF WAS AN ITALIAN MAID, IDA—IN HER THIRTIES AND NOT UNATTRACTIVE. SHORT, SQUARE, WELL-BUILT. I REMEMBER her best, during my first few months at the hostel, bringing the before-bed snack into the lounge: small sandwiches, tea, and biscuits. (Later, the sandwiches were replaced by foil-wrapped Swiss cheese sections with laughing cows on their labels, and a 9d cinema-type ticket had to be purchased to get the snack.) Leslie claimed to have slept with Ida. I was jealous. After I left, as I have mentioned on page 181, she became pregnant by Peter Rafell, who, as a result, married her. Another of the maids, Mathilda, was a largish woman from Austria, very nice, very efficient, and always smiling. A couple of years after I left, she and Adolf, the cook, were engaged to be married. Unfortunately for her, Adolf turned out already to have been married to someone else. This discovery was made a couple of days before the wedding was to take place. Everything had to be cancelled and all the presents returned. (Apparently, many of them weren't which caused a lot of unfriendly gossip.) It was an ugly scene. Adolf had been a carpenter in Poland, or so the story went, who had been forcibly recruited into the German army in the war and taught how to cook. The buzz at Peace Haven was that he cooked like a carpenter.

Pepita La Bonita

The most attractive staff member was the petite Spanish maid, Pepita, who later married Mick Gaul, the ex-sailor who bought the booze for the Christmas party. I don't know whether they lived happily ever after, but I did see her picture in a poster-size photographic collage on the wall in the new part of the hostel when I visited it in April 2003. She was dressed in a frilly dress and appeared to be at a garden party at the hostel, probably some time in the 1960s. Nobody in the new-century Peace Haven knew who she or any of the others in the collage were.

> *Pepita arrived at Peace Haven not long after I did. Since I spoke a little Spanish, and she spoke practically no English, I tried to talk to her one night when she was off duty and sitting alone in a crowded lounge. My Spanish was at least as bad as her English. Like all good Spanish girls at that time, she had been told what monsters we non-Spanish men were likely to be, so her side of the conversation consisted more or less of one phrase: "No me toca!" Don't touch me. She was wearing a skin-tight navy blue and white striped sweater, and I would be less than honest if I were to claim that I would not have enjoyed touching her. But I was not stupid enough to do something like that. As it turned out Jennifer, whose Spanish was better than mine, came to my rescue and suggested that the three of us go to the Duke of York for a drink. I did not realize that Jennifer was trying to make contact with me more than with Pepita. Eventually Pepita saw wicked England for what it was, a melange of the good and the bad, like her native Spain, like everywhere, and she made it her permanent home.*

Liz Timmins and Mrs. Hazlitt

Early in 1959, Elizabeth Timmins arrived at Peace Haven as Secretary. She ran the office, collected the room and board, and so on. Liz was still in her teens, but she was smart and efficient, and we all liked her. There were no class divisions, either real or perceived, among the staff and the residents at Peace Haven. As residents, we considered Liz and the other staff, including the maids (and even the Warden), part of an extended family. Not too long after Liz arrived, a new Warden, Mrs. Hazlitt, was hired to replace Miss Devitt, who, as I have pointed out earlier, had been fired. She had a lovely blonde daughter, Margaret, who was about five. We wondered, some of us, if Mrs. Hazlitt was using "Mrs." as a title of convenience to explain the little girl. She never mentioned a husband, ex-husband, or dead husband. Nobody I knew called Mrs. Hazlitt by her first name; I'm sure she had one, but I don't remember it—if I ever knew it. She would remain on the job through my years in contact with Peace Haven, that is, until the summer of 1962, and, apparently, for some years after that. Tragically, she died of cancer in the mid-1960s.

Leslie Dunkling and I Hit It Off

THE GREATEST FRIEND OF MY PEACE HAVEN YEARS, STILL A FRIEND AFTER FIFTY YEARS, WAS LESLIE ALAN DUNKLING. LESLIE arrived at Peace Haven about the same time as I did. He had spent much of 1958 working in the British Pavilion at the World's Fair in Brussels. Like me, he was medium tall, though he had a darker complexion than I, and his head was crowned with dark brown hair. For two young men who came from such different backgrounds, we had a lot more in common than one might expect: a love of literature, art, and drama; Catholicism; the enjoyment of long walks and long discussions; and, need it be said, a great interest in pursuing attractive young women.

> *Often, on wintery Sunday afternoons—I remember them now as dark and grey, and (in a world that was still not taken over by consumerism) strangely empty of people and vehicles—we would take the Underground in to the National Gallery or the Tate. There, after looking at some of the paintings, we would each purchase, extravagantly at sixpence apiece, a couple of postcards of that day's favourites. In time, my postcard collection grew substantially; and as it grew, it took on increasing value to me. I still have it, added to over the years from other institutions. Still a source of pleasure. But we went to the galleries to do more than look at the paintings. The galleries were reputed to be good places to pick up girls who had at least a modicum of intelligence. As it turned out, we were never lucky enough to make contact with any of the girls we saw there, though we looked them over every bit as carefully as the paintings, and there was pleasure in that.*

Sometimes, we went to the theatre in the West End, usually when there was a blockbuster, such as *West Side Story* playing.[15] But most often, we went to the suburban theatres, which were easier for us to get to and dirt cheap. At the Chiswick Empire, we saw Henrik Ibsen's *Brandt*, and John Osborne and Anthony Creighton's *Epitaph for George Dillon*. At the fine repertory theatre in Richmond, we enjoyed plays like *Tea and Sympathy* and *The Entertainer*.

We tended to read the same things at the same time. We then discussed these works, *wisely*, as young men will do. *Seriously* and *ad nauseam*, as young men will do. I remember especially Dostoyevsky's *The Idiot*, and a couple of novels that were more or less new at that time, Alan Silitoe's *The Loneliness of the Long Distance Runner* and Boris Pasternak's *Dr. Zhivago*. Leslie introduced me to John Updike's *Pigeon Feathers* and *Rabbit Run*, and I have been an avid fan of Updike ever since. But we were not only *reading* novels. We both made attempts at *writing* novels. Neither of us succeeded in finishing one at that time, though we both, in the years immediately following, completed novels that were for the most part embarrassingly bad. Here is an excerpt from one of my attempts, which I intended to call by the horrible title, which I thought clever at the time, "Flow Gently Sweet Acton." You may notice that it has *some* autobiographical content!

> *For the first time that spring, warm air blew on Patterson Road, and the smell of London changed from moss to linen. Henry, as he opened his window and breathed in deeply, felt the air as a harbinger of summer. It was Saturday morning. His mood was good.*
>
> *At breakfast, the other people in the hostel, those that had bothered to get up for breakfast, seemed happier because of the weather. The turkey tracks on Mabel's fifty-year-old eyes were oilier, the angle of Carol's dress as she bent over her bangers was jauntier, and John, Margaret, and Zuzu ate their sausages and fried bread with more zest than one might expect after a winter eating them day after day. In the kitchen, Ludwig, the balding Polish chef who, the story had it, was a carpenter who had been forced into the German army and trained as a cook—we all joked that he cooked like a carpenter—hummed* Oh Susanna *as he scraped a brown flipper over the griddle.*
>
> *In the dining room were seven tables for four, covered with red and white chequered oil cloth, most of them now empty, as it was almost past the nine o'clock time-limit for breakfast.*
>
> *Henry carried his breakfast to the corner of the room and sat with Margaret and Carol.*

---

[15] Leslie and I went to Her Majesty's Theatre, where *West Side Story* was playing, very early on a Saturday morning to line up for the few tickets that were available for each day's performance. While we were in line, a man rolled new posters on to the hoardings outside of the theatre. When he had gone, I slipped out of line, went around to the side of the theatre, and easily unrolled one of them, as they were simply rolled on wet over an identical previous poster. I took it home to Canada with me, but it disappeared from my parent's home some time in the 1960s. It was probably thrown out.

> *"'Ello 'Enry," Margaret said as she watched him sit down. "Sleep well?"*
>
> *Carol coughed and sputtered good morning, choking on a bit of her banger at the sight of Henry, perhaps remembering the night before.*

As you can see, there can be little doubt about the quality of this excerpt.

As I had been raised a Catholic, I provided a pivot around which Leslie's interest in Catholicism could turn. One day he told me he'd made up his mind to enter the Church and asked me if I would sponsor his baptism. He made the arrangements, and the deed was done one evening in a darkened, otherwise empty church, Our Lady of Lourdes, by Father Buckley. I don't remember our going to Mass together, except one Sunday morning after an all-night party. Leslie had a friend, Jackie, a spectral-thin young woman with artistic ambitions, who lived with her husband on a converted barge in the Thames at Chiswick. It was the high kick of fashion to live on a barge in the Thames in the 1950s. Because the river was tidal, and the tide at the time of the party was going out, the barge gradually settled on to the river bottom on an angle of perhaps ten degrees. If you didn't know the change was going to happen, you might wonder what incredible stuff they'd spiked the punch with.

It was well past dawn when we left the party, and as there was no public transportation at that time on a Sunday morning, we decided to walk back to Acton and go to Mass at a church that Leslie knew along the way. We did that. What trouble we both had keeping awake through the peace and quiet of a Latin Low Mass!

On fine weekend days, we often went to Gunnersbury Park, sometimes to play on the pitch-and-putt golf course, but more often just to walk around the park. We also walked along the river in Chiswick and in the park in Richmond. Many complex philosophical, literary and political problems were solved—or so we thought—on these walks.

A Job Offer from Madrid

AS SPRING FLOWED INTO SUMMER, THE WARM, SUNNY SUMMER OF 1959, I MADE PLANS TO GO TO GREECE WITH JOHN DAVISON. WE would hitch-hike to Brindisi and take a ferry from there to Pireaus, travelling steerage for the equivalent of about £5. Early in July, John had a one-man show of his paintings at the Woodstock Gallery in Mayfair. His work was commented on favourably by the art critic of *The Times*, who especially liked the summery heat he felt emanated from John's Etruscan landscapes. Getting any kind of notice from *The Times* was a major achievement. But the paintings did not sell well, and John lost money on the exhibition. He was disappointed and upset.

At the same time as I was talking to John about going to Greece, I had other irons in the fire. I had written to the Instituto Garrett in Madrid and a couple of places in

Casablanca, hoping to find a place to teach English as a second language. If I had taken the Brindisi option, it would have changed my life in a measurable way. I would have gone to Greece with John and returned to teaching at Harlington in the fall. But on June 13, the day before my twenty-fourth birthday, I received a letter from Peter Garrett, the owner of the Garrett Institute, which read as follows:

> *With reference to your letter of 8th. June, we still have one or two vacancies for teachers of English for the coming academic year, i.e. October 1st. 1959 to June 30th. 1960.*
>
> *We pay 3,500 pesetas per month for a 36 hour week to first-year teachers. There is a week's paid holiday at Christmas and the same at Easter. All official expenses such as taxes, Work Card dues, etc. are met by the Institute.*
>
> *If you are interested in this, could you let me have further details of your experience in teaching English, place of work, type of students, etc., together with the copy* [sic] *of at least one reference from a former employer and a small recent photograph of yourself. You would then later be informed of an interview in London.*

I replied, giving him the information and documents he requested. In the meantime, I arranged to do a summer course in Spanish, run by the Universidad de Zaragoza in Jaca, a town in Aragón. At this point, I ruled out the Greek option, though I was upset at letting John down. I did not have a definite commitment in Spain, but I felt that even if the Garrett job fell through, I'd be able to find something else in Madrid or elsewhere.

On the 18th of July, I received the following letter:

> *68 Broadway,*
> *Stoneleigh,*
> *Epsom, Surrey.*
> *17th July 1959.*
>
> *Dear Mr. Keough,*
>
> *I work in Madrid under Mr. Peter Garrett in the "Instituto Garrett" where, I believe, you have applied for a teaching post.*
>
> *Since I am on holiday in this country, he has written to ask me to see you in order to give you some more information about the job and to clear up any questions you may have concerning it.*
>
> *I understand that you will be leaving for Zaragoza on the 25th of this month, so obviously it will have to be soon. I suggest that we meet in Central*

London within the next few days. Therefore, I wonder if you could telephone me so that we can fix a place and time to meet that will be convenient for both of us.

If you could ring me either Sunday or Monday morning I am sure to be home. My telephone number is EWELL 5167. I hope these times are convenient for you.

Yours sincerely,

Hywel Davies

I "rang him up," as they say in England, on Sunday the 20th, and we agreed to meet at the Spread Eagle pub on Woodstock Street, just off Oxford Street, at 7 p.m. on Wednesday, July 22, for what was in fact a job interview. The pub was familiar to me, as I had gone there with John Davison and some of his friends after the opening of John's exhibition just next door in early June. Hywel and I got along well over a couple of pints of bitter. He said he would recommend that I be hired. And I was. A few days after I arrived in Jaca, sometime around the beginning of August, I got a letter from Peter Garrett, offering me a job.

When he heard about what I was doing, Dick Whitehead, a new resident at Peace Haven—he had arrived late in May—decided to come with me. Although I didn't know Dick very well, we had become friends in our short time together, sharing our love of the films of Jacques Tati and our interest in Lawrence of Arabia. Besides, Dick had started going out with one of Jennifer's friends, Hilary, who was also going to Spain to teach English, and we had spent some evenings together as a foursome at the movies and at the Duke of York. Dick and I planned to hitchhike to Spain. When it came down to it, we found the hitchhiking so bad that we did most of the journey by train.[16]

Eulogy to Peace Haven

IN MY YEAR AT PEACE HAVEN, I MADE MANY GOOD FRIENDS, ENJOYED MY FIRST EXPERIENCE OF TEACHING, AND BECAME IMMERSED IN AND built up an appreciation for and love of England. As well, I had a most successful year romantically, lots of casual girlfriends, one serious romance. But most of all, I loved Peace Haven and its late-Victorian architecture: striped brick, pitched roofs, turret, stained-glass windows, hammer-beamed Games' Room, and splendid wood panelling. And I loved the routine of day-to-day life there: the gong that announced that meals were ready to be served, the late-evening snacks, the sharing of bedrooms, bathrooms, lounges, and meal tables. The place filled one of the great vacuums of life, because we were in the best sense an extended family, and there was always someone *there*, even if only a transient or passing friend. Not that there weren't squabbles and disagreements among the people who shared the splendid space that made up the hostel. But between the house and its ambience and myself there was never a squabble. In that year, Peace Haven was

---

[13] See *That Summer in Jaca*

itself the most important character in my life. It was a privilege to have lived for a short time within its walls.

Epilogue

A name is frequently all that is left to us of a human being, not only when he is dead but even while he is still alive.
Marcel Proust, *In Search of Lost Time*, 1913-27

IN APRIL 2003, I RETURNED TO PEACE HAVEN FOR ABOUT A WEEK'S STAY. IN THIS CHANGEABLE WORLD, IT'S AMAZING THAT THE HOSTEL, forty-five years after I lived there, still existed and was still operating under the auspices of the IFL. There had been changes, of course. A two-story addition, respecting the style of the original architecture, had been added to the back; motel-like units, each with its own bathroom, had been joined to the main building, the dining area had been connected to the house by a fine, greenhouse-like glass passageway, and an exterior fire escape from the top floor had been added. Dinner was no longer available, though there was a microwave for the use of guests in the dining room. In the laundry room, where I had spent many a horrid hour washing my clothes with a scrub board over a sink, there was an industrial-size washer and drier, used to process the dirty sheets and towels produced by the operation. In the morning, a chef came in and produced an English breakfast: bangers, beans, eggs, bacon, fried tomatoes, and toast. Maids arrived to strip the beds, do the laundry, make up the rooms, and clean the public areas. By noon they were gone. There was no live-in help anymore. There was still a Warden—at that point in time, Pam Matthews—but she was referred to as the "Manager," the word "Warden" apparently having gone out of style. She was helped by a part-time Assistant-Manager.

It was Pam who asked me if I knew Pandit O'Nath, who had preceded her as Warden/Manager. I said I didn't think so. But when she told me he had been in charge of Peace Haven from the sixties to the nineties, I felt I should contact him to try to find out what had happened to the people I had known in the hostel so many years ago. As Pandit was now the Treasurer of the IFL, when I returned to Canada, I wrote to him via Peace Haven about joining the organization once again. In the meantime, Pam had given him a small album of pictures I had compiled and left at Peace Haven. Here is part of his response, written in his inimitable English:

Hello Terry

Glad to receive your [IFL Membership] Application Form via Peace Haven.

<u>Now to your album</u>: It was really a very pleasant surprise to see the old faces and the photographs. I immediately recognized most people in that album other than those of yours taken with different girls in romantic moods! I see that you

have dated some of the incidents in 1961, so there is a strong probability that I must have met you at some stage, may be in the lounge or perhaps in the Duke of York? Certainly your face (60's style) looks familiar. Looking at these photographs reminds me of many past things. As I was not a resident at Peace Haven I did not have any direct contact with the residents at that time. I came to scene in early 1960. As you are now aware that in October 1967 I took over as the Warden of Peace Haven and continued to manage it for 30 years until July 1997 - that is a life time! I have lots of fond memories and have made numerous friends with the people from many countries. I do remember Bill and Beverley Wood, [friends of mine from my home town in Canada, who lived at Peace Haven from 1961-62] Leslie Dunkin [Dunkling], Rosemary, (Paddy, Sybil and Mathilda - all three have passed away ages ago). You talk about the maid called Pepita - I could not attend Mick Gaul & Pepita's wedding Reception party at the first floor in the Co-operative Hall in Acton High Street though in those early days before my direct involvement with Peace Haven and not being a resident, I was not aware of what exactly went on between the residents, socially. For example, I don't seem to remember any of your girlfriends, Danielle, Jennifer, Lorraine [Loralie], Denise and others, perhaps because I used to come to Peace Haven only in the evenings and during the weekends to do some voluntary work for the IFL in the office located opposite the kitchen, now used as a table tennis room. Of course I knew Mrs Heslin, Elizabeth Timmins and Maisie Hart who were handling the office affairs. Adolf, from Poland, who liked his whiskey in his beer, worked as a cook until he retired around 1969 and died about 10 years ago. Mrs Heslin's daughter Margaret was a very clever little girl, Rosemary a religious sort and Emily the quiet one who emigrated to Australia but soon after suffered some mental illness and later died. In a photograph taken in the garden, the man standing behind Margaret is Wally Bridger (a friend of Mrs Heslin and mine) who was then the Chairman of Peace Haven's management committee; he also died several years ago. You may remember 'Billy' the dog who, on occasions I used to take for a walk in the park. A lot has happened since. You may be interested to learn that I have also experienced romance at Peace Haven - I married a Spanish girl who also worked for all those 30 years as my deputy. We worked very hard throughout to keep the hostel running viably. It all looks quite different than when you were there. No doubt you must have noticed the new building extensions in the main house and the one annexed to the staff quarters built in 1984 and 1993 respectively, and the covered way between the main house and the kitchen around 1994/5. This later improvement has tremendously enhanced to the friendly atmosphere at Peace Haven. The latest one has been named after me; a plaque and a photograph has been displayed on the wall in that lounge. . . . I could write a book about what has happened after you left England but right now I am only trying to refer to how you describe your memories.

Anyway I do not want to bore you with this saga. That is all in the past. Life must move on.

Good luck.

Yours sincerely   Pandit O'Nath 27.08.2003

A New Beginning

In the summer of 2006, the International Friendship League (IFL), struggling to survive with fewer than 500 ageing members, sold Peace Haven. The purpose of the organization seems somehow to have been lost in our modern world. Besides, the hostel had been losing money for some time. People are no longer willing to share a bedroom and use a common bathroom. The group that bought the hostel, Rooms and Studios London Ltd., has retained the Peace Haven name. It has renovated the building, creating studio suites, which are rented out by the week or by the month. The interior rooms that were heritage designated by the Borough of Ealing have been maintained.

Peace Haven November 1958 – July 1959 and After

Terry in Front of the House

Terry & Leslie in the Garden

Garden View of House 1961

The Long-Term Residents

Terry on His Bed in Room 10

Leslie Dunkling

Sybil, Mac, Mick, Harold, Rosemary, ?, Terry
Maureen, Danielle, Jennifer

Lounge at Christmas: Jennifer, Harold, Rosemary,
Danielle, Sybil

Dining Room: Liz Timmins, Harold

Frisco, Pepita, Malcolm, Liz, Paddy

Relaxation Time

Terry & Jennifer in the Lounge

Mac and Maureen

Frisco, Pepita, Mathilda, Liz

Terry & Jennifer in the Garden

One of a Series of Photographs of Jennifer
For a Painting by Brian

Rosemary

Parties and Liaisons

Terry and Lorelei

Xmas 1958 Room Party: Mac, Malcolm (front),
Frisco (behind), Adolph (the Cook),
Danielle, Mick

Terry and Denise Duval

Danielle and Terry

The Library: Scene of Many Trysts

Harlington County Secondary School

Nov. 25, 1958 Return Train Ticket

Entering School by Class, Directed by "Lance Corporal" Hopkinson

My Classroom

My Girls

Intercepted Classroom Note

John Davison at Burton Bradstock

Into Morning Assembly   Jerry Street

Return to Peace Haven 2003

Terry and Leslie in the Lounge

My Room – All Spiffed Up

Chapter 9: That Summer in Jaca

RETURNING TO SPAIN

>It is just after midnight 13th Dec. 73. . . . .Life moves on. I work now for the British Chamber of Commerce. . . . We have bought a holiday flat in a village called Trespaderne up in the mountains near the Ebro between here and Burgos. . . . And this is as far as I have got since that 3rd Class train ride from Zaragoza to Huesca 14 years ago when we were talking and wondering together what was in our adventure.
>
>Dick Whitehead, Christmas Card, 1973

>Bliss was it in that dawn to be alive,
>But to be young was very heaven!
>
>William Wordsworth, *The Prelude*, 1805/1850

Jaca in the Pyrenees

THE TOWN OF JACA IS ON A PLATEAU IN THE FOOTHILLS OF THE PYRENEES, BORDERED BY THE RIVERS GÁLLEGO AND ARAGÓN. IN A SMALL CAMPUS IN THIS SMALL TOWN, THE UNIVERSIDAD DE Zaragoza held its summer courses for foreigners in Spanish language and culture. Dick Whitehead and I arrived there to attend the XXIXth session on August 8, 1959.

The history of the Jaca area goes back a long way. The town existed in the first century AD and was the center of the Roman region, Iacetania. The name probably derives from a local pre-Roman word, "iak," meaning "a healthy place." The Romans wrote the word as "Iaca" or "Iacca." Seven centuries later, the first Count of Aragón, Don Aznar, established his residence in Jaca, and the town remained the center of the Court of the Kings of Aragón until 1096, when the capital was moved to Huesca. Later in the Middle Ages, Jaca was a major stopping place on one of the pilgrimage routes that wound through the Pyrenees on the road to Santiago de Compostela. The atmosphere of the town conjures up in the minds of those with active imaginations the elephants of

Hannibal, the trumpet of Roland, the scallop shell of St James, the criss-crossing hordes of Napoleon and Wellington, and the ragtag soldiers of the International Brigade.

Brooding over the area like a large humped wedge is the Peña Oroel. From this mountain area, the medieval pilgrimage trail leads to a splendidly preserved Roman bridge, just to the north of the town, the Puente de San Miguel, under which flows a small, but rapid-flowing river.

> *We would buy bocadillos—sandwiches, made in crusty buns that were pointed at both ends, filled with cheese or anchovies—cool off a bottle of wine in the river, and spend the afternoon swimming in a small eddy near the bridge. We did not make good use of our opportunity to immerse ourselves in the language and culture of Spain. But unlike the Germans, who worked like Germans and learned an impressive amount, or the French, who pretended to be superior to it all, we had a good time. And I suspect the Spanish, in spite of tut-tutting at our lack of work, found us more simpatico than the others.*

In 1959, Spain was still the old Spain. The country retained, late into the 20th century, the wholesome, rural, peasant feel that before the industrial revolution was pervasive throughout Europe. I had been building castles in this old Spain from my Canadian hometown for years. These castles would have made effective travel posters, the sort one sees and romanticizes about, the sort one curses on reaching the country they depict, because next to the castle is a toothpaste factory. But not in Spain in 1959. The castles I had built in Canada were really there. And there were no toothpaste factories beside them. The Spanish still imported their toothpaste (and many other consumer goods) from France. Franco had built up the primary industries; it would be left to the next generation to do the rest.

Dick Whitehead Joins Me

I MET DICK WHITEHEAD ONLY THAT SPRING WHEN HE SHOWED UP AT PEACE HAVEN ONE RAINY SATURDAY AFTERNOON. WE HIT IT OFF immediately. He was a solidly built, medium height individual with a broad forehead and blonde hair. His voice was strong and masculine, and he laughed easily. He intrigued me with his story of being on a six-month run around England in order to avoid the letter which would call him up for his two-year stint in the army. Everyone knew in 1959 that compulsory national service was on the way out, and Dick had no intention of being one of the last to get called up. His attitude did not sit well with his father. The rumor at Peace Haven—probably started by Dick as a joke—was that he was a retired British army general; in fact, he was a mechanical engineer.

When Dick heard that I was going to Spain to study Spanish in Jaca before teaching for the winter at the Instituto Garrett in Madrid, he decided to come along with me. Getting out of the country seemed to be a good solution to avoiding the dreaded letter from the draft board. His decision was no doubt influenced in part because he had struck up a friendship with Lorette, who was a friend of my girlfriend, Jennifer Sharp. The two girls were on their way to Spain to perfect their Spanish in order to become stewardesses with BOAC. Lorette was on her way to Madrid; Jennifer was bound for Bilbao via Paris. Both girls had jobs teaching English in language schools.

I contacted Jennifer when Dick and I went through Paris, and I spent some time with her in León and Bilbao in September before my contract at the Instituto Garrett began. We also celebrated Christmas together in Madrid. But after that, though we kept in touch for a few years, we drifted apart, and I never saw her again. I don't know whether Dick made contact with Lorette in Spain. He came to Madrid over the Christmas period and visited me at the flat I shared with three other expatriates at No. 7ª, 55 Francisco Silvela, but I do not remember anything else about his visit. He was teaching in Zaragoza at the time. If he had not yet met Laura Esteban at that point, he was about to do so. In a way, I have always wondered at my part in this radical change in Dick's life. If he hadn't met me, his life would have been completely different. And we knew each other for such a short time. Not that there was anything horrible about Dick's life. Quite the opposite: he fell in love with a lovely Spanish woman, married her, and in the throes of a happy marriage, they together raised a family of three delightful (and bilingual) children in the northern Spanish city of Bilbao.

Leaving Peace Haven

ON FRIDAY, JULY 24, THE NIGHT BEFORE WE LEFT LONDON, DICK AND I AND LESLIE DUNKLING HAD DINNER AT LUBA'S BISTRO, THAT marvelous and unpretentious restaurant in a made-over garage on Yeoman's Row, a former mews, just off Old Brompton Road, a few blocks west of Harrods. The kitchen was right there in the restaurant, in the Russian style. The food, as I have pointed out before, was basic: stuffed green peppers, goulash, cabbage rolls, each garnished with one of the many variations of Luba's succulent red sauce. You sat wherever there was space at picnic-like tables that held eight people. Often there was a line-up at the door. You could see Luba herself preparing things in the kitchen area. You could buy a bottle of wine at the pub on the corner, The Bunch of Grapes, take it to Luba's, and they would uncork it for you and provide glasses at no charge. The meals were cheap, four or five shillings for a main course. I loved it.[1]

As Leslie was on his way to France, we had decided to travel together as far as Dunkirk. We gathered our essentials into our backpacks in the morning and bid farewell to Peace Haven and our friends there. Jennifer and Lorette had already left, so the more difficult complication of breaking away from them was not part of the process. We walked the mile or so to Acton Town tube station and took the Piccadilly Line to Victoria, packsacks on our backs. I felt rather badly that Leslie was not part of my Spanish adventure. He was, after all, my best friend at the hostel. My friendship with Dick was newly-minted and precarious, but in the present circumstances I felt I had more

---

[1] For more information, see Chapter 8, *A Young Man's Fancy*, and Luba *Gurdjieff: A Memoir with Recipes* (1993; Berkeley: SLG Books, 1997).

in common with him than with Leslie. We were about to share at least some of the immediate future together.

> *We arrived in Dover in the late afternoon, and as we had hours to waste before the ferry left for the continent, we used some of the time in the unprofitable game of throwing pennies at a pylon sticking out of the water near the dock. The real object was to get rid of the pennies, those mammoth and heavy relics of the Victorian age that ate holes in the pockets of a new pair of pants in less than three months. For some reason, I had a pocket full of them, eighteen, and I threw them all at the pylon and felt much relieved.*

But that was really my minor money problem. There were currency restrictions in place at the time, and one was allowed to take only fifty pounds in cash out of the country. I had eighty and was terrified I would get caught with the extra. I had concealed most of the money in the pages of my journal, a stupid place to put it, as the authorities would not even have had to conduct a body search to find it. But, as it turned out, I was not asked how much money I had. Undoubtedly, I looked poorer to other people than I did to myself.

The ferry was a night ferry—the cheapest—and we did our best to get some sleep on the deck chairs. The weather was good, but there was a moon and we were excited, so we did not sleep much. We docked in Dunkirk on a fine July 26 at five-thirty in the morning, and after having scrounged some coffee and a sweet bun at a dockside café, we started to hitchhike. Leslie went on ahead of Dick and me, as he would have a better chance of being picked up if he was on his own. I did not see him again till the following May, when I was briefly back in London on my way to Canada.

By ten o'clock we had managed to get one ride from a local farmer, who dropped us off at his turnoff about twenty miles down the road. We were there for not more than half an hour when we were picked up by a truck with a flat deck that had removable side panels. We hopped on the back of the truck and congratulated ourselves on our good fortune.

We Help a Farmer with His Potatoes

A FEW MILES DOWN THE HIGHWAY, THE TRUCK TURNED ON TO A DIRT ROAD, AND BEFORE LONG BACKED INTO A FIELD WHERE STOOD forty of fifty sacks of newly harvested potatoes. Neither Dick nor I spoke French, and the farmer knew no English. He made us to understand in the international language of gestures that we were to load the potatoes on to the truck. The problem with this kind of language, of course, is that you can gesture acceptance or refusal but you can't argue in any effective way about the terms. In any case, we were in no position to do so, here beside a dirt road in nowhere, France. So we loaded the potatoes with the help of the farmer and a young man who had been standing guard over them.

When we had finished the job, we hopped on top of the potatoes expecting at worst to be taken back to the highway, and at best to be taken at least a few miles along it in the direction we were going. But the farmer drove us further down the dirt road until we came to a rambling, muddy farmyard surrounded by various unpretentious outbuildings. The yard smelt of stale milk, cowshit and rotting straw, as farmyards do the world over. The farmhouse was a spreading, low-slung building that squatted on the land as if it had somehow grown out of it over the centuries, which it probably had. There were pigs, chickens, ducks, geese, and dogs and cats wandering at will. All of them looked as if they wondered what they were doing there. We sympathized—captive beasts of burden ourselves.

We were invited to have a glass of wine in the huge farm kitchen--our remuneration. There we met the older generation, a man and a woman who might have been in their seventies. The woman brought out wine and glasses, sat us at the scrubbed rectangular wooden table that could have seated fourteen easily, and then went to a rocker by the open hearth and took up her knitting, ignoring us. Her woman's work was done. Entertaining us was man's work. The man poured and grinned—he had only a few teeth left, but his smile was friendly—and unlike the other family members, he genuinely tried to communicate with us.

Good will goes a long way in these sorts of situations. We found that we understood each other quite well. He asked if we had been in the army during the war. My French was good enough to get "armé" and "la guerre." I said we were "trop jeune" or words to that effect. He told me I was a "mauvais canadienne," since I didn't speak French. But he was grinning as he said it, showing his few yellowed teeth. I admitted I was. "C'est vert," I said, "c'est vert."

Mal de Tête on the Way to Lille

WE WERE NOT OFFERED A SECOND GLASS OF WINE, WHICH WAS PROBABLY JUST AS WELL. THE MAN WHO HAD PICKED US UP CAME and got us and drove us back to the highway, where we resumed our hitchhiking as the truck of potatoes headed toward Dunkirk.

Already, we were finding out one of the major problems in hitchhiking. Cars go by and by and by, whooshing their way down the highway, empty of all but the driver. Why don't these people who are all alone in their cars pick us up? We stand by the side of the road, packs at our heels, thumbs out, and hope in our hearts. Maybe the next one will stop. But the next one doesn't stop. Nor does the one after that. Nor the one after that. It becomes both depressing and boring. We think, maybe this is not a good spot for the drivers to stop. We pick up our packs and head down the road to a more likely area—part way up a hill, at an intersection—and wait. We search for trees, for a shady area.

We stood by the road until after one o'clock without getting a ride, and we were hungry. So we walked a mile or so to a village we could see in the distance and went into a bar, the only one there. There was nobody else in the place but the bartender. The atmosphere was lonely and strange. The world had become foreign. We ordered some good French bread, some Camembert, and beer.

> *But I had a problem. My beer was absolutely flat. "How do I say that in French?" I said to Dick.*
>
> *"I have no idea," he said. "Your French is better than mine." It was not much of a compliment.*
>
> *And then it struck me. I knew the idiom would probably be wrong, but it was worth a try. I took the flat beer to the bar.*
>
> *"Monsieur?" the barman said.*
>
> *"Ma bière," I said. "Ce à mal de tête."*
>
> *A look of puzzlement spread across the barman's face. Then a flash of understanding. Then a burst of laughter. He replaced the beer. We could hear intermittent giggling as he fussed at things behind the bar, fussing as bartenders tend to do. What a story he would have to tell the locals that night. Mal de tête, indeed!*

Somehow we got ourselves to Lille by five o'clock. Most of the distance we rode in a large Citroën, driven by a man who had been hunting, perhaps fox hunting, though I don't know whether they do that in France. Anyway, he was dressed in breeches and a pink hunting jacket, and he looked as if he'd be at home tally-ho-ing across the countryside. He spoke no English and after a few futile attempts at conversation, we all gave up and rode in a benign silence, showing our good will toward one another with an occasional wan smile.

The youth hostel didn't open till six, so we went into a bar-restaurant that was part of a small hotel. It was nearly deserted at that time of the day. We ordered a half litre of *vin ordinaire*, some bread and some paté. While we were eating, a man of sixty or so with a handlebar moustache asked us in English if he could join us. He was from Portsmouth. "Come here every year," he said. "Visit the old battlefields. Never married. Don't know why. Keeps me in touch with my youth. It was all terrible of course. Best years of my life, though. Good old Great War! Made a man of me." And so on.

Within a half an hour we had his whole life's story. Or so we thought. It had been a lonely life. It still was. We listened politely. But later at the hostel we laughed at him. "Silly old fart," we said. "Probably got his jewels shot off in the war." "Still here looking for them." Things like that. It strikes me now that the man was then probably only in his early to mid sixties. Fifty years ago, in the arrogance of youth, I dismissed his stories as so much old-man claptrap. But if I had the privilege of listening to him now, I would listen carefully. He had experienced things I would (happily) never know.

Paris and Jennifer

THE NEXT DAY, JULY 27, WE WENT TO PARIS ON THE TRAIN. WE HAD ALREADY HAD ENOUGH OF HITCHHIKING; AND AT THE RATE WE were going, we told ourselves, it would take us two weeks to get to Spain. We had the time, of course, but we no longer had the will.

Earlier in the year, at Easter, I had gone to Paris during the school break. I had stayed at a hotel just off Boulevard Ste. Michele, the Rivé Gauche, recommended to me by some English people I had met on the train from London. I still have the light beige 3"x5" room card (#11) they gave me on that occasion, which reads: *Au coeur de Saint-Germain-des-Prés...*"**Rive Gauche" Hotel**, 25, Rue Des Saints-Pères, **Paris 6e**, Tél.: **BAB. 10-52**. This hotel was central and cheap, so Dick and I headed there. But once again, our lack of French caused us problems. We later learned that Dick's stocky blondness and wide forehead made the concierge think he was a German. He refused to rent us a room. We had no idea why, as he had admitted (or so we thought) that there were rooms available. It was the potatoes all over again. We couldn't communicate enough to sort the matter out.

We took our packs and went to a bar at the corner, where we managed to sign-language our way into buying a *jeton*, the token needed to operate a pay telephone. I phoned Jennifer, who was in Paris as a "companion" to a woman who wanted a golf partner. It was an opportunity for her to improve her French, which was already pretty good, on her way to Spain to improve her Spanish. She knew we were coming through Paris, and had negotiated the day off (whatever one it happened to be) with her companionable lady before we arrived. She came to the bar, accompanied us back to the hotel and explained the situation. The concierge was reluctant, as his pride was involved, but on seeing our passports, and probably influenced by the warmth of Jennifer's smile, he gave us a room. That evening Dick went off to see an old friend who was living in Paris, or so he said. I wonder now if he was being kind in letting Jennifer and I have some time alone together.

> *We roamed through the bars on the Left Bank and walked the darkish summer-warm paths along the Seine, hand in hand. We were in love, as young people always are, and had been in love for the past six months at Peace Haven. But our roads, which had come together for a while, were diverging. When we talked of the future, it was a separate future. We did not discuss what that meant to us, to us as a pair, as a couple. We talked about the future, nonetheless, but we talked about it in the abstract. We never stopped and said, "Hey, wait a minute! Where are we going with this?" But it was clear that we were about to follow our own paths. Jennifer was not going to become a teacher, and I was an unlikely candidate to become a stewardess, let alone a steward, in spite of my restrained vivaciousness. That night on the stone pathways beside the Seine, it was dark and romantic and we did not speak of these things. The light of the roadways above filtered through the overhanging summer branches of the trees. We were young lovers in Paris. There is no better place than Paris to be young lovers, and we enjoyed the ambience and breathed the summer romance, and the thought of tomorrow was put away in the beauty of today. Besides, we would meet again, we knew, in Spain. So this was not the end.*

Toulouse and a Lesson in Sausages

DICK AND I DECIDED THE FOLLOWING MORNING TO TAKE A TRAIN TO TOULOUSE. OUR PLANS TO HITCHHIKE OUT OF PARIS HAD BEEN dashed by Jennifer. Someone had told her that the word at the youth hostels was that hitchhiking was terrible in the Paris area. Apparently, there had been a couple of instances in which hitchhikers had attacked the people who had picked them up. There was talk not only of robbery, but also of murder. The facts varied with the teller. But whether the stories were true or not did not matter. Even the perception of violence, once the word got into the community, would make most people wary of picking up hitchhikers.

We were in any event happy to have an excuse to take the train, though we did not admit to each other that we felt that way. Our plan had merely been "adjusted," and we backed up our "adjustment" with other reasons. There was not only the bad hitchhiking to consider. If we took a train to the south of France, our chances of getting a ride would improve. We had not heard of any robbery and murder there, and we hoped nobody else had either. France was expensive, so the sooner we got to Spain, the better. Why Toulouse, you ask? We took out Dick's **Hallwag** map of France. (He had purchased the one for France, and I had purchased the one for Spain; I still have mine, and it is lying now in its red cover on the desk in front of me.) We looked for a city in the south as a target to head for, and there was Toulouse, nearly dead center. We noticed it immediately, because as a larger city its name is printed bigger and bolder than the others around it.

I don't recall much about our short time in Toulouse. At the time, it had a population of about 300,000, but in many respects, especially in the pace of life there and in its architecture, it was still a 19th century city. In recent decades it has become the centre of both the European aircraft manufacturing and space industries. When we arrived there, we got directions to the A. J. Amiens Esperita youth hostel. According to the stamp in my hostel card, we didn't get away until the next afternoon. In the morning, we went out to buy food to carry with us on the road, sausage and bread. While we were doing this, we bit by bit established (once again with mutual relief) that neither one of us wanted to start hitchhiking again. So we checked out the trains heading to Spain. In a postcard from Toulouse on that day (July 30) to my parents, I wrote: *"We arrived in Toulouse last night and missed the train to Irun this morning. We should be in Spain tonight. We are going to spend about a week in Huesca before beginning the course at Jaca on the 8th"*.

That afternoon we boarded a train that would cross the Spanish border at Irun, the same border point from which I had left Spain on my motorcycle nearly ten months before. Our train had coaches of the open type with the aisle running down the middle. We were surrounded by French-speaking people, as one might expect, ordinary folk, who seemed friendly enough, even though communication with words was next to impossible.

> *Eventually, we unpacked our lunch and began eating the sausage and bread. In no time, the people in our section started giggling and whispering to each other. And then the people in the next section joined them. And then across the aisle. We didn't understand what they were saying. But we knew we were the subject of their conversation; and whatever it was they were talking about, they found it highly amusing. Finally, one of the men, through gestures and elementary vocabulary, got the point across to us that you weren't supposed to eat the outer casing of that kind of sausage. So we all had a good laugh together, and we stopped eating the casing. But, you know, it wasn't that bad; and until it was pointed out to us that we weren't supposed to eat it, we were enjoying the casing every bit as much as the sausage.*

Trouble at the Spanish Border

> "Spain," the woman of Pablo said bitterly. Then turned to Robert Jordan. "Do they have people such as this in other countries?"
> "There are no other countries like Spain," Robert Jordan said politely.
> "You are right," Fernando said. "There is no other country in the world like Spain."
> Ernest Hemingway, ***For Whom the Bell Tolls***, 1940

WE REACHED THE SPANISH BORDER AT IRUN IN THE EVENING. IN WHAT I REMEMBER AS DARKNESS, BUT WHAT SURELY MUST HAVE been twilight at the latest, we went into the customs and immigration building. Perhaps because the building was run-down, and the interior was dark and dirty, I remember our border crossing as taking place at night. I was happy to be crossing the border out of France. It was not a country I much liked. The people, in my experience, were sullen and arrogant and didn't give a tinker's damn for your problems as a tourist, when you looked for help in finding your way around their country. This feeling must have been fairly universal, as the government about that time ushered in a campaign to get even the border guards to respond to foreigners with a smile. They didn't do so often. Once in the country, however, I found Spain and the Spanish people friendly and helpful. So I was happy to be leaving the one country and entering the other.

We were in lines, as is always the way at borders. Dick was ahead of me. In front of us were a number of wickets, like old-fashioned bank cages, with metal bars between the immigration officers and the hoi polloi. As we reached the front of the line, two adjacent wickets became free at the same time, so we each went to a separate wicket.

My own first encounter with Franco's officialdom was routine. The man looked at me, looked at my passport, checked the visa I had bought in London, stamped the passport and waved me on. But while I was being dealt with quickly, I could see that Dick was having a problem. I dawdled a moment before going through the gate.

> *The officer looked at his passport, looked at his face, and shook his head. "Thees peecture no looka lika ju," he said. "No—¿como se dice en Ingles?—gafas—eyeglass." Dick, who was flustered by all this, for a moment just looked at the man, who was pointing at the passport photograph with one hand and at his eyes with the other. When he understood what was needed, he reached into his pack, pulled out his glasses, which had the heavy dark rims fashionable at the time, and put them on. "Ah," the man sighed, looking with satisfaction at Dick's face matching that of the photograph. "Bien! Muy bien!" he smiled, stamping the passport and handing it back to Dick. "Welcoombe to España!" It was our first experience of both the horrible nitpicking of Franco's bureaucracy and the basic warmth and humanity of the Spanish people.*

In 1994, Dick Recalls Our First Days in Spain

WE WENT LOOKING FOR A PLACE TO SPEND THE NIGHT. IN MARCH 1994, DICK SENT ME FROM BILBAO A COPY OF A SHORT PIECE HE had written for *Lookout*, a Malaga-based English-language magazine, called "My First Day in Spain," which begins with the story of our search for a room.

Our task upon arrival at Irun had been to find digs. I possessed but 10,000 pesetas [about £55 / US$165—but to put this into perspective: our five weeks at the summer course in Jaca, for room, full board, and tuition, cost us each £20], *in huge green notes, sewn for security into the back of my corduroy trousers* [even I didn't know about that!], *and this had to, and did, last me three months. It meant the digs had got to be cheap. I had no Spanish, and so my good friend and travelling companion, Terry, who boasted that he had more than a smattering, instructed me to wait in the road while he went upstairs to the fonda and enquired if they had a room. Shortly afterwards, he was back down again with the landlady, and standing together in the doorway, they peered at me for rather more than just a few seconds. I felt embarrassed, for I had only just entered the country and really had no idea what was going on. Terry later told me there had been confusion about whether he was accompanied by an amigo or an amiga and the landlady had eventually decided it was best to make a visual check. Morals were still very strict then.*

The story is a little more complex than that. When I asked for a room for myself and my *amigo*, the lady asked me if we wanted a *matrimonial*, one of the Spanish words for a double bed. I did not know this word and thought she was asking me if I wanted a bed for myself and my matrimonial partner. Seeing there was some confusion, and that my Spanish was not up to sorting it out, the woman beckoned me downstairs with her, where we had a look at my *amigo*, which satisfied her that everything was on the up and up. We were fed a decent meal and sold—for 4 pesetas—a bottle of the worst wine I have ever drunk, bar none. In *Ulysses*, Tennyson writes: *"I will drink / Life to the lees,"* and in a sense, that is what Dick and I were doing in our wandering about Europe. But that night with this wine we went beyond that: we drank the lees themselves. It was not a pleasant experience. Probably we should have opted for a 6-peseta bottle, though I don't recall we were offered any choice. This was the *vin de la casa*.

The following morning, Dick continues, *after paying the 25 pesetas our landlady charged each of us for bed and breakfast* [we had paid for the dinner separately the night before], *we went to the railway station to buy RENFE Runabout Tickets, called Billete Kilométrico. We were helped in this process by local Spanish girls, who, in their keenness to practice foreign languages, and especially English, would stand around the station and volunteer to assist people like ourselves to obtain tickets and travel information.*

Our Kilométricos cost us just under 700 pesetas each, and funnily enough, no passport photos or any of the usual Spanish bureaucratic rigmarole was required. These documents entitled us to ride Spain's railways, third class, up to a limit of 3,000 kilometers. This was well in excess of our needs, and I never expended all my little tear-out kilometer tokens. I suppose I eventually threw the thing away, which I now regret. It would have been a great reminder of those pleasant adventures.

There are some things to be said for those of us who are pack rats by nature. I, in fact, managed to keep my *Billete Kilométrico* all these years. It is a dark, wine-colored passport-like object, about 4" x 6", in which are about a dozen ugly brown pages. On the inside cover the railway clerk has written "Pasaporte No. 768487, Canada." There is a circular stamp which reads around the edge *RED NATIONAL DE LOS FERROCARRILES ESPAÑOLES,* and inside that, across the middle, on four lines, *OFICINA DE VIAJES / 30 JUL 1959 / KILOMÉTRICOS / IRUN*. On the first page there is, among other things, *BILLETE NUMERO 170026*, a 3rd Class designation, *3.000 kilómetros,* my name, and the price, which is printed at 501,10 pesetas, over which the clerk has written 675. Ah, inflation! On the next page there are five different stamps, one of which gives the terminal date for the *Kilométrico*, 30 OCT. 1959, and my own signature. The rest of the booklet is taken up with the tear-out kilometer tabs, mentioned by Dick, some pages of rules and regulations, and a small map of the Spanish railway system. We certainly got our money's worth for just under 700 pesetas.

By Train to Zaragoza and Huesca

THE ONLY WAY TO GET TO HUESCA BY RAIL FROM IRUN WAS TO TAKE A TRAIN TO ZARAGOZA AND CHANGE THERE. TRAVELLING THIRD class on what Dick called *"Franco's antique militarized railway system"* was not comfortable. You sat on bench seats of spaced wooden slats, of the sort you find on park benches, in compartments that were connected together by a corridor. Our train, which was a Correo, the milk-run class of RENFE trains, stopped at every outback station along the way, and all of the stations, as I recall, were outback stations. It was the end of July and very hot. At many of these stations, as Dick has remembered, *"hawkers would lurk along the platforms,"* selling drinks to us *"poor parched passengers. Their prices were extortionate, but we consoled ourselves with the thought that these wretched people needed pesetas even more than we did."*

The train was packed. We shared a compartment—reluctantly, but there was no other choice—with a peasant mother whose young baby had a very bad case of diarrhea. She was accompanied by an older woman, who might have been the grandmother of the child. The mother wiped the baby clean with a seemingly endless supply of rags that she fished out of a shopping bag by the bench on her side, and after using them, flung them out the open window, all the while shaking her head and smiling at us by way of apology. The other end of the baby she kept plying with a nippled bottle of water, in order, I suppose, to keep him from getting dehydrated. The smell was horrific, even though we had the window open. So Dick and I spent most of our time wandering up and down the corridor, leaning on the bars that protected the corridor windows, looking out at the desert-like landscape. *"It seemed the houses were mere mud huts, made from clay bricks,"* Dick wrote. *"I was intrigued, but not impressed. I still preferred the Dorset countryside I had left in England. There seemed to be no human beings in these far-flung places, only donkeys and chickens. The heat must have kept people inside."*

Dick's recollection of the mother-and-baby scene recalls an aspect of it that affected him more directly than it affected me. *"Third Class carriages,"* he writes, *"were still in common use on Spain's railways in 1959, and our Correo train from Irun to Zaragoza was crowded with peasants. For this reason, I thought it best to lay the rather posh Jaeger jersey I had with me upon my section of the creaky old wooden seat so as to keep someone else from taking it while Terry and I were in the corridor.* [Taking the seat, that is, not the jersey. The Spanish people in those days were incredibly honest. You could leave almost anything almost anywhere and it would not be stolen.] *But this turned out to be a mistake. Returning to the compartment, I found to my utter horror that the little urchin, who had been sitting on his mother's lap opposite me when we left, had not only been put on top of the sweater but had in the meantime peed on it."* Dick was understandably upset by this situation, but he was unable to do much about it until we reached Huesca and got settled into our *pension* there, when he put his *"smelly pullover to soak in water overnight."*

At Zaragoza we had to change trains and take another *Correo* for the short journey north to Huesca. We had an hour or so between trains, not enough time to go anywhere, but enough time to have a cup of coffee and a sandwich at the station. Dick's account of this event, he says in his accompanying letter, *"perhaps actually took place at Huesca, and not on Zaragoza Railway Station."* I think, in fact, that he must have been thinking of another time and another person, as I always drink milk with my coffee and would never have ordered it black. But the story *is* amusing. *"When we reached Zaragoza, we found it stifling, and its ancient railway station reeked of urine--or perhaps it was my pullover that had started to stink. We sat down inside the Cantina, alongside the Fonda they had on the platform there, and Terry asked the waiter for café puro, adding, as he watched me nod, that this was how Spaniards ordered their black coffee. We were, he assured me, doing exactly the right thing. What we actually got, of course, was coffee and cigars."* [What I should have ordered, if I may carry on the spirit of this urban legend, was *café negro*, or *solo*, not *café puro*!]

While we were drinking our coffee (and, apparently, smoking our cigars), it occurred to Dick that the girls who had helped us in Irun had said we would have to change stations in Zaragoza. We were shown the way by a friendly porter, who kept trying to convince us that we should spend the night at the *Pension Ambos Mundos* and go to Huesca in the morning. If our guide had been able to manage to get us to stay there, he would have collected a gratuity from the *pension*, and even possibly from us. But we were not to be deterred, and having found the station we were looking for, we took the late afternoon train to Huesca. We were, as Dick put it, *"probably the first ever travellers to do the Irun to Huesca run by RENFE in a single day."* In Huesca, we booked into what Dick remembers as a *"curious monastery-like pension,"* but what I recall as a rather seedy, downtown hotel that was four or five storeys tall.

Bugs and *Bisontes in* Huesca

WE SPENT ABOUT A WEEK IN HUESCA. FOR ME IT WAS NOT A GOOD WEEK. I CAME DOWN WITH SOME KIND OF STOMACH BUG. I probably got it from eating a piece of cut watermelon that I bought from a street vendor the morning after we arrived. (Though, when I come to think of it, it's always possible that I picked it up from the *"little urchin"* who had peed on Dick's sweater. If so, Dick got the better part of the deal!) But on that first day I felt fine. We bought for our lunch some bread, sausage—Dick remembers it as *"a stick of what later turned out to be 'cooking' saveloy"*—and a bottle of cheap wine. We wandered around this small and unpretentious city, and ate our lunch in one of its parks. Dick climbed a walnut tree on one of the downtown boulevards in search of walnuts, and we laughed at that. We sat at various sidewalk cafes, smoking our newly acquired brand of cigarettes, *Bisontes*, which had on the package a depiction of an Altamira cave drawings of a bison. We had chosen this brand because we did not like the dark tobacco that most Spaniards smoked. *Bisontes* were made with the light-colored tobacco, more like that of the cigarettes we were used to, that the local people called *rubio* ("blonde").

Our enforced idleness, as we waited for the time when the summer course would begin in Jaca, and underlined by my health problem, gave us a chance to get to know each other a bit better. We talked about the things that interested us, searching for common ground. During the last few days we had spent a lot of time together, but in the great scheme of things, we were essentially strangers. In the short time we had been together in London, we had established the fact that we were both fans of the films of Jacques Tati. One night we went to a cinema in Chiswick to see *Monsieur Hulot's Holiday*. Dick had a booming laugh, and on that occasion he was at his booming best. So much so, that the man sitting in front of us turned around and said, "Would you mind laughing with a little less enthusiasm? I'd like to *hear* this film as well as *see* it!"

When we talked about books, Dick invariably came round to Lawrence of Arabia and *The Seven Pillars of Wisdom*, which at the time I had not read, and have still not read, though I have tried without success to read it a number of times. Lawrence was a native of Dorset, like Dick, and a local hero for him. But since Lawrence had died on a motorcycle, and I had ridden one around Europe the year before, motorcycles were of interest to both of us. Dick was gung-ho on the *Indian*, a large, powerful, and unpredictable machine that was produced in the United States after the Second World War. I had seen one—it had a nifty cigar store Indian head on its gas tank--but had never been on one. My motorcycle, which I told Dick I had bought from the factory the year before, when I was in Milan, was a Motor Guzzi Cardellino, a beautiful red machine that was massively underpowered at 73cc. Its top speed, on the flat, was about 30 miles per hour; in the mountains, going uphill, it could only manage about twenty. But I recounted my adventure with it to him, pointing out that I had manfully rode it along the French Riviera, through Spain to Madrid, and, in the chill of October, north through France to England. (See *Europe on a Motor Guzzi Cardellino*). I explained that I had stored it there for the winter, but that when spring came in 1959, I had taken it to work every day. I don't think Dick ever actually owned a motorcycle, but he was a fan. In a letter of 10 May 1994, he pointed out that he remembered that I had *"proudly owned and rode* [a Moto Guzzi] *in London,"* and that I had *"very kindly loaned it to* [him] *once,"* a bit of generosity I don't recall. *"What,"* he asked, *"became of it in the end?"* The answer to that is simple. Before leaving for Spain, I put an advertising card in a tobacconist's shop in Acton, where it stood proudly with those of the local masseurs (wink, wink! nod, nod!) and the hookers. I was anxious to get rid of it before leaving England, and I sold it for the absurdly cheap price of £25.

My stomach malady persisted for a number of days. It was an odd bug, because as long as I wasn't near the smell of food, I didn't feel too badly. Every evening I would head down to the dining room with Dick, we would sit at our table and get ready to order, and I would say, "I don't think I can do this," and go back to our room on the fourth floor. On the third evening, when I had once again abandoned the dining room, a middle-aged woman who was a hotel employee brought me a cup of highly-sugared herbal tea. I drank it, all the time thinking that the idea was primitive and absurd; but it seemed to do the trick, and as suddenly as I had become sick, I became well. The next morning I was awake and feeling healthy and energetic even before the cocks that lived on the roof of the building opposite greeted the dawn.

Beginning the Course in Jaca

ON AUGUST 8, WE LEFT HUESCA FOR JACA BY TRAIN. I STILL HAVE MY CARDBOARD TICKET STUB, No. 02695, WHICH WAS PUNCHED TWICE, once to make a round hole, once to make a square one. I have no idea why. Once in Jaca, we were registered, given a room, and told that they would collect our fees on the following day. We shared *Habitación 16* in the *Residencia Universitaria*. The residence was a pleasant modern building, the front part containing the administration, the dining room, and the classrooms, and the back part, a two-storey bedroom section. You entered the building through a central foyer. At one end of the complex was a tennis court; at the other, a swimming pool. That first night with dinner we had one limón natural (5ptas) and one cerveza grande (also 5 ptas). I don't know which one of us had what. (And, yes, I still have my copy of the chit!) The next day, we paid our 3500 pesetas each and with a group of others were given an orientation tour of the building.

> As classes didn't start until the following morning, we decided to spend the afternoon by the swimming pool. Eventually, bored with lying around, and not unaware of the possibility of impressing some of the girls at poolside, Dick began fooling around on the diving board, making all kinds of weird and wonderful leaps into the water. On one of these, he went too deep and hit his head, and when he lifted himself out of the pool, he was bleeding rather profusely, bright red seeping out of his blonde hair. At first he was not aware that he had cut himself, and he stood at the pool's edge with a silly grin on his face as the rest of us rushed to his aid. The cut was not serious, but the administrators we went to for help were alarmed, and they shipped Dick off to a doctor, who put a small bandage on his wound.

Our afternoons were often spent at the *Gran Hotel* playing bridge. We borrowed the cards from the bar. They were not like the cards we were used to playing with. Instead of spades, hearts, diamonds and clubs, they had four suits headed by Tarot symbols: blue swords, brown cups, green cudgels, and gold coins. We had great fun bidding with them: "Two cups!" we would proclaim. "Three swords!" our opponents would answer. While we played, we sipped sweet martinis and felt very European. Compared to the other places in town, the *Gran Hotel*, built for tourists, was expensive; so we nursed one or two drinks through the many hours we played. I don't know what it cost to stay in the hotel in 1959, but I recently checked today's price on the internet: the low season rate for a single room is the equivalent about $90 per night—that's more than double what we paid for four weeks room, board, and tuition at the summer course in 1959.

The Pilgrim Cathedral of Jaca

The cathedral of Jaca! Ah, the cathedral of Jaca! A splendid building, its exterior terra cotta color having the usual unfinished rubble look of the churches of Spain, its interior walls and columns of burnished gray stone, the floor of wood—one of the great pilgrim churches of Spain. I examined the interior in detail every Sunday morning at Mass. The Dutch writer, Cees Nooteboom sang its praises in ***Roads to Santiago***:

The mountains that the pilgrims risked their lives to cross lie white and glistening to my right, I am heading for the long broad shape of the cathedral of Jaca as purposefully as a sailor steering for home. It does exist, love for a building, however difficult it may be to talk about. If I had to talk I would have to explain why it should be this particular church that, when I can no longer travel, I will want to have been the last building I have seen. It was the first Romanesque cathedral to be built in Spain (1063) . . . . You can slip it on like a coat; when I go inside I draw it tight around my body . . . . And each time I return here, no matter how long my absence has been, the same joyful emotion comes over me.

All about its interior and exterior are carved figures of animals, real and mythical, snakes, bears, lions, basilisks, and unrecognizable monsters, as if from a mozarabic manuscript. While the priest preached a sermon I could not understand, I examined each week a different part of the church. It was easy to move around in there among the large crowds, as I was no different from the men who slipped out of the door for a smoke while the service was going on. Great smokers the Spanish were in those days. I joined the "guys" on the porch, and we shared our cigarettes across the barrier of our language problem. As Hemingway is reported to have said, "If you want to get along with the Spanish, give the men tobacco and leave the women alone." I was happy to give the men tobacco. As for the women? . . . well, I thought, we'll see.

The cathedral is in the center of the town and seems to grow out of it like some kind of natural phenomenon, a mountain raised by an earthquake, or better still, as it feels alive, some great stone plant. I have often thought that Gaudí must have received his inspiration for his great cathedral in Barcelona, although in a totally different style, from the same sort of feeling. In his case, the plants appear to have been asparagus. I am pleased to hear that this first of the Spanish Romanesque cathedrals, and in some respects the model for all the others, is being proposed to UNESCO as a world heritage site.

Castillo de San Pedro

DURING THE WEEK, WE HAD LANGUAGE AND CULTURE CLASSES IN THE MORNING, SOME OF WHICH WE ATTENDED. IN THE AFTERNOONS, we swam in the *Residencia* pool, or in the river under the splendid Roman bridge, the *Puente de San Miguel*, or went to the *Gran Hotel*, a newly-constructed international-style building that never seemed to have any guests, to play bridge in the bar. In the evenings, after dinner, we would go across town to the *Casa Paco*, where we would drink wine and socialize. Occasionally, we went on excursions by bus, once to the old pilgrimage monastery, high in the Pyrenees, of *St. Juan de la Peña*.

The building in town that interested me almost as much as the cathedral was the *Ciudadela*, or citadel, also known as the *Castillo de San Pedro* (1595), which we used to pass on our way from the *Residencia* into town. It is a large stone fort in the shape of a polygon or star, in superb condition; with heavy, angled walls about thirty feet high and turrets at the five corners. It is a design that was exported by the Spanish to both the Netherlands and South America. This particular fort is entered by a bridge over a moat, now empty of water, but looking as if it could still be filled should the occasion demand it. Even more intriguing than the building itself, however, was the fact that a section of Franco's antique army was still quartered there, even though it had been declared an historical monument in 1951. One morning, I saw a group of them heading out of the old fort on an exercise to the mountains, with parts of what looked like cannons strapped to the sides of mules.

But it was not only Franco's army that was out-dated. His air force was still flying the German Messerschmitt 109s that were made for the Luftwaffe from 1935 till the end of the Second World War. Curiously, in the summer of 1968, in England, on my way back from a holiday in the Cotswolds, I saw some of these ancient aircraft—borrowed from the Spanish air force and repainted with German markings, dog fighting with Spitfires over East Anglia, not far from Cambridge. At the time I had no idea what was going on, but later found out that they were being used to film scenes for the movie, *The Battle of Britain*. What a different world it is now, forty years' later. The Spanish air force now flies state-of-the-art F-18 jet fighter-bombers.

Sometimes before going for a swim under the *Puente San Miguel*, we would take a walk through the arid countryside. I had bought in Huesca a pair of *alpargatas*, the typical rope summer shoe of the peasant, in those days not reinforced with plastic soles, which had strings on them so you could tie them over your ankles. I would wear these on our short walks, believing myself to be very Spanish as I did so. In the fields were many kinds of cereal crops, and everywhere, in enormous numbers, colorado beetles, the beautiful stripped "potato bugs," on which there was a bounty in England. Some of the English students boasted about their intention of smuggling a matchbox full back to England to claim the bounty.

On some afternoons, and often in the evenings after dinner, we went to the *Casa Paco*. To get there, we had to walk through the main streets of the town. We liked this place because it was for the most part outdoors, the tables being set under a rectangular grape arbor that had the effect of dividing the space into a dozen or so open-walled rooms. On a number of occasions, after drinking more wine than we should have, we headed back through the streets of Jaca, no doubt to the amusement—and probably to the amazement—of the locals, who would have understood none of the words, singing to the tune of *Colonel Bogie*:

> *Hitler has only got one ball,*
> *Goering's got two, but they're too small,*
> *Himmler's got something similar,*
> *But poor old Goebels has no balls at all.*

We thought that it was very daring to sing this song in a country run by a fascist regime that a decade and a half before had had an uncomfortable relationship with these strutting Germans, all of whom had met their *Götterdämmerung* in 1945.

In the bar we met a young Scot who was wandering around Spain as cheaply as he could, sleeping in the open, and if you were to believe his story, living mostly on grapes. When we met him in the Casa Paco, he was full of the fact that he had just run into trouble with the police. Apparently, he had been carrying a Uher tape recorder from place to place, recording anti-Franco songs. It was a very stupid thing to do, and the police, given the circumstances, had let him off lightly. They even gave him his machine back, merely confiscating his recordings.

There Had Sufficed a Pretty Outline

BUT A MEETING OF MORE RELEVANCE TO MY OWN LIFE, AT LEAST IN THE VERY SHORT TERM, ALSO OCCURRED IN THIS BAR. IT WAS HERE I got to know Rosalind Evans.

> . . . for there had sufficed a pretty outline, a glimpse of a fresh complexion, for me to add, in entire good faith, a fascinating shoulder, a delicious glance of which I carried in my mind for ever a memory or a preconceived idea . . ..
> Marcel Proust, *Within a Budding Grove*, **Remembrance of Things Past**, 1918

> A face to lose youth for, to occupy age
> With the dream of, meet death with.
> >   Robert Browning, "Likeness"

> Youth means love,
> You cannot change nature.
> >   Robert Browning, *The Ring and the Book*, I, 1056-7

Ros was my girlfriend through the last couple of weeks of the course. She was a short, rather stocky English girl from Birmingham, whose unfortunate billiard-table legs were more than made up for by the prettiness of her face. Curiously enough, at the beginning of the course she had paired up with Dick in a kind of platonic way, in the same way that I had spent my time as a friend of Mireille, a girl from France whose last name I have forgotten. But at some point, in a wordless kind of changing of the guard, we switched partners. Suddenly it had seemed the natural thing to do. It happened completely spontaneously and without any rancor on the part of any one of the four of us. It was what we all suddenly wanted.

Ros was quite clear about the fact that she was committed to her boyfriend at home. He was studying chemistry at Exeter, where she was reading modern languages. I told her about Jennifer. She made it clear that within these circumstances she was happy to have a fling. So have a fling we did. Were we in love? Yes, in spite of the fact that we were both in love with others, we were in love; not love forever, but love for the time being; love with limits that we both were happy with—but love nonetheless.

> *We got together for the first time when I walked her home from the Casa Paco. Our relationship progressed rapidly; and as I put my hand on her thigh under a huge shade tree by the Residencia, she only said in response, "Don't fall in love with me." In the days that followed, we were inseparable. We walked the town, and sat in the bars, and headed together, hand in hand, out into the fields on the edge of town. On our final afternoon together, when Dick was somewhere with Mireille, she came to Room 16. After half an hour of talk and cuddling, I put my hand on her knee. She froze, as girls will often do at this point of no return, and then she leaned into me. I went to the door and locked it. She lay back on my bed and waited for me to return to her side.*

Ros had a friend from England, whose name was Heather. She *was* an unfortunate young woman from a physical point of view: too tall, too broad, too thick, and too dumpy. Mireille and the other French girls cruelly referred to her behind her back as the *vache anglaise*. She squinted too much, because she didn't want to wear her glasses, laughed too heartily, and when she wasn't sulking (and she had reason to sulk), tried far too hard. I felt sorry for her, and so did Ros. We did our best to include her when we went to the Roman bridge or the *Casa Paco* or the *Gran Hotel*. But sometimes the others would abandon the three of us, and I would be left with two young women on my hands. One too many. Maybe even one and a half too many.

John and Stephen and the Red MGA

DICK AND I BECAME FRIENDS WITH JOHN AND STEPHEN, WHO WERE STUDENTS AT CAMBRIDGE. STEPHEN WAS AN EXCELLENT PIANIST, but he had the English disease of belittling the accomplishments of other nations, and he spent a lot of time running down superb 20th century Spanish composers like De Falla and Granados. Neither Dick nor I knew enough about music to contradict him, a fact he must have known; so when he began one of his tirades, we let him have the floor. But in the last week of the course, he became useful. The faculty asked each language group to put together a little concert that reflected their culture, and Stephen found his metier in organizing the English speakers into a concert which represented English, American, and Canadian culture. The only items I remember from this concert are the songs we sang, all of them, under Stephen's direction, from England. We sang *Three Jolly Coachmen*, a traditional drinking song, and *The Umbrella Man*, which is from a late 1930s English musical. Six of us dutifully shuffled our way through these pieces on a makeshift stage at the front of the largest classroom:

> *Tuma luma luma, tuma luma luma,*
> *Tuma-lye-aye,*
> *Have you any umber-, any umber-ellas*
> *To mend to-day?*

John was quite unlike Stephen. He was a hail-fellow-well-met kind of guy, compact physically, with a large grin. He had an older red MGA which he had driven from England, and we often piled four or five of us into it, hanging like balloons with our bums on the luggage rack and our legs in the well behind the seat. I can still see Dick laughing away uproariously as we sped around town, busily going nowhere, but enjoying the wind and the bounce. One day, after we'd gone into a bar for a *bocadillo* and a *cerveza*, we returned to find a puddle under the back of the car and the strong smell of petrol. John drove us to a garage on what gasoline was left in the tank. The mechanic refused (understandably) to weld the crack in the tank, didn't have any idea how long it would take to get a new tank from England, and said he couldn't solder it. What he did was give John a package of sticky plasticine-like guck to effect a temporary repair until he could get the car back to England. The stuff didn't work very well; but John made the best of it, cursing all the time about the amount of gas he was going through.

Pierre, a *Deux Chevaux*, and the *Corrida*

> Antonio wanted to go to Bilbao now, the most difficult public in Spain where the bulls are the biggest and the public the most severe and exigent so that no one could ever say that there was ever anything doubtful or shady or dubious about this campaign of 1959 when he was fighting as no one had fought real bulls since Joselito and Belmonte.
> Ernest Hemingway, *The Dangerous Summer*, 1960

NEAR THE END OF OUR TIME IN JACA, DICK AND I BECAME FRIENDLY WITH PIERRE. PIERRE HAD A PASSION FOR THE BULLFIGHT.

One day he told us there was a great fight coming up in Bilbao. Now, Bilbao was quite a drive in those days over the narrow mountain roads, and so Dick and I hummed and hawed about going. When I wrote this story up first in the 1980s, I remembered Dick being with us on this trip, but when I sent a copy of it to him, he replied: *"Thank you so much for your most interesting letter with the story of the outing from Jaca to Bilbao. Actually, I did not come with you that day. I think it was because when I arrived in this country, all I had in my wallet was 10,000 ptas, then worth £60, and the bullfight was more than I could afford."* (Letter, 20 April 1991) Then I remembered that it was an Austrian fellow named Lance who was with us. So much for the reliability of memory.

Pierre said a bullfight with both Luis Miguel Domínguín and Antonio Ordóñez was not to be missed, and Pierre knew his bullfighters. "Besides," he said, adding the clincher in his good but highly accented English, "If 'Emingway ees in Spain, for sure, he'll be at zis one."

We did not know that Hemingway had been in Spain all that summer of 1959, having been commissioned by *Life* magazine to write another bullfight saga like the hugely successful one he'd published in the 1930s, *Death in the Afternoon*. This time he chose to write about the rivalry between the two brothers-in-law, Domínguín, who was making a comeback from retirement, and Ordóñez, who had succeeded him as the star attraction in the *plaza de torros*. The result of this rivalry, or *mano a mano*, was published not only in *Life* as a series of articles called "The Dangerous Summer," but also eventually in a book with the same title. The Bilbao bullfight we were headed for on the morning of August 21 was the climax of the rivalry, and of Hemingway's book. But, of course, none of us, not even Hemingway, knew this at the time.

Pierre and I had spent the weekends at bullfights. We would pile into his souped-up Citroën *deux chevaux*, with its window-blind roof and pull-on-the-rope door openers, and head for wherever Pierre said a good *corrida* was taking place that weekend. Although he was from the south of France, where the bull is fought but not killed, Pierre was an *aficionado* of the Spanish bullfight. I wasn't much more than a fascinated observer. I never did learn the elaborate series of passes the bullfighter must make, never could tell a *pecho* from a *veronica*, and, quite frankly, didn't care enough to learn the vocabulary. If truth be told, I didn't like bullfights much. What I wanted was the experience of the day.

Pierre was inordinately proud of his *deux chevaux* and treated it with the attention of a lover. He checked it over thoroughly before we left on our bullfighting excursions, poking at engine parts, reading tire pressures, inspecting the skin of the car as a pilot would inspect his plane for hair-line cracks that might rip apart on the road through the Pyrenees and plunge us from a mountain pass into the valley below. I would watch him with rising trepidation as he checked the car, because no matter how sound it was mechanically, that did not make up for the terror Pierre's driving awoke in me.

He fancied himself a world-class racing driver, waiting only to be discovered. He pushed the car—which certainly responded with more than its two horses' worth—as hard and as fast as it would go. He did not turn at switchbacks—and the Jaca-Bilbao road had many switchbacks—brake, accelerate, brake, accelerate—as we dug for the mountain tops and scudded into the valleys.

> *He would accelerate into the switchbacks; then, when I was sure disaster was only a matter of seconds away and I could see us rolling over and over down the mountainside, he would slam on the brakes, and as the car skidded around the corner, floor the accelerator. It was all timing, he said—gas, brake, gas. On this trip we took two French girls, friends of Pierre's, whose names— even whose faces—I have forgotten, and the Austrian fellow, Lance. In the deux chevaux, we were a real carload. But nobody complained to Pierre about his driving; and he drove as if he were a torero, the car his cape, the road the bull, and the rest of us admiring spectators.*

In Bilbao we bought our tickets, the medium-priced *sol y sombra*, for 175 pesetas each, about $3.00. Pierre, as usual, had been right. Everyone who mattered was at this *corrida*. In the presidential box, as *La Presidenta* of the bullfight—the honorary person in charge—was even the wife of the head of state, Doña Carmen Polo de Franco. It was an important fight.

It was on his second bull that Dominguín was gored. The big black bull caught him against the horse of the picador, piercing his thigh with his horn and pushing him against the horse. The crowd gasped. Ordóñez—and Jaime Ostos, the other *torero* on the card—leapt into the ring with their capes and managed to distract the bull. Dominguín was quickly hoisted up by four men and hand-carried out of the ring. Then Ordóñez fought Dominguín's bull and killed him.

I realized at the time that this *corrida* was important and historical, but I had no idea at the time *how* important and *how* historical. Hemingway's book, of course, underlined the hugeness of the rivalry between Dominguín and Ordóñez, but I was always suspicious of his making this bullfight the climax of his book., thinking that it was probably a convenient way for him to organize his account. But when I was in a taxi from the airport into the city in Madrid in 2000, the taxi driver, who was a great bullfight fan, listened to me in awe when I told him I had been in the *plaza* in Bilbao in 1959 when this legendary *corrida* took place. I could see the envy glittering off his sunglasses, as he asked me for more and more detail, all of which I offered him in my crude Spanish.

A Chat with Ernest Hemingway

WHEN THE FIGHT WAS OVER AND PEOPLE WERE LEAVING THE *PLAZA*, WE SPOTTED HEMINGWAY IN THE EXPENSIVE SEATS BELOW US, standing with a too-thin, wan-looking girl of seventeen or so. He wore a brown and white checked pancake cap and a pair of sunglasses with yellow lenses. He carried his head angled slightly forward from his body, a compensation for the bad back that was caused by two consecutive small-plane crashes in Africa.

> *We hopped over the iron barriers down to the expensive seats, groping our way through the leaving crowd to where Hemingway stood soaking in the atmosphere of the end of the corrida: the moving crowd, the light of the late afternoon, the blood stains in the sand. He was friendly, chatting in a relaxed way in his broad mid-western accent. He asked us where each of us was from. Like a politician, he made us all feel important. I was surprised he wanted to bother with us at all, and that he didn't resent our intrusion.*
>
> *But I wanted to know about Dominguin. "How is Dominguin?" I asked.*
> *"He'll be ok," he said. "It's not a serious accident."*
>
> *But in his account in The Dangerous Summer, Hemingway makes it clear that he did not know this at the time. He knew that the horn "had gone up into the abdomen but they did not know yet if there was any perforation." It was not until later that they knew for sure that Dominguin would be all right. The horn had followed the same route as an earlier wound he had suffered in Málaga. That was the good news. But Dominguin would never fight again. The rivalry had been decided.*

We chatted about, of all things, skiing in the Rockies; though I don't remember why, it probably had to do with my telling him where I was from. I asked him to sign my bullfight ticket, which he did.[2] He then left for the Carlton Hotel, where he was staying. The last I saw of him was the broad, checkered back of his jacket as he left the plaza, his hand resting like a grandfather's on the shoulder of the wan young girl, as if for support rather than as a gesture of protection.

It was the last week for Pierre and me to follow the *corrida*. Anything after this would have been anticlimactic; it wasn't planned that way—it just happened. Two years later, on July 2, 1961, at his home in Idaho, Hemingway put the barrel of a shotgun into his mouth and blew off the top of his head. It was the end of his *mano a mano* with life.

On to My Job at the *Instituto Garrett* in Madrid

WHEN THE COURSE WAS OVER, DICK AND I USED OUR RENFE KILOMETRICOS TO TRAVEL BY TRAIN TO MADRID. I HAD BEEN hired to teach English as a Second Language at the Instituto Garrett. Since I didn't start work until the 20th of September, I had some time on my hands. Dick decided to come along with me and perhaps also find somewhere to teach in Madrid. We became tourists again, spending a few days in Zaragoza; and while we were there, Dick walked into a language institute (I think it was called the Briam Institute) and landed a job. As this job started about the same time as mine did, Dick also had some time on his hands, so he decided to come to Madrid with me for a few days. Train travel for us was more or less

---

[2] The original of the ticket was stolen when our house was broken into in Ottawa in 1990. Fortunately, I had xeroxed it in black and white before that as a prize to show to my English literature classes. A copy of that Xerox is on the picture pages following this chapter.

free, and he had to eat and sleep somewhere, no matter where he was, so cost was not really a factor.

On our third day in Zaragoza, we left the Franco Youth Hostel, where we had been staying, which was on the outer edge of the city, and took a bus to the railway station. There, we stood in line for hours, heading slowly toward the wicket at which we could get tickets for the train to Madrid. But as we neared the front of the line, the wicket was suddenly slammed shut. The train, we were told, was full. Then someone explained to us that we could make reservations ahead of time if we went to the RENFE office in downtown Zaragoza, so we did that, getting tickets to board a train on the following day.

> *Since there was nowhere else we could stay as cheaply, we returned to the Youth Hostel, where the staff was much amused by our reappearance. There, that night, we watched a bonfire ceremony of Franco Youth, which, for all its flag-waving indoctrination, reminded both of us more of boy scouts than fascist youth. It would take another fifteen years for this regime to die; but even at this point, it was clear that it was doomed.*

In Madrid, we stayed at the International Youth Hostel in the Casa de Campo. After three or four days, Dick went back to Zaragoza, and I took a train to León to spend a day or two with Jennifer. I don't remember exactly why she was in León, as she was going to spend the fall and winter teaching English as a Second Language in Bilbao.

A Note on the Rest of Dick Whitehead's Life

I saw Dick once more that Christmas; and one final time, with Laura, the Spanish girl from Zaragoza he had married, in London, in 1963. He had remained in Spain, raising a family there. We had been friends for a very short time. But there must have been some magic in our relationship, as we kept in touch, through many changes of addresses, for more than thirty-five years. When I didn't get a Christmas card in 1996, I was puzzled, so I wrote to him with some trepidation. In March of 1997, a letter arrived in Victoria, written in an unfamiliar handwriting, with a Bilbao frank on the stamp. I knew as soon as I picked it up that the news was not going to be good. The letter read, in part: "I am very sorry to let you know that Richard died on the 20th of December. His funeral was held on the 22nd at the British Cemetery in Bilbao. Last February, he was diagnosed as having a malignant tumour at the back of his tongue. He died peacefully. He received your Christmas card, and it made him happy to hear from you, as he appreciated your friendship very much indeed. I hope that we can continue the friendship he maintained with you all these years. With love to you both, Laura." Laura and I have exchanged letters at Christmas every year since Richard's death.

> The places that we have known belong now only to the little world of space on which we map them for our own convenience. None of them was ever more than a thin slice, held between the contiguous impressions that composed our life at that time; remembrance of a particular form is but regret for a particular moment; and houses, roads, avenues are as fugitive, alas, as the years.
> Marcel Proust, *Swann's Way*, **Remembrance of Things Past**, 1913

That Summer in Jaca

Peace Haven in 1959

Luba in Her Kitchen

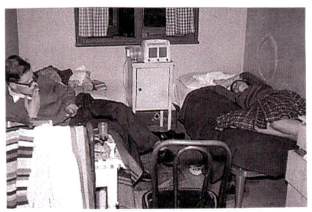

Rm. 10: Dick Whitehead & Jennifer Sharp

LUBAS BISTRO

ONION SOUP	LUBAS RUSSIAN BORSCH
CORN ON THE COB	SOUP DU JOUR
SALAD MIXED	PÂTÉ
PIROSHKI	
FRUIT JUICES (ORANGE, GRAPEFRUIT, PINEAPPLE, TOMATO)	

SPECIALITY

SHACHLIK
BOEUF STROGANOFF
POJARSKY
LUBAS GALUBTZY
CRÊPE A LA REINE
CHICKEN SUPREME
CHICKEN CURRY & RICE
STUFFED GREEN PEPPERS
VOL-AU-VENT
BEEF CURRY & RICE
EGG CURRY & RICE
KOFTA CURRY & RICE
SPAGHETTI MAISON
SPAGHETTI WITH MEAT BALLS
LAMB CHOP GARNI
PORK CHOP GARNI
ENTRECÔTE STEAK GARNI
HOLSTEIN STEAK GARNI
TOURNEDOS STEAK GARNI (if you're lucky)

TRIFLE	ORANGE SALAD
MERINGUE GLACE	CHEESE & BISCUITS
BANANA MELBA	BREAD & BUTTER
PEAR MELBA	CHUTNEY
PEACH MELBA	COFFEE
ICES	RUSSIAN TEA
ICE & CHOCOLATE SAUCE	YOGHOURT
	COCA-COLA
LUBAS SPECIAL CERNIC	ORANGE SQUASH
	LEMON SQUASH

BRING YOUR OWN WINE — NO CORKAGE

Leslie Dunkling in the Garden at Peace Haven

Tables at Luba's Were Shared

Terry Hitching in France

Dick Resting After Lunch

Cursos de Verano Pamphlet

Kilométrico

The Residencia and Pierre's 2CV

Roman Bridge

Terry & Dick at Franco Youth Hostel Zaragoza

Identity Card

Ros Writes from Paris

Moat of the *Ciudadela*

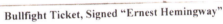

Bullfight Ticket, Signed "Ernest Hemingway"

A Monk at *St. Juan de la Peña*

Keough Painting, *Memories of Jaca (1998)*
In dreams I don my ancient alpargatas,
And walk the fields of Jaca once again.
(In Memory of Dick Whitehead (1939-1996))

Chapter 10: Living in Franco's Spain

TEACHING ENGLISH IN MADRID

I know that my achievement is quite ordinary. I am not the only man to seek his fortune far from home, and certainly I am not the first. Still, there are times I am bewildered by each mile I have traveled, each meal I have eaten, each person I have known, each room in which I have slept. As ordinary as it all appears, there are times when it is beyond my imagination.
                      Jhumpa Lahiri, "The Third and Final Continent," 1999

How one remembers slowly replaces what really was. Like fossils . . .. The same way that mineral particles fill in the shape where a body has rotted away—a kind of lost-wax casting process, as I understand it.
                      John Updike, ***Seek My Face***, 2002

The Spaniards are a mocking race, especially in Madrid.
                      V. S. Pritchett, ***Midnight Oil***, 1971

The Regime of Generalíssimo Franco

PEOPLE HAVE OFTEN ASKED ME WHAT IT WAS LIKE LIVING IN FRANCO'S SPAIN. IT'S A QUESTION THAT'S NOT EASY TO ANSWER. I WAS CERTAINLY NO FAN OF THE REGIME THAT THE GENERALÍSSIMO was running. At the same time, I was never in any way threatened and never felt I had anything to fear. I think we must give the devil—and he *was* a devil[1]—his due.

    Franco was the smartest of the fascist trio of dictators who ruled over Germany, Italy, and Spain for various periods from the 1920s to the 1970s. Hitler—by far the worst of the three—was in power the shortest period of time, from 1933 to 1945—and he did

---

[1] It's estimated that something like 100,000 people were either executed or died as a result of torture in the first couple of years after the end of the Civil War.

the most damage. Mussolini, who in his early years, it could be argued, was the best of the three, came to power in 1922 and after ten years or so of repressive but, on the whole, progressive rule threw in his lot with Hitler and came to grief in 1945. Both came to Franco's aid during the Spanish Civil War (1936-39), so there was a strong argument for Spain to become involved in World War II on the side of the axis. But Franco hesitated when approached by Hitler to allow German troops to attack Gibraltar through Spain. In the end, he refused to get involved in the war in any major way, though a volunteer division of soldiers, the *División Azul* (Blue Division) was sent to fight with the Germans on the eastern front, and up to 100,000 Spanish workers were allowed to go to Germany to work in war industries.

During the late 1940s and early 1950s, the United Nations imposed sanctions on Spain to try to overturn the Franco regime. As usual, this tactic did not get rid of the regime. Its most significant result was to increase the poverty in the country, and in the south, to create conditions that were very nearly akin to starvation and famine. Under American pressure, the sanctions were lifted in the mid-1950s.

By the time I arrived in Spain in the summer of 1959, the Franco regime had been in power for twenty years, and the world had changed greatly in that time. Spain was crawling with tourists, it had American bases and economic aid, and the economy was picking up. I'm sure that those who presented any kind of real threat to the regime continued to be dealt with harshly. As for the rest, their opposition to the regime, freely expressed without fear as far as I could tell, on the streets, in the bars, and in other public places, was generally ignored. At no time did I see any repression of ideas on an individual level. But there was no organized public opposition to the regime, and none would have been tolerated. It felt as if the country was waiting in a kind of coma for what later came to be known as the "National Tragedy" to end. And wait they did. And, apart from some instances of violence in the final years, end it did, slowly and patiently, with the death of Franco in 1975.

Dick and I Travel to Madrid

BUT THE STATE OF THE REGIME WAS FAR FROM OUR MINDS WHEN DICK WHITEHEAD AND I LEFT JACA FOR ZARAGOZA, EN ROUTE TO Madrid, on Saturday, September 5, 1959. We travelled by train, third class, as we still had many kilometres free on the 3,000-kilometre *kilométricos* we had bought upon entering Spain, enduring the hard slat seats, the smelly peasants, and the live chickens they tied on a length of rope to their belts to be killed for food on their journeys.

On the train, I told Dick about smuggling Ros into our room one afternoon when he and the others were down at the river, and how I had silently congratulated myself on not getting caught. I did not tell him at the time a related incident that occurred a few days later, but I told it to him now on the train.

> *I had asked one of the maids to draw me a bath in one of the communal bathrooms. There was a charge. After you paid, they ran the water into the tub and called you when it was ready. When she came to tell me that the bath was ready, she told me that she had seen me and my girl going to my room. She asked if we were engaged (comprometido para casarse), and I said, "Yes," afraid that I might upset her religious beliefs. I knew that once a couple was officially on the road to the altar, even in the 1950s, that the Spanish tended to look the other way, especially when the couple was foreign. But one never knew what the reaction would be, and I was afraid that if the maid went to her supervisor with this story, Ros and I might be in serious trouble. She didn't.*

After spending a planned two days in Zaragoza, which extended to three when we were unable to get seats on a train, Dick and I arrived in Madrid and moved into the youth hostel in the Casa de Campo, a large park on the southern edge of the city, once a hunting reserve of the Royal Family (as Hyde Park was in London), and, incidentally, an area fiercely fought over in the Civil War. The hostel was cheap: the bed cost 9 pesetas a day, 3 meals a mere 42 pesetas.[2] It was while I was at the Casa de Campo hostel that I received the last word I would ever have from Ros: "6th Sept. It's 6 a.m. & I'm on my way to Paris. I've only an hour to get right across Paris, so I thought I'd send you a p.c. of Jaca [the picture on the postcard is of the Roman Bridge]. So far the journey has been hell—hope the second half's not so bad. My address (till 8.10.59) 51, Vernon Avenue, Handsworth Wood, Birmingham 20. Love from Paris. Love, Ros." I never got around to writing to her. As she was unofficially engaged, and I was in a committed love affair with someone else, there didn't seem to be much point. But I had enjoyed our time together and have always remembered it with pleasure.

I Join Jennifer in León

WHILE AT THE HOSTEL I RECEIVED A LETTER FROM THAT SOMEONE ELSE, MY LONDON GIRLFRIEND, JENNIFER SHARP, WHO WAS heading to Bilbao to begin her English as a Second Language (ESL) teaching job. She told me that she would be in León, a five-hour train ride north-west of Madrid, for a few days and suggested that I join her there and travel on to Bilbao with her. As Dick had decided to go back to Zaragoza, where he had been more or less promised a teaching job at the Briam Institute, and I was not scheduled to begin teaching at the *Instituto Garrett* for a couple of weeks, I was free to join her. So I took the train to León, once again using my *kilométrico*.

I had missed Jennifer more than I had wanted to admit. The last time I had seen her was near the end of July, when we'd spent an evening together in Paris as Dick and I made our way to Spain. While I was in Jaca, I was distracted by the summer course and by Ros Evans, but now that I was alone in Madrid, my need for Jennifer, with whom I realized more and more I was genuinely in love, began to close in on me. As the months

---

[2] At that time, the exchange rate was 60 pesetas to the Canadian dollar.

rolled by, my love for her would become something of an obsession—and the more I was obsessed, as lovers everywhere learn, the more dubious about the relationship Jennifer seemed to become—but at this point I was still at the craving stage. I headed to León with enthusiasm.

Jennifer was staying in a *pensión* in the old part of the city. I went there from the train station by taxi, hoping to get a room at the same place. But I was immediately faced with a double disappointment: Jennifer was out when I arrived, and the *pensión* had no room for me. The very severe woman who ran the *pensión* sent me down the street and around the corner to a similar establishment where there was a room available.

Later, when I went back to Jennifer's *pensión*, she had returned from her walking tour of León. She seemed to me to be more excited about the superb stained glass windows in the cathedral than in seeing me again. I did not know then that when you have a break in a relationship, it doesn't start again where it stopped. You have to go back a couple of steps and re-establish your faith in each other. (Besides, the windows *are* magnificent!)

> *We sat together in the public lounge, always it seemed under the hawk eyes of the proprietress. When I left to go to my own pensión for dinner, Jennifer came out with me, and we kissed and cuddled at the bottom of the dark entrance stairway. Later on, Jennifer told me, the severe woman told her with some distaste that she had been watching us kissing and cuddling. Jennifer was a little upset, but only a little, as we were leaving in the morning, and she would never see the woman again. We have here the ugly face of the Catholic Puritanism that generally abounded in Franco's Spain.*

Jennifer Gets Established in Bilbao

THE NEXT DAY WE LEFT FOR BILBAO. THE TRAIN WAS PACKED, AND WE SPENT THE ENTIRE TRIP SITTING ON OUR SUITCASES, RIGHT NEXT to a smelly toilet, constantly having to shift our cases to let people into the cubicle, so, it seemed to us, that they could make it even smellier. When we arrived in Bilbao, we went to a *pensión* that had been recommended by Jennifer's new employers, where we were ensconced in separate rooms. It will seem strange to young people in a new millennium that we didn't share a room. Apart from the fact that our passports, which had to be surrendered in booking into a *pensión* or hotel, were in separate names and from different countries, no one would know whether we were married or not. We could always have claimed that we hadn't had time to get the passports changed. But the thought never crossed our minds. It just wasn't something that you did in the 1950s.

Shortly after getting settled into the *pensión*, we went to the language school where Jennifer was teaching. It was a modest place in the centre of the city, typical of most, a couple of classrooms leading off the second-storey foyer of a four storey building. There we met the owner, a short, small-boned, almost bird-like young man with one of those 1940's pencil-thin Hollywood moustaches and the nose of a ferret. His name was Manuel. He spoke English well. But in no time at all he had made himself *persona non grata* with both Jennifer and me by throwing suggestive remarks at her. That, in spite of the fact that I was there and obviously her romantic interest. He apparently believed the fairy tale, common in Spain at that time, that all foreign women were easy lays. He may also have been overwhelmed, as Spanish men often seemed to be, as Jennifer was a *rubia*, a blonde. I was afraid that she had got herself into a bad situation in taking a teaching job in an institute run by this creep and was a little concerned for her safety. But I need not have been. When he continued to make lewd comments at the lunch he took us to in a café near the language school, Jennifer took the first opportunity she got to cut him off at the knees. True to type, he immediately shrivelled into himself and stopped making the creepy insinuations. And, as things turned out, she had no more trouble with him during her time in Bilbao.

Later, Manuel took us to a bar. On the way, he said, "Watch me pretend to be a Mexican." So he ordered *cervezas* for us, using the sing-song Mexican accent, pronouncing the "z" with an "s" sound rather than the Castilian "th". The bar owner did not react as he served us our beer and a *tapa* of flat anchovies and olives, so Manuel's little bit of fun fell flat. Even in making his little joke he was a loser.

> *Eventually, Jennifer and I were able to get rid of Manuel. We returned to our pensión, where we later had dinner. Afterwards, we went for a walk about the centre of Bilbao, and finding a small park as it grew dark, we sat on a bench and made whatever love one can manage on a park bench. There seemed to be nobody else about. But as it turned out, we were being watched by serious—if incompetent—agents of the regime. It was some time before I discovered what Franco's hombres were up to. On that balmy summer evening in the north of Spain, we had nothing much else on our minds but our love for each other.*

In the morning, Jennifer came to the station to see me off on my train to Madrid. I left reluctantly. In this short time I came to the realisation that this relationship, for me at least, was no passing parade. I was in love. But all of the problems attached to making this a permanent affair, which Jennifer and I had discussed off and on over the past year, remained. She wanted a career as a stewardess with BOAC before settling down; I had no prospects of a permanent job and no idea of a choice of career; we didn't even have a country in common. I was willing now to get to work on these things, but I didn't want to upset the applecart by bringing the topic up again at this time. I was afraid that Jennifer might decide to ease me out of her life if I became a problem in that way. I knew she was in love with me. But I also knew that her love had strings attached, and that one of those strings was non-negotiable: her air stewardess career. Part of my wanting to hang on to her was also attached to my going once more to a new world in Madrid, where I knew no one, and was bound, at least for awhile, to be lonely. She represented to me in my early days in the capital a kind of postal life-line; but even after I had established myself and made a number of friends, she was the focus of my days. On returning to the apartment on Francisco Silvela at lunch time, the first thing I did was to check the mail to see if there was a letter from her.

John Davison Writes about Tarquinia

OF COURSE, I WAS CORRESPONDING AS WELL WITH OTHER FRIENDS I HAD MADE IN LONDON DURING THE PREVIOUS YEAR. NONE OF MY own letters have survived, but six delightful ones from my London painter friend, John Davison, have. I have excerpted the first of these letters immediately below, and have scattered bits and pieces from the others, more or less at the times they were written, throughout this account of my year in Madrid. Everyone's life is more complex than the daily grind would indicate, and these letters offer a glimpse into another area of my life that was rolling by concomitant with my life in Spain.

Like all young men, John was mainly occupied with pursuing girls, and his letters are full of his successes and failures in that area. He was tall, handsome, polite, considerate, confident, and always a gentleman. He also had enormous charm, which he used deliberately and shamelessly. He was often successful in getting girls to come to his studio to be drawn or painted; he was even able occasionally to convince them to pose *au naturel*. But it is clear as the correspondence progresses that he is growing tired of these hedonistic pursuits and wants to hold on to one of these girls and settle down with her.

Yet, John's life was not all fun and games. At the same time as he was engaging in sexual frivolity, he was also thinking seriously about his painting and making a successful career as an artist. And he suffered—as his letters make clear—as much as he enjoyed.

Letter 1

[How John Spent His Summer Holidays]

27 Ravenor Pk. Rd.,
Greenford, Middx.,
15 Sept. 1959

Dear Terry,

So many pleasures are associated with different wines. Tea is an excellent drink, but I fail to recall any occasions when sipping the hot delicate tea my thoughts slip back to sunny days beneath bright sun umbrellas clasping the free hand of a signorina who gazes dark eyed at me from above a cup and saucer.
    Wine . . . red in Belgium in a Brussels students' dive with Annette—in Frankfurt a cool Mosel sparking and fresh with Maxi— Venice . . . hot Italian red thick stuff which made me drunk with Giacometta. Tarquinia 'Est!, est!!, est!!! wine' like Champagne that is Paola, splendid Etruscan woman. All delicious, different like the women

that one meets and drinks with. It was a pity about Greece,[3] but I think that the compensations for both of us have been liberal. I stayed in Germany 2 weeks with Maxi—she is golden. My God how I love her and need her, but one has to be patient and wait.

• • •

It is almost certain that I will live in Tarquinia next year, as an artist friend had offered me the use of his studio to live there, as he is moving into some Medieval Towers after Christmas.

Tarquinia is simply a place that has now become my home. It is where I can live a life instead of always being subjected to habit or duty or artificiality or other unreal pressures.

It is a unique town, Etruscan drunk.[4] The way they speak is different, their looks are different, they are not Romans, and it is easy to see this.

Days spent on the back of a scooter, this is what I remember, with sun blowing in the face and white and pink houses placed in the golden hills whizzing by. Tarquinia high up across a deep valley that a giant has scooped out with his hand (like we would with sand) and sprinkled it into a little heap and watched the grains tumble and slide from the top. Behind Tarquinia lies the sea, blue, right to the very edge, where the hill has slid. Above, the sun is setting, growing in size as a last bid for life, like an overblown red balloon before it bursts. And like a balloon, it hesitates above a tower, one almost expects it to bounce or explode, but it just deflates, to leave only the darkness behind as a reminder that it gave light.

Still, with the breeze in the air, wine in the stomach and heart filled with Maxi—it's a good feeling even when the sun goes down.

Ciao,   John

The Police Pay Me An Oblique Visit

IN MADRID, I TOOK A ROOM (No. 12) AT THE *PENSIÓN IVOR* ON *CALLE ARENAL*, BETWEEN *PUERTA DEL SOL* AND *PLAZA DE ISABEL II*, WITH ITS unfinished opera house, the *Teatro Real*. The location was ideal, as the *Instituto Garrett*, where I was to teach, was at *Calle Hileras 4*, which ran perpendicular to *Arenal* up the hill toward *Calle Mayor* and the medieval-like *Plaza Mayor*, the centre of the old city. It also had the advantage of being close enough that I could return from work for lunch and a siesta. In terms of my teaching salary, all I had to live on, it was not cheap. Full room and board was 605 pesetas a week, or about 2500 pesetas a month, and I was earning only 3500.

---

[3] John and I had initially planned to go to Greece together in the summer on 1959, but, as I have written in my chapter on Peace Haven, it all fell apart when I was offered a job in Madrid.
[4] That is, totally Etruscan as opposed to Roman in feel and culture.

That evening, while I was at dinner in the *pensión*, the maid asked me if I would go to my room and get my passport, as they needed it in the office. I had given it in when I arrived and had had it returned to me, as it was absolutely necessary to have it to do things like change money. I'm amazed now that this request didn't strike me as odd. I suppose I was used by this time to the occasional requests for identification that were a feature of Franco's police state. At any rate, I fetched the passport, gave it to the maid, and continued with my dinner.

> *On my way out of the pensión for a postprandial walk, the owner, a genial, middle-aged man, whose hair was a shock of pepper and salt and who spoke English quite well, called me into his office to give me back my passport. "You know," he said, "that it was the police want to see you pasaporte?"*
>
> *"But why?" I asked, astounded that they would be checking up on me.*
>
> *"It is apparent that they think you are murderer," he said with a mischievous grin, holding out the passport for me to take.*
>
> *"Me?" I said. "But why?" This man, I thought, has a good sense of humour.*
>
> *The pensión owner shook his head. "They say they look for Canadiense who come into España with mujer Ingles—girl Eengleesh," he translated. "Interpol—you know what is that?"—I nodded—"Interpol ask that they find Canadiense. So they come check you."*
>
> *"But," I repeated, "why me?"*
>
> *"It is apparent that they watch you with mujer Ingles en Bilbao. But they—¿como se dice?—'loose?' you."*
>
> *I thought of Jennifer and me on the park bench. Were they watching us then? They must have been.*
>
> *"They are—how you say?"—and he looked out into the hall to see if anyone was listening—"idiotas! Inmediatamente they see is no you, they go."*

It seems that a young Canadian man had murdered someone in France—my proprietor didn't know the details—and come into Spain with an English girl. So they had gone looking for a young Canadian who was with an English girl and they had found me, lost me, and on looking at my passport, for whatever reason, had concluded that I wasn't the one they were looking for. It was a decidedly odd incident and has intrigued me ever since. But I never did hear any more about it.

At the *Instituto Garrett*

THE *INSTITUTO GARRETT* DESCRIBED ITSELF AS *EL PEQUEÑO INSTITUTO DE LOS GRANDES EXITOS*—"THE LITTLE INSTITUTE WITH THE BIGGEST Results." It was located on the top floor of a modern, four-storey building and was reached via a creaky elevator that more often than not had a sign hung on its door: *"¡No funciona!"*—"Out of Order!" One had no alternative then but to climb the stairs. The Institute's claim to fame among the scores of similar places in Madrid was that in its five years of existence it had been the main training ground in the English language for those seeking employment in the Spanish diplomatic corps. But the Institute's main business was in teaching commercial English classes and English as a Second Language classes to the general public.

Class numbers were small and you paid tuition accordingly. The cheapest classes, the ones that were most popular, had a maximum of eight students. If you paid extra money, the amount increasing as the class became smaller, you could enrol in classes of four, three, two, or one. Classes were one hour in length and were held either daily or on alternate days, throughout a six day week. Class hours were 9 to 2 and 4 to 10 daily, Monday to Saturday. Minimum course length was one month. If you were an individual who wanted the Institute to send someone to teach you in your home or office, a teacher would be provided, but the cost was about a third more than individual tuition at the Institute.[5]

My terms of work at the Institute had been outlined in a letter I received from Peter Garrett in England on June 13: "We pay 3,500 pesetas per month for a 36 hour week to first-year teachers. There is a week's paid holiday at Christmas and the same at Easter. All official expenses such as taxes, Work Card dues, etc. are met by the Institute."

Having to teach ESL 36 hours a week in a 6-day week, an average of 6 hours a day, is very hard work, especially considering the fact that the day ran from 9 in the morning to 10 at night, with a lunch/siesta break of two hours in the middle. The 3,500 pesetas (ca. C$60) wasn't much, but one could get by on it. Besides, the pay wasn't the point; what I was looking for was the experience of living in Spain.

When you arrived on the 4th floor by elevator or stairs, you came to a rectangular hall that led you to a door with a frosted window on which was painted *Instituto Garrett*. The Institute occupied the entire floor. Through the door was a square foyer, off of which were six small classrooms and the Director's office. Against the wall opposite the door was a high curved counter, behind which, most of the time, sat the receptionist, Maria Fernanda Solares, known to one and all simply as Maria Fernanda.

My Colleagues at the Institute

ON MY FIRST MORNING AT THE INSTITUTE, ABOUT A WEEK BEFORE I WAS DUE TO BEGIN TEACHING, I ASKED A LONE INDIVIDUAL WHO was sitting at the reception desk reading a newspaper if Peter Garrett, the Owner/Director was in. He showed no interest in me. Without doing much more than glancing up from his paper, he told me that Peter wouldn't be around for an hour or so. So in order to pass the time, I went across the street to have a *café con leche* and a *suizo* bun. When I returned to the Institute, the lone individual was nowhere to be seen, but Peter had arrived. He was tall and blonde, and in his thirties. He was polite, but not quite friendly, and spoke

---

[5] I tutored a young man in his early twenties whose name was Miguel O'Shea—pronounced "OShee" in Spain. His father had come to Madrid in the 1920s and made a lot of money in business. Miguel was trying to pick up the pieces of his life after his parents were both killed in a car accident about a year before I met him.

the English of the public-school-educated upper-middle class of those days. He asked me to come into his office, welcomed me to my new job, and did a run-down of what the job entailed.

He then took me back to the foyer and introduced me to the receptionist, Maria Fernanda, who had arrived in the meantime, and who was, I was delighted to see, a pretty, young Spanish girl with a bee-hive hairdo. She gave me a tour of the place, followed by a copy of my timetable. After that, I went back to my room at the *Pensión Ivor* and continued reading Shakespeare's *Hamlet*, which I had picked up at a bookstore the day before. It was an odd choice, but there wasn't much available in English in the Madrid bookstores in those days, and I hadn't yet discovered the library run by the British Consul.

Howard Dewart, Classical Guitarist

THE TEACHING STAFF, IF I CAN CALL IT THAT, WAS THE USUAL MIXED BUNCH THAT YOU FINE IN ESL SCHOOLS AROUND THE WORLD. During the week before classes, I met most of my colleagues. I discovered that the individual who had been uninterested me on my first visit to the Institute was Howard Dewart. He was short and wiry and had a hawk-like face. His hair seemed to be reaching for the sky. We introduced ourselves. Later on, I learned that he planned to open a music-teaching emporium in the capital—he was a fine classical guitarist—using the £6,000 he had inherited when both his parents (curiously, like Miguel O'Shea's) were killed in a car accident the year before. "I am," he used to boast in a good-humoured way, "a millionaire—in pesetas." I can still see his carefully-honed fingernails. The emporium was a failure.

Allen Clayton, Etymologist

Allen Clayton was a rotund individual of about thirty, who had been at the Institute for three years and knew everything there was to know about everything. He was on the short side. On his nose he balanced a pair of standard, round, National Health glasses. He had precise—and often absurd—opinions on almost anything that came up in a conversation. Why, he asked me one day, do the Yanks use the word "bathroom," which is a euphemism for what really goes on there, instead of the good, solid, English word, "lavatory." I refrained from pointing out to him that "lavatory" comes from the Latin *lavare*, "to wash, bathe," so the two words are really one and the same in terms of their description of the function of the place.

Ian Hastings, Tour Guide

Ian Hastings was a medium-height fellow from Bristol, in his mid-twenties, who worked part-time at the Institute; in his other life, he conducted bus tours for English-speaking tourists. His face had been badly scarred by *acne vulgaris*. He was a decent, unpretentious guy, and I liked him.

Dave Ganderton, Novelist

A much less likeable person was Dave Ganderton, whom I have described in some detail elsewhere.[6] He had ambitions to be a novelist and asked me to read a very bad novel he had written about a Swedish lawyer's adventures in the south of France. I couldn't think of anything kind to say about its plot and characterization, so I did a careful analysis of its style to camouflage my real opinion. He blasted me, quite rightly, for not concentrating on the things that mattered; but I felt that on the whole my ruse had worked, and that I had avoided a much more damning confrontation on matters of substance.

Bob Hendry, Citizen of Spain

Bob Hendry was a horribly sincere, incredibly clean young man, one of those who look as if they've spent the morning scrubbing everything about them, hair, face, body, clothes, even shoe laces. He had been in Spain a number of years and spoke excellent Spanish. One day, shortly before I left the country to return to Canada, he announced that he would be taking out Spanish citizenship. I was astounded that he would align himself to Franco's Spain. "But you'll have to do military service," I said. "Surely you don't fancy being a one-peseta-a-day private in Franco's army!" He replied that the military service was only for a short time, and it was worth it, as he loved Spain and really wanted to be Spanish.

A Cross-Section of My Students

MY CLASSES AT THE INSTITUTE WERE MADE UP OF A VARIETY OF STUDENTS, OF THE SORT THAT ONE WOULD EXPECT TO FIND IN THIS kind of place. The bulk of them were enrolled in beginner classes of eight. These classes, in a way that I discovered was the rule rather than the exception, quickly dropped to five or six, as people decided that learning English was not for them.

Along with these classes, I had a couple of students who had paid for private lessons. One of them was a svelte upper-class lady of about fifty, who wore sweater sets and reeked of old money. She complained—very politely, of course—that with modern artificial pearls being so good, her real ones weren't appreciated any more. She spoke excellent, almost unaccented English, and she was in my class only because she wanted to retain her grip on the language. I liked her. Another student who came for a private class and also spoke excellent English was fine-honing his skills before sitting the exam for the diplomatic corp. He was an extremely bright and enormously confident little fart. (I can think of no better way to describe him.) I happened to be reading McKinley Cantor's Civil War novel, *Andersonville*, at the time—where did I get *that*?—and used it

---

[6] See *Bloomsbury, Brighton, and Blackheath*. I met him again out of the blue a couple of years later in London's Woburn Square. I was doing post-graduate studies at the University of London Institute of Education and he was beginning a degree at University College.

to give him practice in reading. Because the name of the hero of the book is Ira Cahill, my student was confused at first. A name ending in "a" in Spanish is always feminine, and he couldn't understand why Ira was referred to with masculine pronouns.

I enjoyed these one-on-one classes. But all my classes were not as successful at these. I taught a class, for example, to two men, already members of the Spanish diplomatic corps, who were about to be sent to California to study economics. They were given to me because I spoke with an accent similar to a California accent. One of them spoke quite good English, while the other was little better than a beginner; so I found it impossible to teach them both at once. I suggested that they split up, so that they could each take classes at an appropriate level. They refused. They went to the Director and told him they wanted to leave my class because I had a bad accent. Peter Garrett realized what the problem was and managed to convince them to take classes separately with two of the other teachers. I'd be surprised if they did well in California, where everyone, by extension, would also have as bad an accent as mine.

Letter 2

[John is Back at the Old Teaching Grind]

27 Ravenor Pk. Rd.,
Greenford, Middx.,
Sept. 29 / 59

Dear Terry

I'm going to go to Italy again at Christmas for two weeks. It's getting [to be] a madness this running off to Italy, to me I miss it more than any woman. I live now in one long depression, punctuated by weekly bottles of Rhineland wine which make me happy. School is certainly not the same now you and Guy[7] aren't there. No one to talk to or discuss with but just continually exchanging pleasantries with pleasant people and young new teachers who believe every word you say.

Have found a good model called Janet, 19 yrs.-old, beautiful and only lives in the next street. Have persuaded her it is essential I should do some decent life drawing of someone who has a good body—she is posing for me tomorrow.[8]

---

[7] Guy Nelder was teaching part time at Harlington when I was there. He was enormously bright, but vastly under-qualified, as all he had academically were four A-Levels. But they were four A-Levels from a St. Paul's graduate! I found him a bit of a snob, but John liked him. He was off to Oxford in the fall.

[8] The girl is Janet Tubb. She was a serious student of the piano, with concert aspirations. John would eventually marry her and take her to Tarquinia with him. There, he managed to rent a grand piano for her. But she became depressed and began to spend her days sitting and gazing into space. As she was unable to do the laundry, John used to take it to the communal wash house. The local women there refused to let him do it, and they insisted on doing it for him for nothing. It was not fitting that a man should do laundry. When the couple returned to England, Janet got quite well again; but the episode had put too much strain on the marriage and it eventually floundered.

• • •

Pead[9] is blurbing worse than ever (assembly 'til twenty to ten), flapping about to-day saying it was Italy you were teaching in! Forced at last by the children's litter ("It's up to you!") he closed the tuck shop for two days—the brute! It's all all all so bloody I feel like doing ridiculous things at school—and often do. Spend my dinner times lying on my back on the sports field thinking of damn all, dousing the head in cold water enough to see me through calling the register so that I get the names right, sitting slumped in teachers chair, rousing only to say "Keep Quiet" or to mechanically gasp at hot tea which I spill always on the stairs at breaks. Slumping in the staff room while talk flits around me like gnats. "He got B+!" "House mark off Murray!" ZZZZZ – ZZZZZ - ZZZZZ!

• • •

I feel as though I've just woken up—doing lots of drawn heads and two portrait paintings, using what is for me a new approach which started last Easter with a drawing of Annette. The problem now is to retain these qualities while using paint. I think that eventually what I'm struggling so hard to do will reveal itself.

• • •

Well, Terry, I wonder more and more what people like us are meant to do for a livelihood. I've come to the conclusion that if I left teaching this next summer and lived in Italy for 2 years and then bought a primitive cottage about 70 miles from London, teaching, and living with a "housekeeper" and spending all my energies on remaking the cottage so that it was really modern . . . . well, it's an idea.

Ciao, John

P.S. *I always read your letters to my family,[10] who find them most interesting. I leave out bits sometimes. — Hope you don't mind. John*

Maria Fernanda Solares y Yo

Living with Sr. and Sra. Jiménez

BUT IT WAS MARIA FERNANDA WHO, FOR A SHORT WHILE, BULKED LARGE IN MY LIFE. HER FAMILY HAD OWNED A *BODEGA* IN LA Mancha (of *Don Quixote* fame), not far south of Madrid. Through bad management, they had lost the business. In the upset they had moved to the capital, where they lived in a

---

[9] R. J. S. Pead was the Headmaster of Harlington, a year or so away from retirement. I describe him in detail in my chapter, *Peace Haven*.

[10] John was still at this time living at home with his parents. (Interestingly, his father and older brother were also artists.) He moved out in 1960, and, appropriately, found a small flat on Stud Street, which, if I remember correctly, was in Greenford, Middlesex! But he never accomplished his dream of living in Italy, or of inhabiting a cottage far from London. Nor did he stop teaching at Harlington, but retired from there in the late 1980s.

spacious apartment that seemed to indicate that they had salvaged a fair amount of money from the debacle. As I was anxious to get out of the *Pensión Ivor* and move in with a family where I could more quickly improve my Spanish, I asked Maria Fernanda if she could help. She did some enquiring and quickly came up with the Jiménez family, who lived in Apartment 4º, at 34 Eloy Gonzalo.[11] Sr. and Sra. Jiménez—I don't remember their first names, if I ever knew them—were a middle-aged couple who lived in this urban apartment building. They employed with a young girl from the country as a non-live-in maid. The apartment was spacious: three bedrooms, living room, dining room, kitchen, and bathroom, all leading off an l-shaped hallway that ran from the entrance door to the kitchen.

The Jiménez were an old-fashioned couple. They were church-going, respectable people, who like Maria Fernanda's family had come down in the world. They had been on the losing side in the Civil War and had suffered economically ever since. In those days, when the regular evening news on the radio was over, the announcer would cry out in a stentorian voice: ¡*Veinte años de paz! ¡Viva Franco! ¡Arriba España!*—"Twenty years of peace! Long live Franco! Rise Up Spain!"[12] Sr. Jiménez and I used to listen to the news as we ate dinner together in the dining room. (His wife and the maid did not eat with us. They served us, and following the old-fashioned custom that kept women in their place in Spain, ate in the kitchen.) Always, just as the news ended, and before the Falangist propaganda, Jiménez would reach behind him and shut the radio off.

When I had become a member of the British Consul Library, I once brought back to the Jiménez flat a book, written in English, on Franco's life. Sr. Jiménez opened it, pointed out to me a frontispiece picture of a grinning Franco, and immediately dismissed the book as a piece of fascist propaganda. I don't think it was that; but I do think he was right to see it as a piece of writing that was essentially positive toward Franco's regime.

At the corner of Eloy Gonzalo, across from the *Iglesia* metro station, and just down the street from the Jiménez apartment, was a church with two towers, one of which contained a clock, and across from it, another church, whose simple central tower also contained a clock. The churches gave the metro station its name: *Iglesia*. The ringing of the hours by these clocks tormented me every night for a week or more when I was first in the apartment. But eventually I got used to them and didn't hear them any more. Part of the problem lay in the fact that the clocks were out of sync with each other, so that all through the night I would hear first one of them toll the quarter hours and chime on the hours, and then, moments later, the other.[13]

---

[11] Many Spanish apartment buildings in those days had only two apartments per floor. Both were given the same floor number, followed by an abbreviated *derecho* (right: e.g., 4º) or *izquierda* (left: e.g., 4ª).

[12] The idea was, of course, that Franco had been wise enough to keep Spain out of W.W. II; thus, the country, unlike most of Europe, had had 20 years of peace. *Arriba* is difficult to translate, but the word is used in the imperative sense of "Prosper!"

[13] When I returned to Madrid in 2000, I went to have a look at the area of Eloy Gonzalo I had lived in in the 1950s. I wrote in my journal: "The street looks much the same—but busy, busy!—the church on the corner still has its clock, which rang the hours through the night—the second church (also with an hour-ringing clock) is gone."

Letter 3

[In Which John Shaves Off His Beard]

*27 Ravenor Pk. Rd.
Greenford, Middlesex, England,
7th Oct. '59*

Dear Terry,

A fit of madness struck me two day's ago—I became curious to see my own face, which has been covered for five years with a beard. I shaved it off. The result is different. I look like a schoolboy, round-faced, with a rather feminine mouth, which I'm hastily growing a moustache over. I look fat, ordinary, English, and everything which I knew I would look like (but even so, it has been worth it). There are many people, I know, many girls, who have built up a myth about the beard, making it inseparable from my "character," and it is to these people I wish to dedicate this most awful act. They can take it or leave it, hair on the face isn't my only claim to character! Most people say things like "You're much better looking now, but you were more distinguished before." It's been a very good joke, but I'll grow it again starting in a couple of weeks because I'm not prepared to hack at my face for ¼ hour each day. . . . . . I have the feeling I've been caught walking down the street with my trousers off, or the feeling a girl has when the top half of her bikini drops off after doing a rather clever side twist in the water . . . .

Tomorrow is a free day, Election Day. Tomorrow I will spend the afternoon doing some drawings (absolutely bare.!!.) of Janet, who has a splendid body. When art and sex get mixed up together it is most pleasurable.

Write soon, ciao,   John

I Have a Bout with Trench Mouth

A FEW DAYS AFTER I BEGAN BOARDING WITH THE JIMÉNEZ FAMILY, I HAD A DENTAL PROBLEM. MY TEETH AND GUMS SUDDENLY BEGAN to ache, and a short while later, my gums began to bleed. The pain was intense. I didn't know what to do about it, as I knew no dentists in Madrid. When I left some drops of blood on my pillowcase, Sra. Jiménez called Maria Fernanda—it was a holiday morning—who called me back a while later and said she'd made an appointment for me right away to see an American dentist who was willing to examine me in spite of the fact it was a holiday. She also said she'd get out Luis's car to drive me to the dentist's office. Luis was her *novio*, her fiancé, a diplomat in training, whom the government had sent to New York for a year to study economics.

> The dentist, whose name I have forgotten, was a Harvard man, getting on in years, who had settled in Spain in the 1930s. His office was in a medium-rise building, and from it there was a good view down a hilly street to the Bank of Spain building. He said he remembered the trucks lining up there during the Civil War, when Madrid was controlled by the Socialists, and the Franco forces were laying siege and seemed likely eventually to take the city. The trucks were taking Spain's gold reserves to "safety" in the Soviet Union.[14] When he looked into my mouth, he said: "You've got trench mouth."
>
> After sending Maria Fernanda out with a prescription for penicillin, he said: "Do you know an English girl by the name of Molly?"
>
> "No," I replied, truthfully, wondering where this line of questioning was heading.
>
> "Are you sure?" he asked.
>
> "Absolutely," I said. "I don't know any Mollys."
>
> "Well," he went on, "that's odd. I had an English Molly in here yesterday—a young girl, red hair, pretty—with the same problem."

But I was innocent, even if he didn't believe it. In a way, I was sorry it wasn't true. Maybe this Molly would have been nice to know. I don't know how I got trench mouth, but I do know that I'd sooner have got it from Molly than from an anonymous source. The term "trench mouth"—a popular cognomen for this disease—comes from the fact that it was a common problem at the front lines during World War I. Its cause is still disputed. Some believe the imbalance of bacteria in the mouth as a result of poor oral hygiene is the cause; others claim it is a highly contagious condition that can be picked up, say, by using a dirty glass in a bar. My Harvard-man dentist had no doubt about its being a contagious condition. As he had been in the American army in France in the Great War, and had seen trench mouth in the trenches, I believe he knew what he was talking about.

When Maria Fernanda returned with the penicillin, the dentist gave me a bum injection, followed by an oral treatment. Incredibly, I began to feel better immediately, the pain went away, my gums stopped bleeding, and it was as if none of this horror had ever happened. It was a miracle. Over the next week, I had two more oral treatments, and after that, a number of repairs to my teeth, including a primitive sort of root canal. While he was treating me, the dentist complained about how useless his son was. Apparently, he found it impossible to hold on to a job, and though he was in his late twenties, his father still had to support him. Vis-à-vis all of this, the dentist asked me what I did for a living, and when I told him I was teaching ESL at the Instituto Garrett for 3,500 pesetas a month, he charged me practically nothing for all this work, a total of slightly less than 1,000 pesetas. He was a good man.

---

[14] Once they had the gold, the Soviets claimed it was in payment for the military supplies they had sent to the Republican forces. (Spain was reputed to have the fifth largest gold reserves in the world. If that is true, the military supplies were *very* expensive!) The Soviets also tried to get their hands on many of the paintings in the Prado, but these were stopped in Switzerland and held there till the end of the war, when they were returned to Spain.

My Whirlwind Affair with Maria Fernanda

MARIA FERNANDA WAITED FOR ME, AND MUCH RELIEVED THAT THE PAIN WAS GONE—I CAN'T EMPHASIZE ENOUGH HOW MUCH BETTER I felt—I was once again my normal self. I was euphoric to be out of pain. So when she suggested we go for a drive, I was happy to do so.

She took us to a deserted area in the Casa de Campo, where she parked the car. We walked through the parched, autumn fields, with their tall, pale-yellow mounds of grass, and sat under a large oak tree which stood among the pines, young oaks, and cypresses, many of them planted by the Franco regime when this area, which had been a fierce battlefield during the Civil War, was rehabilitated. For some time we sat silently, disturbed only by the sound of the cicadas and the murmur of traffic in the distant city, as we came to terms with what the two of us were doing here.

> *When we stood up to go, Maria Fernanda put her arms around me and said she wanted to be kissed. I was reluctant to kiss her because of my trench mouth, although my mouth felt absolutely normal. She said it didn't matter, that the penicillin would have killed anything living in my mouth. So we kissed. In a short time, she put my hand on her breast and said: "I want you to know something about me right away." What she wanted me to know was that her breasts were small and her bra was padded. "I'm not your typical Spanish girl with her big breasts," she said, grinning shyly. "Do you mind?"*

I didn't mind. Not at all. But I was astounded that this Spanish girl—after all I'd read, heard and seen of Spanish puritanism—was so forward sexually. Later, I reasoned that she and Luis must have participated in some pretty explicit sex, and she was probably missing it now that he was in New York. But as we walked hand-in-hand through the swishing, yellow grass back to the car, I wondered where this was leading, and, especially, where Jennifer would fit into it.

Thus began my short-lived affair with Maria Fernanda. I had not pursued her. She had come on to me like a house on fire. And I was lonely, and in a strange world, and insecure; and I missed Jennifer the way Maria Fernanda undoubtedly missed Luis. Besides, my masculine ego was being stroked, and I liked it. On reflection, I think the whole affair happened because Maria Fernanda and I instinctively recognized that we were both in the same boat: each separated from the one we loved, each feeling the vacuum that moves in when the daily world of physical and spiritual contact, the expectation that it implants, the routine that it becomes, is no longer there. Luis was in New York, Jennifer was in Bilbao, God was in his heaven, and Maria Fernanda and I were at loose ends in Madrid and thrown together by our daily routine.

We were lovers for only a few weeks. At no time did we pass through that romantic phrase, always there at the beginning of true and lasting love (even there in most episodes of false and temporary love!), when we had to be together through as many hours of the day as possible. Although our need for an ersatz partner was rooted in the spiritual, the urges were on both sides essentially physical.

> *Some days we would stay in the Institute during the lunch-break/siesta time, when the place was deserted, the shutters closed to cut out the midday heat, and the lights turned off. Only the sound of the elevator, when it was working, broke the silence. We would make love in the Director's office (Peter Garrett kept a clean desk!) before going our separate ways to eat and relax. We never at any time in those pre-pill times went all the way. The decision not to, never discussed between us, never expressed, was mutual. We both knew this was a temporary affair. Going all the way was too dangerous, in spite of the frustrations that our mutual, silent decision gave rise to.*

Letter 4

[John Has a New Theory on Drawing Heads]

Greenford,
16th Nov. 1959

Dear Terry,

It is a depressing time of year now in England with fog, rain and noisy children. A time of waiting and looking for "kicks"—drink, women and food. But if it is a nerve-wracking time of year, it is also a creative time. When everything is dying or dead it is a real pleasure to make something in paint. I have just finished a painting of Burton Bradstock which has something of the place in it. I used up tubes of greens and yellow on a field of buttercups and then changed it all completely and it now has a continuity of atmosphere throughout. It will perhaps be of interest to you, as you will have also had your thoughts on B. Bradstock and what it was like.[15]

I'm also doing a large painting of Tarquinian buildings. There is a church on the right with huge, sexual, round, half tower things coming from a flat wall. [John has added here a fine sketch of what he is describing, ca.1 inch high by 2 inches wide, and used arrows to draw attention to various aspects of the scene.] There is a narrow twisting road in the middle. Steps here. Most of it is in shadow, but so light that I hope to make the picture sunlit.

At school I have finished a life-size head of a girl. The head is thrust forward expectantly, eagerly, with the lips just slightly parted. [Again, there is a sketch of about the same size, but oriented vertically rather than horizontally.] The whole head receding from this focal point. The eyes underemphasized, smooth—Forms simplified. I made it because

---

[15] John and I had spent the Whitsun Holiday in 1959 in a caravan in Burton Bradstock with John's girlfriend, Christine, and his friends from Ealing Art School days, Evelyn, Jennine, and Brian.

I like looking at certain forms in different girls' faces. It is the head of Annette, the mouth of Maxi, the hair of Paola, etc., etc. It is the sort of thing I like, so I made it. I will put it in a box and keep it for a house or flat in future years.

• • •

Your other letter has just come. You seem to be home-sick. I like your letters because they make me remember that others in the world suffer in the same way. The more we struggle, the less happy we are, but it is inevitable that we do struggle if we are artists.
I'm going to a party now to drink wine!

Ciao,   John

P. S. The girls still ask after you at school. They want to know when your birthday is to send you a present. I said just send it in any case to make sure.

The End of My Liaison with Maria Fernanda

IN THE MEANTIME, I WAS WRITING TO JENNIFER EVERY TWO OR THREE DAYS AND COMPLAINING THAT WHE WASN'T WRITING TO ME OFTEN enough. Oh, what a curse young men must be when they act like this—and they all do—even when the girl they are pursuing is every bit as much in love. And Jennifer was, I'm sure, in love with me. I was a typical, young male pest when I was in Madrid and she was in Bilbao. The fact that Jennifer put up with me attested to her underlying commitment to "us" at some as yet unseen future point. Throughout the next three years, we each moved often to new areas of the world and abandoned addresses with great frequency. We were both careful never to lose contact. But a future for us was just not in the cards. But we never met again after that Christmas in Madrid.

One day, when Maria Fernanda and I were drinking *cuba libres* at the kind of posh cocktail lounge I would never on my own have ventured into, and which would later become a common part of her life as the wife of a diplomat, she asked me if she should tell Luis about us. I immediately said, "No—wait." I'm not sure whether she had arranged it this way, though she probably had, as she was a very bright girl, but this conversation was the beginning of the end for us. Like a balloon that has begun to leak, our little affair slowly started to disappear into thin air. We stopped sticking around during lunch breaks, and we stopped meeting for drinks. One Sunday, we went with a group of Institute staff up into the mountains, where we had a country lunch: *pulpo in su tinto* (octopus in its ink), followed by *cerebros de oveja* (sheep brains), accompanied by the heavy white peasant bread of that region and some good peasant wine. But we went as friends who were part of a group, not as a couple. Sure, things were sometimes a little awkward, but the awkwardness was mutual. So as easily (nearly) as we became lovers, we disentangled ourselves. It really was remarkable, this liaison, from start, middle, to finish.[16]

A Penthouse Apartment in Francisco Silvela

EARLY IN DECEMBER, I ARRANGED TO MOVE INTO A PENTHOUSE APARTMENT AT FRANCISCO SILVELA 55, 7º, WITH JOHN FARMERY, Carlos Pieper, and a black Hispanic from Detroit, Pedro Martinez, who was responsible for the apartment. It had four bedrooms, a living room, a dining room, a kitchen, and a large rooftop deck. Whenever we had a party, Pedro would say to the guests: "If you get drunk, don't toss your cookies over the railing." Pedro was studying medicine at the University of Madrid. He seemed to me to be incredibly rich, as his father, who was a doctor, sent him $100 a month spending money as well as paying all his expenses.[17] The apartment cost 4,000 pesetas per month, 1,000 each. In Canada, I would not have been able to afford my quarter of an apartment as luxurious as this one.

Our Maid, Julia

We had a maid, who came every day except Sunday from 10 in the morning until 8 at night. I forget what we paid her, but it was the going rate for maids and it wasn't much. She cleaned, did laundry (one week I remember her having 16 dress shirts to wash and iron), cooked, and served lunch and dinner. Once over Christmas we asked her to sit down with us for dinner, but she wouldn't do it. It wasn't right, she said. She was a kind and willing country girl in her mid-twenties, had a minimal education—she could read, write, and do simple arithmetic, which was more than a lot of people from a peasant background could do in Franco's Spain—and she was not much to look at. I liked her. Her name was Julia.

My parting with Sra. Jiménez was not exactly friendly. She accused me of leaving because I didn't think her place was good enough. Poor woman. She had been counting on my board money to help pay for, among other things, the new suit they had just bought for Sr. Jiménez. But my motivation for leaving had nothing to do with the Jiménez family, who had treated me very well. I was lonely, and the chance to move into an apartment with three other guys and a maid was too tempting to miss. In terms of learning Spanish, the move was a mistake. My progress slowed considerably, as in the shared apartment we spoke English all of the time, except when we were talking to Julia, who knew no English. But as the months went by, my Spanish improved enough that Julia commented on the fact that I was understanding much better. As she normally made no comments on our activities, I took this as an extraordinary compliment.

---

[16] A year or so later, I had a letter from Allen Clayton, who remained in Madrid until 1961, when he emigrated to Montreal. He told me that Maria Fernanda had married Luis as soon as he returned from New York and had immediately become pregnant. He spoke of this with distain. I thought she had done the right thing—and also the smart thing.

[17] Pedro, because he was black, had had trouble getting into a medical school in 1950's America. So, fluent in Spanish, his mother tongue, he had gone to Madrid. I managed to contact him briefly about ten years' later. He was in New York, running a successful medical practice.

Karl-Ernst Pieper, aka "Carlos"

A few words about the other occupants of the apartment. Karl-Ernst Pieper, or Carlos, as he was always known, was from Borås, Sweden. He was unobtrusive in a thoroughly Scandinavian way, and I liked him for his thoroughly Scandinavian decency. He was tall (I see him standing in a raincoat on a Sunday afternoon as we waited for a train to Toledo), serious, and reliable. He was passionately anti-German, something to do with World War II, the details of which he never revealed, but which must have happened outside of neutral Sweden. Maybe it was just a general horror at what the Germans had done to Europe. He was not much of a thinker. All through January he repeated the cliché, "January is a month of Mondays," which it certainly must have been in icy, snowbound Sweden, but which, though it was quite nippy at times, it certainly wasn't in Madrid. He worked for a tourist agency that catered primarily to Scandinavian visitors to Spain. On one of our Sundays when we were both free from work—Carlos sometimes had to work through the weekends—we went together by train to Toledo. While we were there, we toured the Cathedral, the famous steel-making emporia, and the *Alcázar*, which had famously held out for Franco's side in the Civil War.

John Farmery, Violinist

John Farmery, who also worked at the Institute, and who was responsible for getting me a place in the apartment, was from somewhere in East Anglia. He was medium-height, had an infectious grin, and wore his reddish hair in a disorderly pompadour. He was a trained musician, a violinist, who talked about how boring it was to be in the second violin section of an orchestra, where you are merely providing harmonies to the melody carried by the first violins. He said that people talked about playing second fiddle to others metaphorically, but he had experienced it literally. So he had quit playing and come to Spain to, as he put it, "find himself." (Did he ever find himself?)

A scene in a bar. There were four of us, John, me, and two girls, friends of his. One of the girls was Italian; I don't remember anything about the other. We were standing near a wall, by a zinc-surfaced bar, drinking wine. The place was crowded. At one point, John sneezed in the midst of telling a hilarious story, and a rigid icicle of snot, of which he was unaware, slipped down from one of his nostrils and hung their pendulously. He was talking and laughing, and difficult to interrupt, and we were all embarrassed and uncomfortable. The Italian girl finally took the initiative, reached into the pocket of her suit-type jacket and handed John a small white handkerchief. "Wipe your nose," she said. John took the handkerchief, wiped the icicle off his nose, gave the handkerchief back to her, and carried on with his story as if there had been no interruption.

It was the right thing to do. It dismissed the incident with the least fuss, and in so doing, underlined the normalcy of the get-together. I'm sure there was much more to John Farmery than this incident, but it is all I remember of him.

Letter 5

[John's Move on Roswitha is Thwarted]

Greenford
3 . 2 . 60

Dear Terry

More than ever, I would like to share my life with someone, to sleep with someone every night in a place which is my own and which is beautiful. I'm getting really tired of chasing around making girls unhappy, and for myself, only perfecting the art of being involved and remaining free at the same time.

I am going to Luba's[18] two or three nights a week. I like its relaxed atmosphere and the different girls I take and the different wines to go with the different girls (even more important than the right wine with the right food).

• • •

It will be good for you to come back one day to the school and see everyone you knew. Although the older teachers are exactly the same, the little girls you knew have sprouted breasts like trees grow apples. It's rather beautiful to see these little girls whom I've known for a little while to grow up into young women. Pauline (in your old class—blonde) is turning into a very beautiful girl, as are some of the others you knew.

• • •

A queer situation has sprung up between Evelyn[19] and me. She is living with her sister (about to have a baby) and her brother-in-law (a rich car dealer). They have taken on a "help" who is a most fantastic, elegant, beautiful, German girl (18 yrs. old) to whom, of course, I have offered to show London. Eve rang up and said Paul wouldn't allow me to take her out as he didn't seem to trust me with her (ridiculous). Evelyn, I think, is behind it all, as she doesn't like the idea of sitting around at home by herself. I'm furious because Eve said, "Well, when she meets more people and is freer, it will be alright then." But she hasn't shown the girl anything yet. In fact, Roswitha hasn't been out of the house yet in the 13 days she's been in England. So instead of taking her out tonight, we're all going in a group—her included. I don't mind doing this for a week, but if

---

[18] Luba's Bistro was our favourite restaurant. I have described it in some detail in *A Young Man's Fancy* and *That Summer in Jaca*.
[19] Evelyn, an attractive half-Vietnamese, half French girl who had grown up in England, had been at the Ealing College of Art at the same time as John. She was one of the girls who spent the Whitsun holiday with us in Dorset the previous spring. See *Peace Haven*.

they expect a sophisticated girl like Roswitha to stay at home watching English television every night . . . . . and me to let things drop, they're off their head. It might be funny this evening if I bring it up as a topic of conversation.

• • •

Had a good dinner last night with all different friends, but Eve said Roswitha couldn't come because her sister had pains and thought the baby might come. If so, why didn't Eve stay? How was Roswitha going to find her way to Knightsbridge as Eve was already in London? After driving Eve home, I was asked in for coffee (how could she avoid asking me in?) and damn me if poor Roswitha wasn't there playing cards with Paul. It seems all so wrong, as my date was with her, and I end up with Eve. I don't know what the girl thought, as I couldn't start up a conversation which would be embarrassing for everyone. Still, one can feel deep down when things go well, as just with one smile we feel tied together. She is splendid, and I'm just crazy for the time when I am alone with her to talk and listen and talk.

Ciao, John

Dwight D. Eisenhower Comes to Town

THERE WAS A DISTINGUISHED VISITOR TO MADRID ON DECEMBER 21. DWIGHT D. EISENHOWER, THE OUTGOING PRESIDENT OF THE UNITED States, came to Spain for a day of talks with the man known to his falangist followers as *El Caudillo* (The Leader)—Generalíssimo Francisco Franco Bahamonde. The visit was part of a final tour around the world by the outgoing U.S. president.

After World War II, Spain had been isolated economically and politically by most of the rest of the world because of its fascist government. This government had been ruling the country since the end of the Civil War in 1939. But as the Cold War deepened, and the advantages of having bases in Spain became apparent to the Americans, they were happy to deal with Franco; as they have always been happy to deal with any of the Grendels of this world, provided they get what they want in return. So, in 1953, they hammered out an agreement which offered Franco substantial economic aid in return for bases.

In the Madrid offices and bars, people told the story, undoubtedly initially spread by Franco's *hombres*, that *El Caudillo* had driven a hard bargain. No Americans were to wear their uniforms off their bases, as he did not want Spain to appear to be an occupied country. This prohibition was scrupulously followed. And—you can believe this if you like—the Americans would have to give the Spanish a duplicate of any piece of military equipment that was in the country for more than six months. To get around this problem, so the story continued, the Americans rotated their equipment every five months. The story sounds to me more like Spanish humour than fact. But the economic effect of the

American aid was real, especially when combined with a concerted and successful drive to attract tourists to the country, engineered by forward-thinking Opus Dei economists who had been given seats at Franco's cabinet table, at least in part because they were monarchists.[20] Throughout the 1950s, as a result of these policies, the country began its rapid ascent out of a medieval economy. The primary industries having been modernized by the end of the decade, the basis was laid for the rapid development and prosperity that began in the 1960s and continued thereafter.

> *For a few weeks before Eisenhower arrived, the city was abuzz with speculation about the visit. Many people, thinking, perhaps, more of Spain's past than its future, predicted that Franco would be shot as he and Ike headed through the city in an open car toward El Pardo, the great Bourbon palace on the outskirts of Madrid that Franco used as his headquarters. There was an avalanche of jokes about the visit, told in the bars and offices of the city. One I remember went like this: "The people along the parade route will shout, 'Franco! Y Que!'" Y que is the Spanish pronunciation of Ike, but it means "So what!" So the shout is, in fact, "Franco!—So What!"*

People waiting for the motorcade were lined three or four deep on both sides of the route in the downtown area, and I was one of them. It was the first time I had seen world political figures in the flesh. Helicopters hovered above, clack-clack-clacking away. Sharpshooters appeared and faded, appeared and faded, on the rooftops. Eventually, the speeding open car came by, preceded and followed by other cars and motorcycle outriders. In the back of the open car, Franco and Eisenhower stood, holding a handrail with one hand, waving with the other. I raised my camera to take a picture, but in an instant they were gone, and I got no picture. My momentary glimpse of what some would call greatness had been that—momentary.

Immediately, people began circulating a story about the event. They said that Franco, who was very short, but seemed to be nearly as tall as Eisenhower in the back of the car, had been standing on a box. It may have been true. He certainly went by too fast for me to judge. So, to commemorate the event I was left to take a picture of something that wasn't going thirty miles an hour, a flimsy-looking celebratory arch that had been constructed over the street, on the top of which was a very large photograph of Eisenhower's bald head.

Jennifer Comes to Madrid for Christmas

BUT A MORE IMPORTANT VISTOR ARRIVED IN MADRID LATER THAT DAY. I MET JENNIFER AT CHAMARTÍN STATION, TOOK HER ACROSS

---

[20] Franco declared Spain a monarchy in 1947, thus, he thought, solving the problem of succession faced by all dictators. He refused to consider Don Juan, son of Alfonso XIII, the last king, who had gone into exile in 1931, but groomed Alfonso's grandson, Don Juan Carlos, as a fascist successor. But when Juan Carlos became king on Franco's death in 1975, he quickly moved Spain toward a constitutional democracy. His father, Don Juan, graciously abdicated in favour of his son in 1977.

the city on the Metro, carrying her suitcase for her, and installed her in my room at Francisco Silvela 55. It's difficult now to understand how daring this arrangement was in the 1950s, especially in Spain. The world at that time was set up to make it nearly impossible for unmarried couples to spend a night together in the same room, and girls were especially wary of doing so, as their reputations could be destroyed if those they knew found out they had done such a thing. It was easier to do so in the circumstances we were in, as we were merely passing through Madrid. I wasn't concerned about the attitude of my apartment mates. If anything, they would be jealous. But I was afraid that Julia, our maid, would be shocked. So I took her aside and told her that Jennifer was my *novia*, my girlfriend, to whom I was engaged. I also pointed out that there were two beds in the room. There was no need for me to explain myself, but I felt I owed her at least a palatable lie. When I finished my explanation, she said nothing. But before turning away from me and going back to work, she consciously and deliberately blessed herself.

Strangely, I don't remember much about that Christmas and Jennifer's visit. Once we went out for paella, which in those days was made one day a week by only a few restaurants—usually on Sunday evenings, I seem to recall—at which time it was the only item on the menu. We went often to the *bodega* that was on the ground floor of our apartment building, where we bought small amounts of cheap, Spanish-made copies of French liqueurs, which we would sip on the roof area while waiting for dinner. You took your own bottle to the *bodega* and filled it from the spigots of large wooden barrels. It was fun.

> *There was a party at which one of the guys was making the girls nervous by listening to their hearts, using Pedro's stethoscope—too close to their breasts for comfort. Later, we brought in the New Year in the Spanish way, popping a grape into our mouths as we counted down each of the final seconds. Jennifer, who, like all of us, was a creature of her times, became upset after all the guests had gone and my roommates had retired to their rooms. She had had a little too much to drink, unusual for her, but it was, after all New Years, and the alcohol appeared to be doing its in-vino-veritas thing. She said she felt badly about sharing my room, saying (and I remember her actual words) that she felt she had "let daddy and Susan down." (Susan was her younger sister by three or four years; her mother had died of breast cancer when Jennifer was eight.) I was able to calm her down and she went to sleep. In the morning, it was as if it hadn't happened. Jennifer tended to deal with problems and then forget about them.*

But the visit was, apart from one or two glitches of this sort, a success for both of us. We got along well and continued to cope with "not going all the way." We also avoided any talk about working towards establishing a permanent relationship. Jennifer continued to make it clear, without stating it, that she was not interested in pursuing that route at this time; and with that position I had no choice but to concur.

But as was the case when I left Bilbao the September before, as soon as I no longer had her beside me I knew that I wanted Jennifer in my life forever. I was miserable without her. I survived, of course, as people do, and carried on with the routine of my life, the teaching, the metro rides to and from Francisco Silvela, morning, noon, afternoon, night, the bar visits with friends, parties at the apartment. I wrote long letters to her and waited impatiently for her answering letters, which came often, but never often enough.

Letter 6

[John Philosophizes on the New Birth Control Pill]

Greenford,
Feb. 8th 1960

Dear Terry,

A Swedish club is the sort of thing a country like Spain needs—
"Housed in a disused church, the club at night rollicked to hysterical music and laughter. Blonde girls staggering half-clothed, drunken beneath dim lights! Yes! The local padre had made something for the youngsters to go to after work—somewhere where they could relax and learn to amuse themselves. Blessed by Franco and the Clergy, many clubs sprang up all over Spain and vigorous discussions were held nightly." It is difficult to imagine!

I'm going out with so many girls (a thing I've always wanted to do) that it has begun to be boring, and each evening I wonder how much it has cost me! Last night, I took out the Sicilian girl, but she doesn't interest me. Nothing clicks together, so I'm just pleased that I've written her address in pencil in my address book.

The only girl I wish to take out is this German girl, Roswitha . . . well, it won't be long now. I've abandoned the idea of marrying an Italian girl—they seem to be too much like the Spanish women you described. The Germans (South Germans) seem to have a spirit which I like, if it is possible to couple that with a vital sense of humour . . . .

• • •

Girls seem to play a continual game of "love you, love you not"—with me always trying not to bring up the subject! I am continually arguing, making up, retreating, advancing, flattering, being cruel, giving presents, not sending cards, kissing the cheek, kissing anything—making love out of necessity, hunger, friendliness, drunkenness, or just reassuring them and me. All I want is a companion who'll sleep with me—and they make such a fuss and make themselves out to be so special (although it's just like the others). I find the effort to keep up with them all over-taxing. I even get them mixed up—"Is your 'tummy' better today?" "I don't understand you. It isn't due for two more weeks." . . . . It suddenly dawns on me that it was the wrong girl.

• • •

Good news on the radio . . . . —contraception with the use of one pill swallowed by the woman—100% proof too. I wonder how long it will be before it gets on the market! "Here, darling, take one of these, you'll feel better!" "Well, how did I know it was one of the old sort of contraceptives when she swallowed it!" . . . . "Sold for 6d each in the main school toilet and the gym changing room."

• • •

Friday. At school in the evening there is a dance which is the beginning of a club night for 4th & 5th and Staff. I will go there to see if it is any good. It could be quite interesting to get to know some of the older girls . . . .

Ciao Terry,   Write soon,   John

Epilogue to John's Letters

When I returned to Canada in 1963, I lost contact with John. I later learned that he had continued teaching until the mid-1980s. After retiring, he became a full-time artist. Over the years, he had quite a number of one-man shows in Belgravia, Chelsea, Cambridge, and Oxford, as well as group shows at the Royal Academy, "The World of Drawings and Watercolours" at the Park Lane Hotel, and "The Hot Flash of America" exhibition in San Francisco. The refurbished Dorchester Hotel has six of his watercolours, the St. Andrews Hotel & Golf Course in Scotland has two of his very large oils in their dining room, and his works are held in many private collections around the world. According to Gerry Denning of the Bowmoore Gallery, Marlborough, who marketed his paintings in the 1980s and '90s: "John had met and married a lovely Japanese girl [in the 1980s], and he spent a lot of time in Japan. John died suddenly [in 1998]. He had a heart attack whilst pouring a glass of champagne at a small party he was giving, so he went very quickly and no suffering." John was devoted to his art, and he loved parties and beautiful women. I'm sure he would agree that for him there could not have been a better ending of things.

Jaime Manzano, Painter

ON MY 4,000 PESETA SALARY, I WAS OFTEN DESPARATELY SHORT OF MONEY. ONCE, I HAD TO WALK HOME AT NIGHT FROM THE Institute, a distance of about 6 miles. The metro fare was only one peseta, a minuscule sum at 60 to the dollar. And I had a one-peseta note. But I needed it in the morning to get me to work on time. I left the Institute at around 10 o'clock, and after negotiating the crowded downtown streets, filled with *los gatos*—the late-night revellers known as "cats," who are a part of the night-time scene in Madrid, where people have the reputation of never going to bed—I walked through the quiet and deserted streets of the semi-urban part of the city. By the time I got to Francisco Silvela, 55, it was near midnight. The building's *conserje* was off-duty at 11 p.m., so it was necessary to rouse the man who acted as night porter for all of the buildings in that area. One did this by standing in the street and clapping hands loudly. Usually, once was enough. Out of the shadows of a building down the street, or the corner bar, would come a man with a waist full of keys, who would let you into your building. I don't know why they didn't give us keys to the outer doors. I suspect it was in order to preserve the jobs of the night porters. I don't remember their ever asking for identification. Spain was an honest country in those days.

At the Garrett Institute I became acquainted with Jaime Manzano, who was taking classes from one of the other teachers. I struck up a friendship with him while hanging around Maria Fernanda's counter, something we used to do between classes. We were about the same age. He was short, dark-complected, and bulky in the way of many Spanish men. His head was a large square, which rested on his shoulders, as he had practically no neck. His eyes flashed intelligence and a strong passion for life. Jaime was a serious painter of abstract oils, very much in the 1950's New York expressionist mode. He had an independent income that allowed him to paint full time.

We began to meet two evenings a week in various bars in the *Plaza Mayor* area to practise languages, the first hour talking in English, the second in Spanish, or vice-versa. It was an ideal arrangement for both of us: congenial company mixed with useful language practice. As the weeks went by, partly from the confidence that arises from using the language in a setting in which I knew I would not have to worry about making mistakes, I made great strides in my ability to understand and to express myself in Spanish. I even found myself at times *thinking* in Spanish. I was surprised. It was not something I had willed to happen. It just happened.

Jaime had a one-man show of his paintings, all of which were in shades of gold and raw umber that he claimed he had derived from Rembrandt. The exhibition was in the *Sala Fernando Fe*, on the ground floor of 14 *Puerta del Sol*. It was a moderate success. A few paintings were sold. But Jaime was disappointed in the response. I think he hoped that this exhibition would make him famous.

While Jaime and I were having our conversational practice sessions, near the time when I was about to leave Madrid on a roundabout route back to Canada, we discussed the idea of producing a small booklet containing plates of his paintings—in black and white, as anything else would have been prohibitively expensive—with a text that I would provide and he would translate, or have translated, into Spanish and French. So we cobbled together an approach to art. Jaime came up with most of the ideas and christened them, "Biomorphic Art." I wrote the text before I left Madrid. "Abstract art," I asserted in my two-page essay, with all the confidence of youth, "is essentially interested in projecting an intelligent emotion on to the canvas. Figurative art is reaching towards the same end. This is their inherent sameness. Their difference lies in the accidental choice of forms: the first one uses the world around us as a source of essences and tries to express these essences as they exist in the mind and in the emotions; the second one uses the world as a canvas to be duplicated and intensified. Both of these are valid, individual approaches to Biomorphic Art."

The booklet, eight pages of plates and six pages of wine-coloured text in Spanish, English, and French—6 ½ inches high x 8 1/2 inches wide—was titled on its dark grey cover, **Pintura Actual** (Painting for Our Times). The title page read: *Pinturas de Jaime Manzano—Texto de Terence* [sic] *Keough—Traducciones de Beatriz Simonet*. A few months after I returned to Canada, Jaime sent me a dozen copies of the booklet and asked for a contribution to its cost. I sent him twenty dollars; in the cost-structure of Spain in 1960, it was a reasonable amount for my share.

When I was making plans to return home in April, I decided to borrow $300 from my mother, which would make it possible for me not only to buy my ticket across the Atlantic from Britain, but also go south to Gibraltar to pick up the liner *Queen Frederica* on its way from New York to Naples and travel up Italy, visit Vienna, then across France by train to London. As my route went through Seville at Easter, I decided to stop there for a couple of days to see the world-famous *Semana Santa* (Holy Week) celebrations, in which men in hooded cassocks, looking for all the world like the Klu Klux Klan, carried *tronos* (floats with statues of the Virgin and others) through the streets, each covered with banks of burning votive candles, and the women promenaded in their best dresses with elaborate *mantillas* in their hair. This sort of festival is common throughout Spain, but the Seville version is the most famous. Jaime, when he heard of my plans, suggested that I come to his home in Bilbao and take in the *Semana Santa* festivities there. "*Es lo mismo*," he said. "It's the same." But I was stubborn (as usual) and wanted to go to Seville, not realizing in my youthful ignorance that a visit to Jaime's home was a far better experience than being a tourist in Seville. So I didn't take up Jaime's offer. It was another one of my many stupid life decisions. When I saw Jaime for the last time—he came to the Atocha Station to see me off, the only one of my Madrid friends who did so—he gave me a small abstract watercolour, which I still have.

I Take a Tour of Southern Spain

SO I TOOK THE TRAIN SOUTH TO SEVILLE. I HAD TO PAY, AS MY *KILOMÉTRICO* HAD EXPIRED, BUT THE TICKET WAS ONLY 244 PESETAS. In those days you paid according to how fast the train would get you to your destination. My train was a "*Rápido*," which, in spite of its name, was the slowest and therefore the cheapest train. I complained about it in a postcard from Seville to my parents: "I've just come from Madrid—12 hours—and am dog tired." Today, a fast AVE train does the distance in 2 ½ hours. I spent a couple of days taking in the *Semana Santa* processions. I have pictures of *tronos* and hooded men carrying them. Each *trono* was borne by ten or twelve men. They were heavy and rocked precariously, especially, when like weight-lifters, the men first picked them up and began to move with them down the street, and I wondered if they had ever toppled over and dumped the decorated plaster Virgins and saints and their lit banks of votive candles on to the street. The *tronos* stopped frequently for a rest, and if the place they stopped was in front of a bar, which was often the case, one or two of the bearers would invariably slide out from under the curtains that covered the undercarriage of the float and nip into the bar for a quick *coñac*. It may be my imagination, but as the procession went along, and the *coñac* breaks multiplied, it did seem that the floats were dancing from side to side more precariously than at the start.

As young people will do, on the train I had made a couple of new friends, an American and an Irishman, whose names I don't remember, both like me heading for the Good Friday celebrations. None of us had a place to stay, so we let ourselves be led by one of the hawkers at the station, omnipresent at Spanish railway terminals at the time, to a second-floor room in a house near there. It was completely void of furniture, and the idea was that we would lay our sleeping bags on the floor and commandeer that space as ours. It was basic and cheap, and we were pleased with it. We spent the day together watching the processions. When we arrived back in the room late that evening, there were two more sleeping bags on the floor with two bodies in them. But it didn't matter. There was room for all five of us, and we slept the sleep of the young; and in the morning, we went our separate ways.

Cordoba and Granada

On the way to Granada, I stopped off in Córdoba for a few hours to see the Mezquita, the huge mosque, at one time the largest in the world, which dates from the 500-year period when most of Spain was an Islamic state. I went on to Granada the same day, where I found a reasonably-priced *fonda*, the *Residencia Cantábrico*, at *Serpe Baja*, 14, which was, as their advertising claimed, *Situada en el Centro de la Ciudad*. While there, I did the two sine-qua-non touristy items: the *Alhambra* and the *Generalife*. I also bought a ticket at my hotel to attend by bus a very staged (but very good, as these despised tourist venues so often are) Gypsy Show of flamenco playing, singing, and dancing, which was given in one of the caves the gypsies had traditionally lived in on the edge of the Sierra Nevada, on the outskirts of the city. I don't know whether any of the gypsies were still living in the caves. They certainly didn't live in this one, which was decked out like a night club. After the show, on the way to the bus, I fell into conversation with a young American, who was staying at one of the upscale hotels in the city. He appeared to me to be incredibly rich—he probably wasn't—and I saw myself in his light as incredibly poor, which was closer to the mark.

From Granada, I took the train on April 20 to Algeciras (214 ptas), across the bay from Gibraltar, to await the arrival of the *Queen Frederica*. I had chosen this ship mainly because it was run by Home Lines, the same company that owned the *Homeric*, which I had enjoyed so much on my voyage from Montreal to Southampton in August of 1958. I stayed in Algeciras, because it was cheaper than Gibraltar. In those days, because of a long-running dispute between Spain and Britain over the sovereignty of the Rock, the border was closed at La Linea. So the only way to get to Gibraltar was on one of the ferries, which ran frequently throughout the day. My *fonda*, the *Hospederia Emilia*, at J. Morrison, 31, was run by a man who kept a board in his office covered with postcards from people all over the world who had stayed with him. He asked me to send him one from Canada; in fact, he nearly got down on his knees and begged me, the mark of a true collector. And I did.

Algeciras and Gibraltar

I WAS IN ALGECIRAS FOR ABOUT A WEEK, FROM APRIL 20 TO 26. I HAD HOPED TO SPEND A COUPLE OF DAYS IN TANGIERS, BUT I DIDN'T HAVE enough money to do that, so most days I went by ferry to Gibraltar and took in the sights there. This next-to-last outpost of the British Empire was captured during the War of the Spanish Succession and ceded to Britain by the Treaty of Utrecht (1713).[21] It has been a sore point in Spanish/British relations ever since. Today, the British would be happy to turn it over to Spain, but in a number of referenda, the locals continue to choose to stay with Britain. And the place did have a weird Britishness about it, at least in respect of its food: great English beer (which I enjoyed), greasy fish and chips, and so on.

I had arranged to have my mother send me a draft to Barclay's Bank in Gibraltar for the money I was borrowing from her. I had reserved passage on the *Queen Frederica* at a Madrid travel agent, *Hijos de M. Condeminas*, and set it up so I could pay for it at J. Lucas Imossi and Sons Ltd. in Gibraltar. "I've just ferried across to Gibraltar and the money is there," I wrote in a postcard home, my relief obvious in that simple sentence. I was also able, as I pointed out in the same postcard, to book and pay a deposit "on a Passenger-Freighter leaving Glasgow for Canada on or about the 11th of June."

I did the usual touristy things in Gibraltar. I was amused by the tailless Barbary monkeys, which roam freely around the top of the rock. There is a legend that says that the monkeys will die out just before the British leave Gibraltar. When the population got precariously low in 1944, during World War II, Churchill ordered more of them brought from North Africa, in order to avoid a German propaganda victory. As a result, there are now so many of them that they've become pests. But although the monkeys were fun to watch, my interest was peaked by the cemetery, in which are buried many British sailors killed in the Battle of Trafalgar (1805), most of them only in their late teens or early twenties. Horatio Nelson, of course, was also killed while winning the battle, but his remains were destined for a greater place than an obscure graveyard in Gibraltar. He is buried in St. Paul's Cathedral in London.

> *Every evening when I returned to Algeciras I was amused by the smuggling of coffee, cigarettes, and other items by Spanish domestic workers returning home at the end of the day. Most of the smuggled goods were put into rows of pockets that had been sewn inside the needlessly long and voluminous skirts of the middle-aged women, which they lifted up shamelessly and conspicuously as the ferry crossed, not giving a damn who saw what they were doing (or saw anything else, for that matter), stuffing the pockets one by one. When the ferry reached Algeciras, the women were frisked head to toe, without objection, by guardia civiles, all of them male. Amazingly, not once in my week of crossings did they ever find anything. It was a miracle worthy of St. James!*

---

[21] It was by this treaty that France lost much of its North American territory to the British: Quebec, the Hudson Bay territories, and Acadia (i.e., New Brunswick, and Nova Scotia—except for Cape Breton).

Adios España

AND SO, WITH FINAL MEMORIES OF ILLEGAL CONTRABAND STUFFED INSIDE THE SKIRTS OF SPANISH WOMEN MAKING THEIR DAILY TRIP from Gibraltar to Algeciras, I prepared to make my adieu to Spain. It was a country I had always been intrigued by. My view, of course, was tinged with romanticism, but it wasn't a "castles in Spain" disneyfication of the country. As a boy, I had been thrilled by the exploits of Don Quixote, read in a simplified English version. One of my high school classmates used to bang out *Malageñia* on the school piano. And I loved a 78 RPM record of *Granada*, sung by the inimitable Beniamino Gigli. I had studied Spanish at St. F.X., and, as a background to the course, had learned a fair amount about the history and culture of Spain. When I had actually lived there, I discovered many more things to love: the pace of life, at that time still largely unaffected by the modern world; the patience of the people; the unique music (flamenco, and the traditional classical composers: Granados, De Falle, Tedesco, and so on); the wonderful tradition in art: Ribera, Velázquez, Goya, Picasso, Dali, and so on; the friendly bars; and the beauty of the plains and the grandeur of the mountains: the Pyrenees, the Sierra Nevada. But most of all, I recall the empty highways, alongside of which the peasant villages were huddled, the farmers riding out to their fields on donkeys, their short legs sticking out sideways, as they had no stirrups, looking for all the world like a whole generation of Sancho Panzas.

I have returned to Spain a number of times since 1960 and have been pleased to see the people and the country become prosperous. But I will always be glad that I had a chance to live there while the candle of the old Spain still flickered.

My Spain in the 1950s

Madrid's Plaza Mayor Area

Pensión Ivor in 2000

Francisco Silvela 55 in 2000

Eloy Gonzalo 34 in 1959

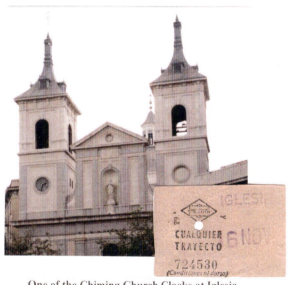
One of the Chiming Church Clocks at Iglesia

The Street of Thread Sellers

A Page of My *Kilométrico*

Eisenhower Visit

Puerto del Sol with Police Headquarters

John Davison (1935-1998)

John at Burton Bradstock May 1959

Harlington County Secondary School (1984)

Evelyn, Brian, & John in His Sunbeam

Part of Letter 4

Paola

PENSION
IVOR
ARENAL, 24, 2.º
Teléfono 48 42 23
MADRID

Habitación núm. 12

D. Terence Keough

Mes de Octubre de 1959   Días del 1 al 11

CONCEPTOS	DIAS													
	Ptas.	Cts.	Ptas.	Cts.	Ptas.	Cts.	Ptas.	Cts.	Ptas.	Cts.	Ptas.	Cts.	Ptas.	Cts.
Suma del día anterior														
Pensión	605													
Habitación														
Baño														
Desayuno														
Almuerzo														
Comida														
Invitados														
Thé, café, leche														
Vinos														
Agua mineral														

pintura actual

pinturas de jaime manzano

texto de terence keough

traducciones de Andrés Simons

Cover and Title Page of *Pintura Actual*

pinturas

exposición

Sala Fernando Fe
Puerta del Sol, 14

21-31 de marzo
6 a 8

..La imagen no representa, en verdad, nada. Sin embargo, lo que aquí es surge en seguida, como si uno mismo, en la avanzada tarde otoñal, llegara cansado a la casa, desde el campo, con el pico en la mano, para instalarse junto a la llama de las últimas patatas que están en el fuego. ¿Qué es aquí lo que es? ¿La tela? ¿Los trazos del pincel? ¿Las manchas de color?

¿Qué es, en todo lo que acabamos de mencionar, el ser del ente? ¿Cómo transitamos por el mundo y cómo estamos en él, con nuestras tantas presunciones y refinamientos?

MARTIN HEIDEGGER

jaime manzano

One of the *Tronos*

Semana Santa in Seville

Gibraltar from the Algeciras Ferry

Chapter 11: The Long Route Home

A BRIEF SWING THROUGH ITALY

The places we have known do not belong only to the world of space on which we map them for our own convenience. They were only a thin slice, held between the contiguous impressions that composed our life at that time; the memory of a particular image is but regret for a particular moment; and houses, roads, avenues are as fugitive, alas, as the years.
                      Marcel Proust, ***In Search of Lost Time***, "Swann's Way," 1913

For at that time in my life I felt capable of anything. Having attempted nothing, I had no sense of my limitations; having desired nothing, I knew no boundaries to my courage.
                      Trevanian, ***The Summer of Katya***, 1983

On Board the *Queen Frederica*

ON APRIL 26, 1960, I MOVED FROM ALGECIRAS, MY LAST OUTPOST ON SPANISH SOIL, TO GIBRALTAR, WHERE I STAYED IN A SMALL, CHEAP HOTEL, THE NAME OF WHICH I HAVE FORGOTTEN. AT 5 A.M. on the 27th, not having slept much, I walked through the dark, deserted, and weirdly silent streets to the ship's launch, which took me along with two other passengers out to the *Queen Frederica*, outbound from New York, which was at anchor in the bay. The ship was an old, two-funnelled liner, built in 1927 as the *Malolo* by the San Francisco-based Matson Line. She was only 17,000 tons,[1] but she advertised herself as something special: "Gleaming white, like an immense yacht . . . every crossing a cruise." And she was in good shape for an old lady. I was taking her on a two-day trip from Gibraltar to Naples at a cost of $42.90. Now that I had left Spain behind me, the voyage felt like the real start of my return trip to Canada.

---

[1] By way of comparison, the first *Queen Elisabeth*, the largest passenger ship in the world at that time, was about 83,000 tons. Most liners were 20,000 to 30,000 tons.

One of the two people joining the ship with me in Gibraltar was Manuel, a very short, dark fellow with a charming Indian face, who came from what was then the Central-American colony of British Honduras. He had an enormous handlebar moustache, which presided over a gentle mouth that spoke fluent English with a pronounced South-American Spanish accent. He was a civil engineer by profession. His country, he told me at some length over the next couple of days, had a new constitution and was moving toward independence. It would be known as Belize.[2] When we were aboard, we asked if we could have some coffee. At first, we were told there was no coffee this early, but then, one of the stewards took us to the entrance to the crew's quarters in the bowels of the ship and supplied each of us with a large bowl of heavily-sugared espresso. Manuel told me it was made in the Turkish style. I didn't like it much, but I drank it. You take what you can get at that time of the morning.

The ship's movie that day was Marcel Camus' soon-to-be-classic *Orpheu Negro* (*Black Orpheus*), a retelling of the Orpheus and Eurydice myth, set in the Carnival in Rio de Janeiro, with a sound track in Brazilian Portuguese with English subtitles. Jobim's haunting song, which runs through the movie, composed by Orpheu in this telling of the story, is perhaps better known than the movie itself, though *Black Orpheus* remains to this day a popular art-house flic.

After the movie, I met an American from New York who called himself James ("not 'Jim'—please!") Something-or-Other. He was, he said, a writer; and to make the point obvious, as a symbol of what he saw as his profession, he carried around with him a nifty little portable typewriter. It was a ridiculous affectation, like a doctor wearing a stethoscope to the supermarket. Many writers carry small notebooks around with them to write down conversational bits they hear and happenings they see. But a *typewriter*! How you would use it on the fly puzzled me, a puzzle that remained unsolved. I never saw him use it. Not once. James had an astoundingly curmudgeonly view of life for one so young—he was in his mid-twenties—and I think his rejection of just about everything was, like his typewriter, a part of his image. He pointed out to me, for example, that the new fashion in men's suits—a tight-fitting line with narrow lapels (not at all like the suit he was wearing)—was an old fashion.

> *"Take Al Smith," James said. "Remember him? The presidential candidate in the late twenties?" I said I remembered him—or, at least, who he was. "He wore those tight suits. Nothing new in that." I didn't point out to him that there was also nothing new in revolving fashions. But this attitude toward fashion, which was typical of his less-than-penetrating assessment of the world around him, helped me to evaluate him. As did his admiration of Hemingway, whose European haunts he intended to seek out. Although he wanted to be seen as an up-and-coming intellectual, he was a superficial thinker and a fraud. After we docked in Naples, I never saw him again.*

---

[2] Independence was somewhat slow in coming: internally in 1964, but not externally until 1981, as Guatemala, which claimed the Belize area, remained a threat. In 1992, Guatemala finally recognized Belize's sovereignty.

Shortly after our arrival there, I wrote a postcard home: "We docked this morning in Naples and I'm staying in a hotel [Albergo Pace, Via Roma, 38]—the Youth Hostel is closed—at $2.00 a night, which is expensive enough when meals, etc., must be bought. Today, I hope to see Pompeii, if I can find out how to get there. I leave for Foggia Monday and then will go to Rome Wednesday or Thursday.[3] It's good to be in Italy, but I can't understand why people say, 'See Naples and die.' It's just another seaport."

I got a train from Naples to Pompey, where I enjoyed the feeling of actually being in an old Roman city, albeit a roofless one, that I could imagine had been burned by barbarians rather than devastated by a volcanic eruption. But in spite of this romantic notion, I was still willing to offer some criticism. On another postcard to my parents, I complained that "Vesuvius, unfortunately, refused to cooperate, and there was hardly a twist of smoke on its crown when the clouds finally cleared." Pompey on that April day in 1960 was not at all overrun with tourists, so I had a leisurely time of it, wandering through the deserted streets with their two-thousand-year-old ruts, visiting the museum, where there are the famous forms of people and of a dog, shaped by their lava encasements. I did not go into the houses with the erotic murals—men, but not women, were in those days allowed to see them—as they charged an extra entrance fee. So, not for the first (or last) time in my life, my poverty saved me from a delightful occasion of sin in experiencing the interior of a brothel, even if it was an ancient one that hadn't seem a hooker in a couple of millennia.

A Visit to Foggia and Padre Pio

THE NEXT DAY I TOOK A TRAIN TO ROME. AT THE STATION EXIT I WAS STOPPED BY A YOUNG MAN WHO ASKED ME IN ENGLISH IF I WAS AN Olympic athlete. I was amused—and a little bit flattered—and regretted that I had to say no. (I'm not sure what this was all about, as the Rome Olympics of 1960 were held from the 25th of August to the 11th of September, almost four months after my arrival in the city.) Oddly enough, a similar incident happened to me in 1967 as I passed through the airport in Winnipeg, where the Pan American Games were held from July 23 to August 6 of that year, though in this case I was only a week ahead of the Games. I have often wondered just what kind of athlete they thought I was. A boxer?—I have a crooked nose—A trap shooter?—A keen eye. Certainly, with my short legs, not a track and field man.

When Denise Duval came to see me in Peace Haven in February 1959,[4] she was full of wonder at what she had experienced in Foggia, like the good Québécoise Catholic girl that she was, seeing in the flesh, the stigmatic, Padre Pio.[5] As a thoroughly lax

---

[3] As it turned out, I went to Rome first and from there took a train to Foggia.
[4] See my chapter on my Peace Haven year *A Young Man's Fancy*.
[5] Padre Pio (1887-1968) was an Italian monk and priest. He received the stigmata on his hands for the first time on September 20, 1918, and experienced it off and on for the remaining fifty years of his life. The Vatican for many years downplayed his stigmata, going so far as to take away all his priestly privileges, except saying Mass, which he was restricted to doing in private. But in the mid-1930s, Pope Pius XI

British-Columbian Catholic guy, I had never heard of him and the huge pilgrimage complex of San Giovanni Rotondo that had been built as part of the cult he inspired. In my case it was not piety but curiosity that took me on this once-in-a-lifetime journey to see a genuine stigmatic, a modern-day Francis of Assisi.

So it came to pass that on May 3 I paid 2,440 lira (ca. $C4) for a second class return ticket to Foggia. There, I stayed at the *Allogio Sorelle D'Errico* on *Viale Cappuccini* (named, one assumes, directly for the monks rather than for the caffeinated brew that takes its name from the colour of their robes), a short walk from the enormous modern church and hospital center that are part of the impressive Pio complex, built on a rising piece of land, so that you have to climb toward heaven to reach it. Following the signs, I went through the back of the church and out on to a kind of esplanade, part of a steady stream of visitors. I joined a group of forty or so people who were standing silently at a respectable distance and staring at a sort of archway on the edge of the esplanade in which was seated a figure as still as a statue—the man himself.

He was wearing vestments, as if about to say Mass, green in colour, and of a subdued classic rather than flowing romantic style. His arms were raised in the way of a priest who is about to say "Dominus vobiscum" or "Oremus" to the congregation in the old Latin Mass. He was short and had a square, one might even say podgy, figure. His round face was graced by a full beard, salt and pepper in colour. His eyes, which never moved and never seemed to flicker, were looking upward to the right, as if trained on some sort of beatific vision that the rest of us were unable to see. He seemed to be in a trance. On his hands, where he had the stigmata, there were deep-red-coloured bandages, unstained, as far as I could see, by blood. He was at the time, and remains in memory, an unforgettable sight.

> *When I tell this story, I'm often asked, "Do you think he was faking it?" The question is reasonable, as the phenomenon is totally inexplicable from a scientific point of view. My answer is always the same. "I can't explain it. It may be psychologically induced—voluntarily or involuntarily—in some way. I would like to be able to believe that it is a sign from another world. I wonder at it—but I can't bring myself to believe in it; there's too much baggage behind it all. Nonetheless, in this context, I am certain Padre Pio was not a fake."*

The Buzz in the Youth Hostel in Rome

Powers Shot Down Over the Soviet Union

THE YOUTH HOSTEL IN ROME DURING THAT FIRST WEEK OF MAY 1960 WAS BUZZING WITH TWO INTERNATIONAL EVENTS. ON MAY 1, MAY Day in most of the Western World, including the Soviet Union, a time to celebrate the causes of the working man—in most countries with worker parades, in Moscow with

---

accepted the stigmata as real. Pio was beatified by Pope John Paul II on May 2, 1999, and canonized as Padre Pio of Pietrelcina (his home town) on June 16, 2002.

parades of tanks, missiles, file after file of goose-stepping soldiers, watched by the dour top brass of the Kremlin—on this day, irony of ironies, the American pilot, Francis Gary Powers, who was piloting a U2 Spy Plane, was shot down over the Soviet Union. These planes were thought to fly too high to be brought down by the Soviets. Eisenhower first reacted by saying that it was a weather reconnaissance plane that had drifted off course. But unknown to the Americans at the beginning of the fiasco, Powers had bailed out when his plane was hit, the Russians had captured him, and he had admitted the true nature of his mission—to spy on the Soviet Union. Khrushchev had caught Eisenhower out in a bare-faced (not to mention "bare-headed") lie. This incident deepened the Cold War for some time.

Princess Margaret and the Jones Boy

The other event that everyone was talking about was the May 6 wedding of Britain's Princess Margaret to the commoner from Wales, photographer Anthony Armstrong-Jones. It was the wedding event of the year, reviving the Mills Brothers 1954 hit, "The Whole Town is Talking about the Jones Boy." On the day of the wedding, Jones was given the title of Lord Snowdon, a move that got rid of the nasty business of Margaret's marrying one of the hoi polloi. The ceremony, the first royal wedding to be televised, was watched by about 20 million people, a huge audience at that time. But behind the glitzy event, the storm clouds were already in place. In 1954, Margaret had planned to marry the love of her life, Group Captain Peter Townsend, who had been divorced from his first wife. But because of pressure from the Royal Family, the Church of England, and some politicians, who were adamantly opposed to her marrying a divorced man, she gave him up, announcing that she believed the church's teaching that marriage was not dissolvable. But, irony of ironies, many years' later, she reversed this public stand on the sanctity of marriage, which it's quite clear that she had never believed anyway, and which had obviously been forced upon her by the powers-that-be. In 1978, after a deepening cold war of their own, Margaret Rose and the Jones Boy had their marriage dissolved by the civil courts, the first divorce in the royal family since Henry VIII went on a divorcing spree in the 16th century. The divorce was a symbol of how much the attitude toward religion had changed, especially at the upper echelons of British society over the preceding quarter of a century.

There is an incidental connection between Armstrong-Jones and my favourite London restaurant, Luba's Bistro. In Luba Gurdjieff: A Memoir with Recipes, Luba says: "One of my regular customers was Tony Armstrong-Jones. He used to come in as a young man with his father and mother. He had lots of travel he would talk about. And then one day I heard he was getting married—to Princess Margaret. I got mad at him. "You're getting married to Princess Margaret and you don't even tell your Aunt Luba?" He was all apologetic. It wasn't official until now and they didn't want people talking. I said, "Good luck to you." I said, "Be careful, Tony. She's a hard woman." He said, "How do you know?" I said, "Don't worry. I know."

On to a Mussolini Villa in Florence

IT WAS WET THE WEEK I WAS IN ROME. THE RAIN WAS NOT CONSTANT, BUT THERE WERE HEAVY SHOWERS NEARLY EVERY DAY, AND THE streets occasionally ran with rivers of water. About half way through my time there, my cheap Spanish shoes, the upper parts of the soles made from a substance resembling cardboard, disintegrated. The new pair of Italian shoes that I replaced them with had fashionable, pointed toes—called "winkle-pickers" in England—a horrible style for my wide feet, so I suffered foot-wise throughout the rest of my journey home, using band aids on my little toes as sideward shock absorbers. But the real effect of this unexpected and undesired purchase was that I had to cut back on my trip. I had planned to spend two or three days in Vienna, but the money to do that was now on my feet.

On May 7, I headed to Florence by train. The youth hostel there, which was four kilometres outside the city on the hill that rises to Fiesole, had been one of Mussolini's villas. From the hostel I took the bus into Florence and did the usual touristy things: the Pitti, the Uffizi, Santa Croce, etc. As the Italians, like the Spaniards, paid no attention to the under-twenty-five age limit which was in those days the policy of the International Youth Hostel Association, there were a number of middle-aged people staying in the hostel. One was a retired American air force man who had spent the end of his career in Germany. He was a burly-looking fellow with a greying King George V beard. A couple of times he gave me a lift into Florence on his Harley Davidson, and I was impressed with the power of the beast, especially when compared to the Motto Guzzi Cardellino I had driven through Italy, France, and Spain a couple of years before. My American friend would drop me off in the middle of Florence and wave me farewell. We socialized with one another at the hostel because we were from the same part of the world, but his brash cynicism coupled with the disparity in our ages mitigated against our becoming friends, even during this brief period when our paths were crossing.

A Return to Peace Haven

THE REST OF MY TOURING IS HIDDEN BEHIND AN IMPENETRABLE CLOUD OF MEMORY. I WENT TO VENICE BY TRAIN AND STAYED, as usual, at the youth hostel there. I visited the glass works. Apart from that, I remember nothing. I was probably running out of steam, saturated by a daily dose of looking at touristy things, anxious to go home and get on with my life. After a couple of days, I got on a train and headed as directly as possible to London. Once again, I went to Peace Haven, where they had no room for me in the rooms and dormitories, but because, as Mrs. Heslin put it, I was "an old friend of Peace Haven," they found me a bed in the staff quarters above the dining room.

Peace Haven had, of course, changed in the year I had been away. Many of the "permanent" residents were still there—Paddy, Frisco, Sybil—and my good friend, Leslie Dunkling. But the place, inevitably, was different; and I, no longer a resident, but a body passing through, felt like an outsider. It was a situation that made me uncomfortable. It was as if I had gone home again, only to find my family had gone elsewhere, and the new people in the place had heard of me but didn't give a damn that I was back. It was a good lesson in the fact that you can't go back to where you were. Where you were is gone. The maids remained the same: Pepita, Matilda, and Ida. Adolf was still in the kitchen; but Liz Timmins was gone from the office, replaced by a West Indian woman by the name of Maisie Hart. And the place seemed curiously empty and lifeless without my girlfriend, Jennifer Sharp, coming down the stairs to greet me at the end of the day.

So the three-plus weeks I spent there have disappeared from my memory. Plays I must have gone to, pubs I'm sure I drank in, meals at Luba's, books read, walks taken, places visited—all gone. And, unlike Proust, I have not found the madeleine to bring these memories back.

Crossing the Atlantic on a Freighter

ON JUNE 10, I TOOK A TRAIN TO GLASGOW TO BOARD THE *ROONAGH HEAD*, A FREIGHTER LOADED WITH ENGLISH SPORTS CARS AND scotch whisky—a cargo for hedonists, if there ever was one, though it wouldn't do any of us on board any good—bound for Montreal, and on through the St. Laurence Seaway (opened as recently as 1959), for Toronto and Detroit. There were eleven passengers, including myself. We boarded the ship on the 11th, as specified in our instructions, but were immediately told that we would not be sailing until the 13th; so, in effect, the ship became a tied-up hotel with free room and board while we waited to sail.

The *Roonagh Head*

The *Roonagh Head* was a small vessel, 9,211 tons, built in Belfast in 1952, and owned by the Ulster Steamship Company. She sailed under the flag of the Head Line / Lord Line. Years later, in 1971, at the end of her days, she was described in a newspaper article, referring to her last trip across the Atlantic from Detroit before being scrapped, as "a handsome vessel, fitted with beautiful passenger accommodations." These accommodations included "a spacious dining salon and lounge to offer the highest standard of comfort." This description jibes perfectly with my memory of the ship. Each of the single passengers was accommodated in one of the four cabins provided for people travelling on their own, a luxury virtually unknown in the world of ocean liners at that time; and couples shared the other four cabins, which were roomy doubles. All of the cabins were outside cabins, fitted with a porthole, through which you could stare at the sea on the ocean crossing, and at the land on the long route up the St. Laurence.[6]

The ship, whose master was Captain Black, left on the 13th as scheduled.

---

[6] There were three "R" class ships built by the Ulster Steamship Company following World War II. The other two were the *Rathlin Head* and the *Ramore Head*. In 1963, I sailed back to Canada from Liverpool on the *Ramore Head*.

The cabins for both passengers and ship's officers were located on the top deck. Only passengers, officers, and stewards were allowed in this area. I would catch glimpses of the crew working below as I went for my twice-daily constitutional around the deck, past the port cabins to the front, past the starboard cabins to the rear, and then the reverse, over and over again.

> *There's not much to do on a freighter besides reading, socializing with the other passengers who have good sea legs—not many—and developing an exercise routine. One day, the Wireless Operator, known at sea as "Sparks," took those of us who wanted to go on a tour of the engine room. You got there somewhat perilously by climbing down a metal ladder that was riveted to the wall. The room was noisy with engine sounds and smelt of grease and oil. I felt claustrophobic, and although the tour was interesting, I didn't like it much down there. It seemed to me to be a terrible place in which to have to work.*

There was plenty of room on the outer deck for chairs, but on the North Atlantic the weather is seldom suitable for being outside for very long, and they were not put out by the stewards until the ship was well into the Gulf of St. Laurence, where the water is calm and in June the weather is warm. The stewards cleaned and tidied our cabins and the officers' cabins and served at meals and in the bar. We dined at two round tables, one headed by Captain Black, the other by either the Chief Engineer or the Wireless Operator, sometimes by both. I was at Captain Black's table, along with a couple of Rhodesian women in late middle age, one tall and willowy, the other, short and stout—a Mutt and Jeff duo. Also at the table were two young women from New Zealand, bound for Canada on the first leg of their journey home, after having lived in London for a year. Tess, the more sociable of the two, was of average height, had a good figure, and wore her strawberry blonde hair in a very attractive shoulder-length cut. Maggie, the quiet one, had black Irish looks, dark hair and blue eyes, was a little shorter than Tess, and a little dumpier. The other person at our table was a 40ish woman, whose name I have forgotten, a lay missionary of the Anglican persuasion, who was eventually heading for Newfoundland. On some of the rougher days in mid-ocean, she and I, blessed, as it were, with good sea-legs, were the only passengers who showed up at the bar for a pre-dinner drink. She was intelligent and a good conversationalist and I grew quite fond of her company and looked forward to our daily pre-prandial rendezvous.

Captain Black's Game of Footsies

CAPTAIN BLACK WAS DUE TO RETIRE WHEN HE RETURNED TO BELFAST AT THE END OF THIS VOYAGE. HE WAS A BIG UGLY MAN, TENDING to fat, with dyed black hair, thick lips, and a left eye whose lower lid drooped. He reminded me of Oscar Wilde, who someone described as having lips like slugs, and of Charles Loughton, roaring through the role of Captain Bligh in the original *Mutiny on the Bounty*. On the first day of our voyage, I heard Captain Black in the Captain's cabin, *sounding* like Captain Bligh, in language that was entirely sailor-like, upbraiding a crew member for drinking,

> *Captain Black had placed the attractive young New Zealand girls on either side of him at the dining table. While this might seem to have been an innocent-enough arrangement, in fact it was not. One day Tess told me that the captain, while eating his meals, was trying to play footsies with the girls, rubbing his shoes against their legs. Rather than being incensed by this behaviour, the girls were amused by it, but at the same time they plotted revenge. Neither I nor the others at the table were aware of what was going on. As he ate, the captain always kept his eyes, one straight and one droopy, roaming the other faces at the table, talking in the slow, sing-song accent of Northern Ireland—a kind of sea-going Ian Paisley—often with a sardonic smile accompanying his small-talk.*

One might argue that he was merely trying to amuse himself and the girls by his actions. But I'm not at all convinced that this was the case. It's more likely that he was just another dirty old man, giving himself a cheap thrill on his last voyage in international waters, where he was king of his realm. At this point in his career, he had, in fact, very little to lose.

I was not told about this situation until after the girls had attempted their revenge on the captain. One evening, when he began once again his game of footsies, the girls, according to their plan, reached down from their respective sides and undid his shoelaces. They had hoped to be able to tie one shoe to the other, but this proved impossible, as it would have required one of them to find some reason to crawl under the table for a couple of minutes. But the girls' attack on his shoes put an end to the problem, and the captain behaved himself for the rest of the voyage. I was the only one of the passengers that the girls let in on their secret, and we three had a good laugh about it.[7]

We Are Damaged by an Iceberg

Of far more consequence to the lot of us was an incident that occurred in the Straits of Belle Isle, the narrow waterway that separates the island of Newfoundland from mainland Labrador. This strait is blocked by ice in the winter months. Captain Black wanted to be the first ship that spring to take this shorter route into the Gulf of St. Laurence, as there was a certain cachet attached to doing so. It was a bad decision, one born out of pride rather than good sense, and the result was that we hit a small iceberg en route. The collision happened overnight, when passengers and crew not on watch were asleep. The captain had used some caution. He had had a man stationed at the bow with a powerful light, but this little berg, like all other bergs, was eighty percent under water, and though it didn't look particularly dangerous, it had a side shelf under the water that

---

[7] In one of his short stories, William Trevor describes an incident that took place in an advertising agency in London, where his narrator was working in the 1960s. One of the guys bet one of the other guys that he would be afraid to go up to an attractive new girl that had just come to work at the agency—in the pub they sometimes repaired to after work—and kiss her on the lips. The guy proceeded to do just that. The girl's reaction? She laughed. Trevor points out that in the 1950s, she would have slapped his face, and in the 1990s, she would have taken him to court.

passed under the ship and hit and bent one of the propellers. When we woke in the morning, we were in a sea of smallish pieces of ice—most of them probably only a few hundred pounds in weight, but still potentially dangerous—which rubbed against the ship as we passed through it. A man was always stationed as a lookout on the bow. We watched his back from the comfort of the library-cum-bar as he stared at the sea. The main result of the collision was that we were slowed down considerably. So the captain's wish to become the first ship through the Straits of Belle Isle came true; but he had, in fact, paid a considerable price for the honour. A freighter's captain is responsible for making a profit on a voyage, and as we were two days behind schedule as a result of our tussle with the iceberg, and would need a costly repair, that profit was at best reduced, and possibly wiped out completely.

Cannon Fire on the Banks of the St. Laurence

As we sailed up the St. Laurence, another incident occurred that is worth a mention. One of the larger shareholders of the Ulster Steamship Company lived on the north bank of the river, east of Quebec City. On his sloping lawn, facing the river, he had a cannon, of the type you see in movies about old ships of the line and in 18th- and 19th-century forts. Whenever one of the company's ships went by, the shareholder saluted it by firing the cannon. We were told ahead of time to watch for this, and when we passed the property, the shareholder waved, put a match to the wick, and let her rip—a loud bang and a puff of smoke. It was an impressive display, but like all fireworks, it was momentary. In no time at all he was gone behind a bend in the river.

I spent a couple of weeks in Montreal, as I thought I might be able to find a job there. During that time, I stayed in Ste. Thérèse de Blainville, just north of the city, with my sister, Joan, and her husband, Erik Frohn Nielsen. I was handicapped in my job applications by the fact that I didn't speak French, generally a requirement in that city. Besides, the economy was in a weak phase at the time, so there wasn't much work available. Morgan's Department Store was interested in my application to work in their display department, since I had had recent experience in that area at the Bay in Vancouver, and you didn't need to be bilingual to do that kind of job. But they took so long to check my references that by the time they finally called and offered me work, I had already decided my best plan was to return to B.C. and look for something in teaching. Besides, I had taken stock of my situation and made up my mind that that was more likely where my future lay, rather than in department store display. So I turned down their offer and made arrangements to go home.

S. S. Queen Frederica

Enroute Home

Postcard Home from Algeciras

Padre Pio and the San Giovanni Rotondo Complex

Rome: The Coliseum

A Street in Pompey

Rome: Admission to the Catacombs

Florence: Ponte Vecchio

Venice: St. Mark's Square

Chapter 12: Interlude in Castlegar

A TEACHING JOB IN DOUKHOBOR COUNTRY

Fuzzy-Wuzzy was a bear,
Fuzzy-Wuzzy had no hair,
Fuzzy-Wuzzy didn't care,
'Cause he was a DOUKHO-BEAR.
Anonymous

To go into teaching was a matter of sheer necessity. My education had fitted me for nothing except to pass it on to the other people.
Stephen Leacock, "Teaching School," in ***The Boy I Left Behind Me***, 1946

An Old Route to a New Job

FOR WHAT PROVED TO BE THE LAST TIME, I TOOK THE TRAIN ACROSS CANADA. PASSENGER RAIL SERVICE OVER LONG ROUTES WAS, EVEN IN 1960, BEGINNING TO DIE, THOUGH WE WERE UNAWARE that this was happening at the time. In little more than ten years, by 1970, it had become a vestige of its former self, destroyed not only by the proliferation of reliable and affordable flights, but also by a continuum of deliberate neglect by the railways of both their equipment and the road bed. They clearly wanted out of the passenger rail business.

I spent what was left of the summer with my parents in Revelstoke, doing very little. Every day I read the advertisements for teaching jobs in the *Vancouver Sun*—there were lots of them available that year, even for unqualified people like myself—but most of them were in the north or in isolated areas I wasn't anxious to go to. For a while it seemed as if I might have to go where I didn't want to go. Then an ad appeared for a position that I was willing to take, teaching English at Stanley Humphries High School in Castlegar, a town south of Revelstoke, near the U.S. border. I applied immediately by letter. A few days' later, I received a phone call from Dave Mitchell, who had been my Grade 5 teacher at Selkirk School in Revelstoke. Mitchell was a tall, thin man who always dressed in a three-piece suit. As he addressed my elementary school class, he had a habit of poking his thumbs under the arm holes of his vest and pulling the vest across to the centre of his chest, where he would interlace his fingers. He said he'd had a phone call from Claude Bissell, the Superintendent of Schools in the Castlegar area, with whom he'd been a student at UBC, asking about my application, and that he'd given me a thumbs-up regarding the job. The next day, August 30, I received a telegram from C. H. King, the Secretary-Treasurer of School District No. 9, offering me the advertised position. I telegraphed my acceptance the same day. An official letter of appointment followed.

As the school year was set to begin the day after Labour Day—Tuesday, September 6 that year—I had to leave for Castlegar immediately. I began my journey by grabbing a ride with my old friend, Bill Wood, who happened to be going that day to Arrowhead, a village at the head of the Arrow Lakes, a widening of the Columbia River, where I was to catch the ferry to Nakusp, a small town situated where the Upper Arrow Lakes met the Lower Arrow Lakes. I would then take a bus to Nelson, and from there, a second one to Castlegar. The route was familiar as far as Nelson, as I had taken it on my way to Notre Dame College in 1953.

Arrowhead was twenty-eight unpaved miles south of Revelstoke on a so-so gravel road. The road was built on alternate sides of the river, so there were two identical small ferries, each holding eight or ten cars, one at 12-Mile and one at 24-Mile, that crossed and recrossed the river on cables, using the current to propel them. The ferry that ran from Arrowhead to Nakusp was a modern vessel that could take a couple of dozen vehicles and whatever passenger traffic presented itself. It was a replacement for the romantic rear paddle wheeler, the *S. S. Minto*, which had plied the river from 1898 to 1954.

> *The Minto had been a fine old ship, 161.7 feet in length, 30.1 feet wide, a smaller version of the sort that once plied the Mississippi and were made famous by Mark Twain. Having a draft of only 5.1 feet, she was able to beach herself at the small communities she stopped at on the way, where planks were run on to the shore to unload whatever had to be delivered and pick up whatever was to be brought aboard. Once before I went on my Notre Dame trip, in 1942, when I was a mere lad of seven, I had taken the train to Arrowhead with my sister, Mary, who was on her way to Nelson to work as a secretary for Jean Poulin, an insurance agent there. We were accompanied by my brother, John, who had not yet joined the army, whose job it was to see me back to Revelstoke safely. We took pictures on the deck of the old paddle wheeler. The Minto belonged to an earlier era and had outlived her time—there were still even brass spittoons in her lounge. Taken out of service in 1954, she was beached at Nakusp, where all attempts to save her were unsuccessful. In 1968, she was taken out into the middle of the lake at Galena Bay, set on fire, and sent to the bottom. Her sister ship, the S.S. Moyie, an exact copy, built in the same year, is beached in Kaslo, B.C., and is now a National Historic Site.*

As I stood on the dock, waiting for this new ferry, a little upset that I would be sailing on a characterless barge-like vessel instead of the romantic *Minto*, I got talking to a travelling salesman—a fairly common breed in those days, now largely gone—who was on his way to Nelson. When I told him I was going there too, he offered to take me with him in his car.

The salesman dropped me off at the bus depot in Nelson, and from there I took a Greyhound Bus to Castlegar. The bus pulled into its depot at the Marlane Hotel, a modern, three-storey affair with a dozen or so rooms, an unprepossessing lobby, a dining room / café, a beer parlour, and a room that was used as a courthouse when the circuit judge was in town. I had reached the small Kootenay town in which I would spend the next ten months. I had mixed feelings about my year-long commitment. After Madrid and London, the prospect of spending nearly a year in small-town Canada was not very exciting. But at the same time, I had good memories of growing up in small-town Canada, and I knew there were aspects of life there that I had enjoyed before and would enjoy again.

Castlegar and the Doukhobors

CASTLEGAR, NAMED AFTER A VILLAGE IN COUNTY GALWAY, IRELAND, IS SITUATED AT THE CONFLUENCE OF THE KOOTENAY AND Columbia Rivers, at the southern end of the Arrow Lakes. It lies about half-way between the larger cities of Nelson and Trail, each about 30 kilometres away. In 1960, it was a town of perhaps three thousand people.

Like most towns at that time, a decade or so before the national chains started moving into small-town Canada, it had a thriving downtown area that served the daily needs of the local people, the stores in connected buildings running side-by-side in the few connected blocks that made up the main street. There was a weekly newspaper (*The Castlegar News*), various garages (e.g., Skyline Auto Service), Mitchell's Hardware, the Palette Café (pronounced "Pal-eh" by the locals, who thought that was the correct French pronunciation), a movie theatre, Central Shoe Repair, Castlegar Sporting Goods, Pitt's Prescriptions, Castlegar Barber Shop, Dutch Maid Bakery, the Canadian Imperial Bank of Commerce, Shop Easy Supermarket, Bob's Pay'n Take-it, various motels (e.g., The Cloverleaf), the Marlane Hotel, and so on. There was also the Royal Canadian Legion with its bowling alley and the arena with its curling rink. In short, Castlegar was pretty typical of small-town British Columbia in the early 1960s. The community was sustained for the most part by jobs in the Celgar Pulp Mill and Sawmill. But there were also quite a number of people who worked at the Cominco Smelter in Trail, to and from which they commuted, in order to live away from the air pollution that had destroyed the vegetation around Trail and made the area look like the face of the moon.

Many of the inhabitants of the Castlegar area are of Doukhobor origin. These 1899 immigrants from Russia, whose name means "spirit wrestlers,"[1] arrived in Castlegar from the original Saskatchewan settlement in 1908. In Russia, they had been much persecuted by the Czar's regime, mainly because of their refusal to have anything to do with any form of violence, which precluded their bearing arms in the Czar's armies, which the Czar's government found unacceptable. Leo Tolstoy, whose ideals they had adopted, was one of those who helped them to emigrate from Russia to Canada. For awhile they prospered in the Castlegar area, running highly productive farms, a grain elevator, a jam factory, and a flax seed mill. But when their leader, Peter "The Lordly" Verigin, was assassinated in 1924, things began to go wrong in the community. There was a split between those—the majority—who appreciated the values of living in Canada and became more and more integrated into the Canadian way of life, and a radical group—later called "The Sons of Freedom"—who clung tenaciously to the old beliefs. This group, mainly centred in Krestova, a village in the Slocan Valley about 40 kms from Castlegar, was constantly in trouble with the government. Their contention was that they should not have to pay taxes, part of which went to the support of the military. They also refused to send their children to school, because they said we taught the glory of war there. Even many ordinary Doukhobors who were averse to breaking the law took their children out of school as soon as they could, at the school-leaving age of fifteen. A favourite tactic used by the Sons of Freedom in fighting the government, a tactic for which they quickly became famous, was to take their clothes off in public.[2] They also tended to go on hunger strikes when arrested. Some of them, in a way that was totally counter to their basic beliefs—but undoubtedly arguing that the end justifies the means—dynamited public installations, destroyed their own cars and trucks, burnt down their own homes or homes of others, blew up bridges, and set fire to schools.[3]

> *In the 1950s, the government of British Columbia, trying to put a stop to acts of terrorism by the Sons of Freedom through education, took away the children of parents who refused to send them to school and housed them in Slocan, in what can only be described as a concentration camp (it had been used to detain the Japanese during World War II). It was not a stellar moment in the history of the province, which was by this action also making its ends justify its means. Though, perhaps, in the case of the province, the approach, in spite of its being morally reprehensible, actually worked, and the younger generation moved away from the radical beliefs of their fathers.*

---

[1] The name was given to them by Archbishop Ambrosius of the Russian Orthodox Church in 1785 and was intended to be derogatory. The Doukhobors promptly adopted it and interpreted it to mean they were wrestlers for and with the spirit of God.

[2] There was a raucous song—which today would be politically incorrect—the chorus sung to the tune of *Ta-Rah-Rah-Bumpteah*, which was popular when I was a student of Notre Dame College in Nelson. There were many verses, of which the following are typical: "We is come from Castlegar, / Nelson can't be very far, / On the corner Hudson Bay, Hubba-hubba holiday," and "We go parading in the nude, / No one seems to understood, / Why we look so very good, / Dressed up in our birthday suit." The chorus made fun of the Doukhobor love of munching on sunflower seeds: "Sun-sun-sun-flower seeds, / Sun-sun-sun-flower seeds, / Sun-sun-sun-flower seeds, / Spit, spit, spit, spit."

[3] Even in the 1960-61, when I was teaching in Castlegar, schools, bridges, and other public installations were guarded 24 hours a day.

As it became clear that the religious fervour of the older generation was not being passed on, the entire village of Krestova, blaming the government for the assassination of Peter Verigin way back in 1924, abandoned their village and trekked all the way to the coast, in what turned out to be a final mass protest. Many of them were jailed for removing their clothes in public and other acts of civil disobedience. But by the mid-1960s, most of the older generation of Sons of Freedom had died off, and assimilation into the mainstream of Canadian society became a fact for the remainder of the cult. By the 1990s the group no longer existed.[4]

Bob Jeffery and I Share a Flat

ON THAT EARLY SEPTEMBER DAY IN 1960, AS I WAS MAKING MY WAY FROM THE GREYHOUND BUS TO THE LOBBY OF THE MARLANE HOTEL, heavy suitcase in hand, I met Bob Jeffery, who I soon learned had also been hired to teach at the high school. We made what are in hindsight some remarkable instant decisions. We first of all decided to share a room in the hotel, thus saving a bit of money while we looked for a place to stay. And before the day was out, we had decided that we might as well look for an apartment to share together.

Bob Jeffery was solidly-built, medium-height, and athletic. He had a mouse-brown brush cut and blue eyes and the look of someone—and I find this hard to crystallize—who had risen to a higher place in life from a rather seedy background. I could see it in his mouth, which had the kind of permanent twist that develops in the faces of people whom life has bashed around. He drove an enormous, older Buick, bright red in colour, with wide white-wall tires and a white vinyl roof, the sort that could easily accommodate six on its roomy bench seats. It was startlingly gaudy, a miniature fairground, epitomizing the bad taste of the time, but I had to admit grudgingly that it was damn attractive on its own terms. It certainly seemed to appeal to the women of the town, among whom Bob proved to be more popular than one would have expected.

I find it incredible now that I would agree to share a flat with someone I had just met and about whom I knew nothing. But we were both young, and young people tend to trust other young people. Besides, as we had both been hired as teachers at the high school, I suppose I just assumed that Bob would be all right.

> *As it turned out, we had practically nothing in common. And when it came to money, he was not dependable. He led a much more raucous life than I did, spending more than he could afford; so he was often unable to come up with his entire share of the rent money, forcing me to supplement what was missing. Then it became a struggle to get him to pay me back. As well, the telephone was in my name, and on one occasion he took the bill—most of which he owed from the long-distance calls he made to his fiancée in Vancouver—and said he'd pay it, and then didn't do so. I was so furious when I got a second notice that he borrowed the money from one of our colleagues to pay the bill.*

---

[4] See Simma Holt, *Terror in the Name of God: The Story of the Sons of Freedom* (Toronto: M&S, 1964).

But in general we tolerated one another's foibles and got through the year together until Bob married in Vancouver during the Easter holidays, at which point I moved into the home of Bill Oleski, another teacher at the high school, whom I had known years' earlier at Notre Dame College, who lived with his diminutive, old mother, and left Bob to share our apartment with his bride.[5]

Mrs. Oleski's Cabbage Rolls

Mrs. Oleski was a post-First-World-War immigrant from Galicia. She told incredible stories of how tough life had been in the old country, of her brothers fighting over their father's boots as he lay dying, of their constant state of near-starvation during the war. She did not cook for us. One day, as I was tearing the outer leaves from an iceberg lettuce to discard them, she said: "Terry. Don't throw away those leaves," and she came over and took them from me. The next day, when we got home from school, there was a large pot of cabbage (and some lettuce) rolls sitting on the kitchen counter. She couldn't bear to waste anything. She told us to help ourselves to these delicious Slavic treats—and delicious they indeed were.

Living at the Reinsbakens

The apartment Bob and I found was a basic, furnished, one-bedroom accommodation in the basement of the Reinsbaken home, within easy walking distance of both the school and the downtown area. The Reinsbakens were immigrants from Norway. Mr. Reinsbaken had built the house himself, bit by bit, as they could afford to buy the materials he needed. It was now nearly finished, only some of their own living and dining area needing dry-walling and flooring. Mr. Reinsbaken finished this area as a Christmas present for his wife, no doubt using the revenue from our rent to do so. Our apartment had two rooms, a kitchen-living room area, minimally but adequately furnished, and a bedroom with twin beds. The bathroom had a shower stall, but no tub. It was on the other side of the unfinished basement, and to get to it you had to negotiate your way around the furnace. Besides our apartment, the Reinsbakens had built a second one on the top floor of their house. That year it was rented to a couple of other high school teachers, Ken and Herm Frey, who became good friends of mine.

Friday's at the Legion

One of the first things that Bob and I did after getting settled into our apartment was to join the Royal Canadian Legion (Branch No. 170) as associate members. We had been told that its bar was considered the most "respectable" in town, suitable even for teachers. Most of our friends and colleagues were also members. Often, on Friday afternoons, after a long week of teaching, we joined other teachers there for a couple of

---

[5] Bill and I sent him a congratulatory telegram on his marriage from the local CPR station, using up, with great care, the full ten words one was allowed at the basic rate. It read: "We'll hold the fort while you've got your hands full." The station agent, Hank Godderis (about whom more later), said: "You guys are terrible!"

drinks, accompanied by rudimentary bar food, and a game or two of shuffleboard. Afterwards, we bowled in the five-pin bowling league. Bob and I were the best bowlers in the league, though he was always a little better than I was, and try as I might—and did—I was never able to top his averages. He was simply a better athlete than I was.

Stanley Humphries High School

"Major" Brown, Principal

THE SCHOOL WAS A BORING, MODERN BUILDING—YOU'VE ALL SEEN ONE LIKE IT—OF A TYPE COMMONLY BUILT THROUGHOUT the continent in the post-war era, its catalogue-source architecture inspired by factory design. The building was even referred to as "The Plant." (How, one might ask, can you fall in love with an *alma mater* like that?) The Principal, Roy Brown, was a huge man in his forties with a brush cut and a naturally scowling face who had been a paratroop major in the war. One never doubted his military background. He hulked through the halls in his two-piece suit as if he were still carrying the burden of his wartime gear. He remained psychologically in the armed forces and retained the attitudes of a military martinet. For example, every morning he issued "Daily Routine Orders" to the teaching staff. (He would have lined us up and drilled us if he could have got away with it!) From the first time I met him, I did not like "Major Brown," as I took to calling him--outside of his hearing, of course. He was far too rigid in both his rules and his opinions.

For the most part, I was able to stay out of Major Brown's way. But at the end of the year, he did something that was reprehensible any way you look at it and confirmed once and for all my bad opinion of him. In my Grade 10 English class, I had taught the son of the Superintendent of Schools, the man in charge of the entire school district, Clause Bissell. Bruce Bissell was a willing-enough lad, but he was as well, unfortunately, incredibly dense. So, when his average came in at a meagre and generous 37%, I failed him. A few days' later, when the pass list for all classes was issued by the principal's office, the superintendent's son was among those who had passed my course. I appealed to Major Brown, but he simply told me that that was the way it was going to be. I was upset about it, but what could I do? I could have gone public, but that would have created a tremendous kafuffle, and as I was leaving Castlegar a few days' later, and had no intention of ever returning, I felt it simply wasn't worth it. The kid, rather than being punished, had benefited. So nobody besides me, and, in a different sense, Major Brown, was hurt by this. I held my nose and gave the Major the final word.

Although I didn't get along with the Principal, I was much appreciated by the students, and that, unquestionably, is of greater importance when you are a teacher. It wasn't that I was easy on them. Quite the opposite. But I made my requirements crystal clear (which a lot of teachers don't do), and I was fair and consistent in carrying them out. There was also, of course, the fact that I was, at 25, not that much older than my students, so they were able to related to me in some respects as one of their own. This small gap in age was even exploited by one of the women teachers, who tried to line me up with her daughter, who was graduating that year from Grade 12.

> *At the end of the year, a number of students got together and presented me with a "Hero Badge" they had made out of aluminum in the school metal shop. It consists of a circle disk, on which is stamped "Hero Badge" in large capital letters, and around the circumference of which, in cursive engraving, is written: "Presented to Mr. Keough—From the Students of SHHS." The disk has another piece of metal attached behind it, which is scalloped at the edges like a rosette, and from its base are a couple of metal ribbons painted in red. A length of butcher cord—an aesthetic failure by any standard, but that hardly mattered in the circumstances—is attached to the top, so it can be hung around your neck.*

Alexander Zuckerberg, Czarist Mathematician

There was an interesting man who substituted at the school whenever a mathematics teacher was unavailable. Alexander Feodorovitch Zuckerberg was an Estonian civil engineer who had been a teacher of mathematics in pre-revolution Russia. He arrived in Canada in 1923, and moved to Castlegar in 1931, brought there by the Doukhobor community to teach their children. He was not a Doukhobor, but he was a Tolstoyan, so his opposition to war and violence made him acceptable to the Doukhobor sect. When he arrived in Castlegar, he bought an island on the river (now known as Zuckerberg Island), where he built a house (now a museum) whose architecture was inspired by the design of Russian Orthodox chapels. When you met him, you knew he was someone special. He was a small, wiry man, who often had a sardonic grin on his face as he listened to the frivolous nature of the staff room conversations. His favourite question, the answer to which I don't remember, was "What is the sine of minus one?" He died in 1961, shortly after I left Castlegar. I did not know him well, but I have always felt it a privilege that I knew him at all. He was a very special man.

New Friends among the Teaching Staff

I MADE A NUMBER OF GOOD FRIENDS AMONG THE TEACHING STAFF. AT THAT TIME, THERE WERE A LOT OF TEACHERS FROM ENGLAND COMING to Canada, attracted, among other things, by much higher salaries than they could get at home. Many of them planned to save a pile of money and return, but for the most part they settled in and stayed. Arriving in Castlegar that year from England were Mike and Shirley Brown, Joyce and Lester Carruthers, Val Williamson, and Ken and Herm Frey.

Mike and Shirley Brown's Marital Problem

I did not get to know Mike and Shirley Brown or Joyce and Lester Carruthers very well, though we intermingled at parties and dances. One night, after a long session of partying, I wound up taking Shirley Brown, who was an attractive, tall, slim brunette, home in Bob Jeffery's car. I heard later that Mike was raging on at the continuing party about the fact that his wife had gone off with me.

> *She had, in fact, come to me and asked if I could drive her home. It was an odd request, as she knew I didn't have a car. I was reluctant to get involved in what appeared to be a marital dispute, but I nonetheless asked Bob if I could borrow his car for the job, and he gave me the keys. When we got to the Brown apartment, Shirley lingered on in the car, as if she were waiting for me to make a move. I was puzzled by it all and did absolutely nothing. I later learned that the Browns were having problems getting pregnant, and I have often wondered if I was being set up as a possible surrogate father.*

Joyce Carruthers' Panties

Speaking of pregnancies, Joyce Carruthers, Lester's wife, became pregnant that fall. Later on, when she had become quite large in the belly, she told a funny story about her road test for a driver's licence. Apparently, as she went to the car with the examiner to take her test, the elastic holding up her panties, stretched to the limit, gave out, and they fell precipitously to her ankles. (You can believe as much of that story as you like.)

Val Williamson, Bruce McLeod's Propeller and Me

Val Williamson was a short, square girl from East Grinstead, Sussex, who immediately she met him, set her sights on Bruce McLeod, a teacher who had just arrived from Melbourne, Australia. Bruce was an attractive young man, perhaps a little short for some tastes, who, as many Australians have done before and since, was on his way around the world. He owned a small two-seater aircraft and dreamed of being a commercial pilot. From time to time he would take his friends up for a ride. His plane was an old-fashioned affair that had to be started by someone's flipping the propeller while he sat in the cockpit and did whatever needed to be done to get it going. He showed me how to flip the propeller, while at the same time cautioning me to be very careful to get out of the way. It was a scary thing to do, and I was damned careful to fall away in a hurry. I don't know whether Val learned to flip Bruce's propeller or not—he certainly did his best to avoid flipping *hers*—but her pursuit of Bruce, which the whole teaching community was aware of and amused by, ended in late winter, when Bruce's girlfriend, Pam, whom he had often talked about, arrived from Australia. They were married quietly in Vancouver shortly after her arrival.

Later that spring, Val began to turn her attention to me, but I was not the least bit interested in her and pretended not to understand her overtures. She was not easily dissuaded, however, and when I mentioned to someone in her hearing that I would be flying out of Calgary on July 12, on my way back to England, she said she would be in Calgary at that time at the Stampede and would meet my train I from Revelstoke. I reluctantly agreed that we might get together for a drink or a meal. She did meet my train, but so did my Aunt Clara and her second husband, Charlie Stringer. My mother had arranged with her sister, while I was at home for a couple of weeks at the end of term, for me to stay with her overnight. I had no way of contacting Val to let her know this. So, we had an awkward conversation, as I explained what had happened; and I left her standing in the station as I went with my aunt to spend the night at her home. I felt badly about having to do things in this way, so I did make an effort to keep in touch with her for awhile by letter. She also had returned to England that summer. But I never saw her again.[6]

Ken and Herm Frey

My best friends in Castlegar were Ken and Herm Frey. Ken was a graduate in geography from the University of Bristol. He was a big, blundering sort of guy, who, though he had a double chin, was not fat. He had a splendid wit. In fact, he was probably the wittiest and funniest man I have ever known. His wife, Herm, who was an Australian, was tall and thin and exceptionally attractive. She was a good match for him, and in her own way was just as brilliant. At the end of that year, when I was on my way to London, the Freys applied for and landed jobs in Victoria. I kept in touch with them and renewed our friendship in 1963, upon my return to Canada from England. After I got back from three years in Kenya in 1968, I stayed with them in Victoria for a few days. The Freys spent the rest of their teaching careers in Victoria, but, regrettably, I lost touch with them sometime in the 1970s, and when Barbara and I moved to Victoria in 1993, they were no longer there.

Romantic Danger at the Little Theatre

I Take a Role in *Monique*

SHORTLY AFTER ARRIVING IN CASTLEGAR, I JOINED THE KINNAIRD LITTLE THEATRE SOCIETY.[7] THIS GROUP WAS STRONG AND ACTIVE, running monthly workshops at which we read plays and performed the sorts of exercises one does in drama groups: e.g., pretend you are a piece of bacon frying in a pan; be a cat clambering up a pant leg for food; read a line such as "I don't love you any more, Marjory," a number of times, changing the emphasis with each reading. The group chose a detective mystery, *Monique*, a play in two acts by Dorothy and Michael Blankford, which had had a reasonably good run in New York in 1957, as the Society's production for the fall of 1961. I auditioned for and won the major part of the Inspector. At this distance, I remember practically nothing about the play apart from the fact that it was set in France, and its plot depended on a misinterpretation of the initials on an embroidered lady's handkerchief. I also remember, with some chagrin, that on the first night, in the pivotal line in the play, I reversed the order of the names, saying, "The handkerchief belongs to Lynette not Lisette," when it should have been the other way around. I was fortunately rescued by one of the other actors, who said: "You mean 'Lisette not Lynette', don't you?" "Of course," I replied. "How silly of me!" Or words to that effect.

---

[6] In what was perhaps an instance of justifiable revenge, Val stood me up in London during the following year. We had arranged that I would meet her at Waterloo Station one day when she said she was coming to town. I met her train, but she was not aboard. We had no further correspondence after that.

[7] Kinnaird, a village on the edge of Castlegar, was incorporated into the larger town in 1974.

We gave the play three performances, if I remember rightly, in a church hall that had a cramped proscenium stage at one end of the room. Before the first performance, I went with a couple of other cast members to the legion for a pub supper, and we drank a little more (not a lot more) beer than we should have, considering the fact that we had lines to remember. When the curtain came down at the end of the first act, the director looked at us grimly: "That was a hell of a first act you guys wrote out there," he said. We had, I'm sure, flubbed a few lines, but the new ones we created worked just as well as the scripted ones. Later, I talked to some of the audience members about the play, and no one had noticed a problem, even with the Lynette / Lisette fumble in the second act. They thought it was all part of the script.

Sheila Stringer Gets a Bit Too Close

While I was participating in the Little Theatre sessions throughout that winter, I became a good friend of a woman I will call Sheila Stringer, an attractive blonde woman in her late thirties who was the wife of one of the local lawyers. We never saw one another outside of the Little Theatre get-togethers, and there was nothing in the relationship beyond the camaraderie of people who like each other's company.

> *Sheila did not act in Monique, but she was one of the crew doing the make-up and for much of that, she was working on me. By the third and last make-up session, I began to feel that her interest in me was getting deeper than friendship. She didn't say or do anything explicit, but there was an aura about her treatment of me—here and there a hand left too long on my shoulder, remarks about how handsome I looked in a beard—that made me a bit uncomfortable. I dismissed it all as the usual fervour of the male imagination.*

But my instincts in this case were right. A couple of months after the play was over, in mid-January, not long after the second half of the school year had begun, I had a note from her in the mail—even then an odd way for two people in the same town to communicate—asking me if I'd like to do *Sorry, Wrong Number*[8] with her and take it to the upcoming regional playoffs of the Dominion Drama Festival in Trail.[9]

Now, my year in Castlegar was a disaster in terms of romance. For some reason or other, as a young man I was far more successful with girls from other countries than I was with Canadian girls. I had had remarkably successful years, from a romantic point of view, in both England and Spain. But Canadian girls didn't seem to like me. I had had a steady girlfriend, Karen Abbott, in my last year in high school, but that was my only substantial relationship up to that time in this country. And I was now 25 years old. In

---

[8] *Sorry, Wrong Number*, by Lucille Fletcher, was originally (1943) a radio play. It was adapted for television in 1946, and, much fleshed out—was made into a movie in 1948, starring Barbara Stanwyk and Burt Lancaster. There have been many subsequent renditions, and it has remained a favourite of amateur groups.
[9] The Dominion Drama Festival was begun by Governor General Bessborough in 1932. Amateur theatre groups competed regionally, and the winners came together each spring for a week in which awards were given in acting, design, direction, original writing, and production. It was discontinued in 1978.

general, I blamed my lack of success on two things: first, I did not have a car; and second, I was being very careful with my money most of the time, as I was saving to go to Europe, or trying to amass enough money to further my education. There had been a number of short romances at Notre Dame College, but nothing to speak of in my two years at St. F.X. When I lived in Vancouver for a year, after graduating from university, I had only one extended relationship, and that was an on-again off-again thing with a married woman who had just broken up with her husband, and saw me, I suspect, more as a sympathetic ear than anything else.

So, when Sheila Stringer sent me her note suggesting we do *Sorry, Wrong Number* together, considering that I was in a desert from a romantic point of view, I was sorely tempted. Doing a play together was a perfect cover for spending a lot of time in each other's company, and I was sure that that was what she had in mind. This play was an ideal one through which to build a romantic liason, as it required only two players to bring it off, the on-stage character, Leona Stevenson, who is confined to her bed, and a series of male voices she hears on her telephone. But in balance the situation seemed to me to be enormously risky, and even though I was as frustrated as only a young man who doesn't have a girl friend can be, the possibilities frightened me. I could see peril everywhere: dangerous liaisons in unexpected places, getting caught in compromising situations, rumours circulating in the school and in the community, the possibility of some sort of legal entanglement. So, after dithering over it for a few days, I followed Sheila's lead and sent her a note through the mail, claiming that the burden of my school work was too great to get involved. We saw each other after that at meetings of the Little Theatre, but our relationship had become awkward, and we both did our best to stay out of each other's way.

Weekend Excursions

The Ghost Town of Sandon

OFTEN ON WEEKENDS IN THE SPRING, A FEW OF US SINGLE MALE TEACHERS EXPLORED, IN AN UNORGANIZED WAY—THE GROUP varying every time—places of interest in the Castlegar area. We went to Sandon, a ghost town near New Denver, about 90 kms north of Castlegar in the Slocan Valley. Here were the remains of a town that grew spectacularly after rich silver deposits were found in the area in 1891. At its height it had 29 hotels, 28 saloons, three breweries, the largest red light district in Western Canada, and a population of about 5,000 people. As there was very little room to expand the town in the narrow mountain valley, a flume was constructed to carry the swift waters of Carpenter Creek through the town's centre, and a busy downtown street, constructed out of timber, was placed right over top of the flume. When the ore ran out, the town was abandoned. In 1955, the creek washed out much of the timber main street, and over the years following, treasure hunters dismantled much of what was left of the town. When we visited it, it was in bad shape. But the value of the site was subsequently seen by the people of the Slocan valley. Since the 1970s, much of the remaining town has been restored and a museum established by the Sandon Historical Society, a group of volunteers from the New Denver area.

The Ainsworth Hot Springs

We also, on a couple of occasions, drove to Ainsworth, which is about 75 kms from Castlegar on Kootenay Lake, on the road to Kaslo. We went there to swim in the hot springs, which at that time were not nearly as developed as they now are. The great fun in going there was to swim in the warm waters of the two natural, adjoining caves, especially when there was still snow on the ground outside.

Nude Parade in Krestova

But the most memorable excursion was one Bill Oleski and I took to Krestova, the Sons of Freedom village in the Slocan Valley, one Sunday afternoon in May. I had not been there before, and, curiously enough, for one who was born and raised in Castlegar, neither had Bill. As it turned out, we arrived in the village on the very day, and at the very time, when twenty-five or so of the community decided to have a protest march.

> *Out they came from one of the farms, the women in the front, dressed as they always were in their Russian peasant outfits—ankle-length skirts, scarves on their heads—carrying a large sign with writing in Russian and English. The men followed close behind. All of them were singing one of the marvellous Doukhobor hymns. It was a parade of old men and old women. The young people stood by the road and watched. In a field across from them were a couple of dozen of their own burnt-out cars and trucks, burnt by themselves as part of an earlier protest against what they saw as the excessive materialism of their lives. Down the dirt road they marched, stopping eventually at an open space, where they erected their sign and listened to a speech from one of their members. After the speech was over, they began to sing another hymn. In the meantime, the RCMP had arrived with their interpreters, who began negotiating with the group to try to calm things down. But whatever they tried to do was unsuccessful; and the protesters, continuing to sing their hymns, began carefully taking off their clothes. Eventually, they were all singing in the nude.*

The main point they were trying to make concerned the land, which they contended could not be bought or sold. I'm not sure who the audience of the protest was meant to be. Krestova is totally rural, no main street, no stores. If Bill and I and the RCMP had not been there, the only audience would have been the other village people (most of them young) who were not actively involved in the protest.

Plans to Return to London

DURING THESE FINAL MONTHS IN CASTLEGAR, I WAS SAVING AS MUCH MONEY AS POSSIBLE TO FINANCE A YEAR AT THE UNIVERSITY OF London to obtain my teaching qualifications. As a result, I had to make some sacrifices I would not otherwise have made. I did not buy a car, even an old one, although it was awkward not having one in a society in which everyone else owned one; and I spent as little money as possible on clothes and entertainment. One night, in his apartment on the top of the Reinsbaken house, I was encouraged by Ken Frey to apply to King's College on the Strand in London, where he had earned his teaching qualifications a few years before. At the same time as I made this application, I applied, as a back-up, to the University of London Institute of Education. The powers-that-be at King's indicated that they were willing to consider my application, but they insisted that I present myself for an interview, an absurd requirement for someone applying from another country thousands of miles away. I wrote them a declining letter, asking if they had noticed that my name was not Rockefeller. But as it turned out, my failure to get into King's didn't matter, as I was promptly accepted by the Institute of Education. Considering that King's was at that time one of those small, snob-ridden English institutions where I would have been constantly bucking the absurdities of the class system, I am convinced that the Institute, the least of whose virtues was that it was in the vanguard of the latest educational theories, was by far the better place for me. And so it proved to be.

My Castlegar year had been an interesting one, a kind of experience in a Canadian context that I had not had before. But throughout that year, it always felt as if my life was running on the spot. This town in the Kootenays did not hold my future, of that I was sure. When I spent a couple of weeks in Revelstoke after the end of term, an old friend of my mother's, Mary Geohogan, suggested to my mother that I was probably going back to England because I had a girlfriend there. About one thing she was right: I did have an English girlfriend, Jennifer Sharp, with whom I was still in constant touch by mail. But Jennifer was in Washington, D.C., flying here, there, and everywhere as a stewardess with TWA. I was certainly anxious to see her. But it seemed unlikely that I would see her again soon. Anyway, the real love of my life at that time was England herself. I was most anxious to get back to her, and I knew she would be waiting for me with open arms when my ship docked in Liverpool.

Major Roy Brown, Principal of SHHS

Castlegar

The Reinsbaken House & Bob's Car

Stanley Humphries Jr. / Sr. High School

Kitchen / Living Room of our Flat

Principal Roy Brown on the Left

Track Meet Day Parade at SHHS

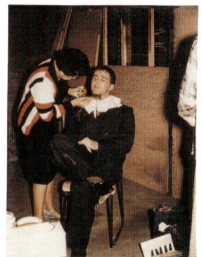

Terry Being Made Up for *Monique*

Bill Oleski (Front Row Right)

Val Williamson (Centre Right)

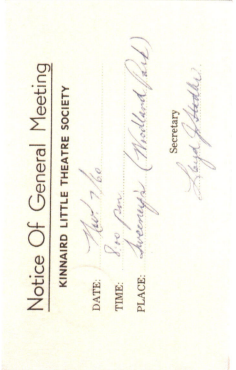

Monique

Terry Made Up as the Inspector

The Frey Flat: (From Lower Left) Herm Frey, Pam McLeod, Stella Crawford, Jim Crawford, Lester Carruthers, Terry, Joyce Carruthers, Ken Frey

S. S. Moyie in Kaslo in 1961

Ainsworth: (Left to Right) Terry, Lester Carruthers, Mike Brown, Unknown, Walter Macintyre, Don Cunningham, Bob Jeffery

Kaslo: Ken Frey (left) and Terry

Sandon Main Street 1961

Krestova

The Demonstration is Set Up

Burnt-out Cars and Trucks

RCMP and Interpreters

Interpreter Goes to Negotiate

The Demonstrators Disrobe

Chapter 13: Return to London

THE ROAD TO WOBURN SQUARE

I arrived at Paddington early and had a first-class compartment to myself, but it was filled before we started. Something about those five other masked faces, buried in their evening newspapers and magazines, at last landed me back in England: the chosen isolation, that hatred of others, as if we were all embarrassed at having to share our means of travel, even though it was first-class, with someone else.
    John Fowles, ***Daniel Martin***, 1977

When the interview was over, he escaped out into the crescent, and as he walked down through the squares—Woburn Square, and Russell Square, and Bedford Square—towards the heart of London, he felt himself elated, almost to a state of triumph.
    Anthony Trollope, ***The Small House of Allington***, 1864

I<small>F YOU ENTERED WOBURN SQUARE FROM THE SOUTH END, OUT OF RUSSELL SQUARE, AS I DID FOR THE FIRST TIME IN SEPTEMBER OF 1961—ITS FENCED CENTRAL RECTANGLE WITH THE ROAD WRAPPED</small> around—it looked like a miniature when compared to the other Bloomsbury Squares, Bedford, Tavistock, and, especially, Russell, one of the largest squares in London. Now, nearly fifty years later, the serene ambience of the Square has been irretrievably altered. The modern building housing the University of London's Institute of Education has uprooted and destroyed the square's south-east end, and on the south-west, new university buildings have spoiled forever what was once a fine and narrow balance.

In the fall of 1961, it was a thrill for a student of English literature to be moving into "a room in Bloomsbury," with all its literary associations, even if few of these were directly connected with Woburn Square itself. The square had, like me, been an onlooker of the literary scene. It had watched pass by the likes of Thomas Gray and William Cowper in the eighteenth century, Thackeray and Mrs. Humphrey Ward in the nineteenth, all of them walking north from their homes in Russell Square. It had seen Charles Dickens rushing by, on his way from Tavistock Square (to the north and around the corner) to Tottenham Court Road and Oxford Street. It had known the mortician-like figure of T. S. Eliot, out for a lunch-hour stroll from his office at Faber and Faber, which was located on the corner where Russell Square begins to bleed into Woburn. But, most of all, it had known the Bloomsbury Group. Directly to the north, at 46 Gordon Square, the Stephen sisters, Virginia and Vanessa, had held their Thursday evening gatherings, attended by Clive Bell, Leonard Woolf, Morgan Forster, Maynard Keynes, Desmond MacCarthy, and many other minor lights. From Bedford Square came Ottoline Morrel, with Henry Lamb or Bertrand Russell in tow. From down the street at No. 51, Lytton Stratchey, his mind preoccupied, perhaps, with what to do about Carrington, arrived on his spider legs, looking, one may assume, as usual, for flies.

In the centre of the square was a narrow, iron-fenced rectangle, reached through a locked gate, as is the custom in London, the keys of which only the residents of the square possessed (none of them available to resident students), was a perimeter concrete path around a grass centre. On both sides of the road, outside the fence, were attractive electric lamps which had once been gas lamps or had been made to look as if they had once been gas lamps. Around the square, various university departments had taken over the older undistinguished low-rise brick buildings. It was in two of these, side-by-side, at Numbers 25 and 26, that the Institute of Education had the hostel for male students in which I would spend my year. Nearly next door to this building was the Courtauld Institute. Across from it and down the square toward the Russell Square end stood Christ Church (1833), which contained an altarpiece in memory of Christina Rossetti which had been designed by Burne-Jones. The Church, an undistinguished (and thus undervalued) nineteenth-century Gothic pile that I often gazed at from my room across the way when I needed to find peace of soul, was demolished in the early 1970s to make room for the Institute's new glass and concrete building, already referred to, which could give peace of soul to nobody but an engineer.

Planning My Return to London

I LEFT CANADA FOR ENGLAND AND MY YEAR AT THE UNIVERSITY OF LONDON INSTITUTE OF EDUCATION A MONTH EARLIER THAN I HAD originally intended (bored with staying a moment longer in the interior of British Columbia), crossing the Atlantic on one of the large ocean liners that were then coming to the end of their era, though nobody realized it at the time. In Castlegar, where I had spent the year teaching high school and saving money to return to London, I had made my booking on the *Empress of England,* a new ship, and one of the last of the many Canadian Pacific "Empress" vessels that had plied the oceans of the world since the late 19th century. In the 1960s, smaller towns like Castlegar did not have travel agents, so the only thing for me to do was to book passage on a CP ship at the local CPR station. These years were the last before the jet airliner had put paid to travelling to Europe by sea, a development that made it possible for every small town to have its own travel agency and for everyone with a week's holiday a year to pretend to be an international traveler.

Hank Godderis, CPR Station Agent

I had originally planned to leave Canada about the middle of August. Then one day, quite suddenly, I decided that I couldn't wait until then. The prospect of getting back to a city I loved was too enticing for me to hang around in Canada any longer.

> *I went to the CPR Station to change my booking. The agent, Hank Godderis, whom I had known vaguely in the mid-fifties (he was the father of my Notre Dame College friends, Gene and Bud Godderis) thought I was canceling: "You can't do that!" he barked. He was a hulking man with a mouth that turned down at the corners, making him appear always to be angry. He was, of course, as I later realized, worried about losing his commission. In his attitude I got a dose of the pig-headed tendency to fly off the handle he was famous for within his family. But when he realized that what I wanted to do was to change my reservation rather than cancel it, he reluctantly agreed to do so. In a pre-computer age, this involved sending a telegraph message to a central CPR booking agency and waiting a day or two for a reply. So, in a short time, the change was accomplished with no difficulty beyond the bother I had caused Hank Godderis in making it.*

When I had known Godderis's sons, the family lived in Rossland, not far from Castlegar, and occasionally on weekends Gene and I would hitchhike there from Nelson. Hank and his wife, whose name I've forgotten, hated each other with a passion and vehemence that one usually sees only among former lovers, their hatred for each other the only thing in life that they both worked at together. But as good Catholics, they were adamantly clinging to their marriage—such as it was. Their *modus vivendi* was to see as little of each other as possible. They did this by Hank's working as a CPR telegraph operator on the graveyard shift, while his wife slept, and she working the day shift as a nurse in the local Catholic hospital, run by the Sisters of St. Joseph of Newark (of which Mary, one of my sisters, was a member), while he slept. When he wasn't sleeping, he wasn't around, so I hadn't seen much of him.

It was an error to go to England early, as I had nothing to do there except spend money, which I had too little of to get me through the year. But I couldn't stand the idea of returning to my parent's home in Revelstoke for the summer, which at that time seemed to by my only option. I'm not sure why I didn't try to find a summer job. I certainly could have used the money. What it came down to, if truth be told, was that I had worked hard the previous ten months and felt the need for a holiday. But most of all I was itching to be on my way, and that was the prime motivation.

By Train to Calgary

AFTER SPENDING A FEW DAYS WITH MY PARENTS IN REVELSTOKE, I TOOK THE TRAIN TO CALGARY, ENJOYING ONCE MORE THE spectacular scenery of the Rocky Mountains, taking special interest in the areas I had worked in in 1950 on my first summer job as a 15-year-old laborer on an "Extra Gang." Extra gangs were put together to do jobs that only required doing once. The one I was part of was given the very heavy grunt work of extending the sidings into which, in a single-track system, one train went in order to let another one pass. With the diesel engine about to replace the steam engine, longer trains could be run through the mountains,

creating the need for longer passing places. We worked ten-hour days six days a week for sixty-five cents an hour. In the remote Palliser area, where the railway is squeezed between huge cliffs and the always-raging Kicking Horse River, we used to get some relief from our back-breaking work by looking up at the mountain goats, high on the cliffs above us. At Beavermouth, a swampy area where the Beaver River joins the Columbia, the mosquitoes nearly ate us alive. But it was only the beauty of the areas I saw now. I have described the working conditions we endured on this gang in greater detail in my chapter on growing up in Revelstoke. At Calgary, I was met by my aunt Clara and her second husband, Charlie Stringer, whom she had married in late middle age, after her first husband, Jimmy Donovan, had died. My mother had arranged for me to spend the night with them before leaving for Montreal.

My First Flight on a Jet Aircraft

THE NEXT MORNING, CLARA AND CHARLIE TOOK ME TO THE AIRPORT. IT WAS THE FIRST TIME I HAD FLOWN ON A JET AIRCRAFT—THIS ONE, a Boeing 707, courtesy of Trans Canada Air Lines (later to become Air Canada)—my initial foray into the new age of travel. On the way to Montreal, we stopped at Toronto for a break that was long enough to walk to the terminal and have a look around. In those days, passengers got off the aircraft by descending a stairway to the tarmac. As I descended, I noticed that at the front of the plane crews were busy refueling it. As soon as I got to the bottom of the stairway, I lit a cigarette. I was immediately pounced on by security: "Do you want to blow this plane up!" the man shouted. "Put that thing out!" I complied grudgingly, grinding my perfectly-good new cigarette (I hated the waste) under my shoe. I was humiliated, not because I was yelled at by security, but because my behavior had revealed the fact that I was not a seasoned airplane traveler. Therein lay the rub.

In Montreal I stayed at the Windsor Hotel. I did not have a reservation. As I registered, the desk clerk asked me to pay for the $14 room. It's likely (in those pre-credit-card days) that he was afraid I would skip out without paying. I certainly had that impression. I thought: "I'll show him!" And I produced from my wallet my only $50 bill—a lot of money in those days—to pay for the room. But the clerk showed no emotion as he counted out my $36 in change, so my little gambit to illustrate that I was a man of substance had proved ineffective, and, in a way, I was humiliated again.

Across the Atlantic on the *Empress of England*

I DON'T REMEMBER MUCH ABOUT CROSSING THE ATLANTIC ON THE *EMPRESS OF ENGLAND*. I MET A NUMBER OF ROYAL CANADIAN AIR Force people who were on their way to the Canadian air base in Lahr, Germany, oddly, for air force people, by ship. One girl in particular, whose name I did not write into my address book and have completely forgotten, I spent considerable time with. She was a slim, medium-height blonde, who looked good in her uniform, which she wore off and on, but not every day. There was no romance in our relationship. We weren't even friends. We just kind of spent time together.

When I arrived in Liverpool, a letter was waiting for me from my old girlfriend, Jennifer Sharp, addressed to the ship's arrival, from Kansas City, where she was based as a stewardess with TWA. I was delighted that she had taken the trouble to welcome me back to England from mid-western USA. It doubled my happiness in returning to England. Jennifer and I had been corresponding regularly since our last rendezvous in Madrid, more than a year and a half before. She said in this letter that she got the odd flight to London, and she hoped some day we could get together there. Once about a year later, when I was working at a language school in Blackheath, east of London, she called on the telephone. But I was not in the school at the time. We each were drifting into our new lives, and the old fires were slowly going out. We never met again.

Return to Peace Haven

SO I ARRIVED IN LONDON ON JULY 20 AND WENT ONCE AGAIN TO PEACE HAVEN, THE HOSTEL IN ACTON IN WHICH I HAD LIVED FROM November 1958 to July 1959. It was my London home-away-from-home. The place seemed to be pretty much the same as it was when I had last been there, a little more than a year previously. Even the weather seemed to be an extension of the warm sunny days that I remembered from the day that I left. It felt as if a year had not passed and I was entering the house again the day after I had left it.

Leslie Dunkling

There, I again met my friend, Leslie Dunkling, who had by that time moved out of Peace Haven and was living in a housekeeping room at 66 Maldon Road, only a few blocks away. I arrived on what proved to be a bright, summer afternoon, and I found Leslie, who knew when I was likely to arrive, on a bench in the back of the garden, reading the orange Penguin edition of Dostoevsky's *The Idiot,* as if he were a man of leisure. Once we had dispensed with the usual greetings, he astounded me by announcing that he had become engaged to a French girl, Nicole Tripet, who was from Courbevoie, a suburb of Paris. She had been in London for only a short time and was staying at Peace Haven when Leslie met and proposed to her. All of this happened just a week before I arrived. Leslie's initiative was the beginning of the end of bachelordom for our group. Although we didn't know it at the time, the lot of us would head to the altar within the next couple of years, including my good friend, John Davison; and also Jim Honeybone and David Hepworth, both of whom I would meet at the Institute, and, of course, myself.

> *Leslie's engagement was a brave act, and at the time appeared even, perhaps, to be a foolish one. He had no money. He was working as a tourist representative for American Express at Heathrow Airport, holding up cards with names on them at lines of disembarking tourists, a job without a future. To save money on transportation, he had acquired a small motorcycle, reminding me of the Moto Guzzi Cardellino I had bought in Italy and used in my 1958-59 year at Peace Haven. He said, as we drank a cup of instant coffee in his Maldon Road room: "Now that I'm getting married, I've got to start thinking in pounds rather than shillings."*

I was not surprised at Leslie's determination to improve his financial situation. He had shown me during my year at Peace Haven that he was adept at finding unusual ways of making bits and drabs of money. He used, for example, to send letters to women's magazines, suggesting household hints, for which he received a one pound payment on publication. It helped that his first name could be either male or female. At times he even used pseudonyms—it didn't do to win too often—which I considered daring, as the cheques he received had to be cashed by signing the pseudonym followed by his own name. It's perfectly legal to do this, of course, but I didn't know that it was. It was one of the many things about survival in a hostile world that Leslie, who had grown up in working-class Acton, understood—and I, who had had by comparison a sheltered upbringing, did not. And I was jealous of his entrepreneurship and the bits of extra money he was earning in this way.

Although one pound wasn't much money, even in those days, its value can be gauged by looking at the cost of staying at Peace Haven: a shared room, with breakfast and dinner all week, plus lunch on the weekends, and a snack each night before bed, brought to the lounge at 9 p.m. by a maid—originally fancy sandwiches and tea—cost only £4.15.0 a week, about C$15. To economize, the management eventually replaced the sandwiches with sweet biscuits, crackers, and those awful Swiss cheese things that come wrapped up in individual pie-shaped foils, each with a laughing cow on the label, many kinds, all tasting the same. But even taking into account the lousy cheese, the price of room and board was an incredible bargain.

Maureen Graham Relieves a Lonely Summer

I MADE SOME ATTEMPTS AT GETTING A JOB. ONE STILL DIDN'T NEED A WORK PERMIT IF ONE WAS A COLONIAL: CANADIAN PASSPORTS STILL proclaimed "A Canadian Citizen is a British Subject." But when a man at a service station, in response to my application to be a "forecourt man" (i.e., a pumper of petrol), asked me if I was "good at figures," I gave up. The horror of this sort of rudimentary temporary employment, which I'd escaped from Canada to avoid, even though I could have used the money, I simply couldn't face.

It was a lonely summer. Leslie was working during the day and occupied with Nicole in the evenings, and I didn't know anyone at Peace Haven with whom I wanted to spend my time, or meet anyone with whom I wanted to strike up a friendship. With the new residents, Harold and Mac, I had nothing at all in common. Paddy and Sybil, the two single, middle-aged residents, who were in the hostel when I was there a couple of years' earlier, were still there, older now and sad to contemplate. Sybil still painted watercolors in the garden, which we all (I think, now, rather unfairly) laughed at. Paddy? What did Paddy do? For the most part, he kept to himself, an expatriate Irish little-person living a lonely life on the edge of a world full of people decades younger than himself. I read an eclectic mixture of things, including, for example, Leslie's copy of *The Idiot*, my own Penguin of *Crime and Punishment,* a book called *Islam,* by Alfred Guillaume I had picked up in a used book store, and English translations of the plays of Jean Anouilh, which had been recommended to me by Leslie. When I wasn't reading, I explored London. One Sunday, I went to listen to the haranguers at Speakers' Corner in Hyde Park. Some days I dropped into the "Duke of York," a five-minute walk from Peace Haven, for a solitary pint or two. This comfortable pub was run by a former bodyguard of the Aga Khan and guarded behind the bar by a pair of huge German Shepherds. It wasn't wise to put your hand over the bar.

One week, my loneliness was relieved by a lightning romance with a slim redhead, as fiery as the cliché says that redheads are, Maureen Graham, who came to the hostel from her home in Dundee, Scotland. She had journeyed south on her holidays looking for the sun, a concept I found amusing, since England can only be noted for sun in a place as sunless as Scotland. But her week was a good one, weather wise, as was most of that summer.

> *Maureen, in her eagerness to go home with a tan, exposed too much of her delicate Celtic skin for too long to the torrid English sun one afternoon in the garden at Peace Haven, and got a painful burn. That evening at supper she complained about her bra grabbing her burn, so I suggested facetiously that she take it off for the evening. Later, in the lounge, after the nine o'clock treat, I asked her to go for a walk. When I kissed her and held her, I was happy to find that she had followed my advice. I was too naive at the time to realize that she'd done so not because I wanted it but because she wanted it. Afterwards, in the lounge, late at night, we lay on the floor and indulged in some heavy petting. But on the next day, and in the few days that followed, Maureen was unwilling to repeat these pleasures. I did not have the experience of John Updike's narrator in his novel, Villages, which is set in this time-period: "With each date she gave him an inch or two more of herself that he could claim as his henceforth; there was no taking back these small warm territories." Maureen operated differently.*

After Maureen went back to Scotland, we corresponded for a few weeks. It was a correspondence based more on good manners than on any real commitment to our future as lovers. There really had been nothing in our relationship but a holiday romance. We had a good roll in the hay, and once that was done, it was apparent that it was going nowhere. I don't remember who was the last to write. But the letters soon dried up, and I never saw her again.

Two Rallies in Trafalgar Square

Oswald Mosley's Fascists

DURING THE LATE SUMMER, WHILE EXPLORING LONDON, I HAPPENED UPON TWO RALLIES, ONE IN AUGUST, THE OTHER IN SEPTEMBER, both quite by accident, both in Trafalgar Square. One of these was a fascist harangue by Oswald Mosley, delivered from the base of Nelson's pillar, which was decorated with a cascading picture of the fascist leader wearing a double-breasted suit and accompanied by the question: "Mosley: Right or Wrong? Questions Answered 2'6." The money was for a pamphlet. Mosley, who had shown so much promise in politics before he took a hard right turn in the thirties, was now a pathetic older man; his right arm raised above his shoulder to emphasize a point, thumping away at a cause that in 1961 was hopelessly passé. Even Landseer's magnificent lions seemed more bored than usual.

Campaign for Nuclear Disarmament (CND)

The other rally, on September 17, was staged by a group calling itself the Committee of 100, made up of the leading members of the Campaign for Nuclear Disarmament (CND). The playwright, John Osborne, recalls the rally in his autobiography, *Almost a Gentleman*:

> *It was well into the second week of September 1961 and the Committee of 100's campaign for a mass sit-down on Trafalgar Square on Sunday the 17th had been shrewdly stage-managed. The preliminary meetings I had attended were overlorded by experts in dissidence, those who would have been most at home in the days of Babylon, locked in canonical disputation and Deuteronomical intrigue among the tribes of Israel. The beginning of the fanaticism that was to expand and impose itself on every aspect of life—from the anti-smoking lobby to animal rights—was stirring, a rabid, venomous and neurotic collection of factions, united by their frightening brand of righteous ruthlessness.*

After the rally, I wrote up my impressions, thinking I might work them into an article for a Canadian publication, but I got busy with my schoolwork and put them aside. Here is a part of what I wrote:

> *The weatherman had predicted a fine, sunny day, but it had been raining since early morning, not good weather for a rally. When I arrived in Trafalgar Square about four p.m., the rain had stopped, but heavy clouds still hung overhead. There were perhaps five thousand people there, most of them in their teens and twenties. Shouts of "Ban the Bomb!" sometimes singular, sometimes in chorus, came from every side. Leaflets were being distributed which warned of the holocaust to come. A young woman, dressed in slacks and a floppy sweater, her child strapped papoose-like into a knapsack on her back, was selling a socialist paper called* The Left. *Her image, carefully planned and executed so as to appear accidental, was part of the ban-the-bomb culture.*
>
> *The rally was designed as a non-violent protest against the very existence*

of nuclear weapons. Everywhere were signs: "PROTEST AGAINST THE H-BOMB," "PORTSMOUTH YOUTH DEMANDS TO LIVE," *and so on. On each was the splendidly-conceived logo, instantly recognizable, that distinguishes the movement, a circle split vertically with a pie slice out of the center of each side of the bottom, the whole thing looking, ironically, like a rocket going up. The titular leader of the group is philosopher and mathematician, Bertrand Russell, a scholar, humanitarian, and long-time pacifist, now in his ninetieth year. He looked healthy enough, but very old and frail and dried-up. In his younger days, Russell had a reputation as an inveterate pursuer of women. But it was hard now, looking at this minute, wrinkled, cricket-like man, to imagine his furtive love trysts with the gargantuan Lady Ottoline Morrell, among many others, that enlivened his pied-à-terre in Bloomsbury fifty years before.*

The original idea was that the participants in the rally were to march down Whitehall into Parliament Square, where they were, in the tradition of Gandiesque non-violent movements, to sit down. The participants were told to offer no resistance to the police but were to refuse to co-operate if asked to move. This plan was frustrated by a last-minute ban on demonstrations in Parliament Square, backed up by a concentration of some five thousand police. The demonstrators, after a few sporadic and half-hearted attempts to break the police cordon, decided that Trafalgar Square would do as well for sitting, and so they went there—and sat.

Until recently, on the whole, the authorities have tended to ignore the activities of the Ban the Bomb demonstrators. Two years ago [1959], and again last year, at the Aldermaston to London marches, the police acted more as guides and traffic regulators than law enforcers. Now a change has come about. I talked to a man of about fifty, who, like me, was in the Square as a spectator. He said he was in complete sympathy with the rally but hadn't taken an active part in it because of his job. He was a teacher. Some of his pupils, he said, were sitting in the square.

By eight o'clock, the crowd had swelled to at least ten thousand people, most of them, like me, observers and curiosity seekers. Police vans and buses had carried off about eight hundred. As each van passed the church of St Martins-in-the-Fields, which stands on the north of the square, a crowd of perhaps a thousand hissed and shouted wildly. Those arrested were, by and large, sincere, ordinary people; but there were also the famous, including playwrights, John Osborne and Shelagh Delaney. The artist, Augustus John, who was dying at the time, had made a Herculean effort to be there. He had sat quietly at the foot of one of Landseer's lions. He was not arrested. Also avoiding arrest, were actress Vanessa Redgrave and novelist Alan Sillitoe. The total number arrested and charged, under an obscure 1839 Act originally promulgated to deal with Chartism, was 1314; they were fined from two to five pounds each.

When I left the square I went into a coffee bar in St. Martin's Lane. The waitress asked me if I'd been to the rally.
"Yes, I was there," I said.

"Bit silly, ain't it love," she said. "Ain't nobody goin' to change nothin' no matter how much they marches and sits."

I Move into Woburn Square and Get a Job

EARLY IN SEPTEMBER, A COUPLE OF WEEKS BEFORE THE BAN-THE-BOMB RALLY, I HAD CONTACTED MISS STEPHENSON, A TALL, TRIM, middle-aged woman with a little grey hair, a lot of dignity, and a smile that looked as if it could be mischievous, who was in charge of residential accommodation at the University of London Institute of Education. I knew I could move in early, as the instructions I had received were that "Overseas students may arrive, by arrangement with the Warden, any time after the first week in September." From Miss Stephenson, I got permission to move into my room in Woburn Square in the first week of the month.

As a result of moving in early, I found myself with an unexpected temporary job, a *teaching* job at that, in a school in the East End of London. It happened this way. As my information suggested I get in touch with the Overseas Student Adviser, and as I had nothing to do with myself until term began at the beginning of October, that's what I did.

When I entered his office, at the north end of the Senate Building, I was glad to see a stocky individual of indeterminate age whose humanity was evident in the disorder that pervaded his desk. He was on the phone, but he smiled at me and motioned me to sit down on a chair across from him. Then he held his hand over the mouthpiece and asked me what I was going to be teaching. "English," I said. "Have you had any experience?" he asked. I told him I had taught in Middlesex, Spain, and Canada. "I'll call you right back," he said to the phone and "rang off," as they say in England.

"Would you like a temporary job replacing a chap who's ill?" he said.

I couldn't believe what I was hearing. I had, after all, come to this office merely to check in, being an obedient chap, without enough to do to keep myself cheaply amused. And, here was a chance to earn some money (without having to prove I was "good at figures"), and I needed any money I could get.

So this Overseas Student Adviser, who on further examination I saw was a bulky, middle-aged man with round glasses, and a mid-Atlantic attitude he was putting on, I'm sure, for my benefit, explained the assignment to me and set me on the road to a three-week stint at Raine's Foundation Boys School, Arbour Square, E1. On a memo form, which I still have, he gave me the address and phone number (STEpney Green 1066) the name of the Acting Head, Mr. Lyons, and a sparse map with directions by tube and bus.

Three Weeks at Raine's Foundation School

RAINE'S SCHOOL WAS A FIVE-STORY, LATE NINETEENTH-CENTURY RED BRICK BUILDING WITH A SMALL PARK, KNOWN AS ARBOUR SQUARE, leading up to it, a bit of beauty that contrasted sharply with the dismal part of the East End in which it stood. Inside, the stairways by means of which one mounted these many storeys were wide and wooden, the walls there and everywhere else wainscoted in dark wood. I liked the place instantly. It looked like a school with its red brick and pitched roof. And it smelled like a school—as if the grimy male odor of generations of dirty young boys had managed to permeate even the woodwork, and being constantly renewed, constantly seeped back into the atmosphere of its rooms.

Separating the Sexes

But I describe only my part of the school. Raine's was rigorously divided into two parts: one for the boys, one for the girls. And the twain were never supposed to meet. Not only did the playground have a high, solid fence running down its middle, but also, on each floor, there were wrought-iron gates between the two sections, so that the boys and girls could see one another but not get close enough to inflict any serious damage. Although I wondered at the strict separation of the sexes that the gates enforced, as the school was run by the Church of England I wrote them off as a demonstration of religious Puritanism, though the more I taught mixed classes in future years and saw what a distraction the opposite sex is in the teen years, the happier I became with the idea of this sort of division.

The Headmaster and His Staff

The school, as befits a 19th century pile, was old-fashioned in other ways as well. The Headmaster's office was an oak-paneled study-like room that would not have been out of place had it belonged to a fellow at an Oxford college. It seemed even more incongruous when one considered the industrial near-slum area surrounding the school that provided the bulk of its pupils. Mr. Lyons looked at me from behind his round glasses, and after we had exchanged the usual language formulas that are considered *de rigueur* in such circumstances, slid out from behind his massive oak desk, which was neat as a pin, and took me to the classroom-sized room where the teachers gathered, peon-like, when duty was not calling them elsewhere (slumping into dirty lounge furniture, upholstered in wine naugahyde that looked bad enough to have been rejected by the Salvation Army as no longer of any value to humankind.)

Academic Gowns

Attached to this room was a cloakroom, where the teachers, as befitted the poor and underprivileged, which they were in England in those days, hung their mangy coats and dirty scarves. (Why, I ask myself now, did I want to become one of them?) In this cloakroom were the academic gowns that they were required—in an absurd pretense of scholarship—to wear in class and about the building. These were useful in covering up their shabby suits, but also, in the absence of a brush, in wiping extraneous material off the blackboard. I was lent the gown that belonged to Mr. Shivas, the man I was replacing. I wore it, as one can imagine, with considerable pride.

Victorian Toilets

In the bathroom reserved for teaching staff was one of those round-topped, porcelain Victorian toilets with a fitting round-topped wooden seat, made of some sort of

Victorian adamantine wood (bog oak, perhaps?), still as good as ever a hundred years later, the top of the bowl wrapped around like a condom and decorated with the most exquisite flower designs, both inside and out. It was so beautiful, I was even somewhat reluctant to pee into it. On the wall next to the toilet, as if juxtaposed as an example of modern ugliness, was one of the usual British, public, toilet-paper dispensers, which grudgingly dispensed slippery-smooth paper one small sheet at a time. On the top of each of these sandpaper-sized sheets was written, "London County Council," in case you might forget who was in this instance your benefactor; and on the bottom, "Now Wash Your Hands Please," in case you might spread horrible diseases about the city.

Jimmy Britton, Senior English Tutor

I was into only my second day of teaching at Raine's when Mr. Lyons came by the staff room and told me he'd had a call from Jimmy Britton, the Senior English Tutor at the Institute, and that he was coming that afternoon to see me. I had no idea why he was coming, and Mr. Lyons didn't give me a chance to ask, but I was curious rather than concerned about the visit. Britton, a wiry man in his thirties, who was the faculty expert on teaching poetry, arrived in time to watch me introduce a second form group to *Treasure Island*. I had begun by putting Stevenson's map of the island on the board and having the class copy it and discuss it. Britton sat through the class and more or less told me afterwards in a kindly way that he was unimpressed. "Not enough solid content," he said. (And he was right.) But he said he had not come to vet my teaching. Rather, he was upset at the Overseas Adviser's sending me to Raine's as a supply teacher. "One could be put off teaching for life by a bad experience at this point," he said. But as it was obvious— even if my class had been a wash-out from an academic point of view—that I was coping with the situation without any serious trouble, Britton went away satisfied that at least, as he said, he had made sure that everything was all right. There was also a bonus. This session of paid teaching was accepted by the Institute as equivalent to the three weeks of vacation practice which was "normally undertaken immediately before the University session opens" in one's home district. When I had previously made enquiries about this requirement, I had not been able to get a satisfactory answer as to how I was to proceed. There had been some mutterings of Christmas and Easter vacation time, and I was glad to see now that all speculation of this sort had been brought to an end.

Basil Dowling, New Zealand Poet

There was one interesting man on the staff at Raine's, Basil Dowling, a New Zealand poet—you'll find him represented in anthologies of New Zealand poetry—who had been living in London at that time for some years. Dowling, who stood out among the other teachers because he wore a rather fancy-pleated forest-green academic gown (over his shabby suit), was at this time a little unsteady on his feet. He had been hit on the head by a javelin at a school track meet in the early spring of that year and had only in September returned to work. He listened sympathetically to my complaints at having to teach Addison and Steele to a third form class, especially from a dilapidated, ink-blotted, red-covered edition that had been edited in 1894 and looked as if it had been printed about the same time and used continuously since.

Officialdom Catches Up with Me

In my last week at the school, with typical mid-20th-century British inefficiency—how did these people ever build and sustain such a massive empire, I wondered?—I received official confirmation of employment, on the official "Employment of Supply Teachers" form, from one F. S. Constant, Divisional Officer, in the Education Officer's Department of the London County Council. It told me I was to "take up duty as a supply teacher" at Raine's and "remain there" until the return of Mr. Shivas. Better late than never, I suppose.

Overseas Students are Lectured on Behavior

BUT MY TEMPORARY JOB AT RAINE'S WAS NOT QUITE THE END OF MY INVOLVEMENT WITH THE OFFICE OF THE OVERSEAS STUDENT Adviser. On the day the term began at the Institute, October 3, 1961, there was, among many other things, a meeting called to which all overseas students were to attend. A group of perhaps fifty students gathered in the room assigned for this meeting. There were blacks from Africa, people of various colors from the Indian subcontinent and other parts of the empire and commonwealth. There were, at most, eight or ten whites, three of whom I joined at the back of the room. A fellow Canadian, Howard Johnston, with whom I was to act the following Spring in the Institute's dramatic production of *The Dark of the Moon*, and who was later a Member of Parliament in Ottawa, and two Americans from Columbia University, who were at the Institute on some kind of exchange program.

The speaker harangued and warned and generally condescended to the audience. He did not tell the gathering that they were to behave like civilized people now that they were in the capital of the empire; but he might as well have. It was my first real experience of the racism that is always under the surface in England. It was unstated in any exact sense, but it was nevertheless up-front, blatant, arrogant, and out-of-place in the 1960s. Wogs still began at Calais.

When the harangue was finished and the meeting was breaking up, the speaker beckoned us whites to the front of the room and spoke to us in sentences riddled with italics. (At the time it did not occur to me that we had, in a sense, in gathering in a group, made our own unconscious racist statement.) "What are *you people* doing here," he said. "*You* shouldn't have been told to be here. *This* wasn't for *you*. It was for *them*."

Later that day, in the Marlborough, the pub in Torrington Place around the corner from the Institute which became our local for the year, I met for the first time James Burston, the principal History tutor, a confirmed, middle-aged bachelor, who liked to hold his tutorial seminars over a pint of beer, and who lived in, of all places, the Reform Club. When I mentioned the overseas student meeting to him, he said: "It's all very well to complain about racism. But things aren't quite that simple. For example, we get students from India applying here who give as their qualifications: B.A. Bombay and then in parentheses (Failed). We don't get that sort of thing from America."

But enough of Burston for the moment. We'll be seeing more of him later in the session.

The Beginning of a Great Year

AND SO BEGAN MY YEAR AT THE UNIVERSITY OF LONDON INSTITUTE OF EDUCATION. IT WAS A YEAR IN WHICH I HAD TO COME TO TERMS with the sloppy thinking that pervades all teacher-training faculties and the textbooks they employ—and this place was purportedly one of the best in the world. The level of thinking peculiar to the social sciences was particularly onerous in the Institute, as the philosophy of liberalism being developed there was imposed with a fervor that can only be described as religious. The professors, each one a pope in his own specialty, possessed the truth about how their subject-area should be taught, and like all people with the truth, they did not look kindly upon opposing ideas. I was not in agreement with much of what they promulgated, but as I did not want to be burned at some sort of academic stake, I kept my mouth shut most of the time. But not all of the time. During my final teaching practice, I had a huge argument over the way a play should be taught after a class visit to Central Foundation School by my tutor, Mrs. Moore. It probably cost me a "distinction" on my diploma.

In terms of human contact, though, it was a splendid year. I made many good and lasting friends and took away with me a raft of fond memories. And it was at the Institute that I met the woman who was in the following year to become my wife.

Return to London

CP Train by the Kicking Horse River 1961

Calgary Airport: Aunt Clara, Charley Stringer (r), and a Friend

Empress of England

Maureen Graham Tanning in Peace Haven Garden with Mrs. Heslin's Daughter, Margaret

Rallies in Trafalgar Square

Oswald Mosley's Fascists
August 1961

**Bertrand Russell's Campaign
for Nuclear Disarmament**
September 1961

Raine's Foundation School (2003)
Now a Community College

Christ Church in Woburn Square

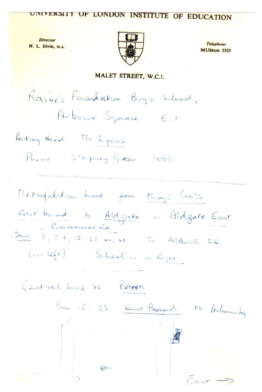

Direction to Raine's School

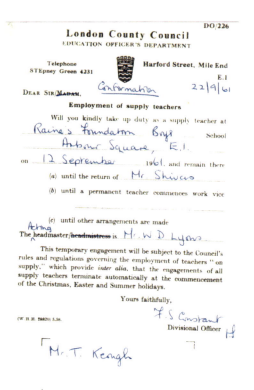

Supply Teaching Appointment

Terry at Speakers' Corner
Hyde Park, August 1961

Tuition for Fall Term ▶

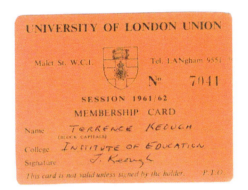

New Institute of Education Building
In Woburn Square

Bill for Room and Board, Fall Term

Chapter 14: Autumn at the Institute

EN ROUTE TO A PGCE[1]

> An intractable phenomenon of writing a memoir is that you begin to miss the people you are writing about. I found myself wanting to call up people I hadn't seen or spoken to in more than thirty years.
>
> John Irving, "Slipped Away," **The New Yorker** (Dec. 11, 1995), 77

> It had been for himself so very soluble a problem to live in England assimilated yet unconverted.
>
> Henry James, **The Portrait of a Lady**, 1881

The Hostel on Woburn Square

THE FOUR-STOREY BRICK BUILDING, BLACKENED BY DECADES OF LONDON SMOG, THAT HOUSED THE MEN'S HOSTEL OF THE UNIVERSITY OF LONDON INSTITUTE OF EDUCATION ON WOBURN Square was part of a square-long row of similar, joined buildings that ran along the west side. The interior was divided into fifteen good-sized rectangular double rooms, each furnished in a spartan though adequate manner with pairs of single beds, bureaus, bookcases, desks with matching straight-backed chairs, and comfortable, vinyl-clad easy chairs, all in a modern plain style. There was a sink with hot and cold water. Above the sink, on the wall, was a cabinet with a mirror door. The room was arranged so that there was a sleeping/working area at the window end and a lounging/socializing area at the end where you entered the room from the hallway. A high, double-hung window opened out on to a minuscule balcony, which was fenced in by ornamented wrought-iron. What you did was throw up the bottom sash, bend over, and step out.

On each floor there was a bathroom with a shower. On the ground floor was a small common room. As a group we ordered in—and paid for from the £1 per person per session hostel fee for social activities—various papers, including *The Guardian, The*

---

[1] The Post Graduate Certificate in Education (PGCE) was the University of London equivalent of a Dip. Ed., a B.Ed., or an M.Ed. graduate degree at other institutions.

Telegraph, and *The Times Educational Supplement*, the latter to provide us with information regarding the job-market. I remember looking with romantic interest at ads for places like Thailand and Samoa, though in the end I got a job through the usual method when a tutor recommend me to a London headmaster she knew. In the basement of the hostel, lighted from the street by a rectangular well, was a breakfast room, where we were dished out our breakfasts through a hatch by a distant but not unfriendly Irish couple, Patrick and Mary, who also cleaned the rooms and changed the linen and towels once a week. All of this, plus dinner every day at the women's hostel at 15 Bedford Way, the next street over to the east, *and* full board on weekends, cost £44 ($C135) for the term, October 2 to December 14, a bargain any way you look at it.

Jim Honeybone's Newfangled Stereo

MY ROOMMATE FOR THE YEAR WAS JIM HONEYBONE. HE ARRIVED ON THE MORNING OF OCTOBER 3, THE FIRST DAY OF TERM. Immediately, before unpacking the rest of his stuff began to set up his stereo, the first I had seen with speakers separated from the amplifier and player by lengths of wire. This was cutting-edge technology at the time. In fact, *stereo* technology was itself very new. I had first run across it at a party at a flat in Knightsbridge owned by a relative of my painter friend, John Davison, a couple of years before. There, the system had been one of those long rectangular pieces of furniture with the speakers at either end. We sat across from it, beer in hand, and *listened seriously* to the demonstration record, as bowling balls, trains (steam whistles at the fore), and sundry moving objects rumbled from one side of the box to the other.

Jim's system, oddly it seems now (when one might not be surprised to find one as an option on a new clothes drier or bathtub), contained no radio. The consequence of this omission—and perhaps the reason for it—was that Jim didn't need to cough up the Institute's charge of "5/ for wireless sets (not battery)" or obtain the necessary wireless licence. This licence fee was used to support the BBC, which was in those days the only radio network allowed in the country. It broadcast on three frequencies: the Light Program (popular music for the unwashed), the Home Program (the last generation's popular music for the undereducated masses), and the Third Program (music and comment of an esoteric nature, the more esoteric the better, for the 15% of the population who were allowed access to the superb education given by the grammar schools). Philistines (that is, most of the young people) listened to Radio Luxembourg, an American-type station that beamed the music that most young people wanted to listen to from outside the jurisdiction of English law. There were also pirate stations which were trying to break into the market, some of them (appropriately for pirate stations) on ships off the coast.

Jim's good friend, and later mine, David Hepworth, arrived at the hostel with a battery radio, for which (though he didn't need to pay the Institute fee) he should have had a licence. He didn't have one, so he risked a fine if a licensing inspector happened by at some point in the year. In those pre-transistor days (the device had been invented but was not yet universally in use), one needed a small "A" battery (about twice the size of a pack of cigarettes) and a large "B" battery (about the size of a squared-off loaf of bread) to power the tubes (in England, "valves") of a radio. These were attached externally with wire leads. It was all very clumsy and very heavy. But it did mean that beaches, public parks, and otherwise quiet neighbourhood streets were not invaded by pimply punks carrying enormous ghetto-blasters, weighing nothing, half as big as their owners, and for the most part consisting of speakers, with which their owners proceeded to destroy a peace that (to pollute St. Paul to the Philippians) clearly passeth their understanding. Honeybone did not disturb *my* peace with *his* system. I don't think he had more than half a dozen long-play records. Among these were Mozart's "Jupiter" Symphony and a selection of songs by Eartha Kitt, both of which I enjoyed.

Jim and Jean, Rosemary and Terry

FROM THE BEGINNING, JIM AND I GOT ALONG WELL. HE HAD A ROUND FACE AND DEEP-SET, SPANIEL-BROWN EYES THAT WERE BOTH ALERT and piercing. His dark-brown hair was parted straight on the right side of his head, and he was often occupied flinging back the hank of it that hung over his forehead. He usually wore a suit, beneath which were an oxford-cloth, chequered shirt, a tie, and a sleeveless sweater. He was neither short nor tall, fat nor thin. When we met for the first time, he looked to me the way a typical 1950's Oxbridge student should look. He had done his university degree at Caius College, Cambridge, from which he had just graduated with a degree in history.

Jim had a broad grin and laughed easily. He was by nature and upbringing a conservative; but through the year at the Institute, which was a hotbed of progressive educational theory (much of which, in the next generation, would pollute a large portion of the English-speaking world), he developed a wish to be an educational radical. This attitude led him to turn down a teaching job at Rhodean, one of the better public schools, where he would have fitted in well, to take a job in a new comprehensive school in Notting Hill, at that time a rapidly declining area of London. The experiment was not a success. After marrying Jean Price, he moved to a job in the much more civilized wilds of Ormskirk, Lancashire.[2]

Curiously enough, Jean, who was from Liverpool, shared a room in the Institute's Bedford Way women's hostel with *my* future wife, Rosemary Latter, who was from Cambridge. We ate dinner with the women students at Bedford Way. In time, we began in a normal way to form liaisons with particular people, with the result that most of the time we sat together during our meals. I don't remember much about the meals, so they can't have been half bad. One peculiarity I do recall is Miss Stephenson, the Warden, cutting corners by buying mushroom stems rather than whole mushrooms at the Covent Garden market. Another is the habit we developed of getting after-dinner coffee for each other, and David Hepworth's being amused when I for the first time asked for cream and "a small half" teaspoon of sugar. The "small half" amused him.

---

[2] Jean and Jim eventually moved to Banbury (of "lead a cock horse" fame), near Oxford, where they raised a family, while Jim taught in a college and established a thriving business producing teaching aids for history and social studies classes.

> *During the months of our courtships (does anybody "court" anymore?), we as courting couples will, got up to things in our respective rooms that were fraught with potential embarrassment if somebody else, like a roommate with a key, unexpectedly appeared. These things we referred to as "18th-Century Activities." In order to avoid embarrassment, we adopted a system which was used by undergraduates at Caius, in which we hung a shoe on the handle on the outside of our room doors as a warning. But sometimes we forgot, and on at least one occasion, Jim, who tended to be absent-minded, even failed to see the shoe on the handle of the door he was opening, or at least to take it in, unlocked the door, bounded in, took a quick and startled look, and then swung around and took off at the speed of light, much more to the amusement than the embarrassment of Rosemary and myself.*

A Honeybone World

ONCE, DURING THE WINTER TERM, JIM, WHO LATER TOLD THE STORY WITH A GOOD DEAL OF GLEE, WAS STOPPED BY A POLICEMAN about midnight as he returned from an illicit late visit to Jean's room—guests had to be out by 10:30 p.m., though nobody really policed the rule. Apparently, someone had been robbed in nearby Russell Square and the police had fanned out on foot, looking for the culprit.

What's your name?" said the constable.

"Honeybone."

"Honeybone?" said the constable. "That's an unusual name."

"Not to me," Jim replied, a little too flippantly, thrusting his hands tightly into the pockets of his suit jacket, a stance he sometimes adopted when nervous.

"What've you got in your pockets, then?" the constable asked.

Jim, who had been on a quick trip home the day before and had dropped in to see Jean on his way back to Woburn Square, pulled out the contents, a safety razor and a toothbrush.

The constable told him to continue on his way.

Jim was seriously into religion at this point in his life, much to the consternation, apparently, of his atheistic parents. Every Sunday morning he marched down the square to Christ Church, which was High Anglican (Jim had no use for broader forms of Anglican worship), for the morning service. At about the same time, Jean Price and I would walk the eight or ten blocks to St. Patrick's in Soho Square, the closest Catholic Church. Rosemary, I think, usually spent the morning playing the piano at the hostel.

Part of Jim's high-church attitude was reflected in his love of Milton. When he was alone in our room, he read aloud and histrionically from *Paradise Lost*. But "read" is the wrong word. He *declaimed* the lines in the most stentorian of voices. If the window was open, I would hear, on my way into the building, the ways of God being justified to man, or at least to Jim Honeybone, as the lines roared out into the square. And he didn't sit as he read them. On a number of occasions I entered the room to his pacing up and down with Milton at arm's length, as if he were some kind of incarnation of Don Quixote de la Mancha, spreading the good news into the darkness visible of Woburn Square.

New Friends at the Marlborough

David Hepworth

AFTER HE HAD FINISHED PUTTING TOGETHER HIS STEREO EQUIPMENT (BY, IN FACT, PUTTING IT APART) AND DONE A CURSORY UNPACKING of his other things, Jim invited me to join him and some of his Cambridge friends for lunch at the Marlborough, a pub around the corner from us. David Hepworth, Jim's best friend from his days at Caius, who was later also to be a good friend of mine, was the son of a prosperous building contractor. He came from Cleckheaton, Yorkshire. He was built squarely and strongly, as one might imagine a Yorkshireman should be built. His Yorkshire accent was slight. When I commented on that fact, David claimed that he spoke a different English from his mother tongue when he was in the south of England, a dialect which he had had to learn in order to survive in Cambridge. By the same token, he had to be careful to remember to revert to his mother tongue in order to survive when he went home for the vacations. He wore large, squarish, brown-plastic glasses, which kept slipping down his nose, making it necessary for him to push them back up with his index finger. When he laughed, he often laughed so hard that tears ran out of his eyes, at which point he would remove his glasses and wipe his eyes on his sleeve. His straight, medium-brown hair was combed back from his forehead in a pompadour.

> *That first day at the Marlborough I apparently told the story of my dog, Pedro, and the grocery delivery man in far-away Revelstoke of the 1940s—or so David told me month's later, having been much amused by it. I have told this story in my chapter on Revelstoke, but let me tell it again in this different world. My mother was talking to the delivery man when the dog, a good-natured, black, mongrel spaniel with a white tie (perhaps of similar breed to the delivery man), began to nuzzle up to him. "Pay-dee!" admonished my mother, for that was our nickname for the dog. "No," said the delivery man, "pay day is Tuesday."*

David had a good deal of humanity and sensitivity and reacted emotionally, though strongly and quietly, in his relationships with the world. He was a good friend to Mary Ann, a black girl from Sierra Leone, whose surname I have forgotten. Her father was the Minister of Education there. They used to spend hours together in David's room, and I used to wonder, with my filthy mind, what was going on in there. But the answer, I think, was nothing but kindness for a black girl a long way from home. David was also a good friend of a male black from Sierra Leone, whose name was "Tuesday." (Remember "Friday" in *Robinson Crusoe*?) He did not, however, spend hours in his room with *him*, as he did with Mary Ann. Eventually, early in the second term, David met Margaret, who was somebody's executive assistant somewhere in the city (though we would not have called her that then), who, though in no way unattractive, was like himself, square. They were a good pair, two good people, very much alike. A year or so later they married and moved to Acomb, Yorkshire, where David had taken a teaching position.

"Bossers"—David Boswell

One of the other people I met on that day was David Boswell, also a graduate of Caius, who looked like an ideal candidate for an Anglican vicarage, but who was actually much involved with the Society of Friends, or Quakers. "Bossers," as we called him, was quiet and respectable, but he also had a fine sense of humour and was, in his way, eccentric. He always wore his wrist watch, for example, in the handkerchief pocket of his suit jacket, suspended from his lapel buttonhole on a chain. He was very bright. Once, during a boring lecture on education and health, given to a large group of about 400 in the Assembly Hall by a woman who insisted on calling funguses "foonj-eye," I passed him a note: "Add the next line: 'Christmas comes but once a year'." He returned it, cleverly, with "Usually in November." Bossers was medium-height and had a trim frame, like a wedge that thins rapidly from the shoulders down. He had the sort of kinky hair that stands up on one side of the head and makes its wearer look as if he's about to take off side-ways.

Autumn Term Class Routine

ON THE FIRST DAY OF TERM, OCTOBER 3, 1961, WE WERE TOLD TO GO TO THE ASSEMBLY HALL IN THE SENATE BUILDING AT 9:30, WHERE we were divided into those with Surnames A—L and those with Surnames M—Z, filled out our registration forms, and paid the term's tuition of £62.10.0d (C$190). Those of us whose subject was English then proceeded to the Small Hall, where we met our tutors: Nancy Martin, Jimmy Britton, and Marianne Moore (always "Mrs." Moore, as in *A Passage to India*, apparently in deference to her age, at most, late forties), and the younger crowd of Mr. Stevenson, Mr. Pattison, Mr. Whitehead (whose first names I have forgotten), and Jocelyn Emberton. Mrs. Moore, who was assigned as tutor to me by some mysterious bureaucratic power, was grey-haired and a bit overweight. She was the specialist in drama and reading. I was a bit disappointed in being assigned to her. Nancy Martin and Jimmy Britton were the groovy ones to be with.

After registering, we had the rest of that first week free. I've always admired the English capacity to organize this sort of academic schedule, full of positive negatives: not too soon, not too quickly, and not too long. We didn't register till October; we waited a week before classes started; we had classes for only five weeks; we followed this short term with three weeks of teaching practice—but only Monday to Thursday, as we returned to the Institute on Friday (mornings only) for the regular Friday lectures. Then, teaching practice over, we had what they called "The Last 3 Days of Term" (2½, actually, as the last day, Wednesday, December 13, was over at noon).

Can anything be more civilized than that? Unfortunately, it was not only a question of civilization. In England, the spectre of the class system is always lurking in the background, in this case, leisured education for the leisured classes. We future teachers were hanging on to this leisured-class group for a while (mainly so our tutors could be a part of it) by our clean (as yet unbitten) fingernails, before forging forth into a world of very hard, gruelling, nerve-wracking, underpaid and under-appreciated work.

But beneath this leisured approach, all other considerations aside, lies a profound understanding of the length to which human beings, teachers, students, and administrators, can extend themselves in a learning situation before they tire and begin to fake it. The maximum is about six weeks. At that point, the whole caboodle needs either to shift gears (in our case, we shifted into teaching practice), or to have a week's holiday, which was the common procedure in schools in England at that time.

From October 10 to November 13, we followed the same weekly routine. In the mornings, on Mondays, Tuesdays and Thursdays, we had lectures and seminars from 10:20 to 11:05 on History of Education or Philosophy of Education. These classes were followed, from 11:20 to 12:05, by lectures (or tutorials with no more than 8 to a group) which were concerned with specific areas of the teaching of English: Children's Reading (Moore), Children's Writing (Martin), Poetry in School (Britton), What Can One Do in a Grammar Lesson? (Pattison), Drama in School, The Scope of English Teaching, Mass Media, Voice and Speech of the Teacher, et cetera, ad nauseam.

In the afternoons, from 2:00 to 3:30, we worked in a workshop format on such things as play production. On Friday mornings, there were three large lectures, one after another, in Beveridge Hall, (which held 400), named for the Minister of Education who had set up the post-war education system, still largely in place in 1961. These lectures were also piped into the Small Hall next door for the overflow crowd (late risers, another 100 or so). The subject matter was anything that could be fitted into three areas: Principles of Education, Educational Psychology, and the English Education System.

So, here was our leisurely student world. On Mondays and Tuesdays we had no classes before 10:30. On Wednesdays, the sole get-together was a tutorial at 11:20. On Thursdays and Fridays we had what was seen as an early start—at 9:30. (There were no classes on Friday afternoons, of course. That would be decidedly déclassé.) Every day we had a copious two hours for lunch. And the entire term for these classes was remarkably short—5 weeks. Considering the mainly inane and boring nature of Education as a subject of study, for me this leisurely approach was a lifesaver. I loved it.

Teaching Practice in London's East End

Introduction to My School

I WAS ASSIGNED TO DO MY TEACHING PRACTICE AT CENTRAL FOUNDATION BOYS' GRAMMAR SCHOOL, COWPER STREET, CITY ROAD, E. C. 2. Head Master: J.P. Cowan, M.A. (Cantab.). This school, in the east end of London, served an area that was largely commercial and industrial, not as good an area as my friends at the Institute were being sent to; but, I suppose, it might have been argued, it was an area good enough for a colonial from Canada, who would have grown up in the midst of wild creatures, and who was thus not only used to the behaviour of savages but also would know how to handle them. Its graduates would need all of the qualities expressed in the school motto, *Spe.Labore.Fide*, to get anywhere in the world; and even with a liberal sprinkling of each of these sterling assets, piously imposed by those who set up the original foundation, the odds were against them.[3] In response to my informing the school by letter, as requested by the Institute, that I would be descending on them in November, I received the following note:

> *Dear Mr. Keough,*
>
> *Thank you for your letter—we shall look forward very much to welcoming you here on Monday, 13th November, when your teaching practice, I believe, starts. The school is best reached by underground to Old Street Station (Northern Line); Cowper Street is the first turning on the left off City Road going towards Moorgate. The school is half-way down on the right.*
>
> *Yours sincerely,*
>
> *J.P. Cowan, M.A.*
>
> HEAD MASTER

At Central Foundation, the timetable was made up of 7 class periods per day. I taught 4 classes Mondays, Tuesdays, and Wednesdays, and 5 on Thursdays. I was supervised by John Roden, the man whose classes I was mainly taking over. He observed me on my first day, and though he was instructed by the Institute to stay with his student teacher throughout the first week, when he saw that I could handle the situation, he left me to my own devices.

---

[3] When I returned to London in 2003, I went back to Central Foundation School, which is still operating in the same place and in the same building. My visit there, unfortunately, fell within the Easter break, so the school was closed. There is a picture of it in the following chapter, *Bloomsbury, Brighton, and Blackheath*.

> *John Roden (a horrible name for a teacher—the students, of course, called him Mr. Rodent) was a large, genial man in his forties, with square, rimless glasses, who had a great love of Wagner's Ring, on at Covent Garden at the time, and a strange and obsessive interest in the minor English poet, George Barker. He especially liked the sonnet, "To His Mother," in which the mother in question is described as being "large as Asia," and which has the fine last line, "And she shall move from mourning into morning." (He brought these aspects of this sonnet up often enough that I still remember them decades later!) "Terry," he would say, coming into the staff room, "I've just been thinking about what you were saying about Barker's "Mother"—and off he would go.*

At the time, both Roden and I were unaware of Barker's Canadian connection as the long-time lover of Ottawa-raised writer, Elizabeth Smart, then literary editor of the English *Vogue* magazine. Smart gave birth to and raised four of Barker's children while he continued most of the time to live with his wife and legitimate family, clearly indicating that in spite of her surname, Elizabeth was not very. Smart's one successful book, *By Grand Central Station I Sat Down and* Wept—surely one of the great titles in all literature—has since the seventies (it was published in 1945) moved from cult status to something more in the main stream, or, at least, that is what is asserted by those who claim to have been able to read it through to the end, and even by some who have not.

Christians, Jews, and Mrs. Moore

THE SCHOOL HAD AN ODD STUDENT BODY, HALF CHRISTIAN AND HALF JEWISH. THIS MIXTURE PRESENTED SOME PROBLEMS IN HOLDING THE assembly with which all schools in England began each day, and which, by law, had to be *religious* (i.e., in the non-Roman-Catholic system, that generally meant *Anglican-religious*). At Central Foundation, we would march into the assembly hall in the morning, teachers on the raised platform at the front, students herded by the prefects into their places in the body of the hall, and when all that had been attended to, and a suitable pause had been allowed to make itself felt, in would SWISH (in capital letters, or so it seemed) the Head Master, J. P. Cowan, M.A. (Cantab.), in all his greatness, complete with cap and gown. The problems involved in accommodating the religious differences were solved by having the religious readings taken from the Old Testament, and the hymns from those without clear-cut Christian content. This arrangement, I'm happy to say, satisfied both Jews and Christians.

Twice during this teaching practice I was visited by Mrs. Moore, who always announced ahead of time exactly when she was coming, so one could do one's best. She also prescribed the type of subject matter she would like to see taught. On her first visit, I was to teach poetry. In observing the class, she was much impressed when, during a discussion of the ballad, "Sir Patrick Spens," a lad in the front row offered to recite from memory in the next class "The Minstrel Boy," by Thomas Moore. (No relation, I think!) "I can't imagine why he would want to do something old-fashioned like that," she said, meaning (a) recite, and (b) recite "The Minstrel Boy," which is far too sentimental to appeal to *good* modern taste. But then, although useless in itself, the offer of the boy was an indication to her that I was inspiring the class, and she encouraged me greatly by saying, "You know, I think you are going to be *very* good."

> *I was relieved that Mrs. Moore had not noticed the pimply Jewish lad in the second row from the front (she was, as usual, at the back of the room), his religious persuasion identifiable because he was, like most of the Jewish lads, wearing a yalmaca. Somewhere in the middle of "Sir Patrick Spens" I had glanced in his direction and inadvertently noticed that, between his desk and his body, standing bolt upright out of his fly was his rigid, circumcised cock. In a trice I looked away, and did not look back again until near the end of the class, when, glancing his way—my trepidation covered by apparent nonchalance—I was relieved to see that it was gone.*

This event, whether designed to shock me or upset my classroom routine with my tutor in attendance, or whether just a manifestation of uncontrolled male adolescent sexuality, convinced me once and for all of the benefits of co-education, in which sort of system it was unlikely to happen. In fact, I spent the rest of my career in co-educational institutions and never experienced this sort of grossness again.

On her second "visit," Mrs. Moore asked to see me teach drama, her specialty. Now, at the Institute the theory was that the students had to act out the play as they read it, even though they had never seen the lines before, had no experience in acting, and, in some cases, were not very fluent oral readers. Otherwise, the philosophical basis of this theory went, they are merely *reading* the play and they will not then experience it as drama.

So, with Mrs. Moore smiling encouragement from the back of the room, I moved my mind away from the old music hall song "Don't have any more, Mrs. Moore," and we began to act out the assassination scene from *Julius Caesar*.

> *I put Caesar on a chair on top of my desk at the front, where he was in tottering danger of coming to some real as well as imagined harm, and after murdering such lines as "low-crooked curtsies, and base fawning spaniel," the conspirators proceeded to climb on to the chairs around the desk and dispatch with daggers of the imagination the noblest Roman of them all. "Et too Broot," said Caesar, showing a total ignorance of what should have been his mother tongue—and to me, added—"Is that Latin, or something?" "Fall down," said one of the conspirators. "You're supposed to be dead." "Wait a minute," I said. "Just flop down on the desk, Caesar. We don't want you to hurt yourself for real." So Caesar slid to the top of the desk, and his killers waved their imaginary daggers in the air.*

And so on. It was as close to chaos as one can imagine. Mrs. Moore loved it. She flashed her perfectly-arranged (though rather large) teeth at me and said: "You know, I think you are going to be *very, very* good."

Dinner with David Reynard and "Ducks"

THE HEAD OF THE CENTRAL FOUNDATION ENGLISH DEPARTMENT, DAVID RENYARD, A MAN IN HIS EARLY FORTIES WITH THE KIND OF soft, unwrinkled complexion that made him look younger than his years, in spite of the grey in his hair, asked me to bring my girlfriend (about whom I had told him) to what he called "an informal Saturday-night dinner" at his house.

He was a kind man whose main claim to fame was his friendship with Alex Comfort, who at that time was known only as a minor poet. David remarked one day with his usual chuckle that Alex had told him that the missionary position in sex was the only one officially approved of by the Catholic Church, a fact that he subsequently made use of in one of his poems. "That's the sort of thing Alex digs up," David said. He was subsequently to dig up a lot more positions than that, and become very famous and moderately rich through the sale of his *Joy of Sex* books. It is clear now, though, that it was essentially the bourgeois acceptability of the brilliant dirty drawings that made the books so successful, rather than Comfort's text. But it was, after all, the Sixties, though we didn't yet realize what that meant in 1961, a period when the main-stream publication of such books was possible for the first time in history, and when everything about sex (no pun meant) was up for grabs. Comfort just had the right idea at the right time.

> *In the course of that evening, when the ladies were in the kitchen doing the washing up, as ladies did in those days, I asked David why he had not considered becoming a head master. He said that he had fully intended to do so, but that when he should have been pursuing it, the long illness and death of his first wife had made the idea impossible. Now that he was in his forties, it was obviously too late. I had not even known that there was a first wife. I could see that the question had hurt him, and I was ashamed. When I think of him now, I think of this moment—and of the old-fashioned, roguish slang he used in calling his wife "Ducks."*

How the Term Came to an End

WHEN TEACHING PRACTICE ENDED, THE FOLLOWING ROLLICKING, TONGUE-IN-CHEEK, HAND-WRITTEN INVITATION WAS SENT TO Rosemary:

Lord Boswell (Bossers, to friends) and multi-millionaire

(tailoring) Mr. D. Hepworth hereby issue an invitation to

> *Miss Rosemary Latter*
> *and friend*
> *(Canadians, for this purpose, may, if ladies so desire, be included)*
>
> *to an after-dinner drink*
> *(quality, but not quantity guaranteed)*
> *on Thursday Evening*
> *Nominal Reason for Celebration (if required)*
> *End of Teaching Practice*
> *Only Forbidden Subject: Teaching Practice*
> *Facilities for 18th Century Activities will be provided later in*
>
> *the evening, so will lovers please refrain from disturbing the*
>
> *peace of less-Lawrentian-type guests until drinks are over.*

And so ended, in a friendly and civilized manner, the autumn term at the Institute. David, Jim, Jean, and the rest, headed home for the "Vac." I moved once again into Peace Haven, as I had found a temporary job in the pre-Christmas Post Office in Acton.

And as for Christmas itself, that was nicely taken care of when Rosemary asked me to spend it with her family in Cambridge.

MY SHORT CAREER AS AN ACTON POSTMAN

> Lord Houghton spoke and sat by me at luncheon: he showed off one of the new "halfpenny cards" (which are to come into use tomorrow) on which he had written a note in Italian to his sister. They are neat little articles, with the stamp printed on the back: you send them open through the post. [September 30, 1870]
>
> John Bailey, Ed. The Diary of Lady Frederick Cavendish, 1923

IS THERE ANY INSTITUTION WHICH BELONGS MORE TO THE NINETEENTH CENTURY THAN THE BRITISH POST OFFICE? THE ACTON BUILDING I worked in over the Christmas holidays was built in that era. From the look of it, some of the dirt (inside and out) had been there for a hundred years or so. It was, in a word, grotty.[4] The supervisor was a string-bean of a man with steel-framed, round glasses, crinkly hair, and, a bad temper, for which I did not blame him, having to try to get some work out of the British workman of 1961. The men had an attitude that was common in the post-war years—do as little work as possible, an attitude that by the 1960s had effectively destroyed many British industries that had been hugely successful in pre-war international trade, many of them dating back to Victorian times.

I was assigned to learn the Bollo Lane area, near Acton Town tube station. You began by sorting mail into a board, a bank of narrow, vertical slots above a counter-like desk. Each slot had the name of a street or part of a street into which you fine-sorted mail

---

[4] I'm happy to say that the old Post Office building was replaced in the 1970s.

which had already been rough-sorted for your board. Once you had your mail sorted, and had taken it out and delivered it, you could go home.

> *I shared my board area with Erik, who taught me the rudiments of sorting. He was a bouncy, short, and rather rotund youngish man with coke-bottle thick glasses. His accent was ultra-low-class London; so much so, that I often had trouble understanding what he was saying. One phrase I remember clearly, however, as I found it funny, contained his instructions as to which part of the board we would each work on: "This 'ere part," he said, "is mine, an 'at air part is urine."*

After a couple of days, I had learned my board well enough to get myself into trouble with the other sorters. It seemed to me that it made sense to sort my board as quickly as possible, get out and deliver what I'd sorted, and go home. But the union people, each alert to the danger of someone's making it obvious how under-worked they really were, taunted me into slowing down. They were not vicious, but they were unpleasant, and I was unhappy in their midst from that time on.

When I combined this go-as-slow-as-possible attitude with the mind-destroying boredom of the job, the situation became unendurable. So at the end of the week I told the supervisor I was quitting. *Now.* "But," he said, glaring at me through his thick, round glasses, "you can't do that. You're the only one who knows that board. If you leave, how will I get those people's Christmas mail out to them in time?" This appeal to sentiment was disingenuous. I told him I didn't know how he was going to get the mail out, but I did know that I had to leave. When he saw it was hopeless, he grudgingly wished me luck. I walked out of the building feeling guilty; as I had, in fact, left him in the lurch, and in the end he had been understanding.

That evening, I wandered the nearly-deserted streets of Acton, so familiar to me now they were like home, down Creswick Road to Horn Lane and the High Street. I knew I should not have quit my job at the Post Office. I needed the money I wasn't going to be getting. But I was relieved I had done so. Rosemary was not expecting me to arrive in Cambridge until Christmas Eve, and that left me a week with nothing to do and the expense of keeping myself for that time. I was bothering myself with all of this when just off the High Street on Mill Hill Road I saw a big brown teddy bear in a shop window. The bear gave me a plan.

Back at Peace Haven, I telephoned Rosemary (Cambridge 58485) and told her I was at loose ends, but that I had found something for her that I thought she'd really like. She consulted with her parents, and they said why didn't I come up a few days early. So the next day I bought the teddy bear. I named him "Aloysius," after the teddy bear kept by Sebastian Flyte in Evelyn Waugh's *Brideshead Revisited*. The following scene, in which we learn the teddy bear's name, occurs when narrator Charles Ryder follows a young man he doesn't at that point know into the hairdressers:

> "That," said the barber, as I took his chair, "was Lord Sebastian Flyte. A most amusing young gentleman. . . . What do you suppose Sebastian wanted? A hair brush for his

> *Teddy-bear; it had to have very stiff bristles, not, Lord Sebastian said, to brush him with, but to threaten him with a spanking when he was sulky. He bought a very nice one with an ivory back and he's having 'Aloysius' engraved on it—that's the bear's name."*

In Acton, I packed my suitcase, tucked my Aloysius under my arm, and took the underground to Euston Street Station, where I boarded an evening express for Cambridge.

Christmas in Cambridge

> The loveliest confusion of gothic windows and ancient trees, of grassy banks and mossy balustrades, of sun-chequered avenues and groves, of lawns and gardens and terraces, of single arched bridges spanning the little stream, which . . . looks as if it had been "turned on" for ornamental purposes.
> Henry James, "Cambridge," ***Portrait of Places***, 1883

Getting to Know the Latters

ROSEMARY MET MY TRAIN AND WAS DELIGHTED WITH ALOYSIUS. WE TOOK THE NUMBER 1 BUS TO HER HOME AT 7 KIMBERLEY ROAD, ONE of a series of very modest, two-story brick row-houses that were built on patriotically-named streets just after the Boer War. It was not an area in which university people were generally to be found; it was town rather than gown: though G. G. Coulton, the well-known medievalist, had at one time lived at number 90. On the ground floor of the Latter house, a hall ran along the left side from the front door to the breakfast room (so-called), off of which was a minute kitchen. From the hall, doors led off to the right to a small living room and a smaller dining room. Each of these rooms, like the breakfast room, had a coal fireplace for heat. I was to learn that two rooms were not to be heated at the same time, as that was an extravagance; and there was no sign of extravagance at 7 Kimberley Road, even at Christmas.

A reversing stairway between the dining and breakfast rooms, with a landing half-way, led to the second floor. There were three small bedrooms leading off the hall, a bathroom, and a warming closet around the hot-water tank, where spare towels and sheets were kept. From the window in the bedroom at the back you could see a small garden, about as long and thin as the house. There was heat only in the bathroom, provided by an electric element that was attached to the wall, and I soon discovered that it took all the time you needed to do your morning ablutions to heat the room, at which point you had to remember (on pain of something not too short of capital punishment) to turn the element off, a movement one might be excused in forgetting, as Cambridge can be damnably cold in winter. I quickly learned that it was a good idea to stay in bed in the morning until someone else had used the bathroom and warmed it up a little.

Veteran Bert

Rosemary's parents were, on the English scale of things, lower-middle-class. Her father, Herbert ("Bert"), had served as a Tommy in the Salonika campaign during the First World War—one of the "Gardeners of Salonika," as they were known; because, as there was no fighting to do in that area, their officers kept them busy digging and re-digging their positions. In this respect, he was lucky. It certainly beat fighting on the Western Front. Every November 11, he joined his diminishing group of veterans in London for the Remembrance Day Parade, until, in the late Sixties, he stopped going, as there were only four of them left. Through all the intervening years, a precious signed photograph of the twit who had been Bert's gentleman-officer—lip-long moustache, the scowl of command—sat on the drawing-room mantelpiece in the place of honour.

Herbert had spent his life as a clerk in the Post Office. He loved to show you how to tie the postman's knot, used to keep the mail bundled into sorted categories for delivery. Although retired, he nearly always wore a suit and tie, even when he was sitting in the breakfast room in the morning reading his beloved *Daily Telegraph*. He dressed this way as a statement of class, but I don't think anyone would be fooled into putting him even a notch or two higher in the ever-present English class system. In his generation, men chose a style of hat: his was a homburg. He went alone to the splendid low-Anglican Round Church on Sunday mornings, and afterwards, was allowed a sherry before mid-day dinner (never two) by his wife. He had a bad heart—a problem which a few years' later (in 1970) killed him. In many ways, he was a gentle man, if not a gentleman, trying to cope with the absurdities of England's class-ridden society, and, on the whole, I liked him.

Bi-Polar Marguerite

Marguerite Latter (neé Smith) was another matter, a tall, large, red-faced, bombastic woman, used to ruling the roost, a pre-Thacherite "Attila the Hen," who fought with anyone and everyone who dared to question her absolute authority over any situation. She was selfish in the extreme, and lied, cheated, stole from, and terrorized everyone she came into contact with, not excluding her husband, her children, their spouses, and her life-long friends and companions. In these circumstances, it's difficult for me to admit that we got along reasonably well. Though I despised her, I never let her have the satisfaction of hearing me say so; and though she criticized me constantly at second-hand (through Rosemary), she never took me on face-to-face. A couple of times, in the summer leading up to my wedding to her daughter, she offered me "advice" by letter on how to dress and otherwise conduct myself in public. But on the whole, we sparred with each other through intermediaries, never in a hand-to-hand fight. Years later, when Rosemary and I had parted for good, she apparently expressed the opinion that I was "really a rather first-rate chap," better than any of those that Rosemary later took up with. I think she appreciated the fact that she had met an opponent worthy of her.[5]

---

[5] Marguerite lived until about 1990. In her last days, she suffered from dementia and was put into a home. Looking back on her behaviour, I have become convinced that she was what used to be called "manic-

How We Spent the Christmas Holidays

WHAT DID WE DO IN CAMBRIDGE THAT CHRISTMAS? WE WENT TO HEAR THE CAROL SERVICE AT KING'S COLLGE CHAPEL, AS BERT, having got a couple of tickets from one of the college porters, a friend of his, very kindly gave them to us. I disgraced myself by admitting that I had not heard of the service before. "But it's broadcast all over the world," I was told by Marguerite. We sat in the plebeian part of Wolsey's chapel, an area appropriate for friends of mere porters, where, defeated by the huge English choir-screen that even in the churches keeps the classes firmly in their places, we were able to hear but not to see the service. The lower classes, one assumes, are blessed with a Superman-like vision, perhaps God-given, that the middle and upper classes lack; so their being where they can't see is at most a minor irritation. To have to *see* the service in order to believe it is really happening might show a paucity of faith: "Blessed are those who have not seen and yet believe," sayeth Our Lord.

We borrowed bicycles and rode to Grantchester, where we were able to answer in the affirmative Rupert Brooke's lines:

> *Stands the Church clock at ten to three?*
> *And is there honey still for tea?*

We took the bus to Trumpington, scene of Chaucer's *Reeve's Tale*:

> *At Trumpyngtoun, nat fer fro Cantebrigge,*
>
> *Ther gooth a brook, and over that a brigge.*

In the church there, we rubbed the brass of the crusader knight, Sir Roger, and read the 19th-century poet's tribute to him:

> *Here stands, his earthly journey done,*
> *Sir, Roger, knight of Trumpington.*

We punted up to Byron's pool, where perhaps Rupert Brooke's personal clock tower was once standing at ten to three as he went skinny-dipping with Virginia Stephen (later Woolf)—though, on second thought, considering it was Virginia, perhaps not.

We cycled out to the American memorial cemetery, with its row on row of white crosses, one for each American airman who had flown from the many bases in East Anglia over occupied Europe in World War II and not returned.

And, the circumstances being right for both of us at this time, we admitted that we had fallen in love. One evening, we announced our intention to get married to Marguerite and Herbert. Their answers:

Marguerite: "You can't." (Like the virago she was.)

Herbert: "What are his prospects?" (Like some character in a 19th century novel.)

---

depressive," as her swings of mood can only be explained by a bi-polar diagnosis. See my chapters, *Bloomsbury, Brighton, and Blackheath*, and *London Last Hurrah* for more on this.

A WEDDING IN PARIS

> His grace the Bishop of Nancy said to me: "You are going to Paris.
>
> It is a place of perdition."
>
> Edmond de Goncourt, *Journal*, 1872
>
> Paris was always worth it, and you received return from whatever you brought to it.
>
> Ernest Hemingway, *A Moveable Feast*, 1964

I RETURNED TO LONDON ON THE 28th OF DECEMBER, STAYING OVERNIGHT AT THE HOSTEL ON WOBURN SQUARE, AND ON THE 29th travelled by train and channel ferry to Paris to be Best Man at Leslie Dunkling's wedding to Nicole Tripet, which took place twice, as is the custom and law in France, on Saturday, December 30, 1961, first at a church, and later at the town hall. I carried with me, wrapped in newspaper in a shopping bag, the wedding present I had bought for them, a Spanish salad bowl that was gaily decorated with Mediterranean herbs and flowers. The Tripets found a cheap hotel near their home for me to stay in, which was a blessing, as I was stretching my finances to the limit to make this trip.

> *The afternoon before the wedding, as Leslie and I were out for a walk in the streets of the Parisian suburb in which the Tripets lived—men being useless during wedding preparations—he told me he'd had his hair cut that morning by a ravishing female barber. According to Leslie, the girl had pressed her breasts against him nearly the whole time she was cutting his hair. I didn't believe him, but I said nothing to contradict him. His story, a good beginning of the marriage celebrations, perhaps, had all of the elements found in a Freudian transfer.*

That evening I ate with Leslie and the Tripet family in the Tripet home. Each course of the meal was served separately in the old French way. The food was superb. And they joked about my marrying their younger daughter, Francine, in which case they would lose both their daughters to foreigners.

An Odd Way to Spend New Year's Eve

ON NEW YEAR'S EVE, THE WEDDING FESTIVITIES OVER AND THE BRIDE AND GROOM SAFELY SHIPPED INTO THE FUTURE, I BEGAN THE return journey to London, where I had planned to spend the evening at a residents' party at Peace Haven. But things turned out differently. The Channel crossing was rough, and people were puking their guts out, except in the bar, where the good sailors were imbibing instead of expelling. There I met a fellow about my age whose name was Michael something-or-other. He'd run out of money in Italy and had given up his passport to the consul in Milan in return for their bankrolling his trip back to England—a "distressed British subject." As it turned out, they had given him enough money so that he was less distressed than I was. I was nearly broke. Distressed British subjects, in exchange for their passports, were apparently expected to return home in some comfort.

When we piled on to the electric train on the English side of the channel, it was early evening and the snow was falling in large, heavy flakes. After a very long time and a lot of sparks from the overhead wires, the train moved from East Folkestone to West Folkestone, not a considerable achievement in three hours in view of the size of Folkestone. And there we sat until after midnight. The New Year—1962—arrived on this stuck train, uncelebrated by its annoyed passengers. About 12:30, we finally began to crawl toward London, where we arrived at a wintry and bleak Victoria Station at about a quarter to two and headed out into the nearly-deserted winter streets.

Here and there, as we trudged through a couple of inches of snow, we saw groups of the Bayswater rich in funny hats and tuxedos sloshing their way from one house to another, like characters in a Waugh novel. Michael and I walked, not at all like New Year's revellers, with one small suitcase each, to Marble Arch, where there was an all-night Wimpey's hamburger place. (Was there ever invented a hamburger as bad as a Wimpey's hamburger, with its slimy meat and slippery fried onions?) There Michael phoned an American woman he knew, an architect, who lived in the neighbourhood, to see if we could go to her place. The answer, not unexpectedly, was no. So as the night wore on, we began to walk toward Acton, a long way away, down Bayswater Road and Notting Hill Gate, till finally on Holland Park Avenue we entered the Holland Park Station, which had just opened for the morning. There, we caught a train to North Acton Station and walked to Creswick Road. We were just in time for breakfast at Peace Haven. After breakfast, I said goodbye to Michael, whose short entry into my life—about 18 hours—ended. He was, I seem to remember, on his way to his mother's place. She would probably become, upon seeing him arrive, the next distressed British subject.

A few days' later, when Rosemary came down from Cambridge, I returned to Woburn Square to begin the second term at the Institute.

Autumn at the Institute

University of London Institute of Education College Rooms, 15 Bedford Way, W.C.1

WARDEN: Miss Stephenson
TELEPHONE: Museum 2930

23rd January 1961.

Dear Mr. Keough,

Thank you for your letter of 16th January about residence in the college hostels next session.

It is likely there will be a place to offer you, and I should be glad to know if you would consider sharing a double study bedroom with another student.

I am enclosing an application form for admission, and will write again later to confirm the arrangements, and your address for the session.

Yours sincerely,

M. Hopkinson.

T. Keough Esq., Box 915, Castlegar, B.C., Canada.

INSTITUTE OF EDUCATION UNION SOCIETY

Coming Up Dance

in the
ASSEMBLY HALL
THE JACK DENNIS ORCHESTRA

SATURDAY OCTOBER 14th   7.30 p.m. to 11.30 p.m.

Bar Facilities   Spot Prizes
Admission 3/6d.   Single
               Dress: Informal

Front End of Room No. 14

North and South Views of Woburn Square from Our Balcony

Jim Honeybone in Room 14

Rosemary & Terry

Raine's School Playground

Michael Benton, Chris Oprey, David Boswell and Aloysius

Honeybone's Desk and Bed

David Hepworth & Margaret

Christmas in Cambridge

7 Kimberley Rd. (Black Doorway)

Marguerite & Herbert

Terry at Mattinglea

Rosemary in Breakfast Room

Rosemary at Grantchester

Terry Gets the Best Bedroom in Cambridge

American Memorial at Mattinglea

A Wedding in Paris

Leslie, Mrs. Tripet, Terry

Wedding Party: l to r: Unknown, Mr. Tripet, Nicole and Leslie, Mrs. Tripet, Terry, Francine

Chapter 15: Bloomsbury Brighton, and Blackheath

FiNAL TERM & WEiRD VACATiON JOBS

> It is perfectly true, as philosophers say, that life must be
> understood backward. But they forget the other proposition,
> that it must be lived forward.
> **Kierkegaard**

AS 1961 MOVED ON TO 1962, IT BECAME INCREASINGLY CLEAR THAT THE "WINDS OF CHANGE," AS THAT OLD FUDDY-DUDDY OF A PRIME MINISTER, HAROLD MACMILLAN, CALLED THEM, WERE blowing over Britain and out into the rest of the world. London was becoming markedly different from the place I had lived in a few short years before, in 1958 and 1959. It seemed that anything was now possible and that nothing was safe, as the old order was being changed, subverted, and to a great extent, buried. Penguin Books, prosecuted in 1960 for publishing an unexpurgated version of *Lady Chatterley's Lover*, had won its case, arguing successfully that the book is not obscene. This victory opened the doors for the unexpurgated publishing of countless other novels which had, at the very least, suffered from extensive bowdlerization. Satire once more became the fashion. In 1961, both the magazine, *Private Eye*, and the irreverent, *Beyond the Fringe*, blasted on to the London Scene. But these events were merely the opening salvoes in what was to become the Swinging Sixties. In 1962, *That Was the Week That Was* shocked and delighted television audiences with its hard-nosed satire of established values. Later in that year, a new group released its first hit, "Love Me Do." They called themselves "The Beatles," and the country was buzzing more about their weird hair-dos than their music. And in the world of intimate relations, the birth control pill was changing the code that governed the way males and females behaved toward one another. The old rules were being tossed on to the garbage heap of sexual history. "Not sweating the small stuff" and "doing your own thing" became the catchwords of the decade. In the midst of this changing world, I returned to this quickly-changing London, to the University of London Institute of

Education, blissfully innocent of the fact that my own life would be caught up in this changed world and these changing values before my marrying in September.

A Room in Bloomsbury . . . Again

All we want is a room, . . . in Bloom . . .sbury.
Song from **The Boyfriend**, "A Room in Bloomsbury," 1953

I ask nothing better than all reviewers, forever, and everywhere, should call me a highbrow. If they like to add Bloomsbury, WC1, that is the correct postal address, and my telephone number is in the Directory. But if your reviewer . . . dares hint that I live in South Kensington, I will sue him for libel.
Virginia Woolf

FROM MY ROOM IN WOBURN SQUARE, IN THE WINTER, WHEN THE LEAVES WERE OFF THE TREES, I COULD JUST ABOUT SEE THE HOUSE IN which Virginia Woolf had lived in Gordon Square. I was pleased to be a part of her neighbourhood, albeit half a century too late, to be living in the area that gave its name to the writers and artists who were later to be known as the Bloomsbury Group. One could still imagine, without too much difficulty, their walking by below my miniature balcony: John Maynard Keynes, Lytton Stratchey, E. M. Forster, Duncan Grant, Carrington, and the rest. And isn't that fantastic creature on the other side of the square, out for a stroll from her home on Gower Street, wearing a massive sun hat, a dress that flows over her willowy figure, and a shawl that's running in the wind, perhaps on her way to a tryst with Bernard Russell, the inimitable Ottoline Morrell?

With these fancies running occasionally through my mind, I began the routine of the spring term, January 10 to March 21. In format, it was essentially a repeat of the fall term: lectures, tutorials—and, of course, teaching practice, which ran from February 19 to March 15. But the term was not all work, by any means. I continued with my usual off-hour enjoyments. I spent many quiet times tasting the literary goodies I could not afford to buy at Dillon's University Bookshop on Malet Street, watching on one occasion the Queen Mother (pearls aglitter) and her entourage arrive (sirens blasting), cops crawling through the store. I have no idea what she was doing there. I don't think she was much of a reader. The Royals have always preferred horses to books. But what a kafuffle to cause if she were just there to pick up a novel or two. Weekend evenings, we often went to the Marlborough for a pint or two; and, if I felt stakey, one of their marvellous fat bangers, more filler than meat, but ever so tasty. On one or two occasions, we met nodding acquaintances from the Royal Academy of Dramatic Arts (RADA)—just around the corner from the Marlborough—and went with them to parties they knew about or had heard about. We saw a few of their plays, dirt-cheap for students, at, I think, sixpence, including a fine production of that old chestnut, *The Importance of Being Earnest*.

My Debut on the London Stage

AT THE INSTITUTE, SOME OF US WERE ALSO INTO DRAMA, THOUGH OF AN AMATEUR VARIETY; AND IT WAS IN A PLAY THERE THAT I HAVE subsequently jokingly referred to as my debut on the London stage. We mounted a production of Howard Richardson and William Berney's late-1940's Broadway hit about witchcraft and preachers in the American south, *Dark of the Moon*. I had a small part, playing Floyd, a country lad one straw short of a thatch. I even had to sing a few lines solo:

> *John the Baptist was a preacher, some folks say he was a Jew,*
> *Some folks say he was a Christian, but he was a **Baptist** too!*

These lines were picked up by the entire ensemble, all of us part of a southern Baptist congregation, and we sang our evangelical hearts out.

> *A St. Pancreas weekly newspaper, the name of which I have forgotten, in a positive review of the play, lauded the piece of straw I hung from my mouth (from a broom I found in the green room) and the foot or so of string I played with in my hand. No comment was made on my singing. Rosemary's mother, who came down from Cambridge with her father for one of the performances (we did, I think, three), said she felt humiliated by my playing such a pathetic character. She felt humiliated because I was playing a pathetic character? I guess your review all depends on where you're coming from.*

Other small parts were taken by Rosemary, Jean Price, and Jim Honeybone.

One of the lead characters, a community leader in the story, was played by a tall, thin, balding fellow from Texas, whose name I have forgotten. He, of course, had the best accent of the lot of us. But the main lead, the Preacher, also produced an accent that was very convincing. He was Howard Johnstone, a fellow-Canadian from Salmon Arm, B. C., a few years my senior, who had done a lot of acting at UBC when he was a student there. In 1975, in Ottawa, we once again crossed paths. He had been elected Social Credit MP for my home riding of Okanagan-Revelstoke. In late May of that year my father died, and in the newspaper obituary in the *Revelstoke Review* which Howard had read it was mentioned that I lived in Ottawa. So Howard called me up and invited me and my wife to have lunch with him in the exclusive world of the Parliamentary Restaurant. Barbara and I went to his office in the Centre Block, had lunch in the restaurant, and watched him try to get recognized by the Speaker during the daily Question Period. (He failed.) I don't know if he expected me to arrive with Rosemary. If he did, he didn't show any surprise when I arrived with Barbara. Probably he never knew that Rosemary and I were romantically connected. Howard and I had never been friends.

An Old Colleague from Madrid

One day on Gower Street I ran into Dave Ganderton, whom I had known in Madrid, his scraggy, ill-trimmed, full beard touched with additional grey, his weak mouth still ready to take offence. We had taught together at the Instituto Garrett. He had written a bad novel about a Swedish Lawyer he called Advocat Elvis, who had a series of adventures in the South of France. Ganderton's wife, even weirder-looking than he, with her bulbous lips and rectangular head, the long side horizontal, was Swedish, and they had lived in Sweden for a number of years. In Madrid, they had a pet rabbit in their apartment they called Olé. One Sunday evening I dropped by there with a couple of friends from the language school to be met by the news that the Ganderton's had just eaten Olé for dinner. We were horrified. "D. Seclève-Ganderton, F.I.L. / Teacher of Languages," as his business card read, was not the sort of person I had ever wanted to know. I let the renewal of our acquaintanceship – it had never been more than that— lapse.

An Evening at the Reform Club

A HIGHLIGHT OF THE TERM WAS AN HISTORICAL PUB CRAWL IN THE AREA OF PALL MALL THAT DAVID HEPWORTH ARRANGED FOR THE two of us with his history tutor. W. H. Burston (always *Mister* Burston to us), was the author of tomes such as *Principles of History Teaching,* and editor of, for example, *The History of History Teaching Collection,* neither of which my life has been long enough to read. We met at the Reform Club, one of the great London clubs, built for the Liberal Party by Sir Charles Barry (1795-1860) in 1841 to celebrate the passing of the Great Reform Bill of 1932.[1] Burston, an old bachelor (fifty something?), lived there on a permanent basis, an arrangement I still find distinctly odd. It never occurred to me at the time, but I think now that Burston was probably homosexual. Of course, in the early 1960s, he would have been most unlikely to have admitted his sexual preferences, as buggery was still technically against the law. Oddly enough, though, that very night, in one of the pubs we visited, the question of marriage and the place of sexual gratification within it arouse for some reason or other. Burston immediately gave a dissertation on the fact that there were plenty of facilities in London to take care of that problem.

On entering the club, David and I gave our names to the Porter. Burston came to get us from one of the side rooms, a tall, heavily built man with a large, round face and thinning hair, and we were ushered up the magnificent, wide, central staircase, often imitated in other buildings, which leads to an enormous mirrored wall, before doubling back on itself, to the left and to the right, with two narrower staircases rising to the floor above.

We were ushered through a thick oak door and into a huge room, the likes of which we have all seen in cartoons and read about in novels: clusters of comfortable wing-back chairs around low, round, coffee-type tables, floor lamps beside them for reading *The Times*, walls densely paneled in rare woods, a floor to ceiling bookcase stretching along one of them, a series of windows along another. Here and there were individual club members or small groups of members. The atmosphere was as hushed as one might have expected to find in Stephen Leacock's Mausoleum Club. We sat at one of the clusters, and Burston asked us if we'd like an after-dinner drink. When we agreed it was a good idea, he pushed a buzzer on the wall beside him.

---

[1] Barry, of course, was also the architect of the Houses of Parliament, in conjunction with Augustus Pugin.

> *A few moments later – like a scene in a P.G. Wodehouse story – a section of the wall of books opened as a door, and a tall, balding man, dressed in an evening suit, who seemed a little too old and fragile still to be working for a living, emerged and came toward us.*
>
> *"Smith," Burston said to him (Smith? Was this a movie I was in?), is there any of that 1927 port left?"*
>
> *"No, Sir," said Smith, "but we do have some '36."*
>
> *So we compromised on the '36. When Smith delivered the port, Burston told him we would be coming back about 10 o'clock. He knew it was late, but would it be possible to have some bitter available for us at that time.*
>
> *It was, of course, possible. So after we had toured a number of pubs in the area, and been given a history lesson about each of them, we returned to the Club. Smith came through the bookcase again, this time with three silver-plated pint mugs of beer, each mug glistening with a fog of condensation, matching at that point, to some extent, our minds.*

The evening was a wonderful experience. I was even willing to ignore the fact that Burston was in many ways an unregenerate English twit who enjoyed dripping the names of club members who were prominent politicians at that time and earlier. Selwyn Lloyd, Burston said, though Foreign Minister in the present Tory government, was a member of the Liberal Reform Club. In the dining room at lunch today, according to Burston, he had said, "What a pity that the Americans hadn't stood behind Anthony [Eden] at the time of the Suez Crisis [1956], as they said they were going to do." The world, he said, would be a better place if they had done so. And John Profumo, Minister of Defence, had dropped in for a drink that very afternoon on his way home from the house; and he had said he had heard this comment right after the crisis, straight from the horse's mouth, from Anthony himself. None of us, of course, at that time knew that Profumo would a short time later be disgraced by his relationship with high-end good-time girls, Kristine Keeler and Mandy Rice-Davies, in what was to be known as the "Profumo Scandal." But the fact that he had been sleeping with these two was not what forced his resignation. There was a security problem, as the girls were also bedding down with a spy from the Russian embassy. When faced with the consequences of his whoring, Profumo lied to the house. It is the lie that led to his having to resign from the government[2]

When we left the club, we walked home through Trafalgar Square, up Charing Cross Road to Tottenham Court Road, and through the streets and squares of Bloomsbury to our hostel in Woburn Square. It had been a wonderful evening and we had both enjoyed ourselves immensely. I wrote up that evening in detail in my journal, since, unfortunately, lost, in which I speculated that the evening had been more unusually wonderful for me than it had been for David, who was, after all, an Englishman. But I think now that it was probably as foreign to his Yorkshire background as it was to my Canadian one. Maybe even more so.

---

[2] After the scandal, the joke was that he now called himself John Fumo, since he had dropped the pro.

Brighton—Home of the "Dirty Weekend"

"Oh, do go to Brighton. Everyone goes there now; you really do see the world at Brighton. Now, in London one sees nothing."
Anthony Trollope, **Miss Mackenzie**, 1865

The sexiest place in England is, without doubt, Brighton, my adoptive hometown of four years. Not only is it synonymous with the Dirty Weekend as no other seaside resort, but 99% of the people you meet here came for a dirty weekend and never went home.
Julie Burchill, "Brighton Rocks," **The Guardian**, August 28, 1999

Interview at the Royal Automobile Club

DURING THE FIVE-WEEK EASTER BREAK, I TAUGHT AT WHITTINGEHAME COLLEGE, A BOARDING SCHOOL WHICH CATERED MAINLY TO JEWISH boys.[3] It was located in Brighton, on Surrenden Road. Motto: *Lignum vitae est his, qui apprehenderint eam*, which may be translated as "The stuff of life goes to him who takes hold of it," or something like that. The advertisement for the job was in the *Times Educational Supplement*, one of the papers we subscribed to at the Woburn Square residence. I applied and was asked to go to the Royal Automobile Club (RAC) on Pall Mall for an interview early in March. The interview was a surrealistic affair. I entered the club, dressed in my best (i.e., only) suit, which got cheaper-looking as I penetrated this world of the privileged,[4] and was guided by the porter to a high, wing-back chair in an enormous room set up into numerous small conversational units of four, with dozens of other high, wing-back chairs.

> *Here and there throughout the room small groups of men sat talking and sipping drinks. I also sat . . . and sat . . . and sat. Fifteen minutes went by, twenty, half an hour. Then, out of a group of three men sitting right across from me, a rotund, short man in his sixties came over to me. He had been watching me all this time. He was Mr. J. Halévy, M.Sc. (Oxon), the headmaster / owner of Whittingehame College. Apparently, I had sat to his satisfaction, as he offered me the job, provided that my testimonials were satisfactory. He asked me to bring my satisfactory testimonials to the RAC, which would send them on to him.*

This I proceeded to do. On the 28th of March, in Cambridge, I received the following letter from the College, incorrectly addressed to Timberley rather than Kimberley Road:

> *We have now received your testimonials forwarded by the R.A.C. and these have been placed before Mr Halévy on his return to School today.*

---

[3] Whittingehame College was named after Arthur James Balfour, Lord Balfour of Whittingehame (1848-1930), who was Prime Minister from 1902-05, and a cabinet minister in various governments throughout the rest of his life. He made a speech in 1917, later known as the Balfour Declaration, in which he advocated a national home for Jews in Palestine, thus giving a huge impetus to the Zionist cause. The college no longer exists.

[4] When compared to the Reform Club, however, the RAC was decidedly second-rate.

We are now pleased to offer you a post on our teaching staff for the Easter holidays, and if you wish to accept the post kindly confirm. As you know, the dates are 5th-30th April.

I Arrive at Whittingehame College

IN MY JOURNAL, I RECORDED MY ARRIVAL IN BRIGHTON: "I STEPPED OFF THE TRAIN, GAVE MY TICKET TO THE GUARD AT THE GATE, AND WENT in search of a cab. The Taxi driver was an old man, who stood wide-legged, like a pair of pliers, beside his taxi, as if he had spent the greater part of his life at sea and was still compensating for the roll of the ship. He gazed at me from behind a white—pure white—beard, with sharp, blue eyes. Apart from the sailor's legs, he looked somewhat the way Hemingway had looked when I met him at that bullfight in Bilbao in 1959.[5] We purred off in silence to Surrenden Road."

> *My first impression of Whittingehame College was that everything was in a state of affable disorder. I asked a boy to show me to the office, and he showed me to the wrong office. I then met a woman in the hallway who took me to another office, once again the wrong one; and so it went, until I finally found myself talking to Mr. Tatman, the Head Teacher. I describe him in my journal: "Mr. Tatman has a little less of the disorder and a little more of the affability that seems to pervade this place. His face is long and elliptical and seems somewhat out of focus at the bottom because of a double chin which runs from ear to ear, almost like a beard of skin." I grew to like Mr. Tatman, who, as the weeks passed by, turned out to be a far more laid-back and easy-going individual than the efficient administrator I had at first labelled him to be.*

I was placed in the student residence, a brick building with horizontal granite stripes, in a room of my own, bathroom down the hall. The matron, Mrs. Cooper, who, it seemed from the slur in her voice, had been drinking, settled me into my room. It was right across the hall from her room, which was right next door to the headmaster's room. The headmaster was not in residence at the time. Mrs. Cooper was a largish, rather attractive woman of about forty, with chestnut-brown hair (probably dyed), who I soon learned had been for many years the headmaster's mistress. (Head-mistress?)

Shortly after settling in at the college, I sent a postcard to Rosemary: *"6 April 62. It's just occurred to me that there's no second post on Saturday, so you'll probably not get the letter I'll write this afternoon till Monday. Give my love to Aloysius and all the other bears about the place, try to avoid (if that's ever possible!) the recurring crises at 7 Kimberley Road, and don't forget that there is more than fruit grows in the orchard under the trees. Te quiero much. Terry."* Imagine having a *first* post on *Saturday*! And a *second* one on weekdays! The crises referred to are, of course, those constantly created by her mother, some of which will be referred to in detail later in this chapter. I have no idea what the orchard reference is about.

---

[5] See *That Summer in Jaca*.

I Meet My Teaching Colleagues

OVER THE NEXT FEW DAYS I MET MY COLLEAGUES AT THE COLLEGE. THEY WERE AN ODD BUNCH OF FULL-TIME, PART-TIME, AND temporary teachers like me. It was the sort of staff that is usually found in a place such as this: the questionably-qualified, the social outsiders, and those who are passing by and have stopped for a while to earn a little extra money.

The Reverend Norman Daines

One of the oddest was Norman Daines, who had been an Anglo-Catholic priest but was no longer functioning as one. He was 36 years old, fat, round-faced, and red-complected, with slicked-down black hair that always looked as if it hadn't been washed for a week—and probably hadn't. Like so many people with low personal esteem, he wasn't careful about keeping himself clean.

In no time, he had confided in me about his marital problems. His wife was a quiet, Portuguese woman, a gynaecologist, who had converted to his Anglo-Catholic faith from her Roman Catholicism. A few months after they were married, she had had a miscarriage. She reacted to this unfortunate event by engaging in inexplicable periods of violence. Second and third miscarriages followed, and she went completely and permanently bonkers, blaming all her troubles on having left the Catholic Church.

Daines, who had led a sheltered life up to the time of his marriage, was unable to cope. (Not that it would have been easy for anyone to handle this situation.) He wrote to the bishop to get permission to divorce his wife. The bishop refused. Daines began to pester him with letters. The bishop removed him from his role as an active priest. Daines would not accept "No" for an answer. He continued to write to the bishop, at times even daily. Often, when I met him in the hallways, he would say, "I've just written a note to the bishop." Poor bishop. Poor Daines. But the bishop was not the only one facing the epistolary onslaught of the former Reverend Daines. He also wrote a number of letters to the Pope, which, as one might expect, went unanswered.

Daines was a fanatic movie-goer (at least twice a week), and a regular drinker (including, he admitted to me one day, two pints of cider to help him wash down a couple of sleeping pills before bed). He knew the pubs in the area—perhaps a little too well – and when we asked him for recommendations, he gladly advised us foreigners on the temporary Easter staff—Steve Keril, John Lane, and me – to try *The Cricketers* and *The Clarence*. Lonely, irritable, raging over small incidents, forever finding ways to avoid reality, Daines was himself close to joining his wife on the wrong side of reality. I don't know what happened to him eventually, but I can't believe it was anything good.

The Amusing Glosses of Fred Smith

Another odd character, also one of the regular part-time teaching staff, was Fred Smith. He was a short, wedge-shaped fellow in his thirties, with a big nose and a horrible sincerity. Like most overly-sincere people, he had no sense of humour. When you spoke to him, he leaned toward you, as if he were afraid you'd punch him in the nose if he didn't catch every word. He was a fan of the novelist, John Masters, and he lent me his own paperback copy of *Nightrunners of Bengal*, which I enjoyed reading. But I didn't enjoy the novel half so much as I enjoyed Fred's marginal glosses. "First things first," a character says. (Gloss: "Right again! Just what I've been saying for many years!") "You're not a queen. You're a murderess, a harlot, and a liar." (Gloss: "Plain, hard unvarnished truth. Good for brave Caroline.")

Steve Keril's Triumph Herald

Steve Keril was an elementary-school teacher from the north of England—tall and gangly, awkward, horribly unsure of himself—who had the infuriating habit of referring to me as "lad." "Well, lad, how's it going today?" he would greet me in the morning. But he owned a car, a Triumph Herald, so the rest of us put up with him. He was useful when we wanted to go anywhere, a situation that he understood and tried to take advantage of……., like a homely woman who manipulates lecherous men with promises of sex. "If you aren't nice to me, I won't take you to Arundel today." So there! He made a series of desperate plays for both of the part-time matrons, Kay and Anne, and persisted in doing so, in spite of the fact that he was constantly, and, eventually, rudely rebuffed.

> *One night after we'd been to The Clarence for a few hours, we got into Steve's car to go home. John got into the front with Steve; I got into the back with the girls. Steve refused to start the car unless Anne came into the front with him. She told him to "Get stuffed!"—at first in humour, later in dead seriousness. Still he refused to budge, and we sat in the car in a silence that mingled embarrassment with giggles. After a while, he said he had to visit the bog. While he was gone, John and I took the girls home on foot; it wasn't that far.*

The next day, Steve didn't mention the incident. It was as if it had never happened.

John Lane: Citizen of the World

Although John Lane and I got along superficially like a house on fire, he never let me see much beneath his carefully constructed, north-London image. He had a square Dick-Tracy face, a long, thin nose, and a nervous habit of sticking out his tongue and running it from one side of his mouth to the other, like a cat licking its chops. He was in his mid-twenties and saw himself as a citizen of a larger world than the one he was doomed to inhabit. His vocabulary was spotted with American expressions ("guys") and pronunciations ("tom-eh-toes"), and he told stories of sleeping on beaches in Sicily and of stretching his travel-money by having "no-eating" days. It takes guts not to eat, and for that bit of courage I admired him. But he protected his carefully-constructed image with great care, and I was never able to penetrate it to the real John Lane. He was obviously not very happy with the real John Lane, hidden behind the barrier of the castle he had constructed—cowering, perhaps, afraid of discovery, in a keep that he hoped was impenetrable. And to me, at least, it was.

The Disturbing Problem of Anne

ON THE NIGHT WE LEFT STEVE IN THE BOG, JOHN TOOK OFF WITH KAY AND I HAPPILY ESCORTED ANNE TO HER FAMILY HOME. ANNE WAS A primary school teacher, who was working at Whittingehame to make a little extra money during the Easter break. So we had a common profession. Not that that makes any difference if there is no chemistry between you. Kay was also a teacher. But from the beginning, she and I, using the natural form of mental telepathy we have all experienced when two people are agreed right from the beginning that their acquaintanceship is only just that, made sure there was space between us. Kay was a redhead, quiet, nervous, aloof—and attractive—but we were never going to make it, even temporarily, as a couple.

Anne and I, on the other hand, hit it off right from the beginning; though, because I was engaged, I was more circumspect than I would otherwise have been in following up the opportunity she offered. But I did eventually make a move on her; and I was able to do so, and to rationalize my behaviour, after visiting Rosemary in Cambridge at the end of my second week in Brighton. Rosemary had a cousin, heather Smith, the only child of her Uncle Horace and Aunt Ruthie. Horace was a successful Cambridge businessman, a partner in an expanding chain of carvery-type restaurants, which were popular at that time.

> *During the Christmas vacation, when I was first introduced to the Latter family, I went one afternoon with Rosemary to visit her Uncle Horace and Auntie Ruthie. There I met Heather for the first time. She was a reasonably-attractive brunette, a little square of body and considerably large of bosom. While we were visiting, she disappeared upstairs and came back in a peasant blouse, one of the sort that has a string around the top that ties in a bow at front. The blouse exposed a good amount of cleavage, especially when she bent over to offer me tea and a piece of cake. When Rosemary and I headed back to Kimberley Road on the bus, she fumed at Heather for what she considered a trick to try to attract my attention. I noticed, of course. But the circumstances being what they were, I was not tempted. Well . . . not a lot, anyway!*

April Weekend in Cambridge

Now, on this April weekend visit, all of the family in the area gathered for a picnic near Grantchester: Rosemary's parents; the two of us; her Uncle John and his wife, Thelma; her brother, David, his wife, Alison, and family; and Horace, Ruthie, and Heather. Even Rosemary's miniature maiden aunt, Rosa, who shared a house in Tunbridge Wells with her life-long companion, Dolly, had come up to Cambridge for the occasion.[6] During the picnic, Heather took me aside and suggested that Rosemary had been seeing her ex-boyfriend, a shop teacher by the name of Gerry Fox who lived in London, with whom she had gone out during her years at Royal Holloway College. She had not seen him once, she said, but a number of times. When I confronted Rosemary with this, she admitted she had seen him, though only "a couple of times," and that there was nothing in it but friendship. She insisted that she had never been alone with him, that at all times they were in the company of Jennifer and Trevor See.[7] She was furious with Heather, of course. Though I wanted to believe her, I was troubled by her hesitant admission of having seen him only a couple of times. And always in public. She would not brook being questioned about it, which made me even more suspicious. But I accepted her story. What else could I do? I was engaged to her and wanted to trust her. But underneath, I didn't believe it, and my doubts gave me the reason I needed to be treacherous on my end of the relationship. It was not an auspicious beginning to our married life.

Getting in Deeper with Anne

I WENT BACK TO BRIGHTON, TRYING TO CONVINCE MYSELF THAT ROSEMARY WAS TELLING ME THE TRUTH, AND THAT HEATHER WAS A trouble-making meddler. Considering Rosemary's often deceitful behaviour throughout the years of our marriage, I probably should have broken off the engagement at that point. But marriage arrangements take on a life of their own, and once started, are difficult to stop. Had I realized at the time that I was hooking myself up to a family that was a nest of vipers, I would certainly have cut and run, arrangements be damned. But it was some time before I discovered that as a way of life they preyed on one another, stole from one another, and generally took any chance they could find to one-up one another. They were a horrible bunch, and most of them were marginally crazy to boot!

But I did use my doubts to rationalize my growing attachment to Anne. I was in a near perfect situation to be unfaithful and get away with it. I was going to be in Brighton for only a few weeks. Nobody would ever find out. I told myself it was all part of the burden that Nature has placed on the behaviour of men, the urge to spread their seed wherever the ground is inviting. What made the ground even more inviting was the fact

---

[6] Rosa and Dolly were known in the family as Arsenic and Old Lace. These two old maids, who walked together arm in arm, like creatures out of a Monty Python skit, had inherited a splendid small arts and craft bungalow, complete with expensive furniture and knick-knacks, from a Tunbridge Wells banker and his wife, who as a childless couple had left it to Rosa. A few years later, when Rosemary and I were visiting them in Tunbridge Wells, Dolly took me aside and told me that Rosa intended to leave the house to Rosemary, and would I give her assurance that we would let her live out her life there if Rosa, who was not well, died first. I said that was fine with me, but she should really talk to Rosemary, whose house it would be. Ironically, Dolly died of cancer about a year later, and Rosa was left alone in the house. I don't know what happened when she died.

[7] Jennifer had been a friend of Rosemary's since their days at the posh Perse School in Cambridge. Her family owned a farm outside of Cambridge that is mentioned in the Domesday Book. They had gone on to Royal Holloway College together, where, at college dances Rosemary had met and become romantically involved with Gerry Fox and Jennifer had become involved with Trevor See, a Sandhurst cadet. Jennifer later married Trevor in a traditional military wedding ceremony.

that Anne had mentioned in the pub that her doctor had put her on the pill to try to minimize her considerable menstrual pain. So, here I was in 1960's Brighton with an opportunity to make love to a girl without worrying about her getting pregnant. How the world had changed in the three years since my cautious, and thus frustrating, love affair with Jennifer Sharp.

Nevertheless, I had a conscience, which constantly plagued me as I was thinking of trying to get Anne into the sack. It made me hesitate. I would move toward her, as if I was about to carry on to the next stage of the relationship. But then my conscience would get to me; and as I was making love to Anne, I would be thinking that I really shouldn't be doing this. When I was apart from her, I would resolve to keep things at the level they were at. But when we came together, I would be carried away by the situation, and we would go a little further. Anne was always willing, and it may be that my hesitation made her more interested in receiving my affection than she would otherwise have been. I have often thought: how different my life would have been if I had thrown caution to the winds, broken my engagement to Rosemary, and taken up with Anne. Not necessarily better, but certainly different.

> *Anne had shoulder-length, deep-brown hair, curled out and up at the bottom, as was the fashion at the time. She had a dark, Celtic face, slightly swarthy, as Celtic faces sometimes are. But her eyes, which were large, were cerulean blue, and scintillating, riveting you when you looked at her. At some point, on every day when she wasn't working at her matron's job, she played the splendid grand piano in the college's conservatory. She played at a near-professional level; and as I walked from one building to another on the school's campus, I sometimes would hear her music sparking in the spring air. Most often it was short romantic pieces that she played: among them, Chopin's Nocturnes and selections from Schubert's Impromptus. She said that she found playing these melodious pieces helped her to relax.*

As we walked home from the bar on the night we abandoned Steve, the perfume in her hair drawing me ever closer to her, she told me that her father had been killed just a month before in a traffic accident. On that day, she had been riding into town on her bicycle when she saw a crowd gathered around a figure on the pavement. He had been hit by a car he apparently had never seen coming. The driver hadn't had a chance. I felt I had to comfort her to show my compassion, but it was also the perfect excuse for me to put my arms around her and hug her. I rationalized this move as one of empathy only, but I was moving toward more than that, and when she responded with a hug of her own, I was well on the way to perdition, and, if truth be told, enjoying every minute of it—in spite of my conscience.

I now understood why she was a bundle of raw and projecting nerves. I wanted to comfort her, but at the same time, didn't want to give her the impression that I was seriously interested in her as a lover. It was obvious that she needed and was looking for a strong male to lean on; and, it seemed she had decided at this point to lean on me.

When I kissed her goodnight, which, I said to myself, I most certainly should not have done, she said to me: "You just think I'm easy meat."

Now, apart from the inherent vulgarity of this expression, it was close to the truth. As the days went by, the more I thought about it, the more I wanted to go to bed with her. I did make an honest attempt to get the idea out of my head. I would say to myself, the next time you're with her, just back off a bit. Be friendly, but keep things where they are. I told myself that it would be morally reprehensible for me to get involved further. I was engaged to Rosemary, whom I kept telling myself that I loved; Anne was psychologically damaged at the moment and was in some senses easy prey—"easy meat," as she put it; and my loving her and leaving her might damage her even further. But as I left her that night, she said: "Why don't I come to your room and wake you in the morning?" The idea was irresistible. There was meaning there that went beyond the simple offer of a wake-up call. She knew it, and I knew it, and nothing more needed to be said. The camel was putting his nose in the tent. "I'd love that," I said.

> *Every morning after that, Anne would come into my room to wake me up. It was convenient for her to do so, as she had to be at the school early to get the boys ready for the day, but we both knew it was a ruse for us to spend a little more time together in circumstances that were highly charged with romance. For the first couple of mornings, we just talked for a few minutes about all the things in life that don't matter. She pulled the curtains on my window, letting in the sun, and perched herself on the end of my single bed. But inevitably, after a few days of temptation, we began making out. There was no time for serious love-making in the morning, as she had to rush off to her work and I had to get ready to go to breakfast and teach my classes. But we managed to find times in the middle of the day when we were both free.*

Often, when we were unable to get together, usually because of schedule conflicts, I would hear her playing the piano in the music room, and I was proud to be associated with a woman who had such talent. I began to have doubts about whether my liaison with Rosemary was what I really wanted and to think maybe it was Anne I should be bringing into my life.

Another Aeneas Betrays another Dido

THE DAY BEFORE I LEFT BRIGHTON, WHEN WE WERE LYING SNUGGLED IN MY SINGLE BED IN THE MIDDLE OF THE AFTERNOON, ANNE SAID TO me, "I think I'm falling in love with you." Her admission was not entirely unexpected. I was certainly also falling in love with her. But her declaration precipitated something of a crisis, and I did not know what to say in return. I had now betrayed two women, Rosemary, whom I was about to marry, and Anne, whose vulnerability I had exploited for crass sexual purposes, but whom I was becoming increasingly attracted to. I was averse to telling a partial untruth, even a small one. Which was odd, in a way, as a lie—if this was a lie—would have been minor compared to the other sins I was committing. But

I realized that if I said anything, whether a partial truth or a partial lie, it would sink me deeper into this morass of my own making.

Before I left, I gave Anne my address in Woburn Square. She began to send me long, rambling, love letters that I answered with short enthusiastic notes. In these, I claimed I would write more fully when I was less busy preparing for my final exams. But I'm sure she knew, like Dido in *The Aeneid*, that I, her Aeneas, was about to betray her; though I'm equally sure she wouldn't have put it that way, nor understood the allusion if I had mentioned it. *Quis fallere posit amantem?* Virgil says, referring to Dido. "Who is able to deceive a lover?" These were allusions that Rosemary would have understood and appreciated if I made them to her. And once back in Rosemary's company, I understood the chasms that separated Anne and me. At the time, I rationalized my behaviour by telling myself that this was the Sixties and there was a new morality and that's just the way things were these days and the only thing to do was to put it all behind me. I did my best to do so. But even after all this time, I still feel pangs of guilt, not so much for deceiving Rosemary, who was probably at the same time deceiving me, as for my shabby treatment of Anne, who was going through a bad period in her life and deserved better. When I finished my term at the Institute and left for my summer job in Blackheath, I did not send Anne my forwarding address. I never heard from her again.

Mrs. Cooper Pays Me a Midnight Visit

ANNE WAS NOT THE ONLY WOMAN TROUBLE I HAD WHILE AT WHITTINGEHAME COLLEGE. ONE NIGHT WHEN I CAME HOME FROM *The Clarence*, shortly before midnight, I had just got into bed and begun reading when there was a knock on my door. I thought—who can that be? Was one of the students having a health problem of some sort? I grabbed my tartan bathrobe. When I opened the door, in front of me was a white chenille bathrobe containing Mrs. Cooper, the matron.

> *"Can I come in?" she said. "I've been having trouble getting to sleep."*
>   *"Of course," I replied, trying not to look totally perplexed at this unexpected visit in the middle of the night.*
>   *Mrs. Cooper (I never knew her by any other name) grasped her white robe close to her throat as she walked toward one of my two Morris chairs, studiously looking toward the other end of the room, either from embarrassment or because she didn't want me to get the wrong idea about her visit. I slithered toward the other chair.*
>   *"I thought you might like a drink," she said, stopping before she reached the chair and suddenly turning toward me. She had apparently had a few already.*
>   *"Well, actually . . .," I began.*
>   *"I'll of and get us a couple . . . tonic ok with your gin?" And she was gone to her own room and back—the drinks had obviously been pre-mixed—before I had time to react.*

She wanted, she said to tell me about Mr. Halévy. All his life he had been a Zionist. He had set up schools, one here, and another at Hancross, where he and his wife had their home, to try to teach the Arabs and Jews to get along with one another; so his schools were populated by an international mixture of students from both groups, though the student body remained predominantly Jewish, and the Jewish holidays only were celebrated. She wasn't Jewish herself, she said, "had no religion, really."

Mr. Halévy—she always called him "Mister"—had been a sergeant in the British Army in the First World War. He had always felt strongly that the Jewish community owed a great debt to Britain because of the Balfour Declaration and should therefore strongly support the country when it needed support. Mr Halévy told her that it was only because of Britain that Israel existed today. She didn't know anything about these things, she said, but that's what he had told her. Because of these convictions, he allowed his only son to volunteer for the army in the Second World War, when he was too young to be conscripted. Mrs. Halévy had been violently against the son's joining up. Of course, the inevitable happened and the son was killed. Mrs. Halévy had never forgiven Mr. Halévy, poor man. "They fight constantly," she said, "but have stayed together because of their common interest in education and their both wanting to avoid the scandal of a divorce."

As Mrs. Cooper talked and I listened, the image of Mr. Halévy in the Royal Automobile Club kept walking across my mind: short, rotund, a mouth curved like a new moon, his thick lips covering his teeth like a layer of pain. A prominent Semitic nose. Poor man, indeed. And poor woman. And poor Mrs. Cooper.

So why did Mrs. Cooper want to tell all this to me, in her nightwear and bathrobe in my room in the middle of the night, drink in hand. She was, of course, more than a little drunk. And she was obviously, and with reason, unhappy with her world. But did she want me to make a move on her? To console her with my body? The thought crossed my mind, both of us having drunk more than was good for our powers of judgement, let alone anything else. But I did nothing, thanked her for the drink, pointed out that I needed to get some sleep if I was to teach my classes in the morning, and ushered her out the door. We remained distant friends for the rest of my time at the college, often meeting in the hallway of the residence during the day or early evening. But she never came to my room again, and her odd midnight visit was never mentioned by either of us. It was as if it had never happened.

How I Passed My Days in Brighton

IN MY SPARE TIME, WHEN I WAS NOT MEETING ANNE OR GOING TO THE PUB WITH THE BOYS, I EXPLORED BRIGHTON ON FOOT. THERE IS, OF course, the Pavilion, that quirkish edifice in an eastern mode built by George IV when he was Prince of Wales.[8] I wandered through it once, as if I were a tourist. But most of my

---

[8] George had been secretly (and illegally) married to the twice-widowed Roman Catholic, Maria Fitzherbert, in 1785. He pretended to live with her as if she were his mistress, a nice reversal of the usual man / wife / mistress situation. The Pavilion was completed by John Nash in what has become known,

walks were in "The Lanes," those narrow streets in downtown Brighton full of antique and junk shops. There I bought Rosemary a couple of presents, a large, hollow, pectoral cross in sterling silver, and an amber cross with a silver transit and end caps. For myself I bought a silver-plated beer mug with exquisitely simple lines, the best I have ever seen, the silver badly in need of replating. On a shield with a crown on top was engraved, *Royal Albion Hotel Brighton*, from which it no doubt had been stolen at some point in the past. On the rim, by the handle, is the guarantee of its size, *GR 37 Pint*.[9] I have it still, and use it often, and I have had it replated at least four times in the past half century or so.

But I wasn't solely pursuing pleasure in my spare time. I was also working on a television adaptation of Pedro de Alarcón's *The Three-Cornered Hat* (*El Sombrero de Tres Picos*). The script was eventually finished a couple of years later when I was teaching in Port Alberni, B.C., but it was never in serious danger of finding a producer. I'm not sure why I decided to write it. I had no training in television writing, and I really didn't know what I was doing. I can only put it down to another folly of youth.

As the days went by, I went through the motions of teaching my classes, all of them small: an Upper 4 (5 students), a Lower 5 (3), an Upper 5 (7), a group of Juniors (9)—and an Upper 6 (2) that never met. The students, who had come to Whittingehame from many parts of the world, had names like Chaim Lieber, Sabah Peress, Fayek Baroukh, and Bahman Khazeni. They were all rich kids, sent to the College, I often thought, to get them out of the way. Many of them were neurotic. Most of them spoke English as a second language, so the academic standard was low. It's likely that we temporary teachers had been hired just to keep busy those students who had not gone away for the holidays. The students were well-behaved and the subject matter was elementary, so it was no challenge for me to teach these classes.

Apart from teaching duties, all teachers had to spend a morning, afternoon, or evening every couple of days manning the desk at the entrance of the administration building in order to answer student questions and to issue *exeats*. The students were allowed out for most excuses, but on the Sabbath we Christians were told to remind them not to take the bus into town. We did so, though we knew, as did everybody else, that they merely walked down the hill and around the corner before boarding it.

At the time of the Passover the dishes and utensils were changed and students were reminded about the laws regarding leavened bread, though most of them cheated on the rules by hiding forbidden goodies in their rooms. For the day of the Passover itself, a great feast was prepared and celebrated by the Jewish students and staff. We non-Jews, including the Arab students, were given a fine feast of our own in a different room: roasted chicken breast, a rice medley, a mixed salad, all served with a decent cheap wine. In the background, we listened to the sounds of happy celebration coming from the room

---

almost comically, as the "Hindu-Gothic" style. In 1850, Queen Victoria sold the Pavilion to the town of Brighton for 53,000 pounds, after first taking all its interior furnishings, including the wallpaper.

[9] Curiously enough, when Barbara and I were touring southern England in 1984, without having planned to do so, we stayed a night in the Albion, after arriving in Brighton with no reservation.

next door, where the Jewish students were ensconced. We rejoiced in these happy sounds, and although we did not eat our special meal in a similar celebratory fashion, having nothing to celebrate, we Christians and Arabs were content in our exile.

A Letter Arrives with Bad News

WHILE I WAS AT BRIGHTON, I HAD A MAJOR DISAPPOINTMENT. THE PREVIOUS FALL, I HAD APPLIED FOR AN OVERSEAS TEACHING appointment with the External Aid Office (later CIDA) in Ottawa. Their response seemed to be highly positive, especially regarding the approach I used in my second letter to them: "If I may mix my metaphors, I don't want to upset the applecart by letting loose a bull in a china shop, but I would appreciate knowing if there is any reason I am not qualified for an overseas assignment, as I will soon need to begin looking for a teaching position here for the coming year." Noble Power responded for the External Aid Office that they'd passed my "very funny" letter around the office, and they hoped there would be a position that suited my qualifications.[10]

A few days after the Spring Term ended on March 21, when Rosemary and I were in Cambridge, a telegram came from the Canadian High Commission in London asking if I and my future wife could come there for an interview regarding employment with the External Aid Office. We went up to London on a Saturday for the interview, which took place in a second-floor room in Canada House on Trafalgar Square. The interview was conducted by two career diplomats—one of them with a horrendous cold. It was very informal, without any real content, as the diplomats were as ignorant of the African postings as we were. But it did seem to go very well. When we shook hands at the end of the interview, standing in the hall outside the interview room, we inadvertently crossed through each other, forming a kind of "X" with our arms. "That's a sign of good luck if ever there was one," the diplomat without the cold said. So I was very confident that I would get an assignment.

I had heard from my old friend, Bill Wood, who was in England at the time, living with his wife, Beverley, in Peace Haven, and teaching in a school in Ealing. He said that he had been assigned to a secondary school in Ghana to teach mathematics. But that had been a couple of weeks earlier, and as time passed, I was getting more and more anxious about my own posting. Every day, I would look forward to receiving the letter that would confirm the positive feeling I had had in coming out of the interview at Canada House. And every day there would be only the usual normal letters—much appreciated, but not settling the one thing I wanted to know—letters from Rosemary, from my mother, from one of my siblings.

The letter from the External Aid Office arrived with the morning mail at Wittingehame College as we waited around for the bell to call us into lunch. I opened it

---

[10] I have not made up this man's name. He was, I think, the son of "Chubby" Power, who was a cabinet minister in Mackenzie King's government during World War II.

with great expectations. It seemed as if all my colleagues were watching me, and I was prepared to share my good news with them.

> *When I read the first sentence of the first paragraph, "In spite of our best efforts, it is not always possible to match even the best candidates with positions in the underdeveloped world," I knew that I had not been successful. The second paragraph confirmed that there was no place for me. I was devastated. I had to get out of this public area. I'm sure my face revealed that the letter contained bad news. I excused myself and bounded to my room, staying there for about fifteen minutes, while I coped with the disappointment. As I had to teach in the afternoon, and I had to have lunch, I did my best to put it out of my mind—my best not being very good, but good enough among people who didn't know me very well. I donned as normal a public face as possible and went back to the rest of the day.*

As it turned out, the External Aid Office was not merely mollifying me but was telling it the way it was. Three years later, I was given a job under their aegis at a teacher training college in Kenya. But the letter of rejection that came to me on that April morning in Brighton was a very low moment in my life.

Back at the Institute

ON APRIL 30, HAVING FULFILLED MY CONTRACT, I RETURNED TO LONDON TO COMPLETE MY YEAR AT THE INSTITUTE. I WAS A LITTLE Late—the summer term began on Wednesday, April 25—but I had Mrs. Moore's permission, as I was finishing up my teaching duties at Whittingehame College. The term once again consisted of lectures, tutorials, teaching practice, and, in addition, the final exams. They were, in fact the only examinations in that year at the Institute, not a system I had experienced before, but one that I liked. When I first went to Mrs. Moore's office on my return, we discussed my plans for the future. The discussion was concerned mainly with my application for a teaching job, which at that point I had done nothing about, though there was a job open at a Catholic school in Kensington that I was mildly interested in. But I also mentioned, among other things, that I was working on a television script of the *Three-Cornered Hat*, and that I had plans to write some poetry. Mrs. Moore said I seemed to have "a few too many irons in the fire," but I might benefit from using the Reading Room at the British Museum. She offered to write me a letter of recommendation. A few days later, with her letter in hand, I joined the illustrious group that had historically worked in that *sanctum sanctorum*, including Karl Marx, Bernard Shaw, and Colin Wilson. I was a mite out of my depth.

In the meantime, I went to work renewing my London social life. There was not only my return to Rosemary, but also the usual coffee and beer gatherings with the Institute crowd. I also, of course, resumed contact with other London friends. For instance, on May 2, one of my hostel mates, Douglas Mueller, took the following telephone message for me: *Terry—5:10 p.m. Leslie and wife thinking of coming in for meal at 6:30. Meet at 25 Woburn Square.* I got hold of Rosemary and we all went to a well-known, reasonably priced, German restaurant, *Schmidts*, on Charlotte Street, an easy walk from Woburn Square.

Teaching Practice Exam Lesson

ON WEDNESDAY, MAY 9, TEACHING PRACTICE, WHICH RAN THROUGH TO FRIDAY, JUNE 1, BEGAN, AND I RETURNED FOR THE LAST TIME TO Central Foundation School. A week or so later, I received the following note from Mrs. Moore:

> *Your exam lesson will be on Thursday, 24th May at 9:30. Mr. Stevenson will be coming also. Please let Secretary know as we shall not be arriving together. Would you send me a card or telephone SLO 5349 to say you have received this notice. E.M.M.*

On the day of my exam lesson, Mrs. Moore and Mr. Stevenson arrived at the school and accompanied me to my classroom. As we entered, the students, as was customary in that school, stood. I don't remember what I was teaching or how it seemed to go. But when the class was over and I was discussing my fate with my two examiners, Mrs. Moore seemed preoccupied with what she saw as the horror of students rising on the entrance of the teacher. I had always felt that this gesture of respect was a good idea, but Mrs. Moore was imbued with the new ideas which pervaded the Institute, and she didn't like the gap this token of respect created, in her view, between teacher and taught. Mr. Stevenson, a young man, probably in his late twenties, said he didn't see that it caused much harm. I kept my mouth firmly shut.

So the discussion was essentially centred on this matter of respect and only peripherally on my performance as a teacher. Mrs. Moore said that she thought I had done very well, and would it be all right if she came again, this time with Jocelyn Emberton, another one of the younger tutors, to determine whether I would be granted a distinction. (The Institute worked on a Pass with Distinction / Pass / Fail system. No marks were given.) It was fine with me. And so it happened, a few days later that I was put through another exam lesson. But it was all for nought. When I got my final results in July, I had passed, but there was no distinction. Once again the English class system had interfered. There were only so many distinctions to be awarded, following some kind of formula based on the number of students. None went to overseas students, so I suppose the very fact that I was being considered for one was in itself something of a distinction, like being nominated for an Academy Award. Most of the people who had gone to public schools, and the smattering of girls among the students who were "The Honourable This" or "The Honourable That" were given distinctions.[11] So, some of the rest of us, in the interest of preserving the class system, had to make way for the "Quality."

---

[11] Nancy Mitford, who was herself one of these "Honourables," refers to them ironically in *The Pursuit of Love* as "The Hons." I remain astonished at the deference given to these young girls, even by some of my forward-looking English friends, because of their peripheral attachment to the aristocracy.

A Visit from My Hometown

Early in June, I was visited by Ron Chisholm, with whom I had grown up in Revelstoke (he had suffered in his boyhood from being called "Jism," a slang word for "sperm.") He was on a tour of England and was staying in Bloomsbury at the *Hotel Ivanhoe*, which was within easy walking distance of the Institute. He had always been a consummate bore, one of those brush-cut, fifties-bred, serious people with no sense of humour. I took him out for a beer at the Marlborough and introduced him to a few of my friends; but I was not sorry that I had earlier booked an Institute-sponsored day-excursion, a tour of the new Coventry Cathedral, for the last of the three days that he was in London. A decade later, still single and still serious, he came to a tragic end. He had always been an avid mountain climber. As it turned out, he climbed one too many and fell to his death in the magnificence of the Rocky Mountains, so much more spectacular than he had ever been.

A Job, Exams, and an Engagement

IN THE MEANTIME, THERE WAS MOVEMENT ON THE JOB FRONT. NANCY MARTIN, ROSEMARY'S TUTOR, HAD BEEN APPROACHED BY MR. Flower, the Principal of Kingsway Day College, for recommendations for two progressive English teachers, and she asked Rosemary if the two of us would be interested. Kingsway Day College was a day-release institution in Keeley Street, just off Kingsway in Holborn, right by the Royal Opera House and Covent Garden Market. More or less just down the street from the Institute. It had been established to give further education one day a week to young people who had left school early. They were given a paid day off by their employers to go back to school. Since my overseas job-possibility had evaporated, and since both Rosemary and I liked the idea of staying in central London, it was ideal. So, on the recommendation of Nancy Martin, we applied for the jobs.

On the 5th of June, I received a letter with the following heading: Mr. F. D. Flower, M.B.E., B.A., B.Sc. (Econ.), Principal of Kingsway Day College:

> *Your letter arrived just as I was about to begin this one this morning! We shall be pleased to offer you a temporary full time appointment as a Grade "A" teacher for next year in the College and are inviting Miss Latter to accept a similar appointment. If you decide to accept, I suggest that you both come in again towards the end of term, after your own exams are over, to discuss details of your projected time table with Miss Stovin.*

Rosemary and I accepted the jobs, and eventually we went to the College to see Miss Stovin, Mr. Flower's secretary. But in the meantime, we had the usual lectures and tutorials to attend until the last day of classes, Friday, June 22. Then it was just a matter of getting ready for the exams. These, we wrote over three days, one exam in the morning and one in the afternoon on each day: Wednesday, June 27: Principles of Education and

Educational Psychology; Thursday, June 28: Principles and Methods of Teaching, and The Educational System; and Friday, June 29: Optionals (I did History of Education, and Health Education). We gained entry into the Examination Halls with an Admission Card, upon which was printed a Candidate Number. Mine was 29304. At the bottom of this card in bold type was the following notice, a reflection of the female shoe fashions of the time: *Candidates are no permitted to wear stiletto heels in the Examination Halls.* There are no other prohibitions.

Up to this point, Rosemary and I had not told anyone among our friends that we intended to get married. But now that the year was over, and we were going our separate ways, it seemed a good time to announce our engagement. We decided to do this at my favourite restaurant, *Luba's Bistro*. We invited our closest friends, Jim Honeybone, Jean Price, and David Hepworth to celebrate the end of term by joining us at the restaurant, without telling them ahead of time of our plans.

I had bought Rosemary an engagement ring, as good a one as I could afford—nine diamond chips arranged in a diamond shape—which we unveiled during dinner. We had bought a bottle of wine at *The Bunch of Grapes*, the pub on the corner of Yeoman's Row, taken our place at one of the bench tables, and ordered our delicious stuffed green peppers, cabbage rolls, and other Luba goodies.

After we had finished eating, Rosemary put on the ring and we made our big announcement. It was a complete surprise. David, in particular, seemed to be affected by our decision, saying he hadn't realized that we were *that* serious. But there were hugs and kisses and congratulations all around. Especially, there were questions. When had we decided to take the plunge? Where had we found such a lovely ring? When were we going to actually tie the knot? We answered the questions as well as we could. Everyone was enthusiastic about attending our wedding, which we said would naturally be in Cambridge, Rosemary's hometown. We said that we had scheduled it tentatively for late summer or early fall. If possible, we wanted to do it before the school year began and we had to take up our first jobs at Kingsway Day College.

It was a great way to end the term.

Blackheath

And eastward straight from wild Blackheath the warlike errand went,
And roused in many an ancient hall the gallant squires of Kent.
Lord Macaulay, **The Armada,** 1842

When I was acquainted with Blackheath, the ingenious device of garrotting had recently come into fashion; and I can remember, while crossing those waste places at midnight and hearing footsteps behind me, to have been sensibly encouraged by also hearing, not far off, the clinking hoof-tramp of one of the horse patrols who do regular duty there.
Nathaniel Hawthorne, "A London Suburb," in **Our Old Home,** 1863

B LACKHEATH, A SUBURB A FEW MILES SOUTH-EAST OF CENTRAL LONDON, WAS CERTAINLY NOT AS WILD A PLACE WHEN I WENT there in the summer of 1962 as it was at the time of the Spanish Armada; and it was a good deal tamer than when Nathaniel Hawthorne spent time there in the 19th Century. But the heath could still be a spooky place to cross on foot in the dark, as I discovered one night when I came home too late to get on public transport. There was never much likelihood that I would be garrotted, but I was made uncomfortable, nonetheless, by this expanse of loneliness and emptiness. Graham Swift describes the feeling the heath gives rise to in his novel, **Last Orders** (1996): *Blackheath isn't black and it isn't a heath. It's all green grass under blue sky. If it weren't for the roads criss-crossing it, it would make a good gallop. Highwaymen here once. Coaches to Dover. Your money or your life.*

So what was I doing in Blackheath? I was working there. In order to earn some much-needed money during the summer vacation—all the more necessary as I was getting married at the beginning of September—I had answered an advertisement in the *Times Educational Supplement* for a teacher of ESL (English as a Second Language) at Wilson College, which happened to be located there. I received an immediate reply from the Principal, Miss M. E. Brimicombe, B. A. Hons., outlining the job and asking me to come for an interview as soon as possible.

I travelled to Blackheath from Charing Cross Station on British Rail (Day Return 2/10). At the College, I was interviewed by a 40-ish dour woman in what looked to be a Black-Watch plaid shirt-front dress, frameless glasses, and a tightly-permed, brunette hair-do. She pointed out that "Miss Brimicombe" was her work name and that she was married to a Frenchman who ran a similar institution in Paris. (Just in case I had got any ideas? I had not got any ideas.) They got together on weekends. She projected herself as a no-nonsense sort of person, and so she proved to be; but she was a few notches down from being a dragon-lady. Having found me satisfactory, she offered me a job for July, August, and September, and when I told her, with some fear that it would lose me the job, that I would be teaching at Kingsway Day College in September, to my relief, she happily hired me for July and August only.

I was more than pleased to have full-time work for the two months at the princely salary of £40 a month plus free board and lodging. For this recompense, I would teach from 70 to 120 students, with a maximum class size of eighteen—high for second language teaching. My courses were Direct method (i.e., ESL) English and Commercial Correspondence. **Residential Duties** were spelled out in my terms of engagement: "Supervizing *[sic]* welfare and happiness [happiness?] of students. Supervizing [*sic*, again] at meal times. Making students speak English at all times. Organizing debates, discussions, games. Accompanying excursions and walks. Willingness to help in all social activities." Some of these requirements I was able to fulfill; others, I left to whatever gods there be. Also stipulated were **Duties and Free Times for Temporary Staff**. Duties consisted mainly in being available to students at a table in the foyer in the evenings, and at other times generally keeping an eye on things around the college. "Two days on, one day off in the week for all temporary staff." Free times were also carefully spelled out: "those engaged for more than a month [that's me] have a free weekend a month." Full-time work, indeed!

The Warehouse on Bennett Park Road

B UT I WAS YOUNG AND ENERGETIC, AND I DID NOT FIND THE JOB ITSELF ONEROUS. I WAS, HOWEVER, SURPRISED BY MY FREE lodging. It was not at the College itself, as I had expected, but in a warehouse in Blackheath Village, a mile or so away. Miss Brimicombe had rented a number of rooms on the top floor of this building, owned by a local Sikh, who used to prowl about the place in an intrusive and disconcerting way. When he showed up, unexpectedly—as he often did—suddenly, and without a conceivable reason, I tended to wonder if I was doing something unacceptable, though I had no idea what that might be. I was the only staff member there, but there were a dozen or so students, housed in double rooms. We all shared a couple of bathrooms, one at each end of the hall.

On August 13, having been there for more than a month, I wrote the following description of the place in my notebook:

> *I live in the " village" and not at the college itself. My room is in an old building, solidly put together (the steel girders are bare in one corner), which from the outside looks somewhat like a cross between a manor house and a mausoleum. It is nevertheless light and cheerful, with its good-coloured red bricks and contrasting cream trim. From Blackheath Station, you walk up Bennett Park Road, which is a cul-de-sac, and the warehouse stands rather formidably across the end. On the way, there are a number of large but nondescript houses, now divided into apartments of unknown amenities, and a small new block containing six unfurnished flats, at seven guineas a week, only four of which are rented. In one of the older flats, I see an easel propped up by a window and an atmosphere of work; but I suspect it is there more for show than anything else, as there is a different painting on it every day.*
>
> *The interior of the building is dark and dirty—except for the bedrooms and bathrooms, which are pristine. To get to my room I have to walk up two flights of stairs, which ascend from both ends of a long, gloomy passage that has only two small windows half-way along it. This building has been an art gallery (there are some bronzes on the newel posts of hideous post-Victorian vintage), and a Borstal home. A fellow named Beard [sic], who, I'm told, is the inventor of television, lived and produced television shows here.[12] He carries on, I suppose, the infamy of*

---

[12] John Logie Baird (1888-1946) is one of the candidates for the honour of being the inventor of television. He worked largely on his own, with some volunteer help. On January 26, 1926, he demonstrated his invention in Soho, transmitting a blurred, 30-line picture of the head of a dummy, using spinning discs. As he had no money, the discs were made from hatboxes and were mounted on a coffin lid. The BBC began broadcasting, using his system, in 1929. But in 1936, the BBC adopted the Marconi-EMI electronic

a village whose heath has witnessed the massing of Wat Tyler's mob in the Peasants Revolt of 1386, the creation of the game of golf by James I, and the camp of Cromwell's Model Army during the Civil War of the 17th Century. Each of these was in its way a world-shaking event. Today, things have reached the less-than-thrilling point where there is a sign on the heath prohibiting much more mundane activities. It states that it is against the law to "sort rags and bones or to mend chairs." And I'm sure there's a story in that.

A few days after I wrote this account, we had an unexpected visitor at the warehouse. He had come to see again a place in which he remembered doing some early film work. Back in the thirties, he said. He was charming, but not at all communicative, as he toured the large, empty, dirty rooms on the ground floor, led through them by our ingratiating Sikh landlord. His rugged face had the look of someone whose mind was wandering somewhere in the past, which it undoubtedly was. We thought his visit reinforced the stories about Baird having lived and worked in the building. His name was James Mason.

A Cosmopolitan Student Body

THE STUDENTS AT THE COLLEGE WERE—WELL—STUDENTS. THEY RANGED IN AGE FROM ABOUT NINETEEN TO ABOUT TWENTY-FIVE and came from all over continental Europe. I have always got along well with my students. These ones were not different. With most of them I had only a classroom relationship. Others became friends. In this sense, this school, like all other schools, was a microcosm of the world at large.

Mercedes and Heinrich

There was a girl from Barcelona, who had the odd Christian name, "Mercedes": "like the car," she would say when introduced, who bore a striking resemblance to Sophia Loren. I was able to practice my horrible Spanish on her. (There goes the rule about speaking English at all times!) She was such a pleasure to look at that had I been Gilbert Osmond in Henry James' *Portrait of a Lady,* I would have collected her instead of Isabel Archer, though she at no point gave me the impression that she would have allowed *me* to collect *her.* Nevertheless, Mercedes was good company, unlike one Heinrich, a German student, who kept coming up to me and saying "Excuse the disturbation!" In spite of my correcting him every time and explaining the fact that we native speakers did not say that, he continued to use the non-word, "disturbation." His teacher, he said, had taught him the rule, so it must be right. Ah, the Germans and rules!

---

technology, which transmitted 405 lines. I can find no concrete evidence that Baird actually has any connection with the Blackheath building. On returning to the building in 2004, I noticed a plaque which states that it was used extensively by those who developed the documentary film in the 1930s. Perhaps that is where the truth lies.

Good Food is Better

Miss Brimicombe proved to be as hoard-nosed in her handling of students as she appeared to be at my job interview. A number of students were sent home for misbehaving. One got the boot for stealing one of those cannonball-shaped oil lamps that were used in those days to identify road hazards at night. Two others disappeared after they had taken a sign from Sainsbury's grocery store, *Good Food is Better at Sainsbury's,* and marched into the dining room with it, having removed the *at Sainsbury's* part. (The food *was* pretty bad, made in the mid-century English way: overcooked, under-spiced, unattractive. Though Mercedes, who earned her tuition and board by working part-time in the kitchen, insisted that the food that was brought in to be cooked was of top quality. It was the cooks who wrecked it. At least, I think that's what she said; she may have been speaking Spanish at the time.)

I Am Lovingly Assailed by Germana

I don't remember how good I was at supervising "the happiness of the students," whatever that means, but I did inadvertently make one student very unhappy. She was a tall, slightly built, attractive, Italian girl from Rho, a village near Milan. Her name was Germana. I can see her now, sitting in my class in her newly-fashionable jean jacket and skirt, paying me ever-so-much attention. Within days, she began to show up beside me when I was on duty. At first, I thought nothing of it, but one evening when I was at the duty desk in the main foyer with no one else around, she more or less told me that she loved me. Now, when you are a young teacher, of either sex, this kind of developing infatuation from the odd student is one of the hazards of the occupation. Generally, however, if you are kind but distant, it stays within limits. Not so with Germana. She pursued me relentlessly. The night before she left, as I sat at the duty desk, she leaned over my back and rubbed her breasts against me. "Take me for a walk, later," she said. Pleasant and flattering as this was, and tempted as I was by her suggestion, it was impossible. I had witnessed Miss Brimicombe's ruthlessness in dealing with student misdemeanours, and I had no reason to believe she would be less ruthless with me if she caught me fraternizing with a student in a romantic way. I'd be out on my ear, pronto!

The next day, a day sometime around the end of July, as she was leaving, Germana came over to me, on the steps at the front of the building to say goodbye, kissing me in the continental manner on both cheeks, a perfectly acceptable public demonstration of thanks, but one that had an underlying meaning that the public did not know. She said she would write to me. And she did. On August 12, I received the following letter:

> *I beg you to read this letter not like a teacher, but like a friend. Now that I am at home I miss so much Wilson College, my friends, the evenings passed in the dancing-room (so dirty but so nice!)* [Whatever did she mean?] *I am always sad and not only me, my friends too and when we are*

together, our general topic is our beautiful stay in Wilson College. We are really envying people that now are enjoying themselves in the College.

I wish I were in E.I [English I] all the day long writing your dictations! I hope you have forgotten my talks in the class-room. In the front page of my little book of autographs there is your dedication.

I will never forget Blackheath and a Canadian teacher, one of the nicest persons in the College. Unfortunately I am always down and I am sure that if you saw me, you would say: ``Che pena!``

I hope (for you) that German people are not so talkative as Italian one, because Miss Brimicombe will become mad!

Have always sunshine. Always! Always! I hate it and so regret English weather so much! I hope you will change your mind and you will come to Italy as soon as possible. Looking forward to seeing you again, I remain Yours very, very sincerely,

Germana

I had a second letter from Germana, which has unfortunately disappeared, forwarded by Miss Brimicombe to my North Kensington address in the middle of September, by which time I was safely married. As I did not reply to either letter, I never heard from her again.

Colleagues Muriel and Bruce

The other members of the teaching staff at Wilson College were a rather pathetic bunch. Heading into middle age, they were unambitious, unfocused, and unmarried. Two of them I remember. Muriel was a pleasant woman in her late thirties, who was so lacking in self-confidence that she was forever apologizing, to the point where you wanted to shake her and say, "Stop it!" Her smile, spoiled by teeth that were beautifully white, but misaligned and crooked, was probably the source of her lack of confidence. When she laughed, she tended to cover her mouth with her hand. She was always game to go anywhere and do anything—in a group. An Australian by the name of Bruce (yes, Monty Python had it right! They're all Bruces!) is the other one that I remember. He was also in his late thirties, with tightly-curled, dark brown hair, balding at front, heavy plastic glasses, and a worn blue blazer with brass buttons. He was a joker, constantly making fun of things. But underneath the hail-fellow-well-met exterior, one sensed a great deal of loss and pain. We worked well with one another, sharing the duty days, taking students on excursions, even one to Cambridge, where Bruce and I were in charge of a busload of 32 students. Once or twice, Muriel, Bruce, and I went to a pub in the evening, but there was no chemistry in our relationships, and I'm sure they forgot me as soon as I walked out the door for the last time.

I had been relatively happy in my time at Wilson College, but I was not unhappy to say goodbye to the place. The thought of finding myself in a position where I had to spend the rest of my career there was stultifying.

The Flat in Upper Addison Gardens

AS THE SUMMER WENT ON AND MY WEDDING DATE OF SEPTEMBER 1 LOOMED, IT RAPIDLY BECAME THE AREA OF MY GREATEST concern. On August 13, there is the following entry in my notebook:

> *Today I wrote to the LCC about my pay, and to BC to try to get some pension money back. "The Three-Cornered Hat" is ready to go. All I need is the postage. Tomorrow, I'll take a train into London and start flat-hunting. I hate the thought of it.*

I don't remember how I got involved with a rental agency in Beauchamp [pronounced Beecham] Place in Knightsbridge, though I may have gone there because it was close to Luba's Bistro, and therefore in an area I was familiar with. At any rate, I found a listing there for a furnished, garden-level flat at 7D Upper Addison Gardens, jurisdictionally in North Kensington, but really a part of much-less-ritzy Shepherds Bush. The rent was seven pounds a week, with a one-shot commission of one week's rent to be paid to the agency. The address was convenient, as it was close to Shepherds Bush underground station, on the Central Line, which would take Rosemary and me straight to Holborn, the closest station to Kingsway Day College. The rental agency arranged for me to meet the owner of the flat, so that I could have a look at it, and she could have a look at me. She was a Mrs. Comninos, a slightly-built wiry widow in her early sixties, who was every inch a Kensington lady.

I liked the flat at first sight. It was the lowest unit of a four-story building, one of a block-long streetscape of identical, attached, apartment buildings that might have been fifty years old at that time. Mrs. Comninos owned all of this particular building, which was about mid-way on the north side of the block. I did not doubt that she also owned many others. We entered the flat by descending three or four steps into a window well that led to the front door. Inside, was a hall that ran past the bedroom and bathroom. From the end of this hall, we entered the living room/dining room. The kitchen, which was off this large, rectangular room, was where the hall would have continued if it had extended through to the garden. And it was the garden that sold me on the place. From the dining area, a large window and a glassed-in door gave a view of a neglected garden, a lawn with some shrubs along the crumbling six-foot brick walls on the sides.

> *After we had done our tour of the place, Mrs. Comninos and I returned to the living room area to discuss my renting the place. Immediately, I said I'd take it. But Mrs. Comninos, sitting as erect as a Siamese cat on one of her about-to-be-rented chairs, said that maybe I should have my fiancée look at it before making up my mind. She felt, I think quite rightly, that the woman I was about to bring*

> *into my life should have some say in the matter. But I said, "No, that won't be necessary," as I knew that Rosemary would be charmed by it in the same way that I was. And she was.*

There was some flak from Rosemary's parents—before they had seen the place. They were aghast at the idea of their daughter's living in a *basement* flat in *Shepherds Bush*, ignoring my pleas that it would be better to describe it as a *garden* flat. But once they had visited us there, they were charmed by it as well, as I knew they would be.

Letters from Home

ALL THROUGH THE SUMMER, MY LETTERS FROM FAMILY AND FRIENDS BECOME MORE AND MORE CONCERNED WITH THE WEDDING. MY mother wrote with her usual concerns about religion and family:

> *Revelstoke, B.C.*
> *July 15*
>
> *Your letter came yesterday, glad you like your job, it seems as tho' it were an easy one. I hope things will go along smoothly re your big day, Sept 1st . . . I asked you if Rosemary was an only child but you didn't say, I am presuming she is and naturally religion and the fact of coming to Canada will irk them, but that's life and we have to put up with those things and may as well be gracious about them.*

And my eighty-three-year-old father followed this a week or so later with a blue aerogram in his shaky, difficult-to-read italic hand. Most of his letter concerns what is happening in his life and in the town and is far more interesting than my mother's general rambling. He makes you feel as if you are there with him:

> *Revelstoke, B.C.*
> *July 25*
>
> *I hear Ma down stairs busy getting dinner ready. Wish you and Rosemarie [sic] could be here to enjoy it with us. I can even hear the trucks back on the mountain road. You wouldn't know that country now, it is so altered.*

In early August, I had another note from my mother, more specific about her surroundings than her usual letters, but shorter, as she was frazzled by the presence of the three Hunter children and a very young "nurse maid." She wrote the letter essentially to let me know that I could withdraw much-needed money from the B.C. Teachers' Pension Fund: *I just wanted to tell you that Larry says you can draw out the Pension Money you put in at Castlegar.*[13] *He says you will need to forfeit a percentage but you still should*

---

[13] Larry Hunter, my brother-in-law, was a B.C. teacher, so he had some knowledge of the system. He and my sister, Jo, had left their three kids and a "nurse maid" with my parents while they went to Banff for a

get a couple hundred bucks and I hope you will never have more need for it and I think you should have it so try anyway. . . . It looks as if you will have a lovely wedding. I can't tell you how sorry I am that I can't be present but such is life. . . . I hope you land that pension money, it would give you a nice honeymoon.

Letters from Cambridge

IN THE MEANTIME, I HAD A NOTE FROM ROSEMARY—ISN'T IT STRANGE HOW WE *WROTE* BACK AND FORTH TO ONE ANOTHER INSTEAD OF telephoning (long distance calls were expensive and generally used for emergencies only)—with some bad news. She was working through the summer at a jam factory, and someone had stolen our engagement ring out of her locker there. I had bought it at an antique store in Holborn for £9. The good news was that the house insurance of Rosemary's parents would cover the loss. We later replaced it with a similar ring that had nine small pearls clustered together in a similar diamond shape.[14] It was not a good omen regarding the success of our marriage in the long run.

As upsetting as the loss of the ring proved to be, it was a minor irritation when compared to the troubles Rosemary was having with her mother, who was displaying classic characteristics of manic-depressive behaviour. One day, she'd be totally in favour of me and our marrying; the next day, she would rage at the kind of person I was and say that the marriage couldn't possibly take place. To illustrate her bi-polar behaviour, I have excerpted passages from some of Rosemary's letters to me during the summer:

July 4 *Because I wasn't up before 8:30 this morning, we're not going to book the reception, etc. She has cried because I'm constantly rude and awkward—she says. She's said I'm to leave and live somewhere else.*

July 6 *Mother came storming into my bedroom at 7:30 this morning and said she couldn't go on like this. So she said* again *that she's having nothing to do with the wedding—that I hate her and she no longer wants to have anything to do with me. So nothing's fixed. But don't despair. This afternoon we have been down and bought her shoes, gloves and dress pattern, so I suppose everything is ok again.*

July 9 *A vast improvement has occurred over this weekend and I'm so relieved . . . My mother has also offered to give me her wedding ring, because it is too small and without telling my father actually wears one she bought later.*

July 17 *Mother is cross again because of the way I was wearing my dress, because I had no slip on, because you did not speak to her on the phone, etc., etc.*

---

holiday. "This is just a note," mother writes, "as I am up to my neck today. Jo, etc. came last Sun. and it's been a hectic week, they brought a 12 yr. old to help with the baby so I have 6 extras and I can't take it as I used to."

[14] We valued the ring at £25 for insurance purposes. The representative of the insurance company turned out to be David Earle, a former boyfriend of Rosemary's. At the time, I was ignorant of the fact that she had a propensity for keeping old flames at least partially lit. David didn't ask any difficult questions.

July 23 *I'm so unhappy—I am just sitting on the bed surrounded by all the things that I have spent the day washing and ironing and cleaning, and I am crying so hard I can hardly see to write to you. It's been a dreadful day—I suppose she had to take it out on me because I came to London to see you yesterday—not because of what she's been like today. She went over everything then—sex as usual being most prominent.*

August 7 *Mother has been vile today. She let me sleep until 10:30 and then came storming in because I wasn't up. She got on to me about sex again, saying that that is all there is between us.*

August 12 *Mother and I are now trying to get the wedding dress finished before [Aunt] Rosa comes on Thursday. She went on again about sex yesterday. But today, she's happy and helpful. It's awfully hard to deal with. I'll be so glad to get out of this house and into our nice flat in Kensington.*

Letters from Friends

I HAD ASKED TWO OF MY FRIENDS FROM THE INSTITUTE TO BE USHERS AT THE WEDDING. JIM HONEYBONE, MY ROOM MATE THERE, WAS happy to oblige. David Hepworth, however, begged off in the following letter:

1, Spen Bank House
Cleckheaton, Yorkshire
August 12

Dear Terry,

    Sorry not to have replied to the wedding invitation earlier, but I was calculating whether I would be in Italy or not. Money prevents that. I've been planning all along so as to be able to come to your wedding and, of course, I'm delighted to accept.

    One thing, though. I'd like to be excused the usher's job. I share your aversion to parading in monkey's clothes, but rather more strongly. Also, there is the expense and difficulty of hiring; and I may well be in Ireland immediately before the wedding. I hate officiating in any respect, and I hope you'll allow me to beg off. I hope my reasons don't sound trivial.

    I can arrange my own accommodation in Cambridge at my old landlady's I think. I'll write an official acceptance to Mr and Mrs Latter and probably put in a note to Rosemary to explain about ushering, etc. She may be offended so I count on good Commonwealth support from you.

> *I'll probably come to Cambridge on Friday, August 31ˢᵗ. Would you care for a token wet? I'll show you an interesting pub or two.*[15]
>
> *All the best. Make the most of your last few days of bachelorhood.*
>
> *David*
>
> *P. S. How's the job? I don't suppose in the hectic premarital days you can spare a weekend up here. It'll only cost you the fare.*

I, of course, was not at all offended. Neither was Rosemary. In many ways, David was a private person, and I did not want to force him to do anything he didn't want to do. I was pleased he was making an effort to come to the wedding. That was good enough. As for finding a weekend to visit him in Cleckheaton, that was impossible, as I was only free one weekend a month. I have always regretted not being able to make that trip.

Finally, in the last week of what David referred to as "my hectic premarital days," I received a long and chatty letter from Leslie Dunkling, my best man:

> *Sunday* [August 26]
>
> *England seems a grim place after Italy, but I suppose we shall soon settle in again. We arrived last night and hitch-hiked home from the airport in record time. Anyway, more about our experiences some other time.*
>
> *I should be able to get up to Town* [London] *on Wednesday at the latest for a fitting* [of his morning suit at Moss Bros.]*, so there is no snag there. A little more difficult is the question of when Nicole and I go up to Cambridge. As you'll remember, I'm taking over the China shop* [where he was working] *from tomorrow, when the owners go on holiday. I have said nothing to them about having the day off next Saturday. I thought it would worry them too much—but I have arranged with the assistant that her daughter should come in to help out for the day, and any deliveries I could look after on Sunday. I have to confirm these arrangements tomorrow, but they are fairly safe.*
>
> *On Friday I am bound to the shop until six, perhaps a little later, and the earliest I could get to Cambridge would be nine-o-clock. I was wondering whether I might not do better to stay at the shop a little longer on Friday and get everything straight, then leave early Saturday morning. I don't know whether you have to be in Cambridge on Friday* [I did]*; if not, we could go out in London for a drink. I shall know more about all this once I get to the shop tomorrow, and more still by Wednesday. Why not telephone me at the shop on Wednesday morning (10-1) or any time on Thursday, and we'll make final arrangements? If it's*

---

[15] David was a great lover of pubs. After a successful marriage, in which he and his wife, Margaret, brought up two fine children, and after retiring from a successful career in teaching, David's love of pubs caught up with him and he died in 2008 of cirrhosis of the liver.

obviously to everyone's advantage that we all go up on Friday, I'll do my best to fix things at the shop.

Nicole has bought a dress for the wedding—a good excuse!—but I can't grumble because I bought a pair of dress shoes in Switzerland. I don't know whether we'll be able to continue to go to Italy for silk, Switzerland for shoes, etc., but it's certainly the best way to buy a wardrobe.

If you can manage to get over here one evening this week for a meal, particularly Wednesday or Thursday, let us know with a post-card and that'll be fine. I don't know when you're moving into your flat, but it would be easier for you if you were already there when you came over.

Before I forget, the telephone number at the shop, "Elizabeth Somerset," is PER 3262. I'm sure everything will work out smoothly, but I expect you'll be glad when a few weeks have passed and you've settled down. We looked upon this holiday as a second honeymoon, and it was better than the first. Marriage seems to be like wine, it gets richer and stronger with time.

Be seeing you soon, then. All the best meanwhile.

Les

I have no memory of how all these things worked out. But work out they did, and we all converged on Cambridge and were there for September 1.

The Interior of *Luba's Bistro*

Bloomsbury: Around the Institute

Dillon's, Where I Saw the Queen Mother. Now a Branch of Waterstone's.

Marlborough: Our Favourite Pub

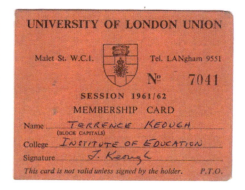

Another Favourite Pub

25 Woburn Square. My Room is Right above Left Door

Royal Academy of Dramatic Arts

Russell Square

H 3557

Mr T. Keough

Dr. to UNIVERSITY OF LONDON INSTITUTE OF EDUCATION COLLEGE ROOMS

Bed and Breakfast
Board Residence from 9th Jan to 20th Mar

Pd. 25/1/62

Cheques and Money Orders should be made payable to University of London Institute of Education and crossed "Westminster Bank, Limited, Bloomsbury Branch, A/c Payee only."
Payment should be made to the Cashier, Room 174 or by post to :-
THE ACCOUNTANT
UNIVERSITY OF LONDON INSTITUTE OF EDUCATION,
MALET STREET, LONDON, W.C.1

The slip attached below should be torn off and sent with remittance
Receipts will not be issued for payments made by cheque, unless specially requested

Board Residence 9 Jan – 20 Mar

BM Reading Room Ticket   8 May 1963

Whittingehame College over Easter

WHITTINGEHAME COLLEGE

TELEPHONE
BRIGHTON 56066/7/8

SURRENDEN ROAD
BRIGHTON, 6.
SUSSEX

HEADMASTER
J. HALEVY, M.SC.

27th March, 1962.

Mr. Terence Keough
7, Timberley Road,
CAMBRIDGE.

Dear Mr. Keough,

We have now received your testimonials forwarded by the R.A.C. and these have been placed before Mr. Halevy on his return to school to-day.

We are now pleased to offer you a post on our teaching staff for the Easter holidays, and if you wish to accept the post kindly confirm. As you know, the dates are 5th – 30th April.

Yours sincerely,

Secretary.

The Administration and Classroom Building

The Conservatory Where Anne Played the Piano

Back View of Administration and Classroom Building

The Albion Hotel Silver Mug

Latter Family Picnic in Cambridge

Heather Smith with Rosemary on the Cam

The Pavilion

My Room at Whittingehame

Teaching Practice in the East End

Cowper Street E.C.2
Central Foundation School at Left

Entrance

Welcome to Central Foundation Boys' School

Playground

Toilet Paper in London Schools

Last Extant Wilson College Laundry List

47, Bennett Park.

WILSON COLLEGE
St. John's Park, Blackheath, S.E.3

Day Return London to Blackheath 2/10

Date................... Laundry No:...............
Name..

Towels, each	....	**Vests**, each
Shirts, each	....	**Briefs**, pair
Pyjamas, pair	....	**Socks**, pair
H'chiefs, each	....	**Face Cloths**, each
Sports Shirts, each	....	**Sports Shorts**, pair
Laundry Bag	....	

The Laundry will retain this part.

Name.................. Date............. Laundry...

Towels, each	....	**Vests**, each
Shirts, each	....	**Briefs**, pair
Pyjamas, pair	....	**Socks**, pair
H'chiefs, each	....	**Face Cloths**, each
Sports Shirts, each	....	**Sports Shorts**, pair
Laundry Bag	....	

Charing Cross Station

Retain this Part.

Name.................. Date............. Laundry No:......

Towels, each	....	**Vests**, each	....
Shirts, each	....	**Briefs**, pair	....
Pyjamas, pair	....	**Socks**, pair	....
H'chiefs, each	....	**Face Cloths**, each	....
Sports Shirts, each	....	**Sports Shorts**, pair	....
Laundry Bag	....		

47 Bennett Park Road Warehouse 2004

7D Upper Addison Gardens Entrance

Wilson College
Gre. 3581 — Office
Gre. 0781 — Miss B's Rooms
Gre. 3970 — Students

My Note of Phone Nos. (Gre=Greenwich)

Garden Alcove at 7D

Coal Stove Area of Living Room at 7D

Terry Outside of 7D

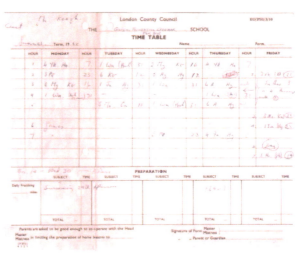
Teaching Practice Timetable
Summer Term 1962

Job Offer at Wilson College

Chapter 16: A London Last Hurrah

KINGSWAY DAY COLLEGE: ON THE CUTTING EDGE

> To disclose yourself, expose yourself, in a whole book is asking for trouble. Self-revelation is a kind of suicide
> Nicholas Wollaston, *Tilting at Don Quixote*, 1990

> It was a funny thing: once you tell your story to others it becomes more like fiction and less like truth. A layer of performance is added to it, removing you further from the real thing.
> Tracy Chevalier, *The Virgin Blue*, 1997

A Wedding in Cambridge

ON SEPTEMBER 1, 1962, IN ST. LAURENCE'S CATHOLIC CHURCH, MILTON ROAD, CAMBRIDGE, AT 3 O'CLOCK IN THE AFTERNOON, I WAS MARRIED TO ROSEMARY ANN LATTER. ROSEMARY HAD TO prepare for this day, as she was a Protestant, by taking "Instructions" from the Catholic padre of the University of London, Father Sheppard, a priest at St. Patrick's Church in Soho Square, the first post-Reformation Catholic Church built in England (1792).

Why did I go through the bother of marrying in the Catholic Church? Partly because I loved the traditional liturgy, even though I had largely rejected many aspects of the theology, both Catholic and Christian. Besides, and more importantly, I knew that if I married elsewhere it would cause a rift in my family. My mother was especially hard-line in these matters. The religious question was not a problem for Rosemary, but as I was later to learn—I did not realize this at first—it was a difficulty for her family of incredibly low-church Anglicans: Herbert, her father, went to a service every Sunday at the Round Church in Cambridge, which is about as low-Anglican as you can get; Marguerite, her mother, though professing a devotion to the Church of England, never went to services at all, except to attend events like baptisms, weddings and funerals.

In the months leading up to the wedding, it was Marguerite who enlisted the help of an adamantly anti-Catholic, former boy-friend of Rosemary's to try to convince her that the marriage was a bad idea. In a letter to me at Wilson College on July 6, Rosemary recounted an early attempt by this fellow to dissuade her:

> *This morning was taken up with entertaining Jimmy. He had got the morning off from school to drive here from London. He says now that he is not driven by purely personal reasons, that he can control his feelings in the matter to further the more important end of my happiness. But he wants to warn me about marrying Catholics. He wants me to wait a year—because you are not offering me enough security, and because I've known you such a short time. He thinks I should consider the feelings of my parents more. In fact, he preached me a long moral sermon against marrying you on September 1st. But he says he does not intend to try and break up the engagement, and he feels a great desire to protect me and look after me. So I thanked him very much and said that I could manage very well and the only person who was likely to disrupt my happiness was Mother and that that would be the only possible result of his interference. So he left a booklet on R.C. for my parents to read and he gave me a little history lesson on the corruption of R.C. which necessitated the Reformation. He said that if you had not been a Catholic he would not have intruded and he does not want you to think of him as a rival for my desirable hand, but someone who has my best interests at heart, etc., etc. It went on and on.*

Jimmy's attempts to turn Rosemary off the marriage continued throughout the summer. But the result was opposite to what Marguerite and Jimmy had intended, and, as one might expect, they were not only unsuccessful, but hardened her resolve to go through with the marriage.

Rosemary wore a beautiful, form-fitting, off-white dress that she and her mother had made for the occasion. She looked absolutely stunning. I was in a morning suit: tail coat, striped pants, white gloves, top hat, etc., rented from Moss Bros. of London. I felt somewhat as if I had donned a costume to act in a play, and in a sense that was the case. (But even I looked fabulous, if I do say so myself!) The ceremony was traditional, to the point where we used a 1936 Canadian silver dollar as a piece of silver to be blessed along with the ring, a symbolic hope for a prosperous marriage. The church was full of Latter family and friends. Nobody from my family was in attendance, but that lack was mitigated by the presence of good friends of both of us from our year at the Institute.

Father Sheppard annoyed me by preaching a sermon on the evils of birth control; but apart from that, and apart from the fact that the organist complained that the organ was a mere pump organ, all went well.

The reception was held in the garden at the Milton Arms, a pub not far down the road from the church. Father Sheppard, who was a graduate of Trinity College, Cambridge, stood around the periphery of the guests, smoking. He was a big man, not fat, but chunky. He was wearing a somewhat disreputable, rumpled, linen jacket. Marguerite later referred to him as "that dirty old man." Some old aunts observed the gathering guests, with narrowed eyes. Suitably hated for the occasion, flowered of dress, their handbags hanging to their knees, they were storing away shards of criticism to be gossiped about later. Lady Ridley, mother-in-law of Rosemary's brother, David, sat on the edge of her chair, ladylike, unaware that her slip was showing a couple of inches below her skirt. Wine and beer and finger foods were served. The sun looked down in favour upon the day. Guests mingled. Photographs were taken.

After a decent time, Rosemary and I went into an upstairs room in the pub, rented for the occasion, and changed into our going-away clothes. Leslie Dunkling, the best man, and his wife, Nicole, brought their rented car to the front of the building, and we left for London amidst much waving and clapping. We were glad it was over. When we arrived in London, the Dunklings dropped us off at our flat in Upper Addison Gardens and sped away. We did not plan to go on an immediate honeymoon, as we had to start our teaching jobs a few days later. We didn't need a honeymoon. We had had enough excitement putting up with the summer-long shenanigans of Rosemary's mother and arranging and going through the wedding ceremony. Besides, we didn't have any money.

The World of Kingsway Day College

ONE OF THE TASKS WE HAD HAD TO WORK AT AS THE TERM AT THE INSTITUTE CAME TO AN END WAS THE BUSINESS OF FINDING A teaching job. I had flirted with an opening for an English teacher at a Catholic School in the western part of Kensington, but the job demanded that I teach Latin as well as English, and I did not feel comfortable with my Latin, which I had dropped at the end of my second year in university. All of this became academic, so to speak, when on May 9 Rosemary received the following letter, scrawled in dashing handwriting on a piece of University of London Institute of Education letterhead, from her tutor, Nancy Martin:

> *I have had lunch with Mr. Flower, Principal of Kingsway Day College. He says to you—and particularly Terry—to apply for any post (Eng - Maths etc!) which was advertised in last week's T. E. S.*[1] *and to ring him up and make a date to see him <u>as soon as possible</u> (Chancery 3725.) The College is very flexible in its requirements and position of staff, and other changes will happen in time, etc. Go and discuss the possibilities*

---

[1] The *Times Educational Supplement* was delivered with the paper on Fridays. Each week in the final term, we checked all the job offers, from all over the world, very carefully, looking for just the right one.

with him—both of you. It's a terribly nice place—so don't be put off by looks!

In haste, NCM

I have referred to Mr. Frederick Dalby Flower, "Fred D. Flower," as he usually signed his name, in the previous chapter. Here I would like to have a closer look at the man who was Principal of Kingsway Day College. In the lengthy obituary in *The Guardian* (Aug.13, 2001), for Fred Flower, MBE, CBE (1915-2001), he is referred to as "one of the great humanist educators of his day, and his skill in providing a framework for the development of unconventional ideas powerfully influenced British post-16 education." He spent the war in the Army Education Corps, organizing educational and recreational events for the Eighth Army in North Africa and Italy, rising to the rank of lieutenant colonel, and being awarded an MBE for his services.

Flower occupied a cluttered office at the college's building, on Keeley Street, in Holborn, off Kingsway, about halfway between High Holborn Street and the Strand. He was a soft-spoken, unpretentious, forward-looking man in his 40s, who obviously knew what he wanted; and when he saw what he wanted, he went about getting it. (In this case, he wanted Rosemary and me.) It became evident early in the interview that his politics and social conscience, like ours, were left-leaning. We did not know at the time that he had been a long-time member of the Communist Party, joining when he saw the horrible result of the Spanish Civil War in 1939, and quitting after the appalling Hungarian invasion of 1956. From that time on, he became a strong force in the framing of educational policy for the Labour Party. Following his retirement from Kingsway in 1978, he was awarded a CBE. We knew nothing about his early life at the time of our interview with him. If we had known about his military background, we would have been impressed. And his political background would not have mattered. A short time after the interview began, he offered jobs to both of us; and, without hesitation, we accepted.

The building on Keeley Street was indeed old and ramshackle, but we were not put off by that, as Nancy Martin had feared. We were young and decidedly biased toward an urban lifestyle; and the moderate decrepitude of the place—still common in post-war London, not yet a forest of glass and aluminium—charmed us.[2] We felt we were on the cutting edge, helping to define the direction in which day-release education was heading. And we were.

Although the jobs had been promised to us, and we had no reason to doubt that they would be ours, we did not receive official confirmation and application forms from the London County Council until August 9. In those years, the bureaucracy, like so much

---

[2] The building has been gone for many years, replaced by a modern office complex. The College, which moved from Keeley Street to the Grays Inn Road area when it lost the Keeley Street building, was amalgamated with Westminster College in 2000 to form Westminster Kingsway College. It now has about 19,000 students spread over six campuses in Central London, studying a wide variety of subject areas, including cooking, acting, painting, tourism, ESL, film, as well as academic courses to prepare students for their GCEs both at O Level and at A-Level. In my time, we might have had a thousand students in total, and our focus was essentially on improving their academic skills.

else in the country, was mired in old fashioned attitudes and out-of-date procedures. It would take the likes of Margaret Thatcher, much as I hate to admit it, considering her horrible attitude toward ordinary people, to turn the system on its head and bring England, dragging and kicking, into the 20th century. The salary was £855 a year (ca. C$2,500), including the London allowance, meant to compensate for the greater expense of living in the capital—it didn't!—and also including a bonus for having a "good honours degree." The money wasn't great, but it was enough to get by on.

From Shepherds Bush to Holborn and Back

THE COLLEGE TERM BEGAN ON SEPTEMBER 10, SO WE HAD A FEW DAYS IN WHICH TO SETTLE INTO OUR FURNISHED FLAT AT 7D UPPER Addison Gardens. The flat provided the basic necessities—furniture, curtains, cutlery, and so on—and we made it feel like home by installing our few books in the built-in shelves on either side of the living room fireplace and adding to the decor items like Rosemary's portable gramophone—a turntable and speakers in a blue suitcase, a twenty-first birthday present from her parents.

Once during those first days, we tested out the route to and from the College. Upper Addison Gardens is in North Kensington, a seedy area at that time, and our closest underground station was Shepherds Bush, on the Central Line, only a five-minute walk away. There, we caught a train to incredibly busy Holborn Station, on the Piccadilly as well as the Central Line, a journey of about twenty minutes (Day Return 2/4). From there, it was only a short walk to Keeley Street. An easy commute.

The students we taught were released by their employers from their jobs with full pay one day a week in order to further their education. Most of them had left school at the school-leaving age of fifteen and taken menial jobs of one sort or another. On the whole, we did not teach them skills directly related to their work, but tried to give a boost to their general education. It was Mr. Flower's contention that a teacher with a tertiary degree, or with the equivalent in life and work experience, could prepare and teach the material in almost any discipline at this level. He did pay some attention to a teacher's background, so Rosemary and I, for the most part, were slotted into courses in English. I don't remember what areas outside of her training Rosemary had to beef up and teach. But I did a course in Geography for partially-sighted people, a course on the History of London (if you can believe it!) for night students, and a course in basic arithmetic for butcher's apprentices.

Most of our classes were held in the Keeley Street building. But there were exceptions. If you walked a short distance up Drury Lane and turned right on Great Queen Street, you came to the City Literary Institute,[3] which contained a library and classrooms, both of which we used, and a staff room in which we could hang out between classes. I taught a number of my courses there. In the fall term, I also taught a course

---

[3] It had been established originally to try to raise the educational level of working-class people, so it was a perfect fit with Kingsway. It was still there in 2007 when I explored that part of London, but it looked out of place in the midst of newer glass and steel buildings, a bit of post-war London: old, shabby, and dirty.

one morning a week at the YW/YMCA on Baker Street, in almost the exact location of Sherlock Holmes' fictional hangout. Fred Flower was spreading his tentacles into the community even at this early date. "Elementary, my dear Watson," he might have said to me, if his name was Holmes and mine was Watson. He would, at any rate, have been amused by the connection. I'm sorry I didn't think of it at the time. We would have had a good laugh over it.

> *The Secretary and Receptionist at the Baker Street "Y" was a young woman in a wheelchair. Her name was Mary. She was a delightful, friendly individual, who had had an accident a few years before which had left her legs paralyzed. As time went by, we became good workplace friends. One day she told me excitedly that she had just become engaged to a young man who, unlike herself, was able-bodied. He didn't give a damn that she was in a wheelchair, she said. He loved her. Not only that, but she had been to see a doctor, who had told her that there was no reason why she could not have children. It was a heart-warming story, and I leaned down, wished her the best, and embraced her. We didn't embrace much in those days, and she was surprised. But she was also pleased. After that fall term, I never went back to the Baker Street "Y," and I never saw Mary again. I wonder if the marriage was a success, and if she managed to have the children that she so much wanted. I hope so.*

In order to earn a little extra money, Rosemary and I each taught an extra early-evening class on Wednesdays. These classes ran from 5:30 to 6:30, and were for people who could not get day release but who wanted to improve their education. It was during this class time that I had the audacity to teach a course on the History of London. It was fortunate that none of my students knew any more about it than I did; and though I sometimes slipped up in my references to the geography of the city, I came through it well enough, and in the bargain learned something I had previously known nothing about.

After these classes, we would go back to the Shepherds Bush area, to the northern end of Holland Road, almost directly opposite Upper Addison Gardens, where there was a little Chinese restaurant on the ground floor of a four-floor walk-up building, that served a cheap and delicious mushroom soup for three shillings a bowl, including bread. This was our treat to ourselves for doing the extra work. When we had finished the soup, we would walk down the street to our flat, where we would complete our dinner with a sandwich and coffee. To eat a whole meal in the restaurant every week would have been extravagant.

Some Kingsway Colleagues

THE FACULTY AT KINGSWAY WAS AN ODD ASSORTMENT, AS ONE MIGHT EXPECT IN A COLLEGE OF THIS SORT, ON THE CUTTING EDGE of experimental day-release. Some people, like Rosemary and me, had traditional academic qualifications and taught more or less traditional academic courses; others, such as Jack Cook, Dorothy Bumpus, and Gaynor Freestone, had been hired to teach students in areas in the workaday world in which they had accumulated a good deal of experience. A special friend on the academic side was John Daniels.

The Many Sides of Jack Cook

Jack Cook was a somewhat rough character in his early forties who had worked for years in a variety of trades, many of them at the apprentice level. He was one of those odd people who, once they have attained a qualification in a particular trade, seek to learn a new area. He had been a chimney sweep, a butcher, and a bartender, among other things. So, in many respects he was ideal to teach courses relating to these and other trades. He did me a favour when I was saddled with an arithmetic course for apprentice butchers by teaching me the arcane formula used in England at that time to determine the price of bacon. I have since forgotten it completely.

> *One day, Rosemary—more angry than upset—came to me with a story that illustrated another side of Jack Cook. He had grabbed her while the two of them were in a cupboard sorting out supplies and kissed her on the lips. She was not amused, and she told him that if he ever did that again, she would make a good deal of trouble for him. He didn't. But he was lucky that this incident occurred in the 1960's, when women were more tolerant of errant male behaviour. In the 1990s she might have taken him to court. In the 2000s she probably would have kicked him in the family jewels.*

In the spring term, Jack invited the entire faculty to Islington, where his amateur theatre group was putting on a production of Gilbert and Sullivan's *Yeoman of the Guard*. Now, at that time, Gilbert and Sullivan's operettas, like all things Victorian, though still popular among the hoi polloi, were deemed by the young and educated to be hopelessly dated. So most of the faculty pooh-poohed the idea of going. Rosemary and I, however, felt that we should show up, at least briefly, and offer some support to a fellow teacher, as objectionable as he might sometimes be.

We talked our colleague, John Daniels, and his American wife, Judy—about whom more later—to join us. We drove in John's small van to the hall in which the performance was to take place. It was a small hall, with a small audience—perhaps fifty or so, most of them probably friends of the performers. We stood against the back wall, not wanting to make a greater commitment. We were late. We came in on a scene in which eight yeomen, singing bravely in a row across the front of the stage to the accompanying piano, dressed in absurd knight-like uniforms, alternately dropped to a sitting and rose to a standing position, as if they were getting on and off a series of toilets. We had trouble subduing our giggles and left at the end of the scene, laughing uproariously as we walked to the car. Our visit had taken ten minutes at the most. But at least we'd shown up.

Jack Cook had dragged himself up by his own working-class bootstraps. I never liked him, but I admired the effort he had made to make himself a better world.

Dorothy Hallam Bumpus and the College Theatre Scene

In later years, long after I had gone on to other places and other things, the College became well-known for its dance and drama programs. But even in those early days, there was a good deal of theatre of all kinds being produced. The inspiration behind the drama and the singing programs was Dorothy Hallam Bumpus, a ball of energy in her thirties, who was able to handle all aspects of theatre production. At the end of October, over three nights, the Keeley Players mounted an excellent production of Oliver Goldsmith's *She Stoops to Conquer*, at Starcross School, on Sidmouth Street, a kilometre or so north of Keeley Street, as the College did not have a theatre of its own. As a Christmas Concert, "Dot" Bumpus contrived to put on a broadly ambitious program at the same location, designed principally to give as many students as possible experience on stage. There were selections by the Keeley Players from the Christmas pantomime, *Dick Whittington and His Cat*; a short piece from the court scene in *Witness for the Prosecution*; an excerpt from Act III, Scene 4 of *Hamlet*; and a selection from the first act of *Saint Joan*. There was solo singing of the old-fashioned type—a soprano accompanied by a piano, looking incredibly earnest, arms locked in a bow at her waist. This theatre program, expanded and specialized in later years, produced a number of well-known actors, including, among many others, Michelle Collins and Steve McFadden, who rose to country-wide fame in *EastEnders*.

Gaynor Freestone Looms Large in Dance and Singing

The dance groups were taught by Gaynor Freestone, a huge woman. I couldn't imagine her actually dancing without bringing the house down, literally as a well as figuratively. But I suppose she must have done so, since she had been hired to teach dance to our students. It's likely that her real strengths were elsewhere, as she also had impressive qualifications in piano and violin, and she could teach singing. At the Christmas Concert, the Dance Drama Group performed part of a modern ballet, in which a group of Priestesses mourn the death of Adonis, as well as some Cha-Cha Dances, and a jazz ballet based on the story of Shadrack, Meshac, and Abednego. Gaynor was in many ways a remarkable woman. She was a no-nonsense type of person who expected (and often got) superb performances from her students, perhaps, in part, out of fear that she might beat them up if they didn't give her their best effort. Her physical size even intimidated *me* a bit.

> *She was a rough gem. One day, when the two of us were alone in the staff room at City Lit, discussing in a desultory way the photographs of Cecil Beaton, especially his then-revolutionary posing of his female models with their legs spread apart, she said, "Women only open their legs for one reason." And when I replied, playfully, "And what is that?" she swung her enormous handbag at me, forcing me to skip back from her. Both of us then burst into raucous laughter, which puzzled a couple of the other teachers who were just entering the room at the time. It was one of those lovely moments between near-friends who enjoy each other's company, but who will never be real friends.*

John Daniels—A Class Act

John Daniels was a medium-height man in his mid-twenties with a large nose and piercing eyes. He had grown up in London in a working class family. After showing great promise academically in grade school, and passing the Eleven Plus examinations with flying colours, he was singled out as one of the working-class children who at that time were sent in token numbers to various public schools and near-public schools. The idea was to begin the process of eliminating the class divisions. (It didn't work.) In John's case, the school was Merchant Taylors' School Northwood (founded 1561). John certainly received a superior education as a result of the experiment, which, while succeeding academically in his case, and no doubt in the case of many others, was a total failure on the societal level. But along with the academic success, there were scars. He was, he said, always ashamed of his parents on those days when parents were invited to the school—they were obviously working class, and in spite of their concerted efforts (often making things worse rather than better), they did not fit into the crowd of middle and upper-middle class moms and dads. They had the wrong clothes, the wrong manners, and the wrong accents, and their lack of confidence made them seem obsequious when they tried to intermingle with the others.

John had gone on to University College, London, and from there had been given a Fulbright Scholarship to the University of Minnesota, where he met and married Judy, his American wife. When they returned with their infant son to England, they found a small house in Hampstead, and John was hired to write reviews for *The Spectator*. As there wasn't enough money in writing reviews to pay the bills, he looked around for other work; and, in a series of steps, he eventually arrived at Kingsway Day College.

For some reason or other, I remember John most of all sartorially: worn corduroy jacket with leather patches on the elbows, tie badly knotted and askew; I see him entering the staff room in his tan raincoat, collar up, epaulets on the shoulders, looking every bit like a probing journalist. He would take out his pipe and fill it with an aromatic tobacco called *Clan*, which came in a pouch decorated with a tartan motif. In imitation, I got out my old pipes, which I hadn't smoked for a couple of years, bought myself some *Clan*, and joined John as a pipe-smoker. I also joined him in his staff-room battles with Bill Kitsis, an American communist in our age group who had graduated from Harvard, fled to London, and was forever proselytising on the theories of Marx and Engels. One thing that Merchant Taylors had convinced John of—rather oddly, one might think—was the fact that there is no such thing as a worker's paradise. He had come to the conclusion that no matter what political system happened to be in place in a society, there would always be a group of elite people running things.

John and I spent quite a lot of time together. Both of us were trying to write a novel. I actually finished the one I was working on. When I showed it to John, he was peculiarly quiet as he scanned through it. I knew then that it was bad. And it was. But he did praise one chapter over and over, and I think it was not just compensation for the rest. It was the one well-written part of it all. John used to talk about getting up at five every morning to write before going to work. But he never showed me anything he'd written.

> *Just as I was about to leave for Canada at the end of the school year, and before I had told anyone about my plans, John came to me and asked me if I would like to take over his reviewing job at The Spectator. I don't remember why he was giving it up. It was tempting to throw up my plans, retain my job at Kingsway, and take on the prestigious task of writing book reviews for such a fine periodical. My travel plans were far advanced. But they were not so far advanced that they could not have been reversed. Besides, there was no compelling reason why I should return to Canada at that time. I probably was fixed on doing so because I was anxious to show Rosemary to my family and friends and introduce her to my country. Rosemary, on her part, was excited about the prospect and looking forward to the move as a great adventure. It had gathered a momentum of its own, and even though it was stoppable, neither one of us wanted to stop it. We were committed. It was what we wanted to do.*

Students and Student Evaluations

OUR STUDENTS AT KINGSWAY DAY COLLEGE WERE NOT, ON THE WHOLE, AMONG THOSE WHO HAD DONE WELL AT SCHOOL. BUT IN many ways, they were not responsible for their failure. They had been short-changed by the class system. It had singled them out to go to inferior elementary schools, where they were not properly prepared to pass the Eleven Plus examination, which in itself was designed to keep the vast majority of the population as underdogs. Fred Flower had long recognized the unfairness of the system then in place. Not only had he as an individual risen above it, but he had also experienced first hand, while he was in the Education Corp of the British Army in North Africa during the Second World War, the unrecognized value and undeveloped capacity to learn in those who had left school early.

Like their grunt equivalents in the Eighth Army, our students had a measure of unused capacity that they were eager to fill. And they had a marvellous humanity about them, beaten down in some cases, but always retrievable with a little bit of acceptance and encouragement on my part.

> *One cold morning, a girl came to me before class and giggled out the fact that her father, who kept his teeth overnight in a water-filled glass beside his bed, awoke to find the water frozen. I wondered at how cold their house must have been. Another day, in the spring of 1963, a small group of students came to me with the exciting news that they had run into a new musical group on the Charing Cross foot bridge. They were called The Beatles, they said. They had weird hair-dos. I, of course, had never heard of this group and didn't pay much attention to the story at the time. But when I remembered the incident later, I wondered that what was then casually possible for the Beatles and their fans would never be possible again.*

At the end of each term there were the usual token gifts, much appreciated, that one becomes used to in the world of teaching: a carnation, a small box of chocolates, a key chain. Occasionally, to provide some kind of balance and keep one's ego in check, there was a vitriolic note from an unhappy student. Sometimes, there was an unexpected thank-you note, profoundly touching, from a totally unsuspected source. I have kept one of these notes, written on a hand-made card from a place with the pretentious name, *L'ECHOPPE d'art*, but a card chosen with great care. The message reads like a poem:

> *Classic course evaluation:*
> *to sum up and say*
> *everythings with nothings.*
> *You've been a great guy*
> *(I feel I have to say this)*
> *In every sense of the word*
> *(Let it be . . . said)*
> *That's part of what I think is important*
> *Thanks for being yourself*
>
> *The feeling of you remains with me,*
> *Let us say none of the rest . . .*
>   Lea Kusters

Nights at the Opera—and Elsewhere

THE ROYAL OPERA HOUSE, WHICH EVERYONE SIMPLY REFERRED TO AS "COVENT GARDEN," WAS JUST A HOP, SKIP, AND JUMP DOWN THE Street from the College. I have used this much worn image because of its relevance to the theatre we experienced there. One of our colleagues, Dorothy Stratton, with whom Rosemary quickly became friendly, was a fiend for ballet, and we were soon drawn in by her enthusiasm. Once we had decided to go to a particular performance of the Royal Ballet, one of us would go down the street to get into the line-up at the Covent Garden box office to get a queue ticket, giving us a time later in the day to come and pick up the actual tickets. The system worked very well for us, as we worked close by.

Dorothy's husband, Ken, was as enthusiastic as she was about the ballet. Ken had lost the lower part of his right arm in a childhood accident, but he had learned to do practically everything he needed to do with clever manipulation of his left hand and his stump. In no time, one had forgotten that he was handicapped. He was the librarian/archivist for the liberal *News Chronicle*, whose archives had been kept separate when the London daily had been absorbed by the right-wing *Daily Mail* in 1960.

It was an exciting time for ballet in London. Rudolph Nureyev had recently defected to the West, and his presence had revived the fading career of Margot Fonteyn, who was then in her forties and had been on the verge of retiring. Nureyev entertained the audience with huge and dramatic leaps, so much so that there was an audible gasp each time he made one. Dorothy and Rosemary were enthralled by him, perhaps a little in love with him, referring to him as "Rudy." They might not have been so star-struck if they had known that his interest in women was purely platonic. But there's no question that we were all amazed by the astounding athletics of his performances. Of great interest to me as well was the young Canadian dancer from Vancouver, Lynn Seymour, who had become a principal with the Royal Ballet in 1959. We saw her in a number of ballets, including one of her great early triumphs, *The Two Pigeons*, on January 25, 1963.

Ken was the one who introduced me to the Folio Society and its beautifully-crafted books—I have been buying them ever since. More interestingly, he told me about a strange society that he belonged to. A group of Londoners had decided to "renew" the Holy Roman Empire. There were eleven in the group, most from the fringes of the journalistic world. The idea was that each member would chose to become one of the Emperors, research the life and times of his emperor thoroughly, and at each annual meeting—having first rented a suitable costume from Moss Bros.—he would describe to the group a short, historically cogent and interesting aspect of his reign. I was fascinated by the idea. If I had stayed in Britain, I would have become an emperor. Of sorts.

Rosemary and I also went frequently to the Aldwych Theatre, with the Strattons or other friends, close by at the bottom of Drury Lane, where in those days the Royal Shakespeare Company performed in winter. A highlight for us was a presentation of *Troilus and Cressida* on Friday, October 19, directed by Peter Hall, with Ian Holm as Troilus and Dorothy Tutin as Cressida. We saw other plays, the details of which have slipped from my memory, but which included the many stars in the company, the likes of Peter O'Toole, Paul Hardwick, Diana Rigg, and Judy Dench.

Old Friends in New Places

W E WERE OFTEN IN TOUCH WITH LESLIE AND NICOLE DUNKLING. SOMETIMES WE WOULD GO OUT TO 28 WALDECK ROAD IN EALING for dinner; and at other times, they would come to our place in Upper Addison Gardens. We had planned to get together on New Year's Eve 1962, but for reasons I have forgotten, at the last moment—and after Rosemary and I had dressed to go out to meet them—the plan fell through. So we went on our own to the Duke of Clarence, a pub just around the corner from our place, for a pint of bitter and a shandy and went home from there a short time later for an early New Year's night.

Also in town that winter was Bill Wood, with whom I had travelled across Canada and on the Continent in 1958. Bill had subsequently married Beverley Rudd. I had grown up with both of them in Revelstoke. They were living in the upstairs staff quarters at Peace Haven. On occasion, Rosemary and I went back to my old hostel to visit them. Once in the middle of winter, the four of us travelled by train to Cambridge, and Rosemary and I showed them the sights of the town and the university. And later that spring, on a warm and sunny Sunday, we went to the south coast near Arundel in Bill's car. We met the Dunklings there and had a picnic near the sea.

In late winter, we invited old friends from the Institute to a Saturday afternoon gathering at our place in Upper Addison Gardens. Included were my former room mate, Jim Honeybone and his fiancée, Jean Price; David Hepworth and his fiancée, Margaret (whose maiden name I have forgotten); Chris Oprey, and Michael Benton. The gathering had been planned for some time, so we were disturbed by what happened the night before our guests arrived. The gravity tank, which fed water from the top of the building into the flats below, froze over, leaving us without water for the toilet, or for anything else, for that matter. (Rosemary had been able to fill the kitchen sink before things froze up completely, so we *were* able to make tea.)

David and Margaret arrived very early, so, as we needed more coal, which I'd forgotten to have delivered, for our briquette-eating fireplace insert—the only heat source in the flat on a cold day—David and I left Margaret to help Rosemary finish putting the finger-food together and went off to get it. The dealer, Thos. Lebon & Sons Ltd, was at 47 Shepherds Bush Green, about a 20 minute walk away. A half a hundred-weight bag (56 lbs) cost 11/6. We alternated carrying this heavy and awkward bag back to the flat.

It was a pleasure to see our Institute friends again, and in spite of what became a grungy toilet, we had a very pleasant afternoon together. In subsequent months, Jim would marry Jean, and David would marry Margaret. Both of the men would continue to pursue teaching careers and raise their families away from the metropolitan area. In 2005, I once again made contact with Jim and Jean Honeybone, who now live in Banbury. We had a fine pub lunch together in October of that year at The Plough Inn, just outside of Oxford. They were still friends with David and Margaret Hepworth. David unfortunately died in 2007, before I had a chance to see him again. I don't know what happened to Chris Oprey and Michael Benton. It's perhaps as well that we did not know at the time of our spring get-together at 7D Upper Addison Gardens that it would be the last time we would see most of them.

A Delayed Honeymoon on Jersey

OUR PLAN HAD ALWAYS BEEN TO SAVE UP ENOUGH MONEY TO GO ON A DELAYED HONEYMOON DURING THE EASTER BREAK. AFTER toying with a number of other possibilities, we found a package to the island of Jersey that was within our price range. We took a train with reserved seats in second class to Plymouth, and boarded a day ferry from there, arriving on the island in the late afternoon of Tuesday, April 9. The sea was rough, as it often is in this area, and Rosemary was seasick almost all the way.

When we arrived in St. Helier, we were conveyed from the ferry to our Guest House—the name of which I have forgotten—bed, breakfast, and dinner for the week provided for £6/9/6 (about C$20) per person. The middle-aged woman owner of the guest house, who turned out to be a large, jolly creature with dyed red hair and a massive bosom—no Jersey Lily, this one—after taking one look at us, immediately asked us if we were on our honeymoon. We said we were, but, not wanting to appear naïve newly-weds, we told what was in fact the truth and emphasized that it was a *delayed* honeymoon. There were two rooms besides ours in the Guest House. An older couple was in one of them, and a young travelling salesman in the other. They were pleasant enough, but we did not get beyond a nodding acquaintance with them.

Apart from the overall beauty of the scenery, which we explored by taking long walks into the countryside—and yes, ladies, those magnificent Jersey cows have eyelashes you would be envious of—there were a couple of tourist sites, both military in nature, which we visited. One was Elizabeth Castle, named for his queen by Sir Walter Raleigh when he was governor of the Island (1600-03), a decaying pile of rock, with 18th-century cannon poking through suspiciously modern-looking holes in the walls, reached at low tide from St. Helier by means of a causeway.

The other was the German Underground Hospital. This unfinished example of Hitler's megalomania, blasted out of solid shale, was begun in 1941, using about 6,000 slave labourers, largely brought in from Eastern Europe, and was originally intended to be an attack-proof regimental barracks, what Hitler saw as the German Empire's Gibraltar. When the invasion of Europe by the Allies became inevitable in 1944, and it became obvious that there would be a lot of casualties, the unfinished structure was converted into a 27,611 sq. ft. hospital. The walls and ceilings are lined with concrete; there are doors to seal the area off against gas attacks; there is central heating, an air conditioning system, and a generator to provide electricity. It's an impressive place; but behind the impressiveness one can see the S. S. Officers with their Luger P.08 pistols and their whips, and hear their German Shepherds—dogs in this case—growling as they bare their teeth at the unfortunate slaves doing the construction work.

> *The 100-yard tunnels that house the museum do not make cosy viewing. By 1941, there were 11,500 German troops on Jersey, one for every four islanders. Recorded Jersey voices echo through the chill corridors, talking about deportation, starvation and, yes, collaboration: of neighbours betrayed for owning a forbidden wireless set, or for sheltering runaway Russian slaves. The Jersey girls who traded in their patriotism for German stockings and lipsticks, for a bit of fun in a time of dread, were labelled Jerrybags and treated to brutal reprisals after the liberation.*
> Jersey: The Tide Has Turned, 𝕿𝖍𝖊 𝕿𝖊𝖑𝖊𝖌𝖗𝖆𝖕𝖍, 12 Jul 2001

Return to Canada on the *S. S. Ramore Head*

WHEN ROSEMARY AND I WERE PLANNING OUR MARRIAGE AND TALKING ABOUT OUR FUTURE LIFE TOGETHER, WE HAD DECIDED THAT WE WOULD teach one year in England and then go to Canada for at least a year or two, perhaps returning to England after that time. This plan became an *idée fixe*, in spite of the fact that we had good and interesting jobs, new friends and old, and the exciting life of a young couple in central London. These reasons probably should have encouraged us to stay where we were. But the decision to go through with the plan also had a couple of strong and attractive prospects: I would be going home, and Rosemary would be off on an adventure in a new country. Besides, the move to Canada didn't have to be forever. (Though, her mother did her best to weep and wail, proclaiming that she would never see her daughter again.)

From about the middle of January, we began to check the *Times Educational Supplement* weekly, looking for teaching jobs in British Columbia. Eventually, we settled on two jobs, one for Rosemary, one for me, teaching English—and another subject not yet named (we were used to that at Kingsway)—in the Vancouver Island lumbering and fishing community of Port Alberni.

I arranged our passage across the Atlantic with the Belfast-based Ulster Steamship Line. I had travelled on one of their Head Line/Lord Line freighters when I had returned to Canada from Spain in 1960, so I was familiar with their system. It was a cheap and interesting way to cross the Atlantic. I booked us on the *S. S. Ramore Head*, sailing from Liverpool on or about July 23—you were never given an exact sailing date on a freighter. You arrived on the date stated, and if there was a delay, you were allowed to use the ship as a hotel (room and meals) from that date until you shipped anchor. We left one day late.

As a B. C. native, I was aware of the ramifications of going into a town on the edge of civilization, especially after one has spent a couple of years in London. I would not have chosen Port Alberni if better choices had been available. But there were no jobs advertised in Victoria, my first choice, or in the Okanagan region, my second. As it turned out, and it was predictable, Port Alberni was a mistake. It was a rough lumbering and fishing town. Although we made some good friends among the teaching staff, Rosemary and I were not happy there. It was the beginning of the end of our marriage. But that's another story, and a subject for the beginning of another book.

Wedding in Cambridge

David Latter, wife, Alison; John Smith (Uncle),
wife Jean; Lady Ridley, Jonathan Latter
(David's son); Marguerite Latter

Bride and Bridesmaids
Carole, Jean Price, Rosemary, Heather Smith

"Some old aunts . . ."

Off to the Milton Arms

In the Garden at the Milton Arms

Leslie Dunkling, The Best Man, and the Groom

London Life

Shepherds Bush Station—Rosemary far left

The Living Room Alcove

Day Return Underground Ticket

At the Door of Our Flat

In the Garden

Chris Oprey, Jean Price, Rosemary in Living Room

Nicole, Leslie Dunkling & Rosemary after Dinner

Chris Oprey and David Hepworth

Kingsway Day College

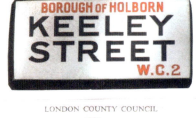

Nancy Martin Job Letter

KINGSWAY DAY COLLEGE
BRANCH AT CITY LITERARY INSTITUTE

Use of the City Literary Institute
by Kingsway Day College Students

Staff Room at City Lit

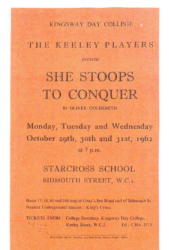

A Positive Course Evaluation

LONDON COUNTY COUNCIL

W. F. HOUGHTON, M.A.
Education Officer

TELEPHONE WATERLOO
EXTENSION 6322/7658
REPLIES TO BE SENT TO THE
EDUCATION OFFICER, QUOTING

THE COUNTY HALL
WESTMINSTER BRIDGE
LONDON S.E.1

EO/FE.13/HE.4

9 AUG 1962

Dear Mr. Keough,

Your temporary appointment as an assistant, grade **A** at **Kingsway Day College** takes effect from **10th September 1962** and you will be paid salary from this date.

Your salary is provisionally assessed at £ **855** a year (including London allowance). A detailed statement of the final assessment will be sent to you in due course.

City Lit in 2004—Hanging On

Holborn Station in 2004

On the Beach in Jersey

Queen Elizabeth Castle

The German Military Underground Hospital

MEADOW BANK
ST. LAWRENCE
JERSEY

JERSEY

Causeway to St. Heliér

An Order for Coal

Picnic at Arundel: Bill Wood, Terry, Bev Wood, Nicole Dunkling

Return to Canada

S. S. Ramore Head

Fare—but not the Roonagh Head

On Deck in the St. Laurence

A Serious Passport Photo